Contents

We wish to express our thanks and dedicate this book to our wives,
Becky Kluesner and Carlene Collier, who have for years put up with:

*Elk bugling in the house
*Turkey yelping in the house
*Stinky scent bags and one spilled bottle of "doe in heat"
*Watching hundreds of hunting videos and pretending to be interested
*Eating wild game they really didn't like
*Mysteriously appearing credit card orders for hunting equipment we couldn't afford
*All the late nights and long weekends it took to put this manual together.

Warning!
Read This Carefully

WAIVER OF LIABILITY

Warning: Some of the information contained herein including maps and hunting area descriptions has been obtained from the US Forest Service, USGS and Colorado Division Of Wildlife and interviews with individuals who claim to have visited those hunting areas. That information, and other information provided herein is believed to be reliable, but no guarantees are made, expressed or implied as to the accuracy contained therein. You agree to hold all parties providing such information harmless and waive all claim of liability on the part of the same for any misinformation that may or may not be provided and for any damages or claims arising as a result of such inaccuracies or misinformation..

Hunting in Colorado involves strenuous exercise at high altitudes and exposure to adverse weather conditions. The areas described in this manual always require strenuous exercise to get to. We do not recommend going to the areas described herein unless your doctor has specifically "OK'd" this type of hunting for you. In addition, hunting Colorado requires that you be able to adequately use map and compass and not get lost in the vast areas in which you will hunt. Also, although we have given indications as to what time of year certain areas are good, weather is unpredictable in Colorado, and you need to use common sense. In all instances, ask the locals before you visit a hunting area about recent events that might affect that area, specifically snow, rain, high wind, avalanches, etc. Specifically, do not go into rugged areas you may not be able to get out of if there were to be a snowstorm.

You assume all risks when you hunt in Colorado, and the areas described in this manual. This is a legally binding waiver of liability.

ISBN: 0-9637585-0-0

Guy Collier & Spencer Kluesner

The Big Game Scouting Report

Colorado's premier "Where To Hunt" guide detailing over 500 trophy hot spots on Colorado public land.

Gamefinders International, Inc.
Denver, Colorado

HOW THIS ALL STARTED

By Spencer Kluesner

Guy and I first met while attending Colorado State University. Over the years, with our good friend Craig Fishel (whom we nicknamed "Fish" for the outrageous hunting stories he told) we hunted, fished and scouted a large part of the Colorado public access lands. While some hunters will hunt the same place fifteen years in a row, we have rarely hunted in the same place more than two days in a row, even if the hunting was good. It always seemed as if maybe we could find a better place, or we just wanted to see new country. This is the reason we've been able to write about so many different hunting spots.

Before we wrote this manual, people were always asking us, "Where do you hunt?" Our reply was always the same "I could tell you where I hunt, but then I'd have to shoot you." But over time we came to realize that (1) we had more good spots to hunt than we could ever really hunt (over 500 spots total) and (2) people were willing to pay for good hunting spots. The result was this manual.

The seeds of our greatest passion, hunting, were planted long before college by our fathers, grandfathers and uncles who all hunted. When I trace back our family trees, and all the hunters who came before us, I realize that hunting is in our blood. It's what we were born to do.

For me personally, coming to Colorado was the fulfillment of a dream I'd had since childhood. I had always wanted to live out west and hunt big game, but was raised in Missouri. I spent several summers out west when my father was a Park Service Ranger. But it was only seasonal work. We always went back to Missouri in the winter where he had a teaching job.

I always felt I had been cheated somehow by not being born an Indian in the old west, or at least a mountain man. As a kid I did a lot of crazy things to prove I had what it took to be one of them. I once read that mountain men had to wade in ice cold water in the dead of winter to set traps. Consequently, at 9 years old, in the middle of winter, I tried wading chest deep in our local creek. By the time I had run the mile home, my pants had completely frozen over except for the creases where my knees bent. I told my mother I had fallen in. I'm just glad I'm still able to have children.

While employed as editor of North Dakota Outdoors Magazine, Spence's father, Leo Kluesner displays some of his story "research."

Spence's family spent their summers in the national parks where his father was a park ranger.

Growing up my greatest influences were my father and grandfather. They religiously pursued two sports, hunting and fishing. So naturally, I did too. My father has a degree in wildlife biology from Washington State University. In his younger years he was a game warden and also the editor of North Dakota Outdoors magazine. As a kid he was even kicked out of the Catholic Altar Boys because the priest caught him ditching church to go fishing

My grandfather spent most of his time sitting around telling us kids hunting and fishing stories. To him, everything in life revolved around the next hunting or fishing trip. He worked not for the sake of working, but so he could have the money to pursue his sports. He was an invaluable resource when I wanted to know where to hunt. He'd been everywhere. He was the only person I knew who had actually hunted wolves in Missouri in the early 1900s. Although he became deaf in his early 40s, he continued to hunt into his 80s. Even in the throes of death, his sport consumed him. After having a massive stroke, while lying in bed babbling away half out of his mind, he seemed for a second to regain his focus, and pointing at me said, "You should be fishin."

My grandfather mostly hunted with his brother-in-law, my great uncle Richard Wilson, who was also from a big hunting and fishing family. Uncle Dick's father had been a well-known fur trapper along the Missouri river who had met a very untimely death by his own gun. He had been a notorious womanizer and had simply wronged the wrong women. During a heated lovers' quarrel, he gave her the opportunity to shoot him, and she blew a hole clean through him with his own 12 gauge shotgun at point blank range. You could see a lot of him in my Uncle Dick, who in between coon hunting stories was always teasing my aunt about "all his girlfriends." He seemed to have a knack for getting the young girls to pay him a lot of attention.

Guy is also from a family of hard-core Colorado hunters. His two grandfathers both hunt. One was a rancher in Gunnison. The other used to own the local RC Cola distributorship and because he was self-employed, had a great deal of time to hunt. Guy has more uncles and cousins than I can count, and they all hunt too. It's a great setup because every time we need to find out about a new area Guy will say, "Oh, I have an uncle [or cousin or some other extended family member] who hunts there. Let's call him." Then we have another good spot to hunt.

Spence's Grandfather Alphonse Kluesner (left) and father Leo Kluesner with their hunting dogs Night and Day.

Guy's mother Gayle Collier growing up in a ranching/outfitting family.

The thing about Guy you'll notice right away is a natural confidence. No matter what the situation, he's always sure he'll come out on top. And he does. The first time they took him out to shoot clay pigeons, he hit 21 out of 25. Before that day, he had never picked up a shotgun. He was only 14 years old. Another time, I personally saw him shoot two ducks out of the air with a 22 rifle. When I saw the ducks fall, I was completely dumbfounded. This air of confidence worked in other ways too. It was as if the girls at our school sensed it or something. I'd love to write down some stories about his exploits along this line, but this book is supposed to be rated "G."

When Guy was a little kid he wanted to be a mountain man so bad that he bought some traps, a big pair of boots and a coonskin cap. A few weeks later he was spotted trapping muskrats on a golf course near his house. He tried to run but his oversized boots slowed him down and the guys in the pro shop chased him down in their golf carts. The police came and took him home. When they got to the door of his parents' house they said, "Mr. Collier, we caught your son on the golf course with all this stuff," producing his traps, a hatchet, a knife, and a whole lot of string. I'm sure his parents thought that all his uncle's corruptive influences had gone a little too far, but by that time there was no way to stop it.

Fish grew up hunting down in the Big Cypress Swamp of southern Florida. I went down and hunted the Big Cypress with him once. Down there they use dogs to drive deer out of the thick patches of woods they call hammocks. One night, Fish's uncle by marriage to his mother's sister (I'm still a little confused by their extended family tree) told me that dogs were good, but as a kid Fish was really the best dog he ever had for driving deer out of the hammocks. Although Fish's uncle Lance divorced Fish's blood aunt, Lance continued to raise Fish as a hunter and a top notch shooter.

Like many southerners I know, Fish played the role of "Crazy Redneck" very well. I met a lot of his relatives down in Florida who were also crazy rednecks. But Fish seemed to be the craziest of them all. I once saw him jump our college fraternity's blazing 10 foot wide fire pit with his motorcycle because someone dared him to. I have also seen him grab the tail of a rattlesnake that was trying to strike him, throw it in the air and shoot it with his pistol. Once, as a college prank, he kicked in the door to the room of a little bald guy named Jimmy Eagleton. Screaming insanely he pointed a loaded blank at him and pulled the trigger. Jimmy fell down with fright and the other guys in the room jumped for cover. The funny thing was, they actually believed Fish was capable of doing something crazy like that. They didn't really understand him.

Knowing Fish personally, I know that it was all a facade. The thing about Fish is that everything he does is a calculated risk. He weighs the odds and remains completely cool under pressure. He's the only person you'll meet who can totally and absolutely control his emotions in a dangerous situation. This calculated control has made him one of the best shots I've ever seen. Hitting doubles and triples all day long while dove hunting is not uncommon for him. Right now he's a commercial pilot for a small commuter line. He's trying to get on with a larger airline, or at least one that pays better. Anyone who does hire him will never regret it. I'd put my life in his hands over any other pilot.

Guy's great uncles Larry Rinehart and Harry Carpenter (both with dark shirts) used to own the Cebolla Creek Outfitting down in Gunnison, Colorado.

Guy (left) and Spence at a college party. Probably talking about hunting.

With these backgrounds and personalities, the stage was set for the three of us to meet in college. The first time we hunted together, we had so much fun that we never stopped. People said our hunting was obsessive. They said we corrupted one another. It's probably true that if each of us had been left to a crowd of nonhunters, we wouldn't have gotten so into it. But we sure had a lot of fun indulging our obsessions.

Usually in August we would quit our summer jobs well before college classes started and hunt the archery antelope season. That kicked off at least a straight month of hunting, sometimes a full six weeks. This estimate of hunting time doesn't even take into account all the hunting the previous winter and the weekends of scouting the entire summer before the season opened.

We had many adventures back then. One time in particular I'll never forget. Guy and Fish took off on their three-wheelers to go check out a hunting spot. Guy went around a turn on a gravel road pretty fast. Fish tried to follow at the same speed. But he had some bald tires on his three-wheeler, and when the road turned, he went straight. He rode right through a barbed wire fence that nearly ripped all the clothes off him. Guy looked down at him lying motionless in a cloud of dust and wondered if he was dead. But miraculously, Fish got up and they rode the 100 yards down to a local bar/grocery store by Walden, Colorado. When they walked in, Fish told everybody inside that he had been clawed up by a bear. And it sure looked like it. They all felt sorry for him and bought him drinks to ease the pain.

It's almost painful to look back on those days because we never realized that they might end. We thought we would just hunt as much as we wanted forever. We never knew how good we had it back then.

After college both Fish and Guy moved to North Carolina. For several years Guy would fly back to Colorado for the hunting season. But I didn't see him much other than one week a year, and we didn't put in the time hunting like we

Fish with his airboat during a 1983 hunting trip in the Big Cypress.

used to. Then one day he called and told me he was moving back to Colorado because he missed the hunting too much. And it started all over again. Guy is a flight attendant and has a great deal of spare time to hunt. I own a small computer software company and have flexible hours. It's a perfect setup for a hunter.

Rugged and beautiful. Colorado has more hunting spots than one person can explore in a lifetime.

Fish, on the other hand, never made it back. He got trapped in North Carolina by his new wife who refuses to become a hunting widow. Fish always was a sucker for a woman. Then again, sometimes I think maybe Fish's hassle free life is the better way to go. Every hunter can sympathize or empathize with the situation. If you are going to hunt, and you are going to be married, you are always going to be in trouble with your wife. It's inevitable.

It's a recurrent theme in our society that men and women will clash over a man's hobbies, whatever they may be. So many women cannot understand or accept the fact that men have hobbies they devote their lives to. They see it as selfishness. For us, it's our way of really living. We're dead inside without it. If they just let us have that release every once in a while, we would be better husbands, providers and fathers.

Guy and I will continue to scout and hunt the Colorado public lands, and write up our areas in future editions of this book. We hope that someday, we can do it on a full time basis. Each book we sell gives us money to put together an even better book the next year. So please tell your friends. We also hope that someday we'll get Fish out here scouting too. We'll keep working on him.

Why We Hunt

By Spencer Kluesner

These days it seems as if every time you turn around you run into somebody who's telling you that hunting is wrong. Growing up I never questioned why I hunted. I just did it because I enjoyed it. It was a family thing. But all the pressure by the growing population of nonhunters has caused both Guy and me to really look at why we hunt.

Let's face it. For most of us the logical rebuttal to someone challenging a hunter about the right and wrong of hunting is the population control argument. We tell them it's necessary because animals will overeat their range and then die a miserable death by starvation. We tell them that you can maintain a much larger herd size by culling some of the population. It all makes sense.

But I don't hunt for those reasons, neither does Guy, and if you really think about it, you probably don't either. You hunt because you never feel so alive as you do when you are hunting. There's a very good reason for this - as Guy would say, "Instinctually humans are predators." Even if you eat tofu and bean sprouts all day long, somewhere deep inside, your predatorial instinct lives. It's just a matter of finding it.

When you hunt you tune into everything around you. You are as much a part of it as any animal. Look at those people who don't hunt. They never realize how far from the earth they've strayed. They could just as well be on the moon as being in the woods - they are equally as out of place in either spot. They don't understand the workings around them and they definitely are not a part of it.

It's kind of like this. Does the tourist who takes his picture next to the Eiffel Tower somehow become a Parisian? No. That's why they came up with the word "foreigner." Likewise, many people who enter the woods are really foreign and oblivious to the things around them. These people whom we have termed "Granolas" have these grandiose illusions about nature. They believe that if you get far enough back in the wilderness, animals are unafraid of each other and of humans, and they are living in some sort of peace and harmony. They think that what comes in and screws up this peaceful coexistence is man. I'll tell you. Animals are competing. They are living. They are dying. They are eating. They are loving. They are doing all the things we do. But they are part of the food chain. And at one time, we were too.

When you hunt you become part of the animal world around you, part of the food chain. You re-learn things you have lost, things that have been dulled by living in the cities and the suburbs. You become alive and live the way humans evolved to live. The nonhunters in the growing suburbia populations have forgotten or denied the animal side of themselves. They want their meat killed where they can't see it die. It's bled, packaged in styrofoam and cellophane, then displayed in a temperature controlled environment. Some people take the moralistic stance of not eating meat, and look pretty sickly as a result. They think they are living naturally but they are not.

I can't say what's going to happen. But for hunters I think it's important to keep this side of us alive as long as possible. There will be more and more of them, but that doesn't mean we will lose. It's important that we band together and defend our right to hunt.

Guy says you should feel sorry for those people - that they don't really know what they are missing and what part of themselves they have lost. He goes out and actively converts people to hunting. I can't count the number of people he's brought into the sport.

Personally, I just have animosity toward them. I think they are weak, and being the predator I am, I am disgusted by weakness. I've found myself referring to them as "half men" and "weaklings" more than once. For hunting's sake, I hope there are more hunters out there like Guy than like me.

Browns Canyon

Big Game Hunting Unit(s): 56, 57, 58

How To Get There:

From Denver take Highway 285 southwest to the stretch of highway just north of Salida.

How To Hunt This Area:

This area is good for deer year round and elk later in the season. By the third rifle season, many of the elk have been pushed onto private land bordering the National Forest. On some of the private land we drove through, a fresh blanket of snow from the previous night was completely broken by elk and deer tracks. So your best bet is to work the public land right along the private land boundaries, or seek permission to hunt the private land.

As you get closer to Salida there is a lot of private land that effectively blocks access to the mountains to the east. You can still get to those spots. You need to drive around the back side of those mountains then take the access roads west. From where they end, you can walk the hillsides down to the private land/public land border.

If you are willing to spend a lot of time walking, you will have a definite advantage over other hunters. The reason is that most of the hunters in this area road hunt. People do have luck road hunting, but you are really limiting your opportunities that way. Your best bet is to spot tracks from the road, then get out and follow them wherever they go.

Rugged pinion-juniper terrain like this offers some of Colorado's best deer hunting opportunities.

The best spots are going to be the steep gullies that drop down to the Arkansas River. They are covered with pinion and juniper trees. Along the sides are rocky outcroppings that provide good vantage points. If you cross an established game trail going through one of the gullies, find an outcropping where you can sit and get a good shot down the gully.

If there has been a lot of snow in the mountains and you have cross-country skis or snowshoes, bring them. One road down into the canyons was impassible during the third rifle season due to heavy snow drifts. If we had brought our snow equipment with us, we would have had a huge hunting area all to ourselves.

Spot 01: **Elk Byway.** From Highway 285 head east on Road 194 which is just south of Helca Junction. Just a half mile up the road to the right are some pinion and juniper trees. We saw a lot of large deer trails in there during the third rifle season. Plus, elk were traveling north and south, paralleling the Arkansas river drainage and at night moving into the wheat fields below. Part of this spot is BLM land and part is private. Just make sure that you stay on the BLM land.

Spot 02: **Road 194 High Point.** Drive to the last gully that runs east just before you hit the highest point on Road 194. You'll be about 1/4 mile from the top. The road will continue up to the ridgetop then drop down on the other side to the Arkansas River. The gully doesn't actually go to the top of the ridge which runs north and south. Instead, it goes up and forms a high saddle paralleling the ridge.

Spence:

A few years ago, Guy spotted a herd of deer just past the saddle that parallels the ridge at about 10:00 AM. There were two good sized bucks, and a lot of does. We flipped for it and I got to make the stalk. Instead of hunting the gully up, I went straight up the hill so that I could come up on the lip of the saddle that parallels the ridge. The reason for doing this was that I could pop into view and only be 100 yards away from the herd. If I came up the gully, they would see me coming.

I got up the hill in half an hour. Sometimes the snow was waist deep, but I was drawing on a lot of adrenaline which made it seem easy. I eased up to the lip and moved my gun into place. I put the crosshairs on at least 20 different deer that were feeding in and out of the pines. But all were either does or fork horns. After 30 minutes, I had scoped and passed on all the deer except one that was in thicker brush. It wouldn't move where I could see if it was a buck or doe. I moved in and flushed it into the open, quickly placing the crosshairs on its back shoulder. All I saw were big ears. No antlers. Another doe. When I got back down to the truck, Guy told me that the two big bucks had slowly moved over the hill just before I hit the saddle lip. I'd missed them by just a few minutes.

Spot 03: **Browns Canyon.** Park next to the Arkansas River where Road 194 ends. Walk north along one of the gullies running up the side of the hill. Deer trails run between the gullies and then around to the steep section facing Brown's Canyon and the Arkansas River. Find a fresh trail and follow it.

Spot 04: **Two Valley Ridge.** From the spot where road 194 ends, walk up the deep gully that heads northwest. It's the farthest gully to the west. Toward the top of the gully, heading north, you will come out on top of a ridge. The ridge runs north and there are open meadows paralleling it on both sides. Stay on top of the ridge because the meadows on either side are only a 300 yard shot away. Elk and deer trails parallel the ridge as the animals prefer to stay in the meadow bottom. This is a good place to sit any time. But it's an exceptional spot for opening morning when the hunters from below will push the game right past you.

Spot 05: **Rock Formations.** Just north of the ridge discussed in the previous spot is a wide open pasture. If you circle to the west of the pasture there are a good number of game trails coming down to the pasture. There are a number of distinctive rock formations that provide perfect high spots to sit and watch for movement.

Spot 06: **North Drainage.** Cross the pasture discussed in the previous spot to the trees on the north side. The trees border a drainage of three creeks that flow east into the Arkansas River. They are dry most of the year but do provide good forage for game.

Guy:

Both deer and elk follow those creek drainages down to the Arkansas River. The upper parts of the drainage are on private land, but right where the drainage goes into the river, you can hunt. When I was there, a train down along the Arkansas River whistled and caused two bucks to stand up about 100 yards away from me. They were both small 3 X 3's and I didn't shoot. I also saw some cow elk down in the drainage. During the third rifle season, the area along the Arkansas River is good for deer and elk. During the other seasons, it's really only good for deer.

Spot 07: **Droney Gulch.** Head farther south on Highway 285 from the turnoff to Browns Canyon. You'll come to a turnoff heading to the west up Droney gulch which parallels Squaw Creek. Going in you will cross some private land, which during the late gun season was completely covered with deer and elk tracks. Take the road up and the minute you get on public land you should start to hunt, paralleling the private land. If you're hunting during one of the earlier seasons you probably need to go farther up. You'll be hunting on a pinion and juniper covered table that forms a base around Mount Shavano. Although it looks flat from the road, there's actually a lot of small shallow gullies where game hides. This table provides some of the area's best deer habitat.

Spot 08: **Longs Gulch.** Take Ute Creek Road 175 northeast out of Salida then take Road 183 down Longs Gulch. During the third rifle season, we saw deer and elk in Dead Goat Gulch and Longs gulch bottoms as we drove from Brown's Canyon to Salida. Unfortunately, there was no public access from the bottom. You have to hunt from the top down, but it's well worth the scramble.

Spot 09: **Aspen Ridge.** Drive Road 221 north past the quarry. On the hillside to the east, we saw a bull elk standing in some thick brush no more than 200 yards from the road.

Spot 10: **Spring Gulch.** From Road 221 walk the gulch west toward the Arkansas River. When we were there, the elk were crossing Aspen Ridge then heading down toward the river through Spring Gulch. They were probably being pushed by all the hunters up on top. It's rough walking, but well worth it. There's no access from the west. Later in the season, the animals establish trails which parallel the river and Browns canyon. For some reason, they are reluctant to cross the river.

Spot 11: **Castle Rock Gulch.** Heading north on Road 187 you will cross some private land where you will see a house. Just past the private land on the left hand side we spotted a herd of deer. They were moving out of the dark timber into the wet meadow bottom to feed in the evening.

Spot 12: **Arnold Gulch/Bald Mountain Gulch.** If you can get down this road, try it. It's a good spot because hunting pressure will push deer into that area from below, above and from along Highway 285 to the north. Also, try the trail over to Cottonwood Creek. When we were there during the third rifle season, all of the fresh deer and elk tracks headed down into that area. The reason became obvious when we were unable to get our 4WD vehicle down there. Deep snow drifts blocked our passage.

Spot 13: **Castle Rock.** We spotted a decent size herd of bighorn sheep on the west face. It's also good deer habitat. If you're lucky enough to draw a tag for bighorn sheep you'll probably be able to pull a trophy off of that hill.

Spot 14: **Shields Gulch.** For some reason we didn't see Road 315 that branches off from 285 and heads up this gulch. But just east of the road, there were deer tracks everywhere. They covered the ground on both sides of the highway. This spot has always been very good for deer. We see them there every time we drive by.

Browns Canyon

(Reprinted from San Isabel National Forest map)

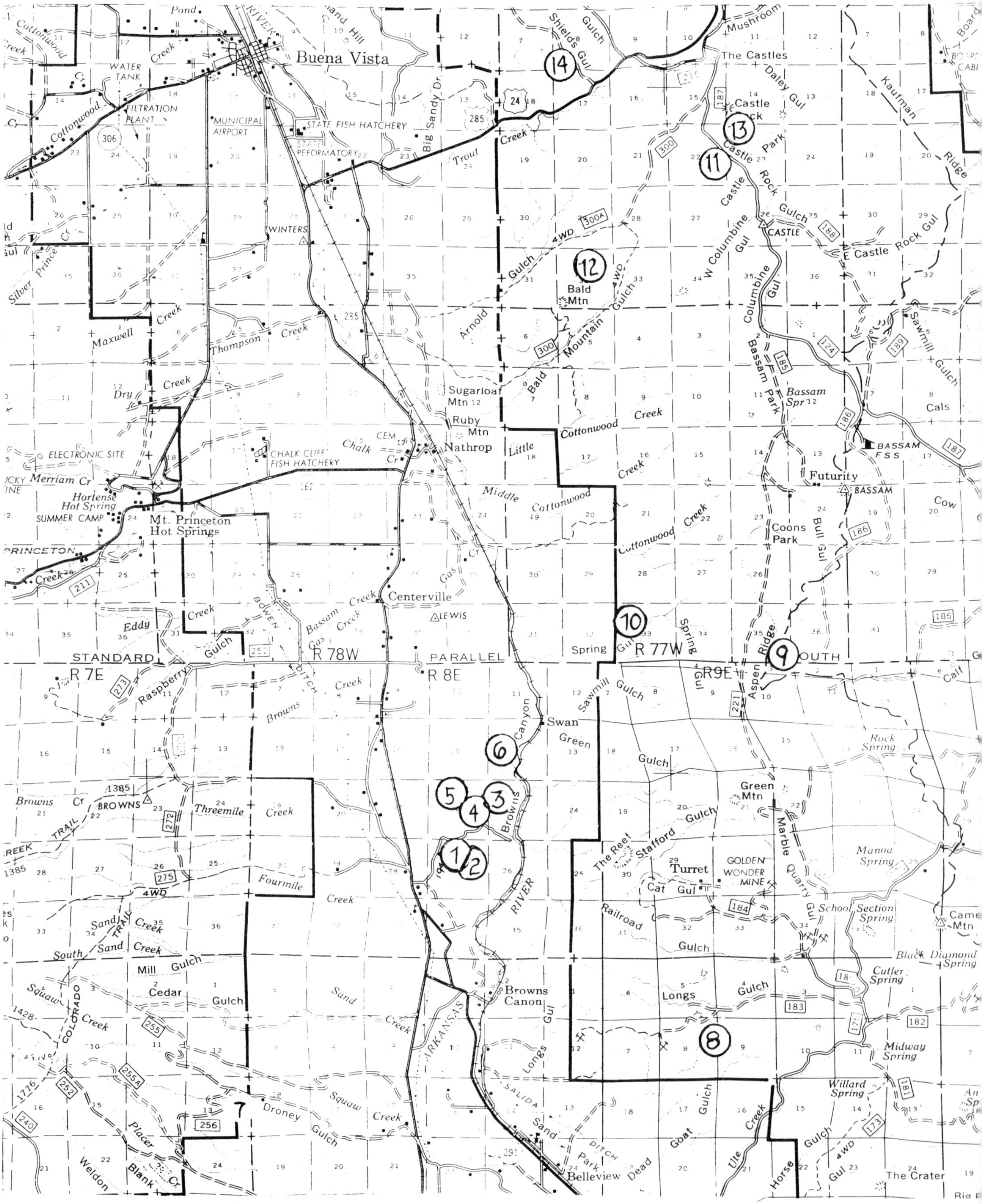

BROWNS CANYON 3-D MAP

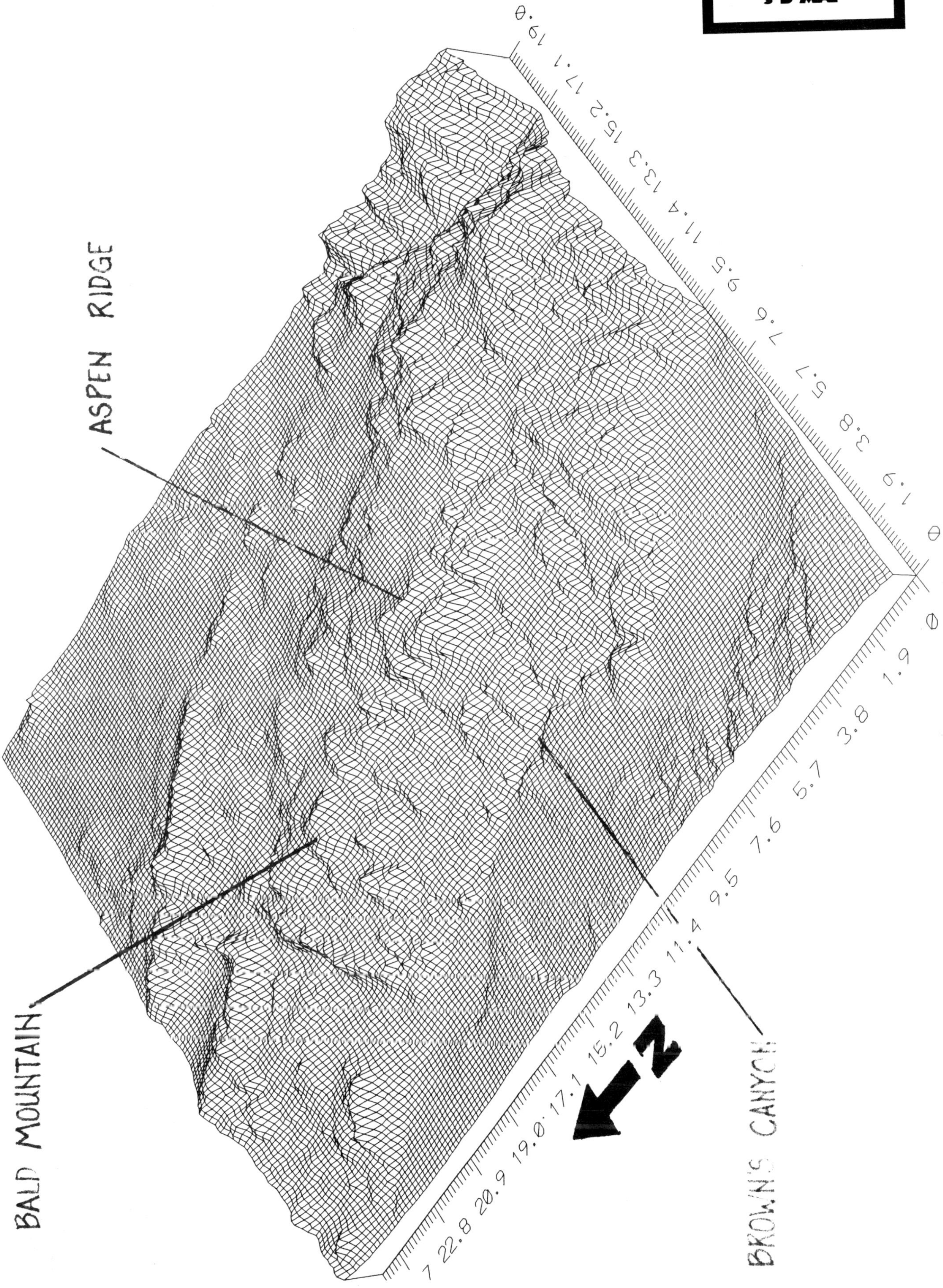

Beaver Creek State Wildlife Area

Big Game Management Unit(s): 59

How to Get There:

Take Highway 50 toward Canon City, but before you get there take Road 67 north at the sign for Cripple Creek and Phantom Canyon. A little way up Road 123 will come in from the right and you will have a choice of either heading up Phantom Canyon to Cripple Creek or going right toward an outdoor shooting range. Go right then take the first left up Road 132. Follow Road 132 all the way to the end.

How to Hunt This Area:

This is probably one of the best deer hunting areas we have seen. Up on the old logging roads we saw deer around almost every turn. They like the clover that grows along the roads. The area is very dry, so waterholes can be very productive. All you really have to do is find water in a remote gully and sit above it in the early morning and evening. We did this one morning and had at least 50 deer come in. After the best hours in the morning we were still able to see a lot of deer. They were sitting back in the woods watching the meadows. We even saw a few elk in there, but this definitely is not an elk area.

Also, keep in mind that if it has been a really dry year and the seeps up on the mountainsides are no longer flowing, the deer are going to be concentrated down in the wet creek bottoms, primarily Beaver Creek.

The vegetation in this area consists of open pinion and juniper forests with dark pines on the higher hills. It's extremely open terrain where field glasses can give a hunter a big advantage. However there's more cover than at first appears to be and you will be surprised at how many deer you don't see at first glance.

Guy poses with an old 9" double beard he shot along Beaver Creek.

Spot 1: **Red Rock Gully**. This gully is unnamed on the map. We've named it Red Rock Gully for the dramatic red rocks located just to the north. As you are going up Road 132 you will see a road branching off to the right along lower Beaver Creek (but don't take that road). Pull over on the left just past where that road comes in and start walking to the northwest. The gully is narrow at the mouth then opens back up as you get farther in. About an hour's walk back where the gully breaks up into many tributary gullies, you'll run into a tremendous amount of deer sign. Back there we also saw the tracks from a young mountain lion whose lair is in a cave on the hill to the north.

Spot 2: **The Turnoff**. Take the turnoff discussed in the previous spot (before you get to the Red Rocks spot there is a road heading southeast along the Beaver Creek). Deer come off of the hill to the east in the evening and early morning to feed in the meadows along the creek. It's a great place to still hunt.

Spot 3: **Beaver Creek**. Along the bottom of Beaver Creek, all the way up to the mouth of the canyon are open meadows interspersed with cottonwoods. This is a good place to still hunt for deer on opening morning. After the first few days of hunting season, hunting pressure will push the deer out of the area.

Spot 4: **West Mill Creek**. From the parking lot located at the very end of Beaver Creek Wildlife Area, walk north up the canyon along the creek bottom. Don't take the trail that runs to the right. Instead stay down by the creek. Right where you see some old drainage pipes, cross over to the other side of the creek. Head west along the bottom of the first canyon on your left which will be West Mill Creek. You'll notice a short rock outcropping farther up the canyon called Strawberry Point.

Head for that.

Spence:

I ran into a group of soldiers from Fort Carson Army Base who hunted that drainage a couple of years back. They said it took them a day to backpack in, but it was worth it. Thousands of deer had been pushed up there by people hunting along Beaver Creek and people hunting in Phantom Canyon. They saw over 500 deer a day but not one other hunter. They all took trophies. It's not an easy spot to get to and you have to be prepared to camp overnight, but there are more deer in there than you can even imagine.

Spot 5: **East Mill Gulch**. From the parking lot, take the trail up Beaver Creek Canyon to the mouth of East Mill Gulch. Walk the gulch up to the fork and take the right hand gully up toward the highpoint you'll see. The point is unnamed, but you can't miss it. While you're walking, look up on the hillsides and you will definitely see deer. We ran into several turkey hunters who complained that all they saw up that gulch were hundreds of deer - no turkeys.

Spot 6: **West Gulch From East Mill Gulch**. At the fork described in the previous spot, go left instead of right. The gulch will take you back up the side of the point and then drop back down into East Beaver Creek. Once again there are multitudes of deer up on the hillsides.

Pinion-Juniper terrain like this is not what you would typically expect when hunting in Colorado. However, it does offer some of the state's finest deer hunting.

Spot 7: **North Sugarloaf Mountain**. From the parking lot, walk the foot trail up Beaver Creek Canyon. The back side (north side) of Sugarloaf Mountain is a good spot for deer. There are numerous deer trails up there that parallel West Mill Creek. You can easily spot them with your binoculars.

Spot 8: **Beaver Creek Bottom North**. Taking the trail up Beaver Creek, just past Sugarloaf Mountain but before you get to the forks of West and East Beaver Creek, you'll come to some open meadows along the creek bottom. The meadows have a lot of deer sign in and around them. They are left undisturbed by hunters because it is difficult to get there.

Spot 9: **East and West Beaver Creek Upper Bottom Lands**. From the parking lot you can walk for as many as 15 miles up Beaver Creek. The farther back you get the less disturbed and wary the deer herds are. If you are fit enough for some extremely rugged hiking, or if you have a sure footed horse, this is the place for you.

Spence:

I hiked back in there about 3 hours and got into spots where I'm sure people rarely go. There were deer out in the open in the middle of the afternoon just standing there staring at me. Also, the fly fishing was great. I caught about 15 trout in two hours. The last one broke my leader.

Beaver Creek State Wildlife Area

(Reprinted from USGS Colorado Springs map)

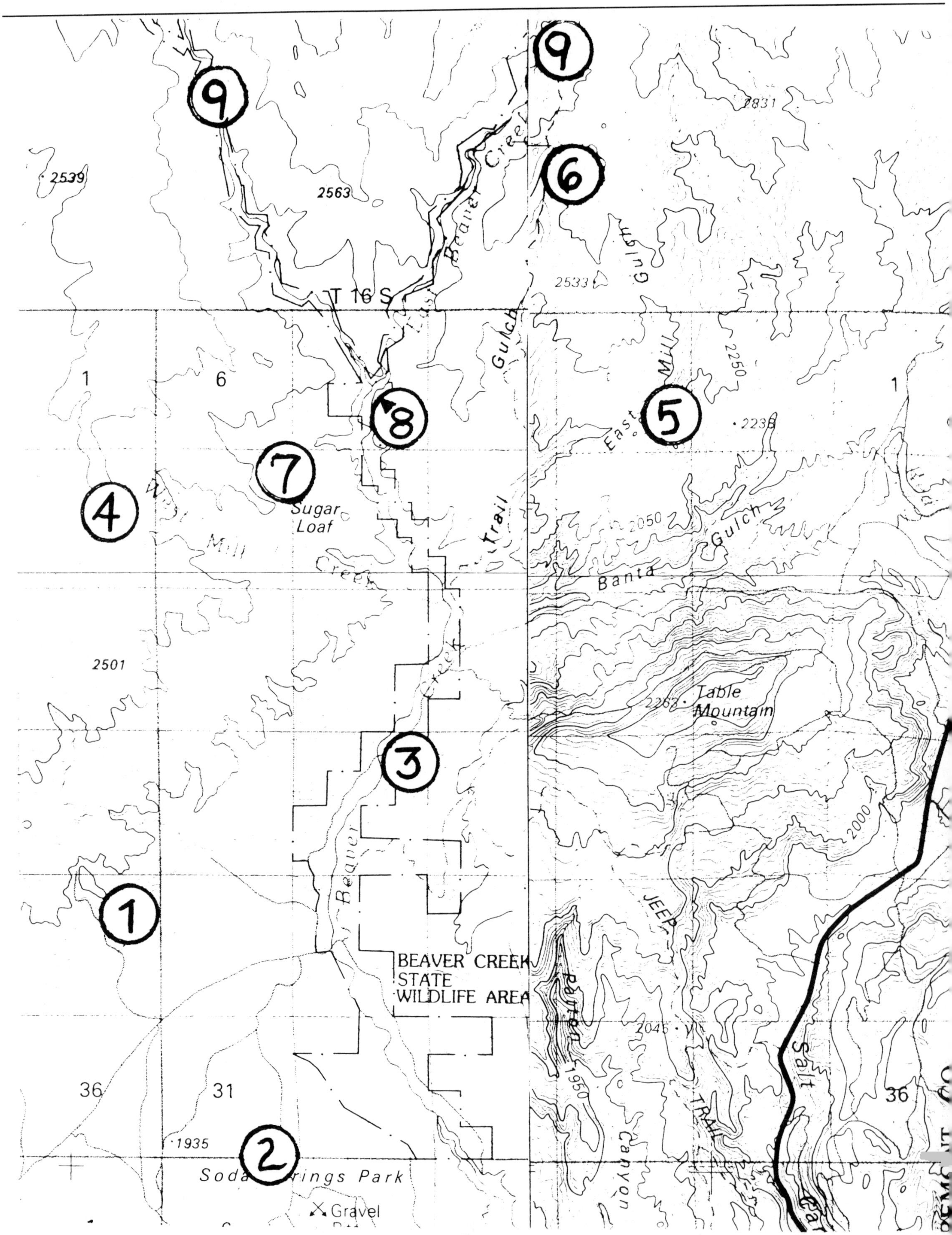

BEAVER CREEK STATE WILDLIFE AREA 3-D MAP

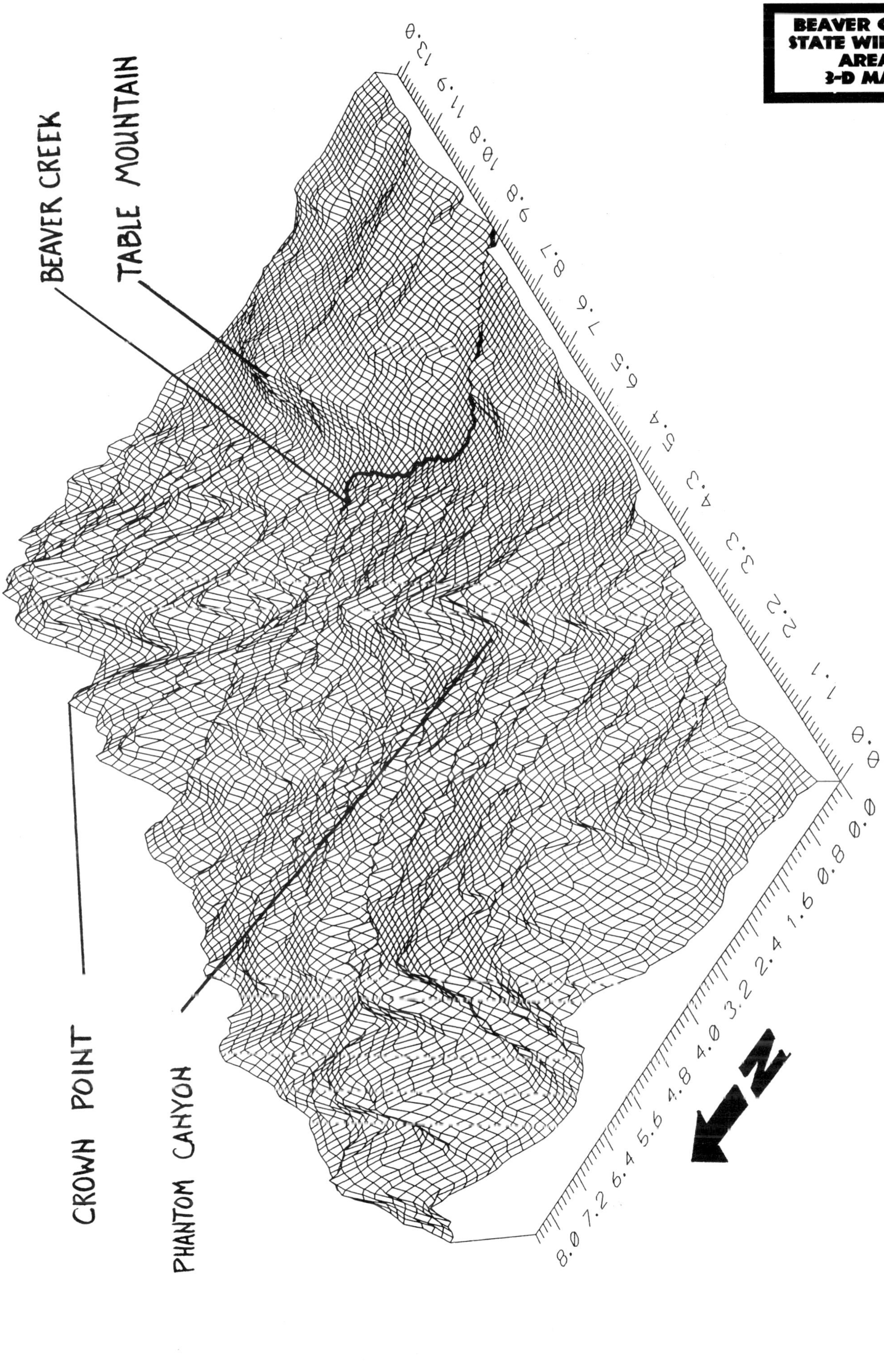

Big Creeks Lakes Area

Big Game Hunting Unit(s): 161

How To Get There:

This spot is located northwest of Walden, Colorado. Take Highway 125 north to Cowdry, then go west out of Cowdry about 15 to 18 miles. Follow the signs to Big Creek Lakes. From Big Creek Lakes take Road 099 two miles south to where it starts to turn east and begins winding around.

There is a lot of water in this area and as a result, a lot of elk. There aren't many deer, but the deer you do see will be extremely large...probably 25 inch spreads or better. Just like the Flat Tops which are discussed in another part of this book, this area contains a lot of downed timber and thick vegetation. It's hard for any animal to get through that stuff, so the elk stick to established, well beaten trails where it's easy to walk. So should you.

Because the game is concentrated on certain trails, tree stands will work well if they are well positioned. Very few hunters in Colorado use tree stands, which actually gives you an advantage. The animals are not conditioned to looking up, and are therefore much more susceptible to tree stand hunters. In recent years, many of the largest trophy deer have been taken from tree stands, which attests to the effectiveness of this method.

Heavy snows push elk and deer down onto the flats like those in the forefront of this picture.

There are a few guides working the Big Creek Lakes area. They concentrate more on Independence Mountain because there's a lot of country up there to hunt. Their horses have a rough time getting in because it's so thick. They have to stick to the trails to get anywhere, and so will you. Stick to Forester Creek to get back in.

Our friends Craig Fishel ("Fish") and Glen Vanderlinden went camping up in this area. In the middle of the night they heard a big ruckus in their camp, and Glen convinced Fish to stick his head out of the tent to see what it was. Fish looked out and said, "Get your gun out Glen, there's a humongous bear coming our way." Glen was from New Jersey and was not used to being around wild animals. He started saying, "Shit, shit, shit" while he frantically dug through his duffel for his pistol. Glen finally looked out to see the bear which by now Fish said had become completely enraged - that at any minute it was going to charge. What he saw was a little rabbit licking an open can of beans. Each time he licked the can, it would bang against a rock and make "bear noises."

Spot 01: **North Fork**. Right outside the National Forest border is a marshy area where many trees have been blown over. Work the little gullies and areas between the ponds you will see. This is a place that doesn't get a lot of pressure early on. Later in the rifle season hunters are going to push the elk from the valleys down below all the way up into the wilderness area where they're harder to find. This is a great trophy spot because very few people around the state know it's there.

Guy:

> I knew a professor at Colorado State University who hunted this area and shot one of the biggest bull elks taken in the 1989 season. It measured at 390 5/8 inches, although it was never entered into the Pope and Young record books.

Big Creek Lakes

(Reprinted from Routt National Forest map)

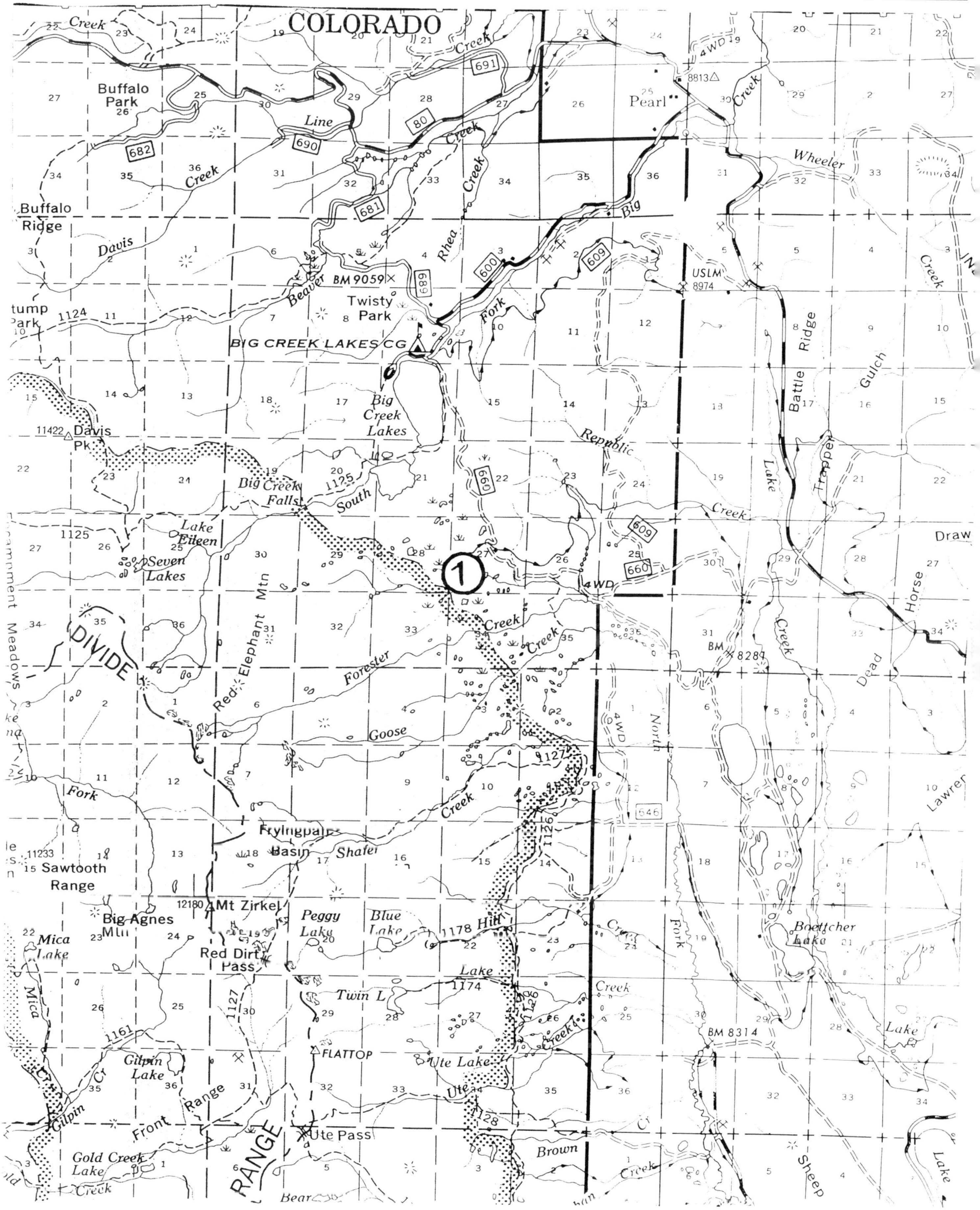

BIG CREEK LAKES 3-D MAP

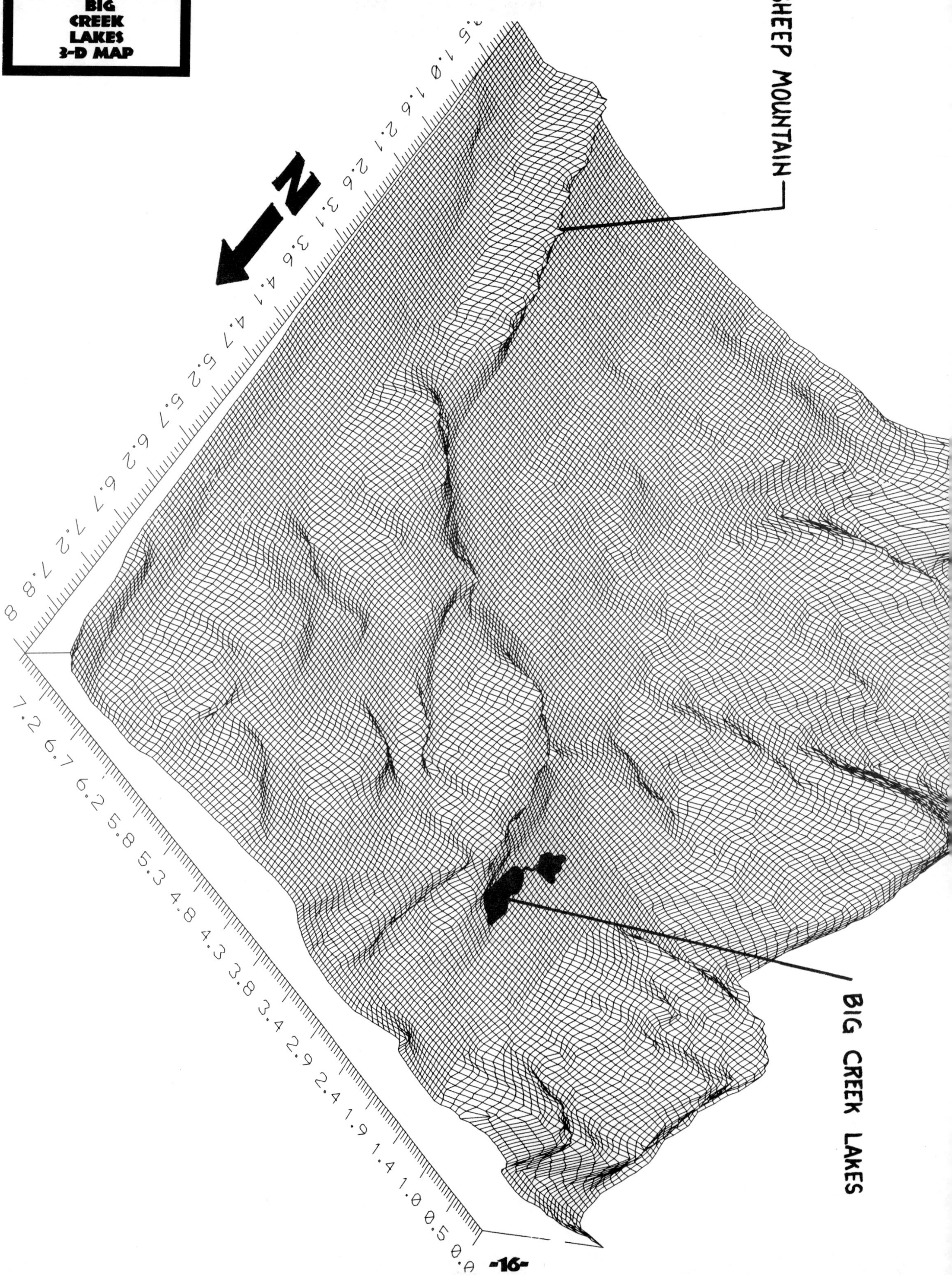

Bull Mountain & Laramie River

Big Game Hunting Unit(s): 8

How To Get There:

To get there head north on I-25 from Denver to Highway 14 which will take you west up the Poudre Canyon. Drive all the way up to Chambers Lake then turn right and go north on the Laramie River Road. This whole valley has a lot of game, especially in the high alpine meadows. Keep driving north (24 miles) to Sand Creek Pass Road, then turn right and go 4 miles to Bull Mountain. It will be on the left side. It's the largest mountain in the area.

How To Hunt This Area:

The face of this mountain has thick, closely packed pines, downed timber and pockets of Aspen with grass and bushes growing between their trunks, plus some open sage meadows to the west. You will find deer and elk feeding in the aspen meadows in the early morning and late evening. They only enter the sage meadows at night. The game trails cross back and forth between the sage meadows to the west and the heavy timber and aspen meadows to the east. You'll find the game bedded in the downed timber in the middle of the day. We've been able to jump them in there by keeping the wind in our face and moving slowly. They cannot always see over the logs they lay between without first moving, which gives their position away to the hunter.

The face of the mountain is very steep, while the top is relatively flat. There are a lot of ponds up top which were formed as a result of the flat terrain. The water has nowhere to go. There are always wallows around the ponds. Tree stand hunting may work well if a wallow is being used during the day. In 1983 Guy took a spike bull elk next to one of those wallows.

The lower southeast side of the mountain has a big treeless area that was formed by a forest fire. The lush grasses growing in this old burn support a lot of elk. Field glasses and long range scopes work very well in there. You can see the elk from a long way off.

Spot 01: **Bull Mountain Face**. You can camp at the base of Bull Mountain and walk directly up the face. Look for trails crossing from the woods (to the east) to the sage meadows (to the west).

Guy:

We hunted this spot quite extensively when we were in college. Spence and I were talking just the other day about how much sign we saw on the face of that mountain. There were at least 15 large elk trails that were used daily. Although we did get deer and elk out of there, in retrospect, we realize we should have gotten a lot more. We were just young and inexperienced. We didn't know how to hunt elk. If we went back there today, we'd surely fill our tags the first day.

Spence:

The funny thing is, when we discussed this area, I asked Guy if he wanted to go back. His answer was the typical "No, I've already seen that country." When we hunt, we like to explore too, and if we go to the same spot, we lose out on that feeling of adventure.

Spot 02: **Ridge Rocks.** Walk to the crest of the hill then head northwest. About a half mile over you will come to a wall of granite. Approximately 200 yards below the wall is a very nice waterhole. It sits about 200 yards back into the woods to the west of an old clearcut.

Guy:

I sat by that waterhole one night and took a 240 pound doe by shooting across the pond with my bow. I did hear several other animals in the timber coming in to water but decided on that deer because it was getting dark so quickly. Both deer and elk come in to this spot to water. We've also seen moose tracks where they waded through the water and ate the water grasses.

Spence:

That was the biggest doe I've ever seen. Its hide was half again as big as one from a 3 X 3 I had taken a week earlier. Getting that thing out of there across the steep mountain face was definitely a job. We carried it out on a pole. At one point, Fish tried to hold on when I slipped and dropped the carcass, and he ended up getting vaulted downhill, doing an aerial flip and landing on his back in a bush. He was pretty red in the face when he pulled himself out of the underbrush.

Spence:

I also had an encounter with a bear back up there. Just to the east of the waterhole is an old clearcut where berries grow. I had been seeing a lot of bear sign in the area. So I took my wounded rabbit call up. I blasted away a couple of times, and surprisingly, minutes later he came in from upwind. I could hear him breathing, but could not see him at all. I had sat down in cover that was too thick. Pine squirrels went off in front of me, then to my right side, then behind. I knew he was circling. Thinking the bear was hunting me, my bow began to feel flimsy and useless. I looked at it and said to myself, "Is that really going to stop a bear." Fortunately, after he circled behind me he got my scent and took off down the hill.

Spot 03: **Refuge Valley**. This spot is located in a valley about a mile to the east of Bull Mountain. It rises up from the sage flats that extend all the way to Laramie, Wyoming. This area will be extremely productive during the second or third rifle season.

Guy:

In 1984 we tried to get in there with our four wheel drive, but the roads were impassable due to heavy snow. However, from the Laramie side we spotted between 200 and 300 elk marching back and forth across the valley. As we approached they ran for the timber. The snow had pushed them down from Bull Mountain. An excellent time to hunt this spot would be the third rifle season, especially if there is an abundance of snow on the ground.

Spot 04: **Chimney Rock Ranch**. This spot is located three and a half to four miles east of Bull Mountain on Sand Creek Pass Road. The area has a lot of rim rock and wide open sagebrush. There are always deer down in the willows along Sheep Creek. If you hunt in there, you will more than likely see a lot of coyotes as well.

Guy:

If you continue north on this road you will cross over into Wyoming and come out at a community known as Tie Siding. I'm always amazed at the amount of antelope I see out on the flats over there. I wish I could catch them crossing over into Colorado.

Spot 05: **Little Bald Mountain**. Near Sand Creek Pass summit is Forest Service Road 177. Drive south on that road approximately 3 miles. You will gain a lot of altitude. Walk the creek bed bottoms you'll see a long the road. They always have deer in them.

Guy:

Last year while driving through there we saw three huge timber bucks crossing the road. The smallest was a very mature four by four and the largest a five by six with excellent mass. We were exactly 2.6 miles up Road 177.

We also got up on top and walked for a while. We found a tremendous amount of elk sign around the beaver ponds you'll see up there. I saw several groups of elk in the distance, but none had antlers. Possibly some were bulls but we were up there at a time when antler growth would have been minimal.

Spot 06: **Sand Creek**. As you continue farther up Road 177 (about 2 miles) the elk sign along the road increases. There are still some big timber bucks up in there, but generally speaking you will be in prime elk country. There are several drainages you can hunt. Look to the aspen stands which will be on the right for the most action.

Guy:

I've seen several big rubs in there. Last year I saw where one bull had rubbed an eight inch thick lodgepole pine completely raw. This got me very excited and I swore I'd be back.

Spot 07: **Pete Creek**. As you continue on Road 177 you will come to a "T." You can turn right on Road 162 or stay on 177. If you turn on 162 it will take you to Dead Man Road and back out to the Laramie River Road. This spot is located along the east side of the road. You'll be hunting on a small aspen/dark timber covered peak at the headwaters of Pete Creek. There is abundant elk sign on every side of the hill.

Spot 08: **Link McIntyre Trail**. Walk up Link Tail along McIntyre Creek and hunt the draws to the north and south. The abundance of elk sign in there is astonishing. We have seen dozens of cows and spikes feeding along the sides and also a few larger bulls. One bull was a five point with impressive mass.

Guy:

This spot is in the Rawah Wilderness. Motorized vehicles are prohibited. Bring along your best boots as well as a strong back. No sissies allowed.

Spence:

I knew some archaeologists in college who surveyed this area. They actually complained about the pesky bighorn sheep and elk coming right into their camp in the evening.

Spot 09: **Springer Creek**. Go back out to the Laramie River Road and head south approximately seven miles to where you will see lots of beaver ponds on the right hand side. That area will be productive during all hunting seasons. It's cool enough for elk during the early seasons and mild enough during the late season. The upper end of the valley is higher in elevation which is where you'll find the greatest concentration of elk. As far as deer are concerned, it's not going to be as productive as the lower part of Sand Creek, but you'll see a few in there.

Guy:

In this spot, when we first got out of the car we were slamming the doors and not being quiet at all. Figuring we would have to hike back in to find our quarry, we were surprised when we ran into a herd of 15 elk not 200 yards off the road. They scattered when they saw us. We tried to move in on them but they were completely spooked and we couldn't close the gap. The elk sign in there was unbelievable. Judging by all the sign we saw on both sides of the road we believe there are elk within 50 yards of the road nearly all of the time.

Bull Mountain and Laramie River Drainage

(Reprinted from Roosevelt National Forest map)

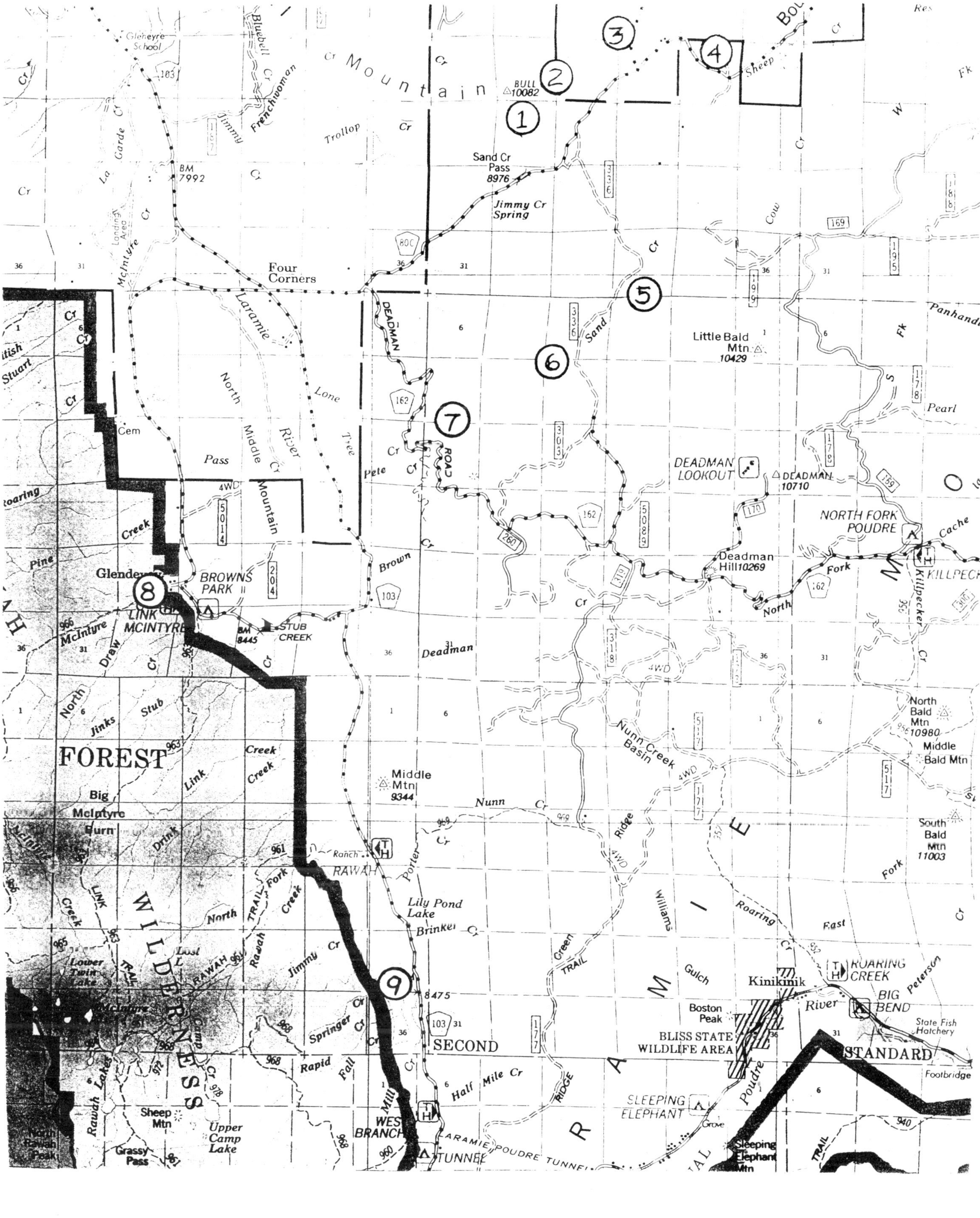

BULL MOUNTAIN & LARAMIE RIVER DRAINAGE 3-D MAP

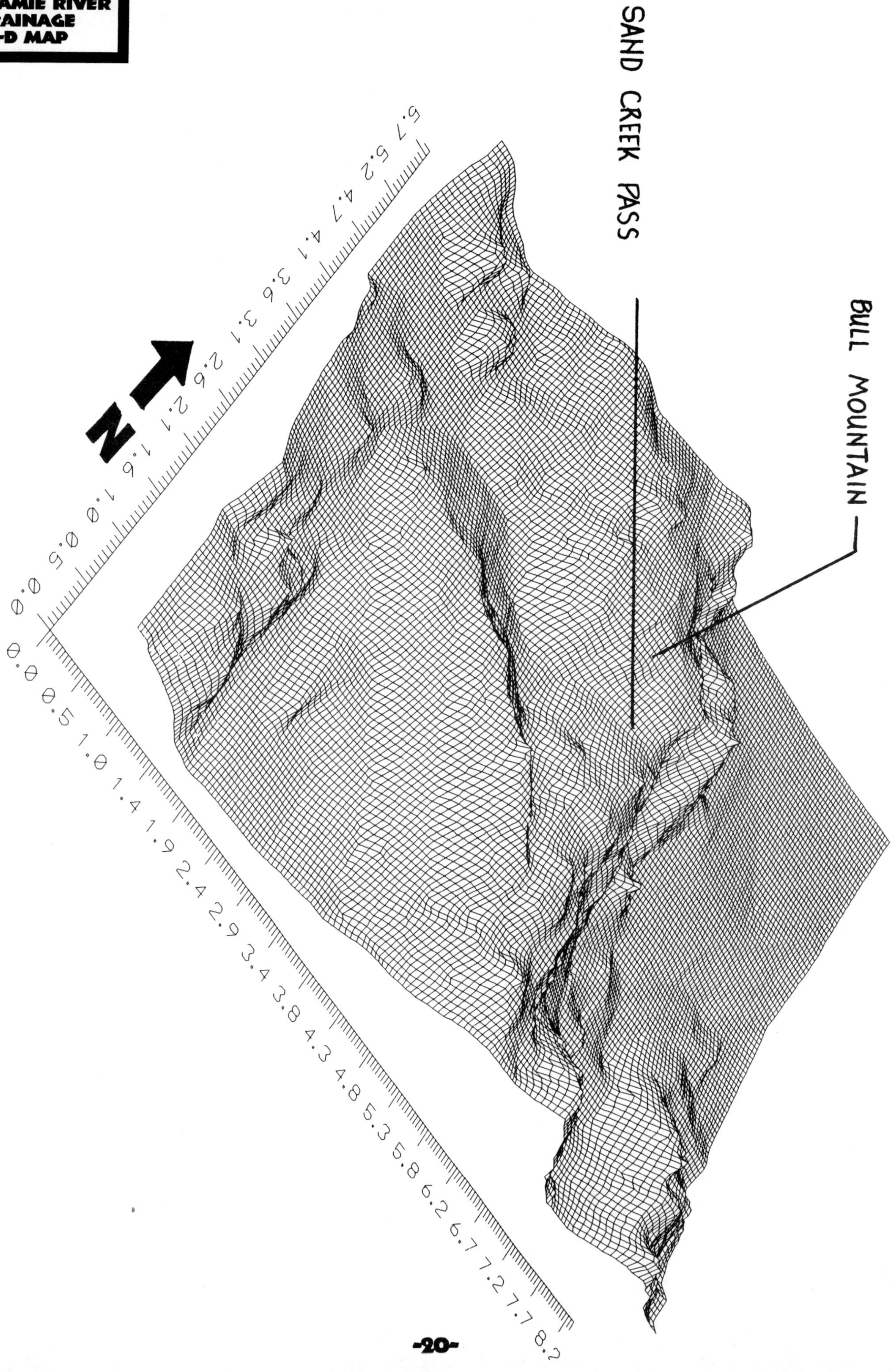

BULL MOUNTAIN & LARAMIE RIVER DRAINAGE 3-D MAP

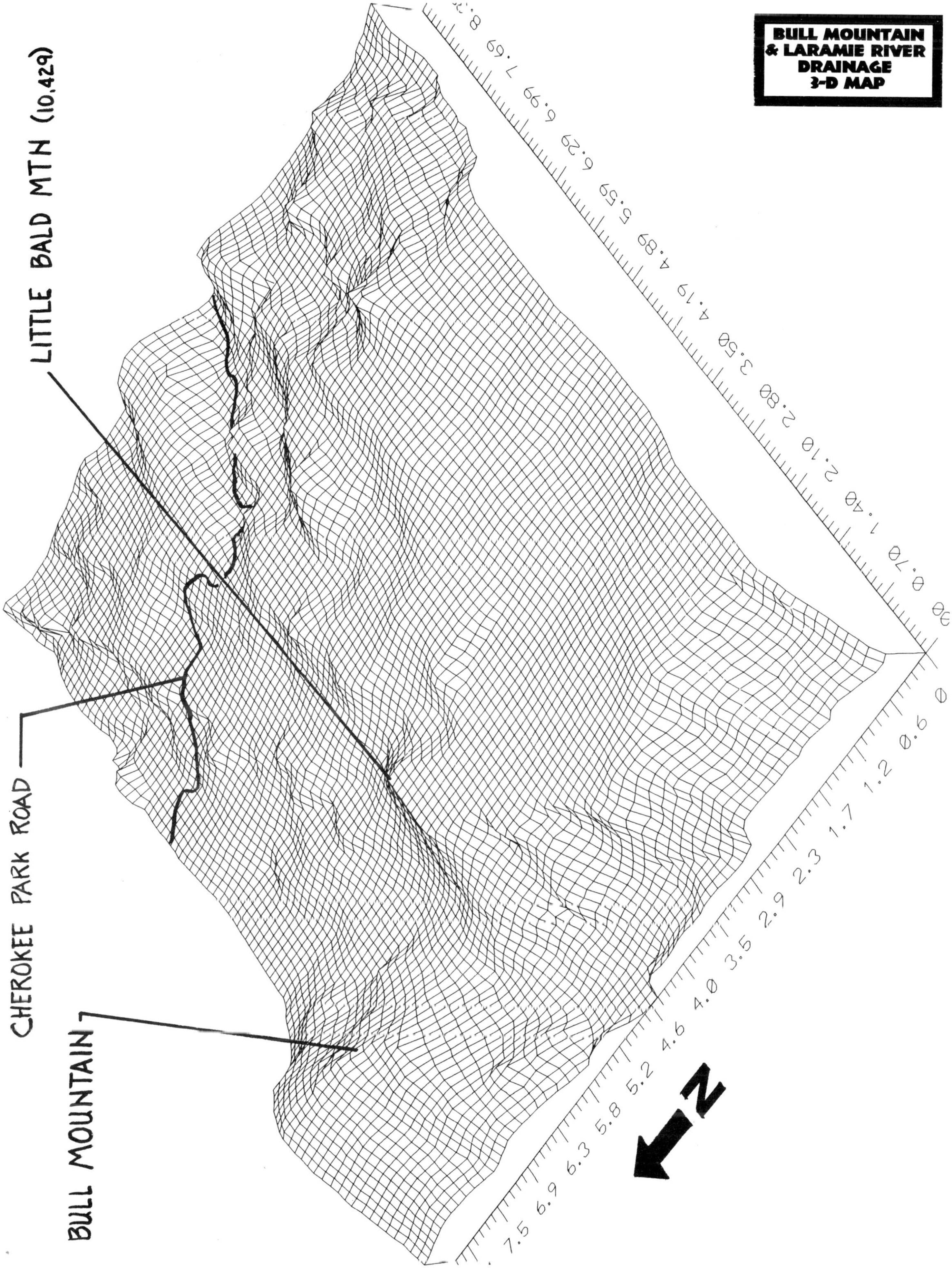

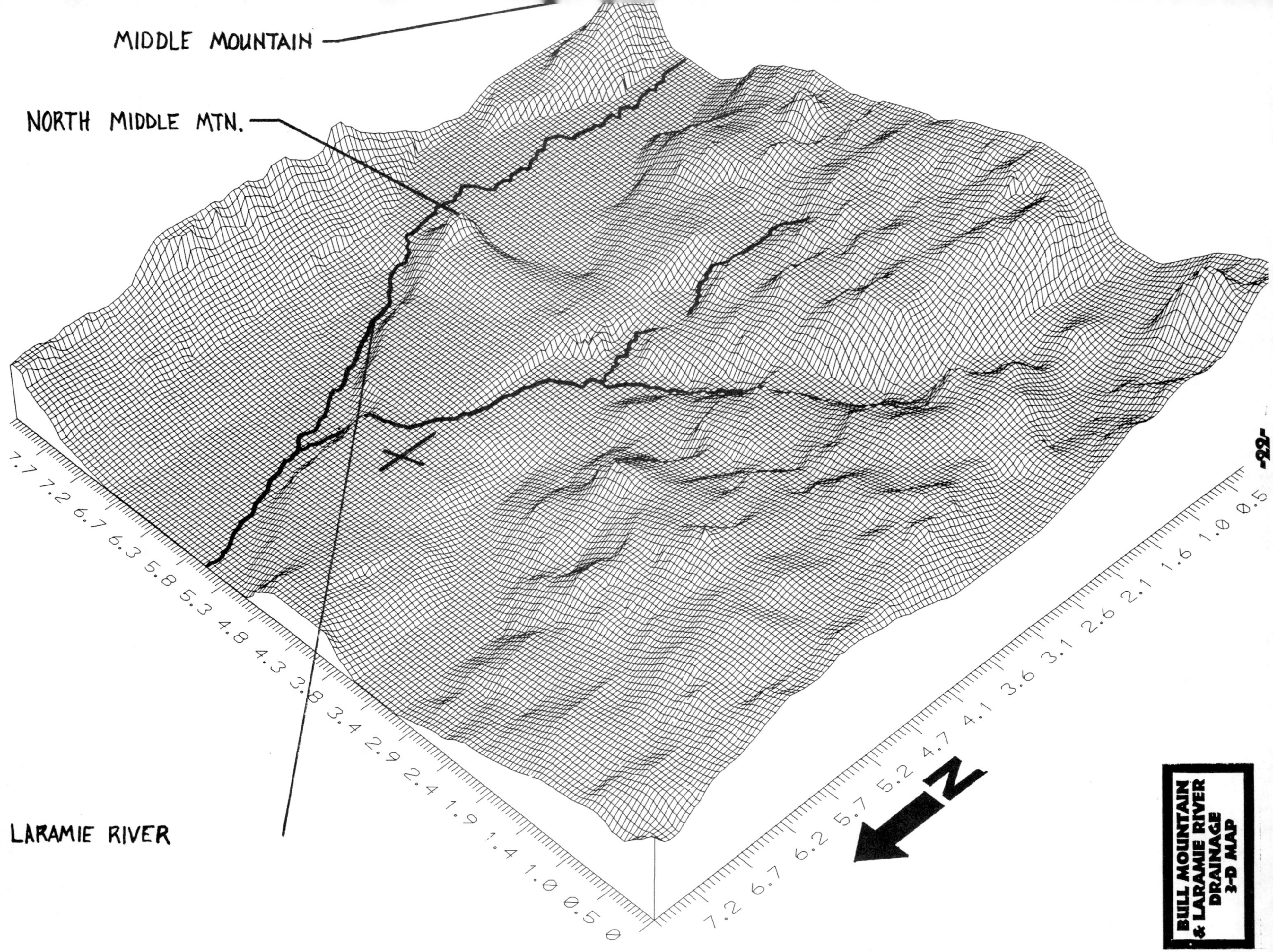

BULL MOUNTAIN & LARAMIE RIVER DRAINAGE 3-D MAP

BULL MOUNTAIN & LARAMIE RIVER DRAINAGE 3-D MAP

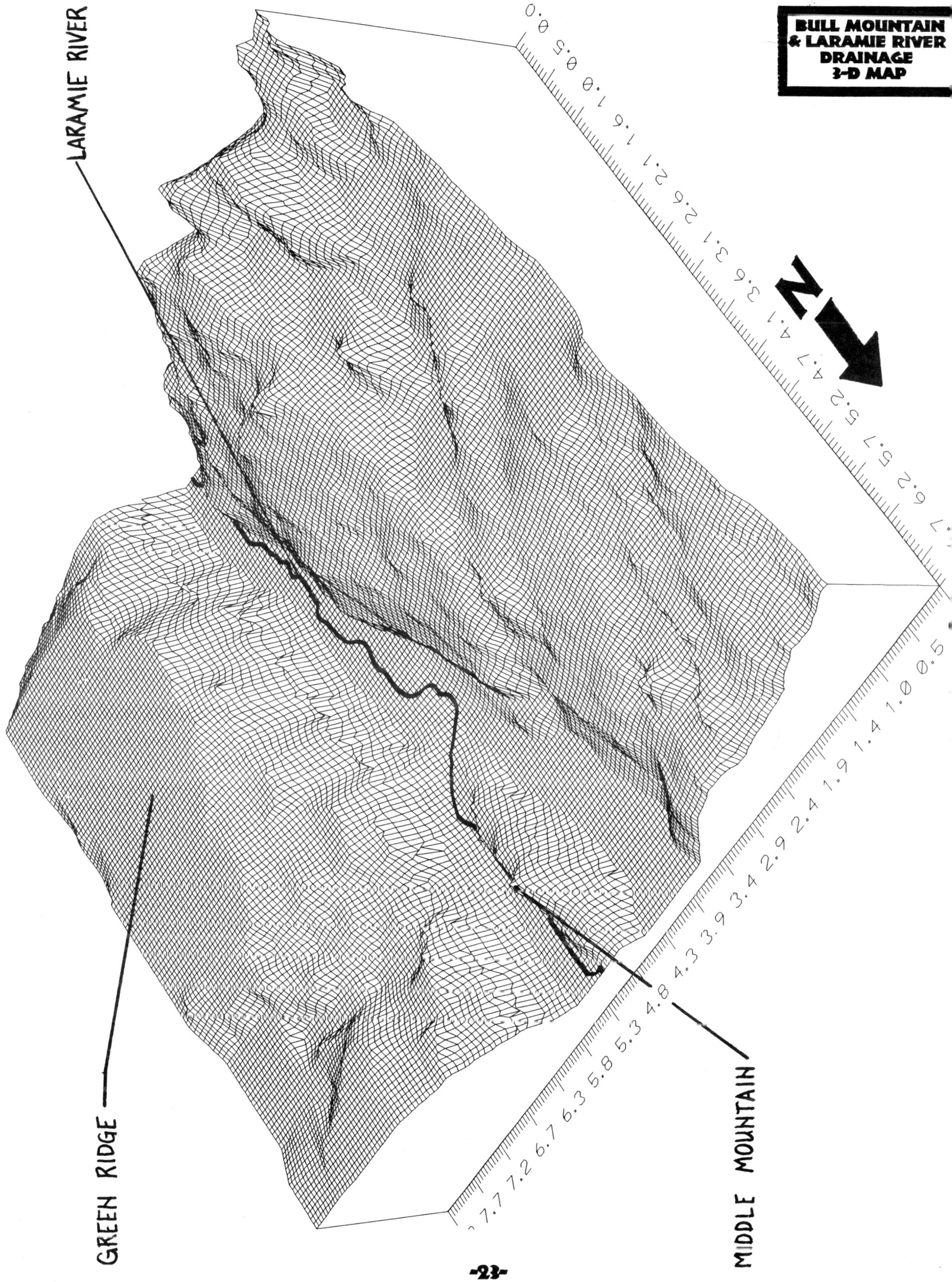

Canon City, Wet Mountains, San Isabel, Sangre de Cristo

Big Game Hunting Unit(s): 581, 58, 86, 84, 69

How To Get There:

You're going to the Wet Mountain valley in the Sangre De Cristo National Forest. Drive to Canon City, then drive up Highway 15 along the Arkansas River valley. All the spots mentioned are either located on the sides of the Arkansas River valley or along Texas Creek after you turn down Highway 69.

How To Hunt This Area:

How you hunt this area depends on whether you are hunting land adjacent to the Arkansas River valley, the Wet Mountains or the Sangre de Cristo National Forest borders.

Arkansas River valley:

In the Arkansas River canyon you will mostly hunt in pinion and juniper forests. It's extremely dry everywhere but the canyon bottom. Try walking up the dry side canyons which feed the Arkansas River valley. You'll find big deer that hide out up there until night when they go down to the river and the surrounding fields. You can also still hunt and catch them going to and from the valley.

If you are lucky enough to find a spring or waterhole up one of those dry canyons, stick to it. A day won't go by that deer don't come to a spot like that.

Wet Mountains:

These mountains are good for both deer and elk. There's a peculiar weather pattern that dumps a lot of moisture on the peaks which are a lot lower than the mountains in the San Isabel forest to the west. There are some alpine meadows up on the highest ridges. But it quickly drops down into pinion and juniper mixed with scruboak. It's very very rugged and often passed up by hunters. Be prepared for a lot of steep walking through brush that tears at your clothes. However, there is no better place for deer, and the elk you find will be less pressured by hunters.

Sangre de Cristo:

The Sangre de Cristo mountain range is found in the San Isabel National Forest. The vegetation there is very diverse. In just 15 miles you can cross 5 different vegetative zones. The topmost zone is alpine. As you walk down hill you quickly enter dark pine and aspen. Just a few miles from that you get into pinion and juniper. A few more miles you hit scruboak. Then four or five miles farther you get into agricultural areas where wheat is grown. The extreme variance in vegetation supports large numbers of animals in relatively small areas.

You will find deer in the 4 lower vegetative zones year round, and in the upper zones during the archery, muzzle loading and first rifle seasons. Elk are concentrated in the upper zone until they are pushed down by snow, although there are always a few in all the zones.

The locals say this area is Colorado's best kept hunting secret. It is always overlooked by hunters who want to hunt the more famous areas like the White River National Forest and Flat Tops Wilderness. If you drive through the town of Westcliffe, you'll see how good this area is. Right there on the fire station wall is a rack from a huge elk shot locally. It's probably pushing 375. That's all the proof we needed to give this area a green light.

Spot 01: **Monument Border.** This spot is located approximately four miles northwest of Canon City on Highway 50. There is a little stretch of BLM land on the right and left side probably 3/4 of a mile long. What's unique about this spot is that it's surrounded by private property and right behind it is the Royal Gorge National Monument. Anybody who has been to the Royal Gorge will remember all the huge deer that pester the tourists for handouts. Most people would skip this place driving by, not realizing that it borders a huge popcorn and peanut butter sandwich fed deer herd. Also, to the north of the road are about three or four hills. You can either pull off to the side or pull over to a little gate you'll see and hunt right up the valleys between the hills.

Spot 02: **Deer Sheds.** This area is located next to Spot 1, but it's on the south side of the road. There's a road that parallels the highway then goes up the side of the mountain. If you walk that road early in the morning you can cover a lot of ground and get back in about a half a mile to the back side of the property. This is another "sleeper" area. People will not usually hunt there because it's small and isolated. Just in case someone does decide to hunt there your best bet would be to hunt the first rifle season. We scouted this spot in March and picked up some huge deer sheds. This is how we know it is going to be really good this year. Many of the big bucks made it through the winter.

Spot 03: **River Crossing.** Take Highway 50 west through Parkdale and back into the BLM land on the other side. You will notice several canyons off to the right on the other side of the river. The good thing about this spot is that there is absolutely no hunting pressure. But there's also one major problem, you have to cross the river to get to it. You'll need a rubber raft, canoe or kayak to cross. Once you're on the other side, you'll have all the deer to yourself. There's a little creek coming down one of the canyons all the way to the Arkansas River. You will notice it on the map. Walk it up to the saddles on top. You'll probably never have to walk all the way to the saddle because you'll run into so many deer down lower.

Spots 04 and 05: **Hinman Gulch & Table Mountain.** This spot is also located on the north side of the Arkansas River. On the map you'll notice a huge flat top mountain called Table Mountain. It's probably about four and a half miles back in. There are several creek beds to hunt and there are a couple of little roads that go up Reece Gulch and Texas Creek Gulch. All three drainages are wonderful hunting spots. Up high on Table Mountain we found one four point (left side) and one six point (right side) shed. And that's just what we found. There's definitely a lot more up there. The whole valley between Table Mountain and Hinman Gulch should be very productive.

Spot 06: **Before Texas Creek.** Right before you turn off Highway 50 at Texas Creek, you'll notice a steep little gully to the southeast. Walk the bottom of this and look up the sides for big mule deer, especially around any pools of water you may find. You can either set a tree stand up in one of the pine trees or you can just find a piece of higher ground overlooking a frequently used waterhole. If there's too much hunting pressure, try going up on top. We saw all kinds of deer up there. But it's a deer only area. Don't expect to run into any elk.

Spot 07: **Back Door Gulch.** This spot is unique because it's right next to private property that runs along Highway 69 and forms a hunting access barrier. If you park right on the BLM land and slip back into the gulch you will probably have the spot all to yourself. We saw sign for between 30 to 40 deer throughout the valley, and they didn't seem to be afraid of humans.

Spot 08: **Farm Fed Deer.** Take Highway 69 south from Highway 50. In this area, alfalfa and wheat fields have been planted right up next to the surrounding BLM land. You can slip in next to that boundary line and wait for the deer to come down and feed in the fields. Or, you can hunt some of the valleys farther back. You'll notice that all of the game trails go to the agricultural areas in the valley. As you drive farther south of this spot you'll notice that all the farmers' haystacks have huge fences around them to keep the deer and elk from eating their harvest during the winter.

Spot 09: **Likely Gulch.** Park right alongside Road 69 where the gulch meets the road. The land adjacent to the highway is owned by the BLM. Follow the creek bed up. It's pretty easy walking. This spot is a little bit more mountainous than the previous ones, with pine trees mixed with pinion and juniper. Despite the increase in elevation and change in vegetation, it's still relatively dry. On top it's flat, which makes for an easy walk hunt. An easy walk is rare in Colorado.

Spot 10: **Spring Road Gulch.** Drive east approximately 3/4 of a mile, then walk up toward the spring. This spot is going to be exactly like Likely Gulch, except that it is much easier to access. As a result, it will get more pressure during the rifle season. With each new rifle season, you will have to walk farther back to find the game. But during the muzzle loading and archery seasons, you probably won't see many other hunters. Once again you're only going to find big mule deer in this area, no elk. We found one really nice shed in there that had 6 points on one side. We got pretty excited because we spotted 20 to 30 deer in a short period of time. We happened to be turkey hunting and we found another spot just up over the ridge called Turkey Gulch. Now we know why it's called Turkey Gulch. There were turkey tracks all over the place.

Spot 11: **McCoy Gulch.** Turn off Highway 69 on Road 1A. About a mile up on the right hand side of the road, after you cross a yellow cattle guard, the terrain will change to rolling hills. We spotted 22 deer right off the side of the road. It's a relatively small area surrounded by private and state land. People tend to overlook the small areas like this one. Walk back into the far corner of the property which is just to the east of McCoy Gulch, and sit on the boundary. That's where the local herd comes through the draw from the private land. It's an easy flat walk. You might even catch elk down in there in the late season if the weather in the Sangre de Cristos has been bad.

Spot 12: **Electric Deer Fence.** This place is about an eighth of a mile farther up road 1A from the McCoy Gulch spot. It will be all private on the left hand side. You will see a corn field with electric fence around it. The deer are thick there. Presumably, they had to put the electric fence up to keep the deer out. There's a little bit of BLM land adjacent to this land which you can hunt.

Spot 13. **Hayden Creek/South Prong And Middle Prong.** Go west on Highway 50 four or five miles past Cotopaxi. Right before you get to Coaldale turn left and you will see a sign for Hayden Creek campground. It goes about five miles back in. There is a circle at the very end. You'll also pass a privately owned campground called Cuddy's where you may want to stay. Despite the fact that it's very isolated, it has hot showers, a swimming pool, and of all things, putt putt golf. It's nice to take a hot shower after a hard day's hunting, especially if the weather is bad.

The lower part of this canyon is mostly pinion and juniper but it gains altitude quickly. Toward the top there is snow most of the year. The South Prong and Middle Prong Creek beds were torn up by elk when we scouted there. In April we saw several bull elk that hadn't completely dropped their racks, which is unusual. All of the deer had dropped their racks, but something was keeping the racks on the elk.

Guy:

As a kid I used to go camping at Cuddy's with my family. Every time we went, we ran into bears. One night, there were three different bears in the campground's trash cans at one time. I was always paranoid that I would be confronted by a bear while fishing in the creek.

Spot 14: **Hayden Creek - North West.** There is a pack trail heading northwest from just outside the campground. It will switch back and forth a couple of times, then head back toward some lakes. All along the trail are excellent places to hunt for both elk and mule deer. Once the heavy snow starts to fall the elk are going to come down out of the high mountain valleys and pass right through there on their way down to the valley by Coaldale. Hunt right where you see one type of vegetation switching to another. In this area they use the dark timber to bed, coming out into the scruboaks and fields to feed. There are several little gullies you can walk up away from the trail. Look for tracks where the trail crosses a gully. If you see some, get off the trail and follow.

Spot 15: **Hayden Creek - Italian Gulch.** Just up from Cuddy's is Italian Gulch. Walking the creek bed up is the easiest way to get access to the higher elevations. Follow the gulch over to where it crosses another trail that also runs south out of the same campground and goes over to Slide Rock Mountain. There are a lot of deer and elk in there. One thing nice about this area is that it won't get any pressure early on. During the archery and muzzle loading seasons, you'll have the place virtually to yourself. They hunt it hard in the rifle seasons, but if you're the first one in, you'll still get some good opportunities.

Spence:

> I don't want people to get the idea that a lot of hunters in an area makes it a bad area. You just have to modify your tactics to fit the situation. You can really use intense hunting pressure to your advantage. Just figure out where the game is going to move in order to get away from the other hunters, and set up an ambush. A saddle is usually the best place to sit. I was once in an area that got so much hunting pressure the deer never even bedded down. I set up and all day long deer walked by as they tried to stay away from the hunters who were walking around making more noise than they should have been.
>
> Also, the game is going to go where people don't want to walk. If you're willing to stay out all day, and work the really rough areas, you're much more likely to get something. At some point in your hunt, you're going to look down into some extremely steep gully and say to yourself, "God, I don't want to go down there. How would I ever get the meat out of there if I got one." When I hear this voice in my head I know I'm at the door of a prime hunting spot. Just make sure you're physically fit, and have enough equipment with you (ie. matches, emergency sleeping bag, food, etc.) to stay overnight if you do have some mishap.

Spot 16: **The Plateau.** This spot is located near the spot with the electric deer fence down along Cotopaxi Road. But you'll be hunting up against the Sangre de Cristos. As you are driving south through the valley you will come out up on top of a plateau. Looking to the right you will see a definite vegetative transitional zone where scruboak and aspen meet. It's pretty easy walking and great hunting.

Spot 17: **North Side Of Sullivan Creek.** Take Road 36 back as far as it goes. It will stop on BLM land and then turn into a foot trail. Park right there and walk the trail back through the scruboak and pine. The deer are thick in this spot. We must have jumped 30 in just a couple of hours. We also saw elk, but that was because the snow had pushed them out of higher elevations. There will always be a few elk in there, but the only time you would want to go to this spot just for elk would be the third rifle season, provided the weather has been cold.

Spot 18: **South Lake Creek.** Just past Hillside take Road 198 and go directly west to the campground. Hunt right along the private boundaries as far as you are willing to walk in. All of the drainages and the area around the lake are good for deer and elk. You might want to pack a fishing rod. Fishing in there can be phenomenal for cutthroats and brookies.

Spot 19: **Brush Creek Lakes.** Take Brush Creek Loop Road to Road 192 and drive as far back in as the road will permit. In the drainages below Brush Creek Lakes is where a huge 6 X 7 bull elk was taken a few years back. Having lived so long, it probably sired a lot of offspring that now roam those hills.

Spot 20: **Middle Brush Creek.** This spot is located south of Brush Creek Lakes. There are a lot of willows along the creek bottoms with scruboaks on the ridges above them. These are great places to find and ambush animals. Game activity will center around whatever water is available. Look for dusting areas and wallows. Try to cover as much ground as you can, moving from gully to gully.

Spots 21 and 22: **Dienza Peak Area.** Take Verdemont Road west to where it ends. From there you'll take a trail running west. The first spot marked on the map is high up and good in the early season for elk and deer. There is a huge knoll right about timberline just below Dienza Peak that holds a lot of nice elk and some deer. They congregate there. Don't be surprised if you glass that spot in the early morning and see a herd bull bugling away. The second spot is good later in the season when snow and cold weather push the elk down into the valley along Green Leaf Creek. You can walk along the creek or take the trail over to Coal Creek. Walk the creek bottoms until you find fresh elk tracks cutting up the hillside. Pay attention to track size. Lone bull tracks will be larger than cow tracks.

Spot 23: **Spring Bear Gulch.** This spot is located between Canon City and Westcliffe. Take the turnoff west from Road 255. There is no road number for the road going down to Grape Creek, but it's right by a huge mound of fill dirt. The access to this spot is through private property. You will notice that a local outfitter has posted all the private property, and there's a very good reason why. This area is very very productive for deer. We drove down there in the evening, and it seemed like every time we went around a turn, we saw another deer. We did not see any trophies, but that doesn't mean they're not in there. With this many deer, there are bound to be trophy animals. The best way to hunt this spot is to walk the ridges down hill and watch the gullies on either side. Several people can work this area using drive and block tactics. You will continually lose altitude until you hit Grape Creek at the bottom.

Spot 24: **Grape Creek.** Spring Bear Gulch road comes out at the bottom of Grape Creek. You may want to take your fishing pole. At one time this was probably a private fishing camp. They set up diversions to create little waterfalls which all have trout behind them. Stick your line in there. It would be a great way to enjoy some fresh trout for dinner.

The canyon itself is steep on both sides. It's flat and open on the valley floor where a lot of grass grows. As long as there aren't too many hunters walking the bottom, you'll find deer there in the evenings and the early morning hours. You could probably set up there on opening morning and shoot your deer from camp. Any one of the little gulches going up from the creek bottom would be productive too. Just walk the bottom and look for tracks going up the hillside. With a pair of field glasses, you can easily spot deer moving along the hillside above. Terrain permitting, you can walk the Grape Creek valley downstream for ten miles until it hits the Royal Gorge and Arkansas River. There are no roads down the creek, just foot trails. We did not walk very far down, so we're not exactly sure how far you can really walk. But it can only get better the farther down you go, because eventually, you will get into areas where the game has never been hunted.

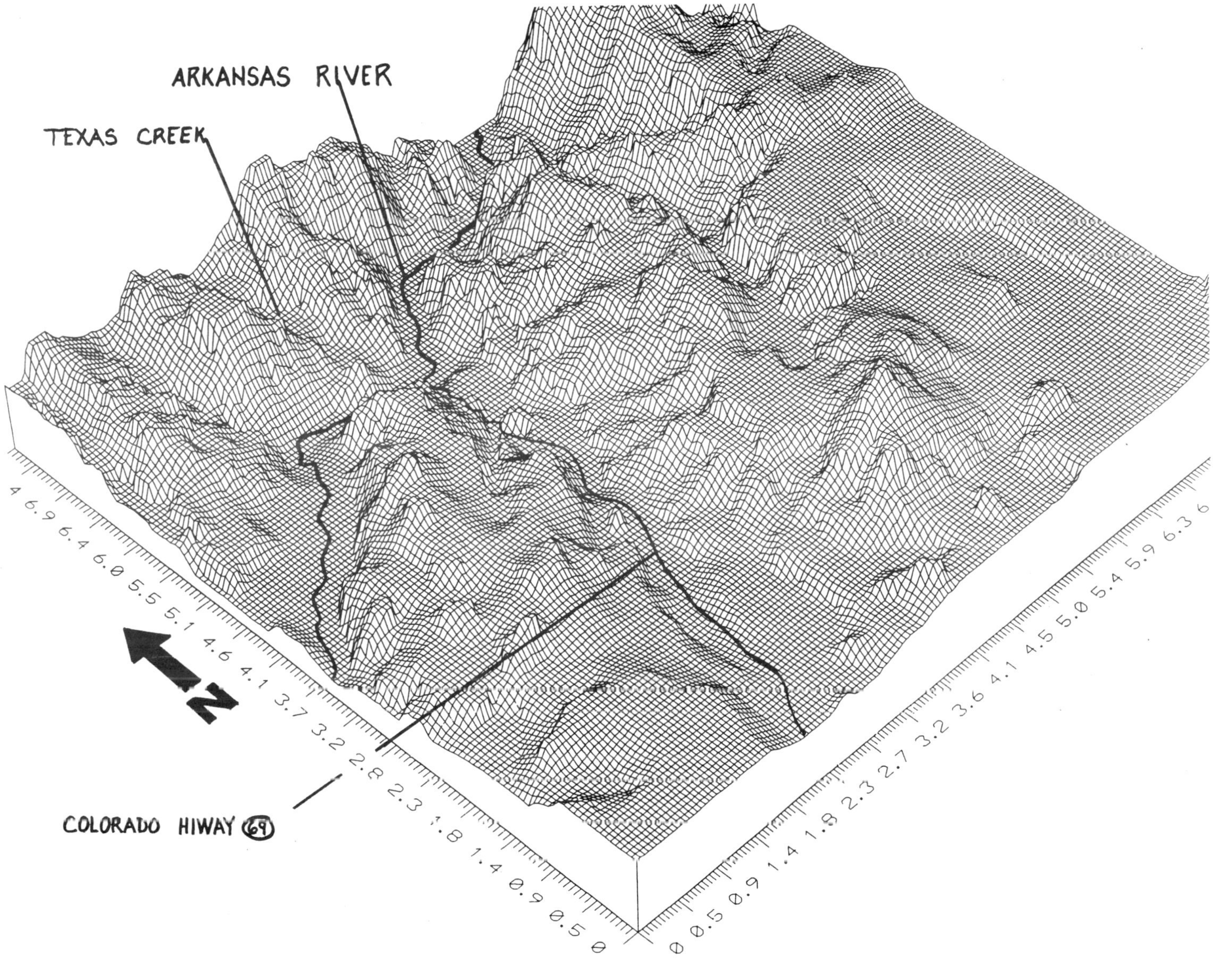

CANON CITY, SANGRE DE CRISTOS.... 3-D MAP

Canon City, Wet Mountains, San Isabel, Sangre de Cristo

(Reprinted from BLM Canon City map)

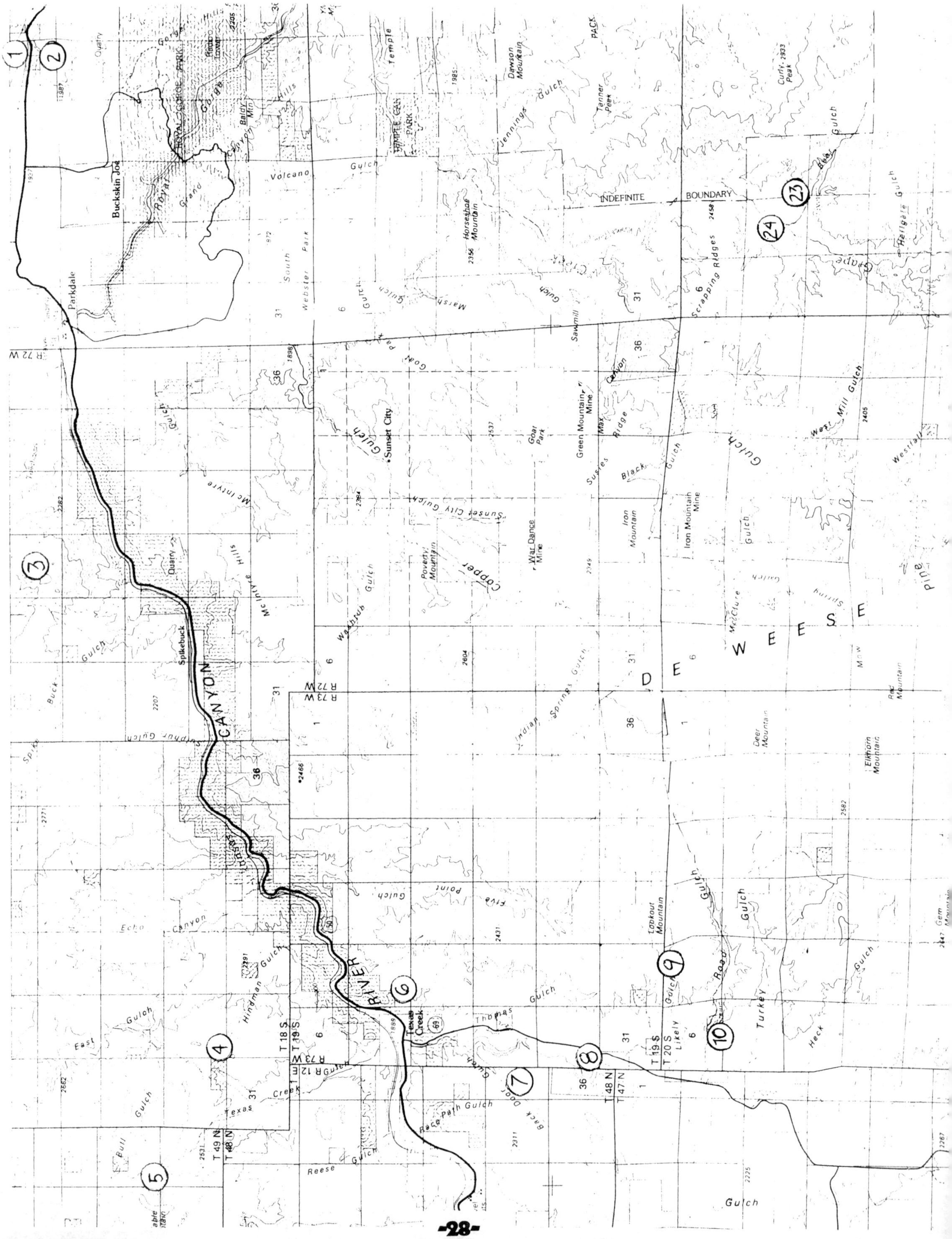

Canon City, Wet Mountains, San Isabel, Sangre de Cristo

(Reprinted from BLM Canon City map)

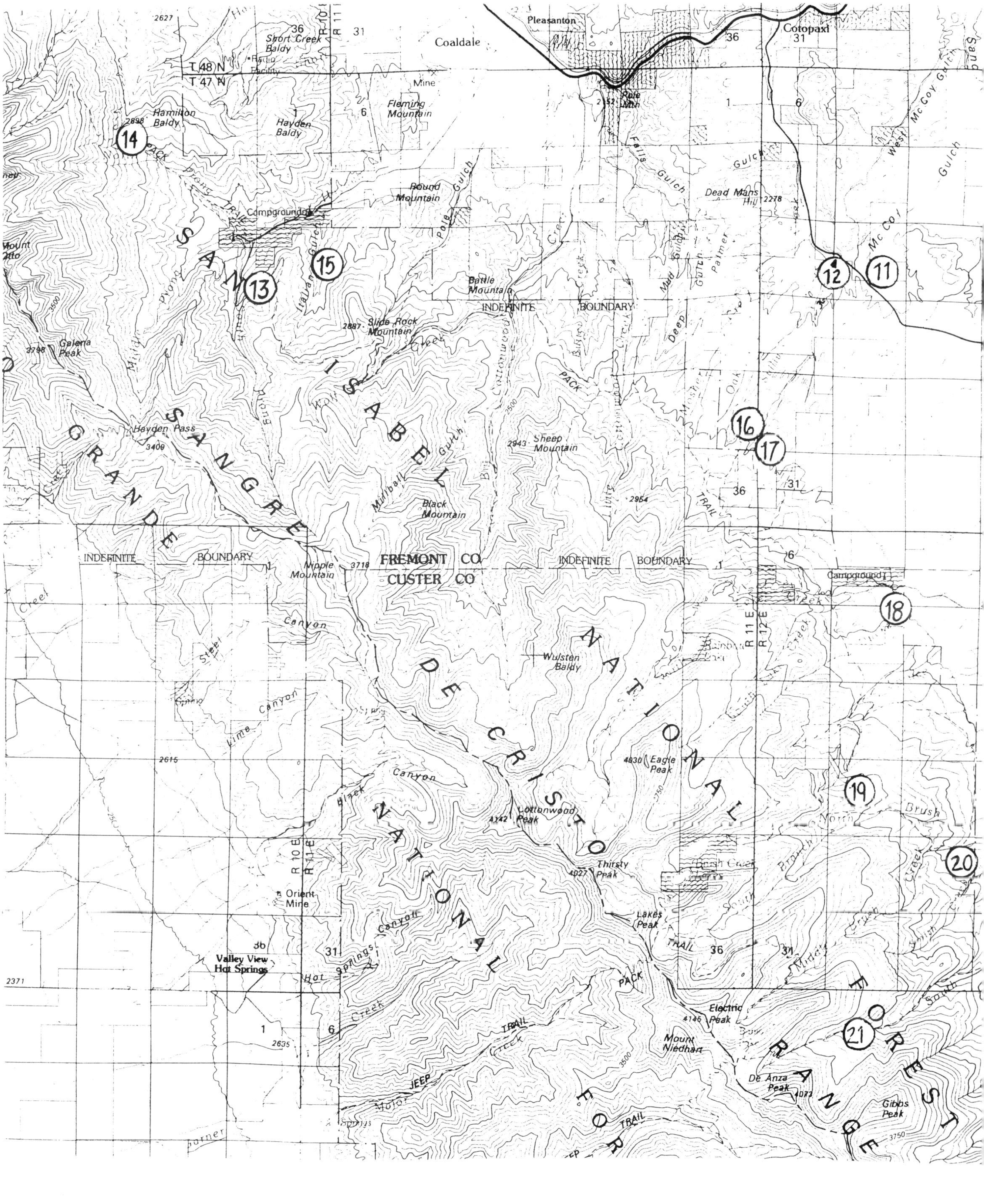

CANON CITY, SANGRE DE CRISTOS.... 3-D MAP

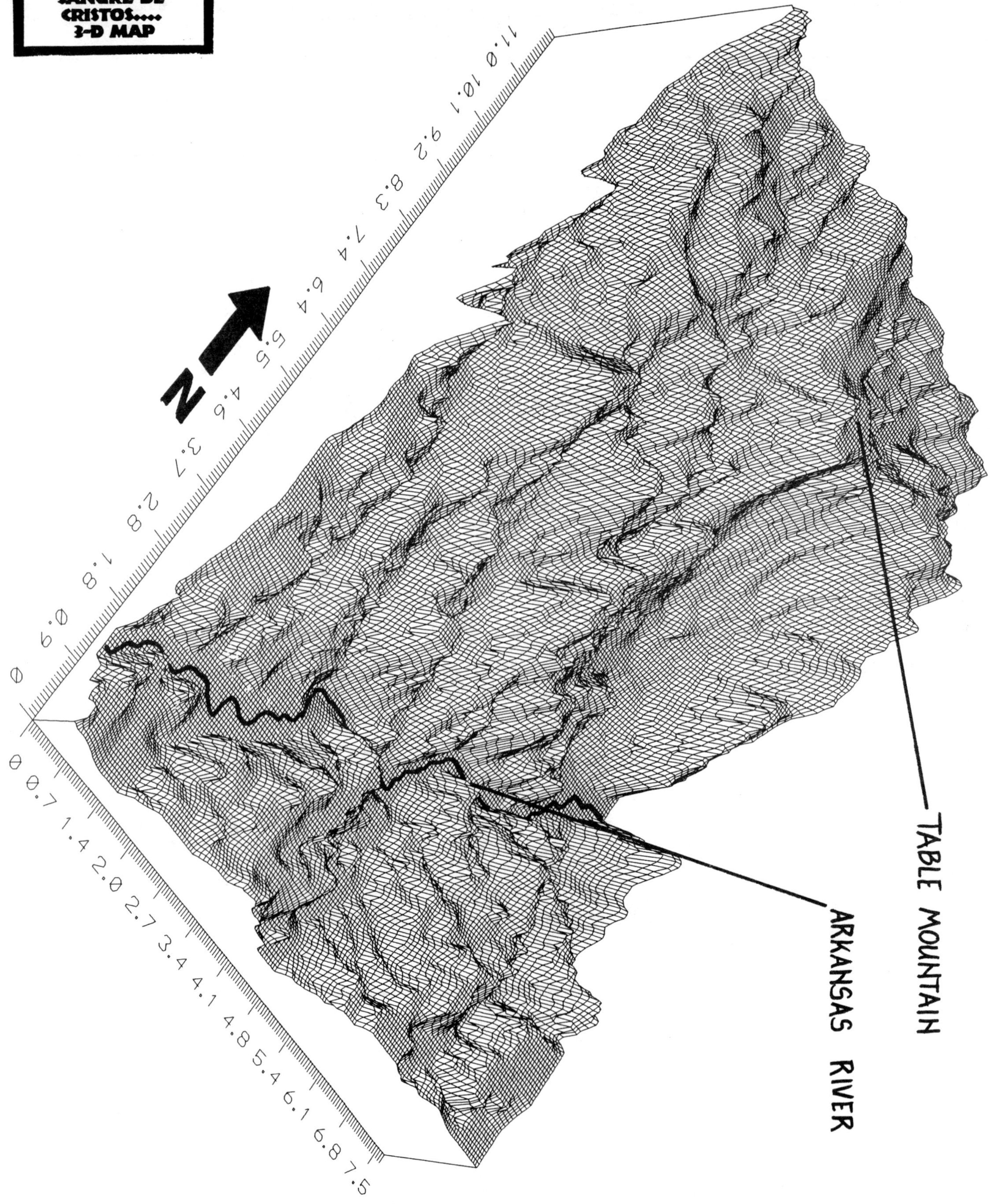

CANON CITY, SANGRE DE CRISTOS.... 3-D MAP

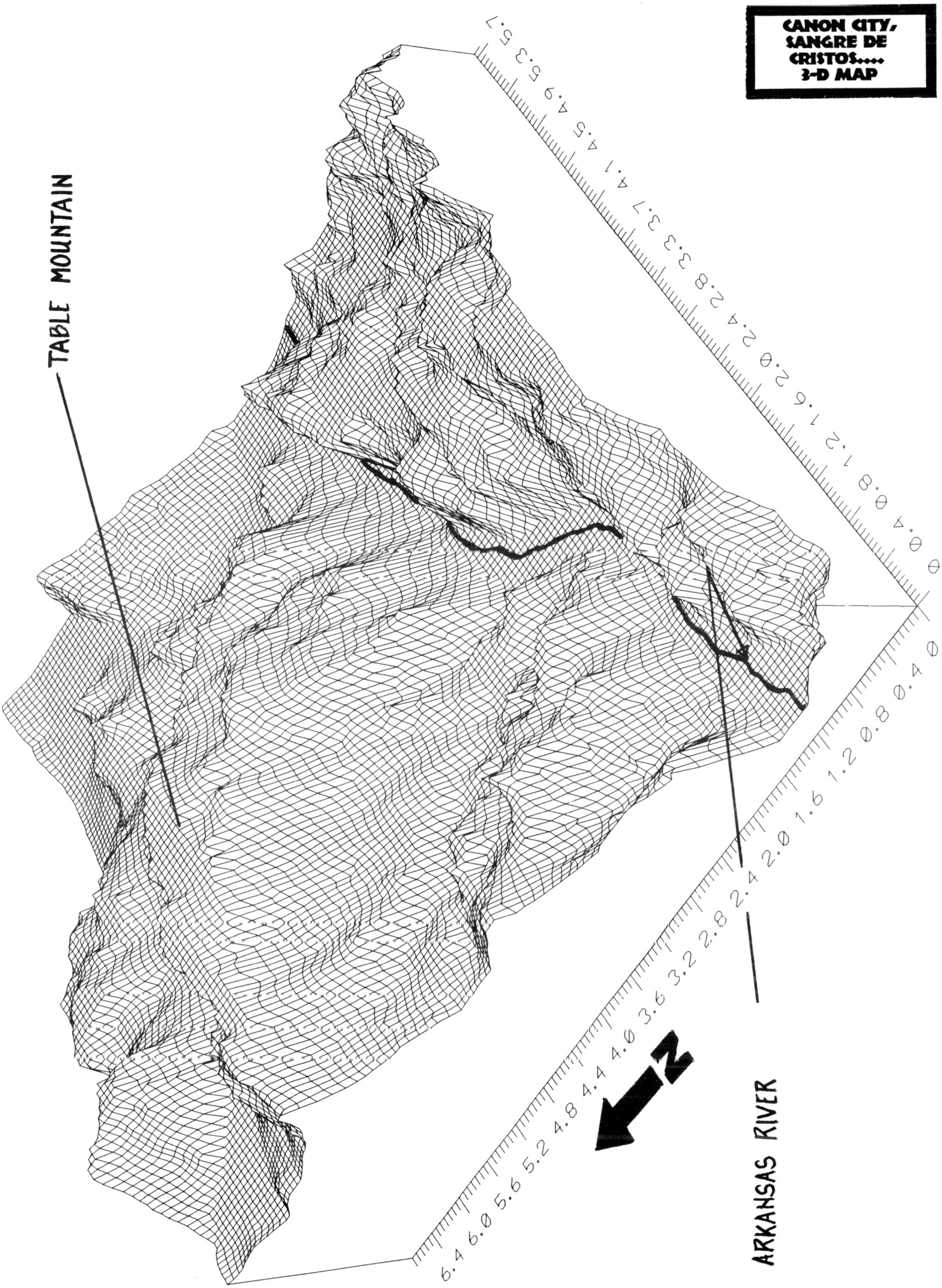

CANON CITY, SANGRE DE CRISTOS.... 3-D MAP

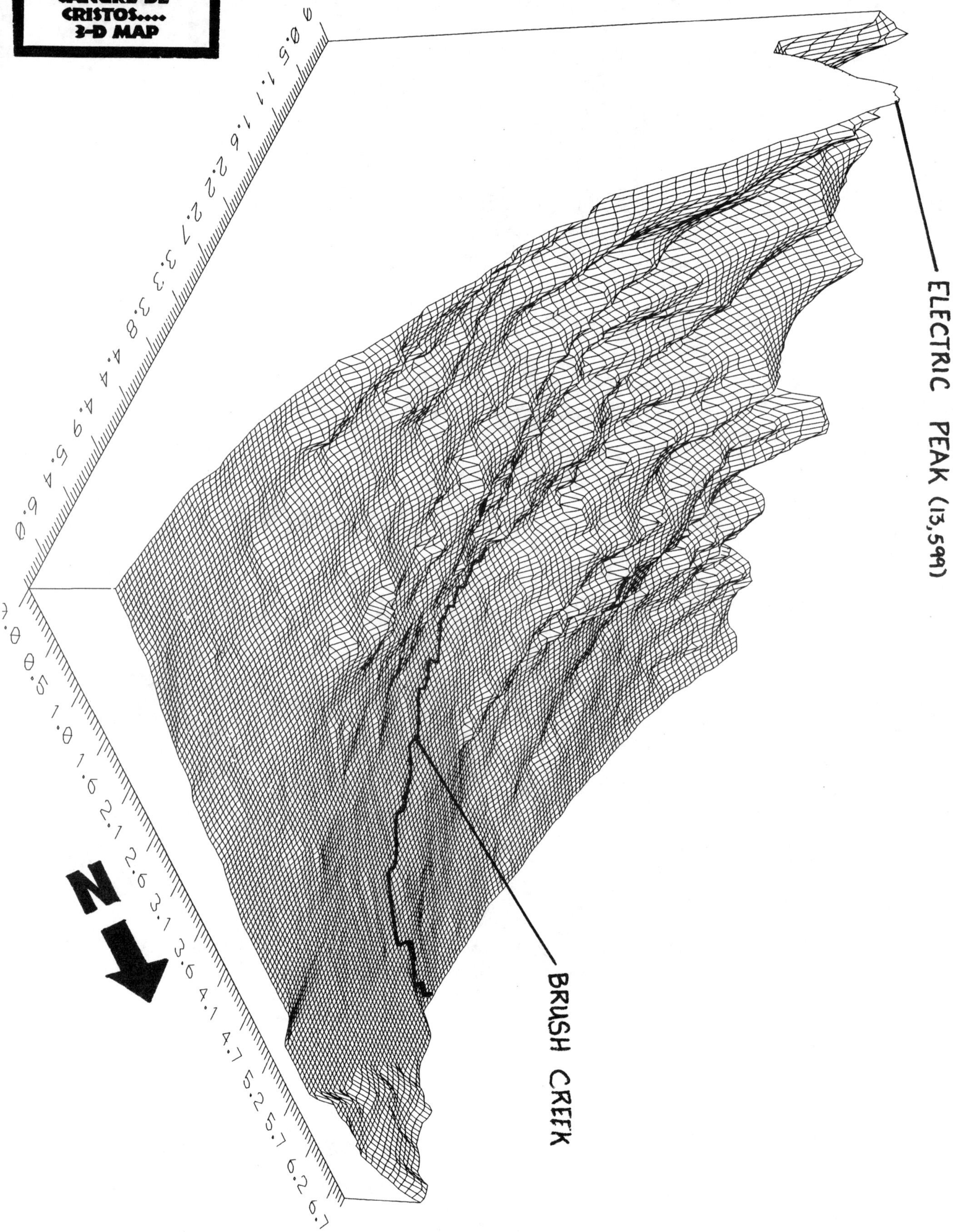

CANON CITY, SANGRE DE CRISTOS.... 3-D MAP

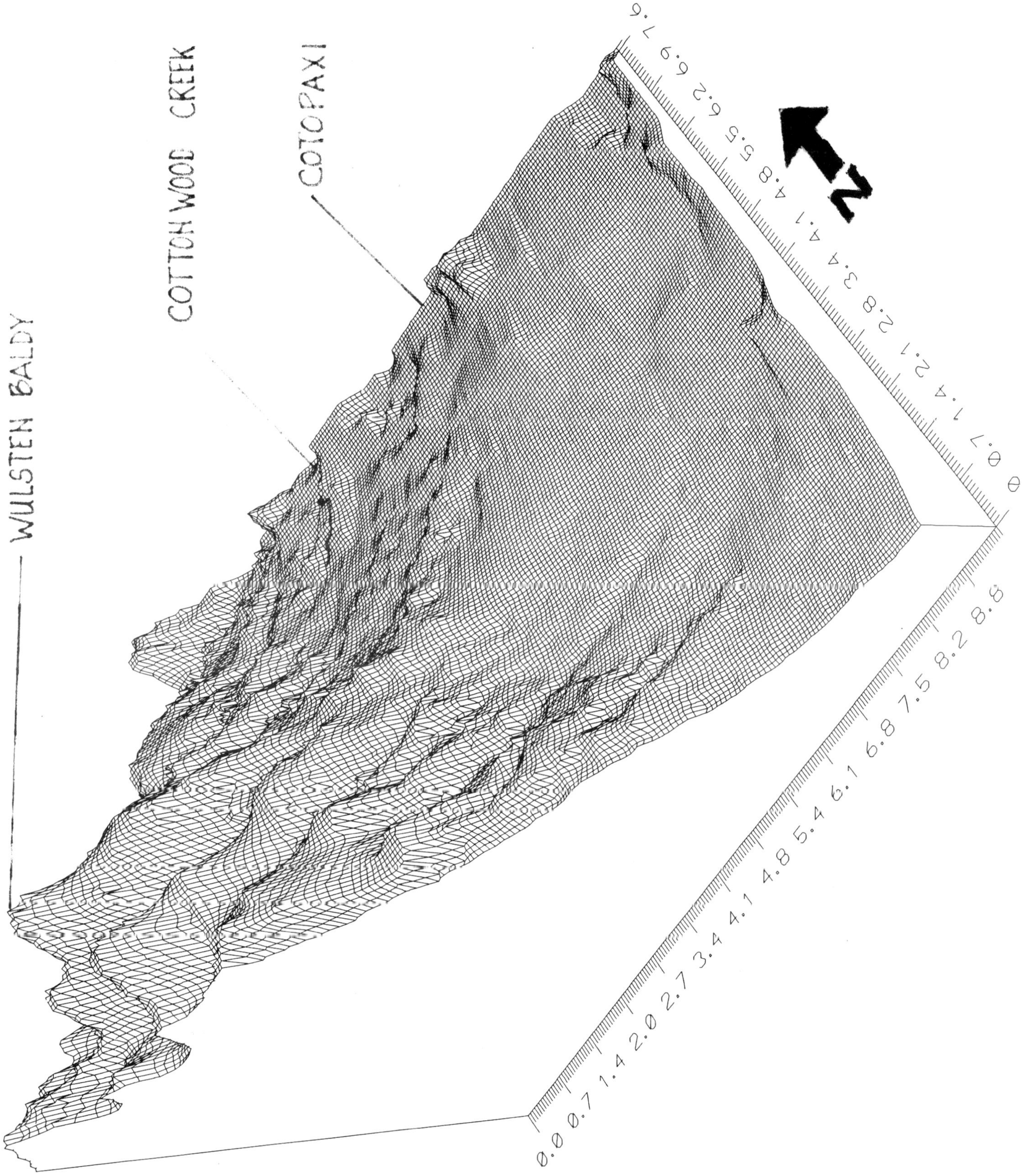

CANON CITY, SANGRE DE CRISTOS.... 3-D MAP

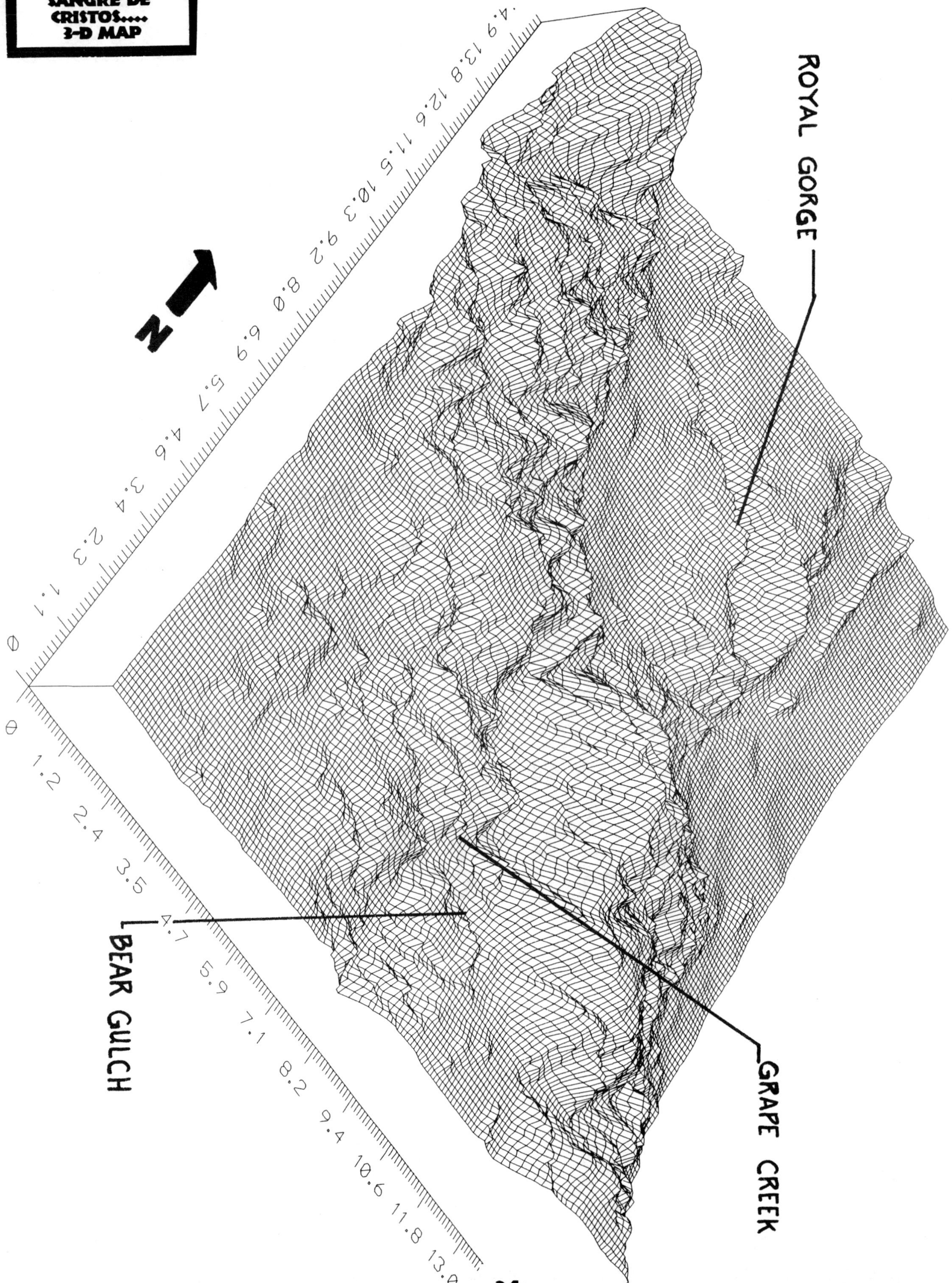

Cherokee Park & Red Feather Lakes

Big Game Hunting Unit(s): 8 (Red Feather Lakes) and 191 (Cherokee Park).

How To Get There:

Red Feather - Take Highway 287 north out of Ft. Collins to the Red Feather Lakes Exit then follow the road up to the spots we've marked on the map.

Cherokee Park- Take 287 north out of Fort Collins until you get to the Cherokee Park Road which is approximately four miles north of the Red Feather Lakes Exit. Then drive west to the spots indicated on our maps.

How To Hunt This Area:

The vegetation in this area is mostly mature ponderosa pines with intermittent sage meadows as well as grass meadows and a few aspen stands. It is relatively open. The best way to hunt this is to glass open areas as well as the sides of sage covered mountains for game movement.

The access is quite limited. There are only a few roads through the area. You will mostly be on foot. There is not even any place to take a four wheel drive. However if you do have horses get back in before first light and let the road hunters push the game to you. Those mountains (the Laramie Mountains) are pretty dry in the fall. So it's best if you can find the creeks that go along the bottoms of each ravine. There you can come across tracks where the elk and deer are coming down to water. Watering spots are always a good place to ambush.

The primary game in this area is going to be large mule deer. You will also see a few scattered elk during the second and third rifle season when the snow pushes them down from Bull Mountain and Thunder Mountain. We hunted the area quite extensively while we were in school up at Fort Collins. We found that hunting during the week was always the best because there weren't as many hunters out spooking the game. Opening day can be quite good if you are the first one in.

Spot 01: **Adjacent To The Diamond Peak Ranch.** Cherokee Park Road intersects one little corner of this spot. There is not a lot of access in the area so be careful where you park. Once we came back and found a nasty note on our windshield saying that most of the land was private. But as long as you know where the public land borders are you'll be alright.

Elk can be found in open meadows like this during the early morning and late evening.

Guy:

Once when we hunted up there we saw three nice bucks run across the road in front of us. We parked the car and moved off in pursuit. After we crossed over a small ridge directly to the southeast we spotted them feeding below. Spence circled around and pushed them back to me. That's where I shot my very first mule deer with a bow. It was only a four by three. But it was large as a result of very good forage. It wasn't a trophy deer, but I consider taking any deer with a bow a major accomplishment.

Spot 02: **Bull Creek Drainage North Of Lost Lake.** Take Road 179 to 180 until you come to the little stop right before the creek. That whole valley offers excellent hunting during the third rifle season. In there we've jumped a lot of elk in groups of two's and three's, but never any large herds. It's steep all the way down to the creek. But if you walk that hill, you will cut plenty of elk tracks. If you take the time to move slowly and quietly, keeping your eyes open, you can sneak up on them after they bed down in the late morning.

Spot 03: **Lost Lake And Adjacent Area.** Take Road 179 to 180 then take your first left. There you'll find open meadows with sporadic hills that provide good spots to sit and watch all the deer moving below. If you are too far for a shot, watch where they go so you can plan a late morning stalk. They'll usually head for patches of timber then bed down. Right around Lost Lake is also a good spot for deer.

Spot 04: **Upper Cherokee Park.** Don't be surprised if you see antelope in there in addition to the resident mule deer. Herds of antelope have moved down into the area from Wyoming. Get off the road and walk toward Haystack Rock. If you set up there before first light, the hunters moving in late in the day will always push deer to you. If you're set up right you'll have a good chance at getting one of the large trophy bucks that have made the area a local favorite. Be patient. You'll probably have to pass up a lot of fork horns and three pointers before you get a chance at a big deer.

Spot 05: **Trail's End.** Park right along the side of the road. It's kind of steep going up the hillside. But once you get up on top you can cover a lot of ground because it gets flat. It's a great area to hunt in during any season. It doesn't get a lot of snow because the slope is south facing. The terrain is wide open with a lot of sage so you can see a long way. Get your binoculars out and stay alert. It will pay off.

Guy poses with a beautiful 6 Pt rack.

Spot 06: **Turkey's Roost.** Park down in the parking lot at Cherokee Park Wildlife Area. You'll have about four square miles to hunt. Walk north from the trailhead to Turkey's Roost. From there you can see down into several different valleys. A good pair of binoculars will really pay off. If you get up there at first light you'll catch the deer on their way back from feeding all night in the fields. This is a great spot to get a long shot off with a flat shooting rifle like a 7 millimeter or 243.

Spot 07: **Lower Cherokee Park.** The good thing about this spot is that it tends to get overlooked. People usually go farther west and leave it unhunted. This is the first spot you will pass while driving up the Cherokee Park Road. It will be to the south. Take the deer trails back into the hills. The terrain is very similar to the rest of the park area, just a little drier. There are also a few bighorn sheep there, so make sure you identify the rack before you shoot.

Guy: We always see deer crossing the road right there. It usually happens when we're coming down at night after hunting Upper Cherokee Park all day. I always say, "Damn, we should have hunted there." But like everyone else, we keep going up high.

Spot 08: **Lone Pine State Wildlife Area.** This spot is located right along Red Feather Lakes Road. Heading north the road will immediately make a hairpin turn and go around the mountain to Lone Pine Creek. At the bottom of the mountain you'll see horse corrals. This is as far as you will be able to drive. In addition to mule deer, there are also bighorn sheep in the area. The best hunting spot is the mountain you drive around going in. An alternative to parking at the very bottom by the corrals is to park by the first sign you see indicating you are entering the area and walk north over the top of the hill. We have jumped many nice 4 and 5 point deer using this tactic. Unfortunately, they have always seen us coming and run off before we could get a shot off. However, we were archery hunting. If you have a rifle, and take your time, you have a great chance of success.

Spot 09: **Upper Lone Pine.** Continue straight up the trail from the horse corrals mentioned in the previous spot. You can walk far into Roosevelt National Forest. Walking the trail you can cover a lot of ground without making any noise. There are hundreds of deer throughout the valley. It will be very productive in there - any time, any season.

Spot 10: **Lower Lone Pine Creek Bottom.** In this spot you can either walk down Lone Pine Creek or straight north over the hill and walk the ridge down scanning the slope to the north. We have seen several deer in there slowly feeding. They had no idea that we were even present. You are probably looking at a three to four hundred yard shot to get one. But it's not that hard because they won't be moving that fast. When you're ready to shoot, whistle and they will stop walking long enough for you to capitalize.

Cherokee Park & Red Feather Lakes

(Reprinted from Roosevelt National Forest map)

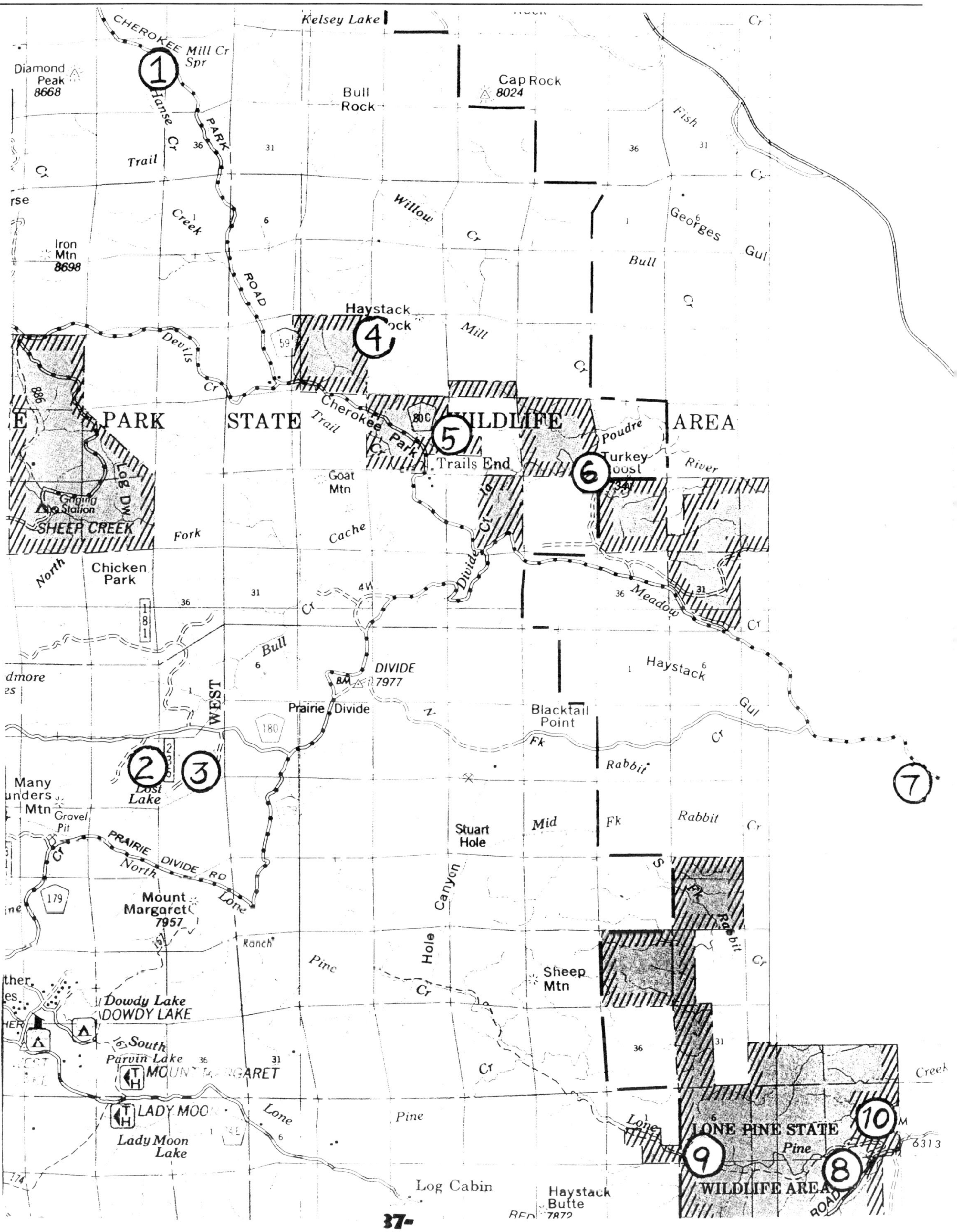

CHEROKEEE PARK & RED FEATHERS 3-D MAP

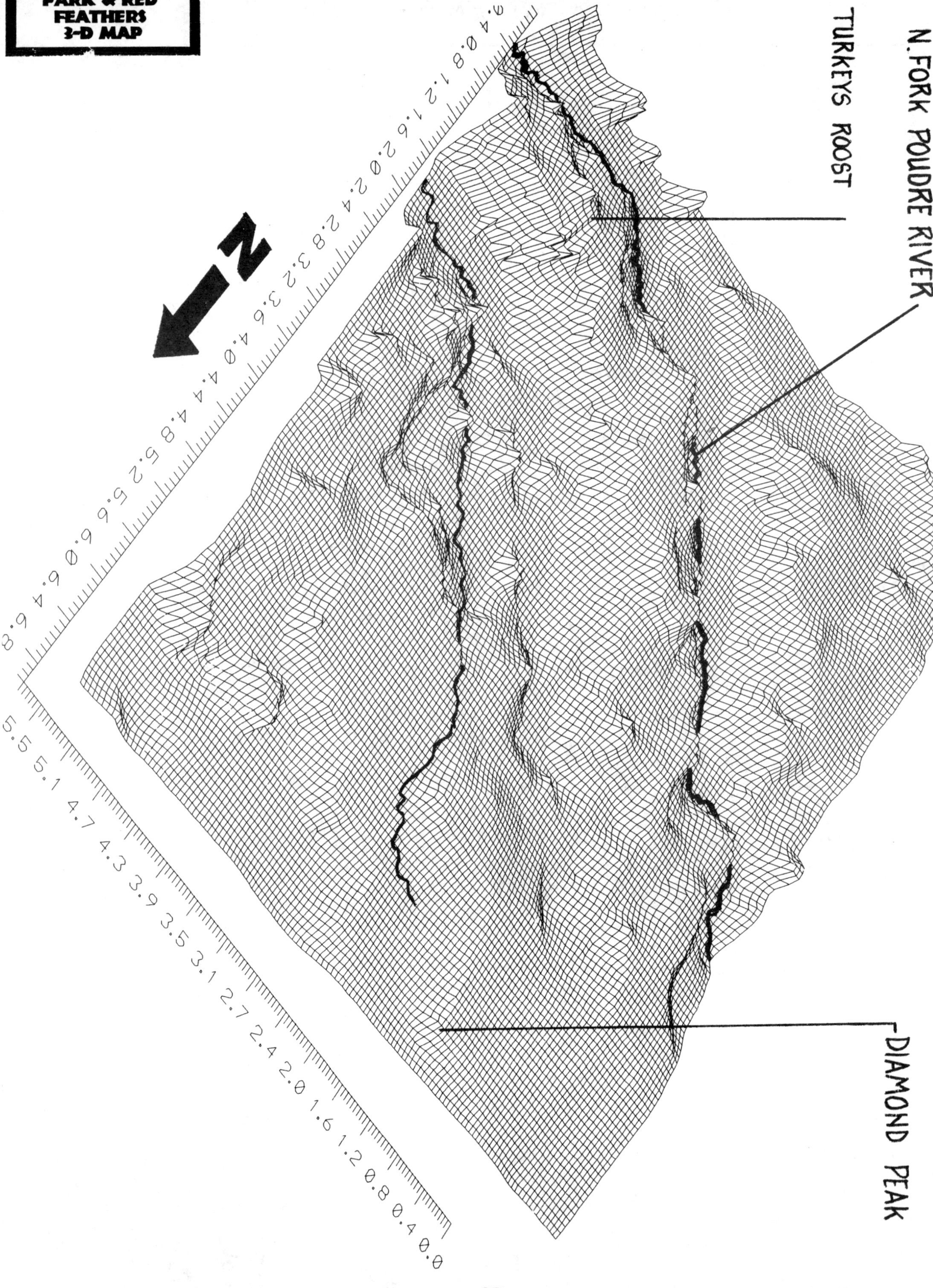

CHEROKEEE PARK & RED FEATHERS 3-D MAP

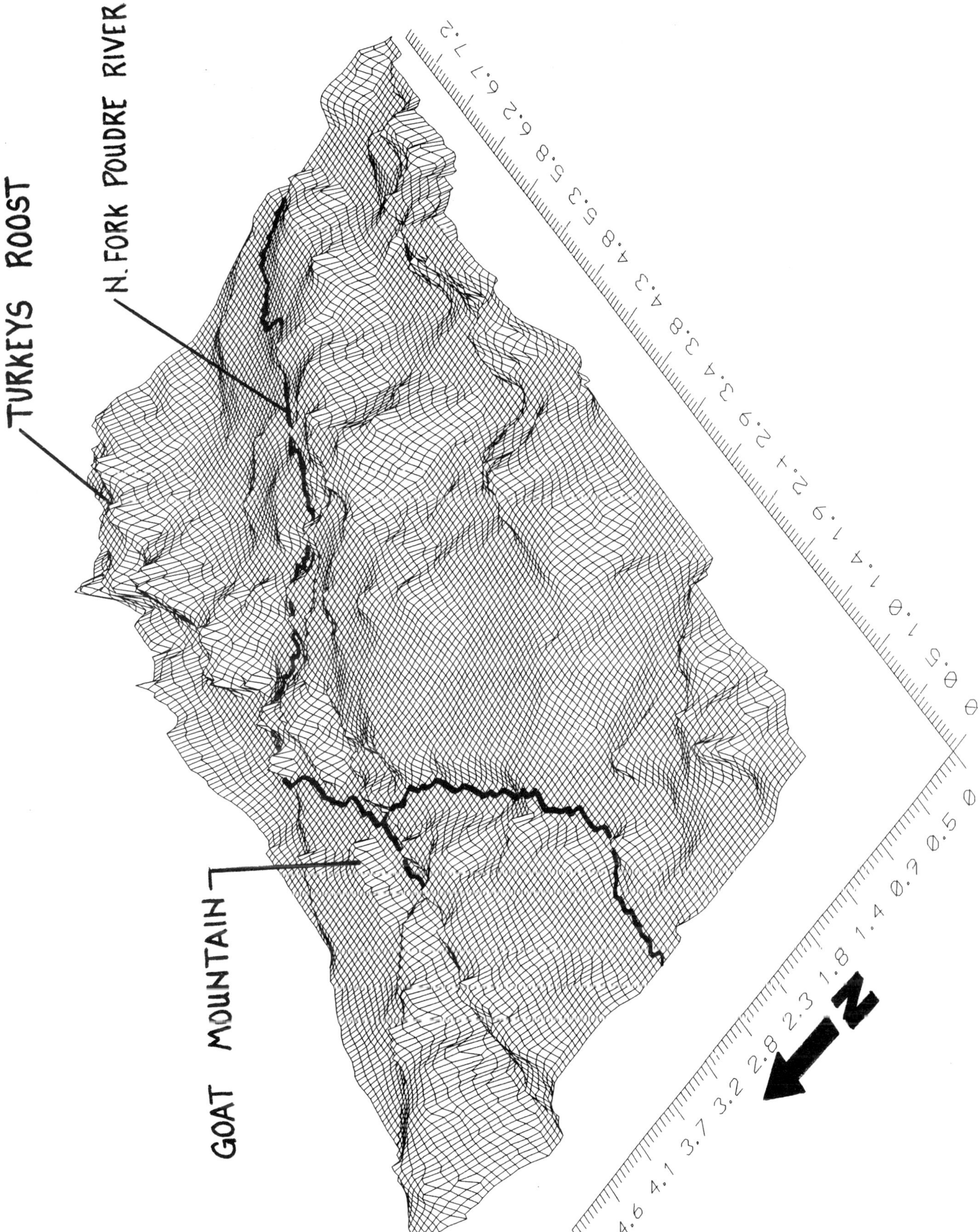

CHEROKEEE PARK & RED FEATHERS 3-D MAP

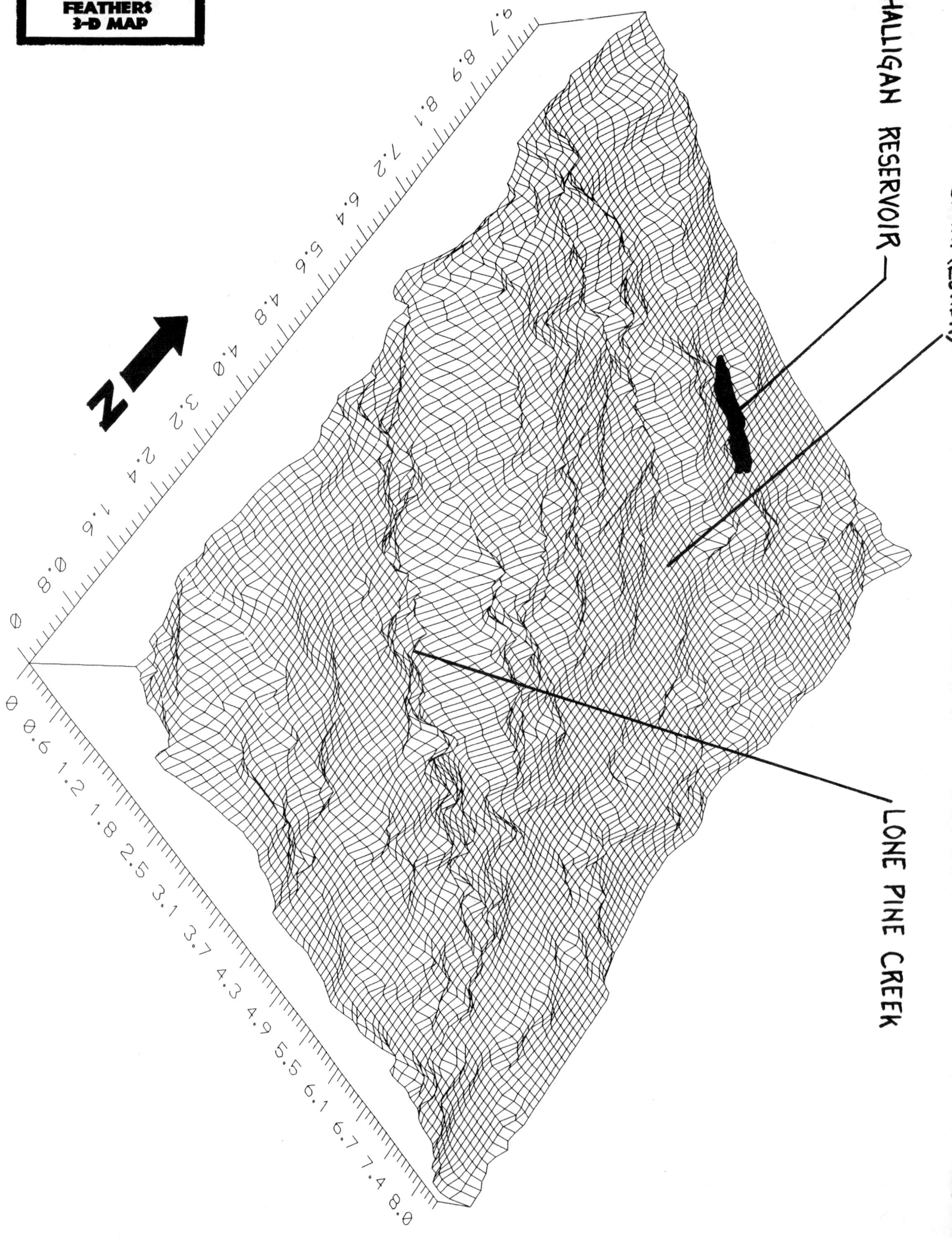

Crested Butte

Big Game Hunting Unit(s): 55, 521, 53, 54, 63

How To Get There:

From Denver take Highway 285 south to the town of Salida. Then take Highway 50 west to the town of Gunnison. From there take Highway 135 north to the town of Crested Butte.

How To Hunt This Area:

This area is known for its dramatic scenery. The mountains are high and rugged. Much of the area is above timberline. You'll need a good pair of hiking boots with ample ankle support. Also, a good pair of field glasses is essential.

We've walked for three, even four hours up the sides of mountains in this area without ever getting close to their tops. Sometimes you hike for hours up to the top of one ridge, only to find you are a week too late and they have moved to another. Also, you may see elk run to the next ridge, and realize that you will have to walk hours more to get to where they just ran.

But this is a place where you can come over a ridge and in front of you see 200 elk. Crested Butte is known for its huge elk. The world record elk came from a canyon west of Crested Butte. It scored 442 5/8.

One thing to look out for are spots that have been heavily grazed by cattle. If you find this go to another place. The elk don't hang around when a spot gets too much grazing pressure. One year we found a great spot up Rustler's Gulch. But when we went back the next week, a rancher had put hundreds upon hundreds of cattle into that small valley. The week before we were waist-deep in ferns and other succulent forage. The next week it had been eaten to the ground and the streams were full of mud. There's nothing wrong with grazing cattle. Cattle can co-exist with elk. But we seriously doubt if the rancher had a permit to run that many cattle in such a small area. Locals at the ski resort told us that this is a common abuse in the area.

When hunting around Crested Butte, the best strategy is to find a high altitude valley that has a lot of elk in it, and at all costs don't disturb them. Move slowly. If you don't spook the elk you can work them for days. If you spook them they may run across a divide and in an hour be farther away than you can walk in an entire day. If you can afford it, spotting game from an airplane can give you a big advantage in this area. Be sure to comply with the mandatory waiting period for game spotting from aircraft.

Guy's Uncles Hugh (left) and Larry (middle) with a big 5 Pt bull in downtown Gunnison.

Spot 01: **Splains Gulch.** Take Road 12 west out of Crested Butte, then drive up the road on the left to Splains Gulch. Despite what you see on the map, the lake to the right is not accessible by road because it has been backhoed. There's actually a road that does not appear on the Forest Service map that curves to the left of the road that is supposed to take you to the lake. Right where the road curves to the left, there's a spot where you can pull off and camp.

If you go straight south from the campsite you will hit a marshy hillside feeding the lake. Elk move through the willows up there grazing on the lush, wet vegetation. A quarter of a mile farther to the south is some dark timber where elk like to bed after feeding among the willows.

Spot 02: **Splains Deer Dust.** Directly south of the lake is a little bit higher ground and some broken pines. Right by a small mound of backhoed dirt, there's a dusting spot for deer. We spotted a group of deer standing on the mound watching the others roll in the dirt.

Spot 03: **Bear Spot.** On the hillside just north of the lake we found established elk trails paralleling the lake's meadow. The trails headed deeper into the woods to the hill overlooking Splains Gulch Road. They paralleled the road allowing the elk to monitor human activity while remaining hidden. There was also a lot of bear scat along the trails.

Spot 04: **Mt Axtell Bottom.** The road up from the campsite by the lake goes a lot farther east than it shows on the map. By driving that road you can get way down into the woods south of Mt. Axtell. A few miles back on the right hand side of the road, you will come to an open area where people have been cutting wood. To the west of the woodcutting area are some woods where we found a number of frequently used elk trails.

Spot 05: **Mt Axtell Gully.** Continue taking the road down along the south side of Mt. Axtell as far as it will go. On your left you'll see a gully going up Mt. Axtell. Follow it uphill through the dark timber. We've seen elk right where the gully comes out at timberline.

Spot 06: **Red Mountain Fence Line.** Take Road 737 northeast toward Carbon Peak, then head east on Road 563 toward Red Mountain. You will cross private property a couple of times. Right where you get to the very last private access gate, there's a road cutting off to the right. It's a very small road that has become somewhat overgrown with brush. Take that road several hundred yards in and you will come to an area that has been cut to put up a large fence for the adjoining private property.

The deer come into the open area bordering the fence. Walk along it. During the evening we saw numerous bucks feeding along the fence line including one very large five point buck.

Spot 07: **Between The Creeks.** Where Road 563 stops at a locked private property gate, park and head north down the steep hillside into the gully. There is a hump of higher ground between that gully and Carbon Creek which is farther to the North. Elk move between the two gullies which have rich green vegetation in the bottoms. Walk the higher ground between the gullies heading west.

Spence:

> Doing this, I came across three bedded elk including one large bull which stood about thirty yards away. Unfortunately I could not take a shot. The brush was so thick that I could not tell if it was a cow or a bull until it ran.

Spot 08: **Upper Carbon Creek.** Instead of walking between the gullies discussed in the previous spot, cut over to Carbon Creek and then walk up the creek to the southeast. The elk sit in the thick timber and watch the meadows along the bottom of this fork of Carbon Creek. Unless it's early morning when the elk will be in the fields, it's best to walk parallel to the fields 50 or 100 yards into the timber where you can still get a view of the meadows. We found this spot to be very marshy and wet at times. We spotted a lot of elk tracks in the mud along the creek.

Unknown hunter takes a large coyote just outside the Cebolla Creek Ranch.

Spot 09: **Upper Squaw Gulch/Table Hill.** Where Squaw Gulch and the upper part of this fork of Carbon Creek join, there's a hill to the North which forms a bench at the base of Whetstone Mountain. We saw a large number of deer tracks there and we also found fresh elk sign. From there an elk trail heads down the steep escarpment into Squaw Gulch. It's a good ambush spot because they will hesitate at the lip before going over the side.

Spot 10: **Whetstone Spring.** From Spot 9, follow the elk trail back along Whetstone Mountain to the northwest. You will come to a natural spring where elk from the area get water. We found a number of fresh rubs in the willows next to the water. Plus, there's a wallow about 20 yards from the mouth of the Spring. It's another good ambush spot.

Spot 11: **Dry Gully.** Continue northwest from the spring discussed in the previous spot to your first little gully cutting up Whetstone Mountain. A sizeable deer herd lives in that dry gully. We spotted numerous deer bedded in the clumps of aspen toward the bottom. Also, if you follow the gully up, you can probably get into a deer herd that hangs out in the trees below a big rockslide on the east side of the gully. We actually climbed up the gully all the way to the top of Whetstone Mountain. There was a lot of elk sign on top where they were crossing in the early morning. But it really isn't a place you want to go. The climb is very tough, and there's no place to hide and ambush an elk. They'll see you way before you get close enough for a shot. Stick to the gullies below.

Spot 12: **Lower Carbon Creek.** Take Road 737 to where it ends on private property. The landowners have it all blocked off so nobody can get up into the Forest Service property. But if you cut directly to the east where the private boundary ends, then head north, you will find a decent spot. The bottom along the creek has been heavily trodden by cattle. But if you walk along the creek bottom about a mile to the east, then take the first draw heading north, there are elk in the aspen on the west side of the draw. We got into a herd that was heading down to the creek bottom through those aspen just as it got dark.

Spot 13: **Copley Lake, Lake Irwin.** According to the locals, the top around the lakes is flat and park like, dropping off sharply on both sides. Hunt the top meadows. The elk herd that feeds up there grazes east every morning then walks back west in the evening.

Spot 14: **Gunsight Pass.** You really need a four-wheel drive to get up to this spot. Glass the ridge and open areas for elk movement to either side, then follow. This is a good place to use a spotting scope.

Spot 15: **Peeler Lakes.** To get there, you need to go up Oh Be Joyful Creek Road. The road gets really muddy. You probably need a four-wheel drive. Walk the trail down to Peeler Lakes (3 mile walk). You can catch elk in the bottom in the early morning, or up on the hillsides later in the morning.

Spot 16: **Oh Be Joyful.** Take the Oh Be Joyful four-wheel drive road as far up as you can go. There is a path at the end of the road which you have to walk to get into the Raggeds Wilderness. You can't go into the wilderness area in your vehicle. Get above timberline if you can and glass the hillsides. It's prime elk habitat. A local four-wheel drive enthusiast told us that he always sees heavy elk sign around the ponds at the top of the pass.

Spot 17: **Queens Basin.** Park and walk the trail up toward Copper Lake, but then head up Queen Basin toward White Rock Mountain. A local rock climber told us about this spot. He was up on White Rock Mountain and came upon a herd of over 200 elk. Also, a local hotel attendant said that he and his friends hunted Queen Basin during the first rifle season. They backpacked in and took several big bull elk.

When we scouted this spot, we only saw a few elk. However the sign was tremendous. At first we thought the area had been torn up by cattle. But upon closer examination it became apparent that the damage was caused by elk. They had turned up the whole side of the mountain. There was dung everywhere and the creek crossings were muddy. Keep in mind that it's extremely steep there and you may have to walk 3 or 4 hours uphill to get to the elk.

Spot 18: **Upper Rustler Gulch.** Take the road up as far as you can go. Then you have to either hike or take a horse up the valley. Toward the top of Rustler's Gulch, to the left of the trail, there's a low saddle where most of the valley's elk cross over to the creek running below West Maroon Pass. They are funneled into that saddle by the cliffs above and below. Sit there and wait.

Spot 19: **South Side of Upper Rustler Gulch.** On the south side of the gulch are woods where the majority of the valley's elk trails are found. They prefer those woods to the man-made road coming up the valley on the north side of the creek. The woods stretch like a finger up above treeline which congests game that wants to stay under cover into a much smaller area.

Guy's uncle Harry took this huge mule deer outside of Gunnison in 1941.

Spot 20: **Lower Rustler Gulch Wallow.** Half way up the Rustler Gulch trail there's a large wallow. You'll see it on your left just before you cross the creek and head up a small rocky embankment. It's huge, at least 50 yards across. Plus, there are a lot of mineral deposits right next to it, so it's a salt lick as well. This is a focal point for game activity in the area. We found elk tracks crossing and crisscrossing from every direction. That morning, hundreds of deer had come into the wallow from the south and left a trail that was at least three feet wide. Every inch of the trail was filled with tracks.

You probably won't catch them there during the day. But you can gauge how many animals are in the area by the number of tracks leading into the wallow. Also, you can follow tracks from the wallow to late morning bedding spots.

Spot 21: **Rustler Gulch Tributary Lake.** Driving the road up Rustler Gulch, you'll get to a gate where you can go no farther. Cross the creek to your right and head up the hillside. You'll be heading east. We found a small lake up there that doesn't appear on the map. Elk stop to water at the lake which is bordered on three sides by very steep hillsides. Sit on one of the hills and watch the woods on the south side of the lake. Elk use them as cover when they come to drink.

Spot 22. **Hill Above Lake.** Above the lake mentioned in the previous spot, to the north, is a hill that flattens out on top and has three small watering holes. The game use those spots as alternatives to watering at the more open lake below.

Spence:

> I ran into a herd of about ten mule deer there including several large bucks. They were all standing in the bushes next to the pond drinking water. Using a mound of dirt as cover, I stalked to within 20 yards. I did not shoot because I was more interested in the elk bugling in the meadow above.

Spot 23: **Last Valley/Rustler Tributary.** Farther up the southern tributary to Rustler Gulch, you will come to a large level meadow surrounded by mature ponderosa pines. This is the last timbered spot before you go completely above timberline. We spotted a good size bull standing in the meadow. He moved off after answering our bugles heading south and downhill. We tracked him through a very steep rockslide area. He was alone, but we were hoping he'd lead us to a larger herd. Farther down, we found tracks where he'd joined up with about 10 cow elk after picking his way through some cliffs that held us up for a good hour. We never did catch up.

Spot 24: **Upper Rustler Tributary.** When we were there, the top of the southern tributary to Rustler Gulch had a tremendous amount of older elk sign. We estimated that two weeks previously, there had been over 100 elk feeding in there. They had headed back down the valley to the south. We found a hunting camp nearby which was probably the reason they had moved out. This spot would have been phenomenal had those hunters not spooked the elk.

Spot 25: **Lower Rustler Gulch Southeast.** A bike trail crosses the mouth of this gulch and runs southeast. You can get there by crossing the creek to the south of the gate mentioned in Spot 21. If you follow the trail about a mile down, to the left is some downed timber where an elk herd spends its summers. Sometimes you can see fresh tracks crossing the trail and follow them up the side of the hill. The last time we were there we went a little bit farther down and followed a draw up the back side of Avery Peak. In the woods directly to the south of the creek we found fresh sign from at least 10 small groups of elk (three to five elk each).

Guy's uncle Lloyd Carpenter took this huge 6 Pt taken in 1952 above Gunnison.

Spot 26: **East Brush Creek Trail.** Take Road 738 up to where trail 545 cuts off down the gully. The south side of the gully is extremely steep. It's made of loose talus type rock and drops several hundred feet down to the creek. Deer use that trail to avoid walking on the steep talus. However we did see some elk tracks going straight down the talus. But the majority of the game stayed on the trail. Sitting along the trail is your best bet for deer.

Spot 27: **East Brush Creek South Side.** If you cross the creek, there's good elk habitat to the south (big dark pines). Follow the trail either toward Waterfall Creek and Double Top or back up to the northeast. You are sure to see a good amount of elk sign in there.

Spot 28: **Deer Creek.** The name speaks for itself. It's open and grassy. We saw a lot of deer without even getting out of the car. We talked to a girl who had ridden her mountain bike up that road one evening and saw over forty deer. It's worth checking out.

Spot 29: **Lower West Elk Wilderness.** This spot is not on the book's map because it is so far from all our other spots. But we thought it was worth mentioning because the locals told us it is one of the best spots in Colorado. To get there, take Highway 50 west out of Gunnison then head north on any of the major access roads.

Spencer Kluesner on top of Mt Crested Butte. Oh-Be-Joyful directly behind.

Crested Butte

(Reprinted from Gunnison National Forest map)

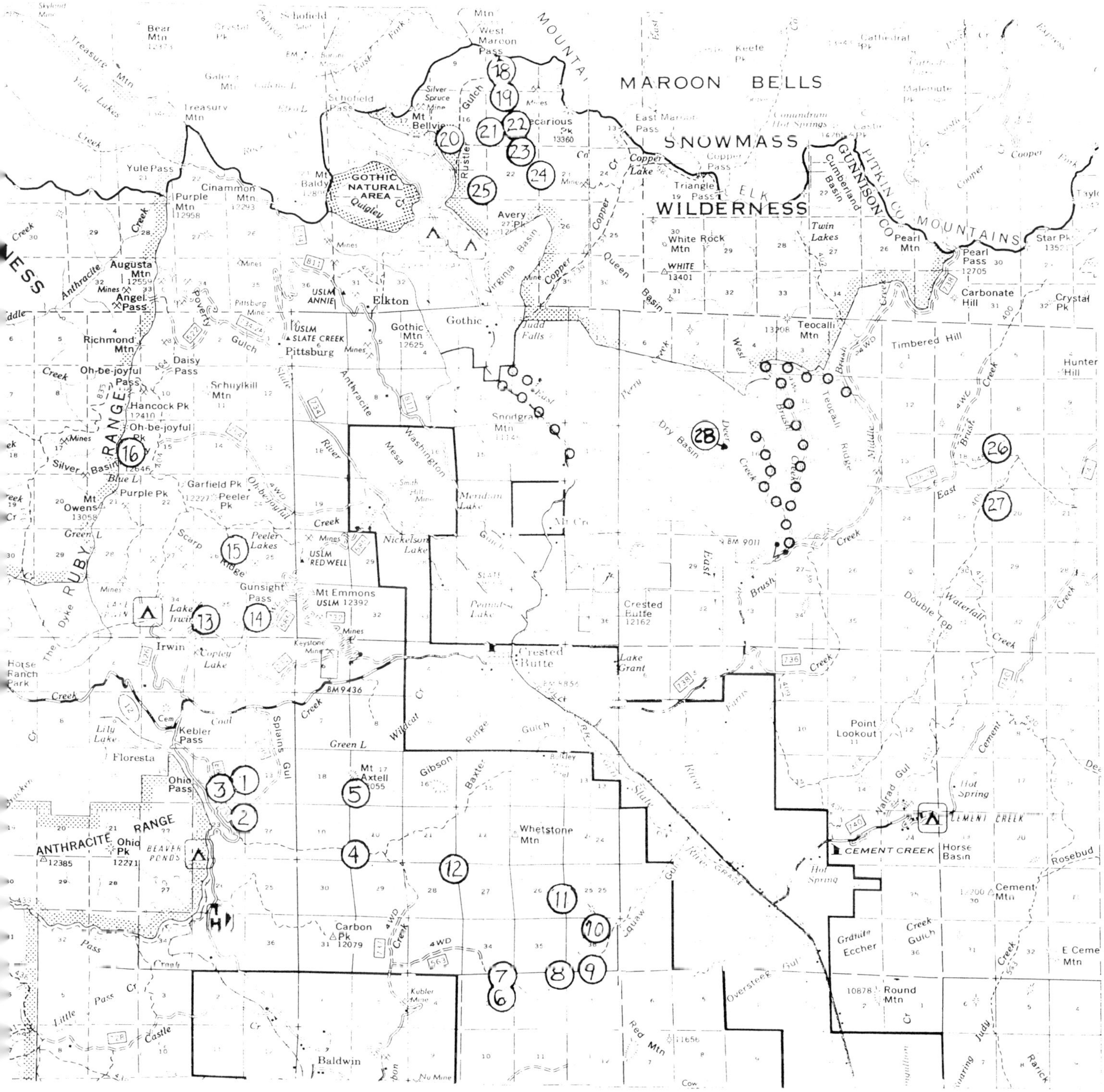

CRESTED BUTTE 3-D MAP

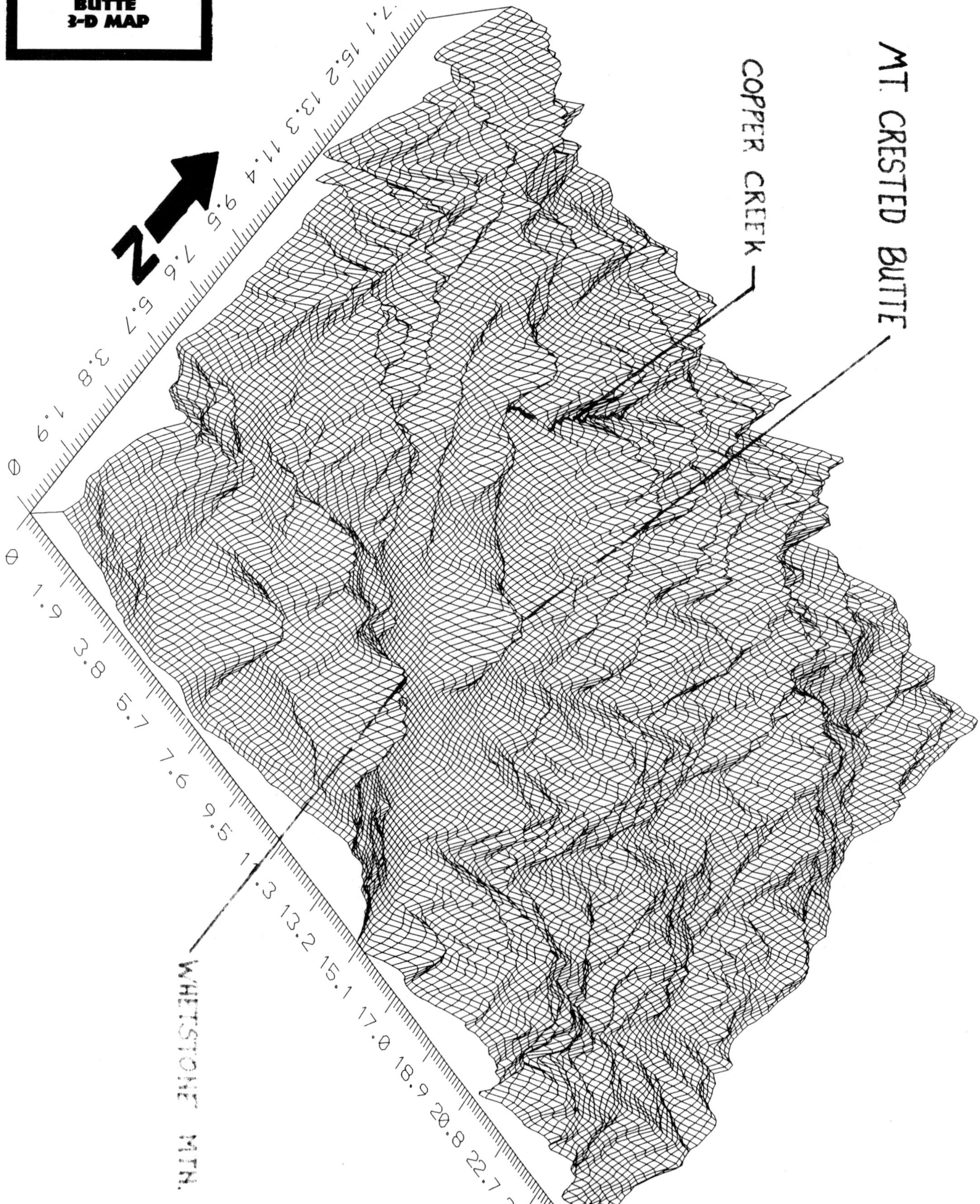

Elk Head Mountains

Big Game Hunting Unit(s): 4

How To Get There:
Take Highway 40 west to Craig, then go north on Highway 13. Approximately 11 miles up you will come to FSR 110 which provides access into the Elk Head Mountains. This is one area that does not offer much access. There are only a couple of roads cutting through the mountains. So be prepared to pack your game out in quarters.

How To Hunt This Area:
What tactics you use to hunt in this area really depends on which spot you are hunting in. There are extreme variations in elevation, and consequently a wide variety of vegetation. As you first enter the Elk Head Mountains, you will be in thick clumps of scruboaks that produce a lot of acorns the game feed on.

Spence:

> I use a really unorthodox tactic for hunting in this type of vegetation. I'll throws rocks (or shoot them with a sling shot) into the clumps of scruboak after the deer have bedded down late in the morning. Lots of times, I'll kick out deer and take a shot as they run into the open. Years ago I used this tactic to take a nice 3 x 3 with my rifle as it bounded across a field in front of me.

Gradually, as you move to higher elevations you'll get into lodgepole pines and aspens. During the early season you want be up high. The elk like the cooler air in the high meadows when the sun isn't out, and the dark cool timber when it is. This area has not been logged in quite a while so you are going to find a lot of mature timber up there. It's easier to hunt in because there's no downed timber and very little ground brush.

These mountains drop down, then flatten out several times which is why we call them "stair step" mountains. We found that where the mountains flatten out, especially where there's aspen stands, the deer like to bed down. If you accidentally jump them, just sit down and wait 20 minutes. They always move laterally (rather than up or down). If you don't spook them by pressing too hard too soon, you can catch up to them farther over and get another chance.

Guy:

> I've seen more bears in there than anywhere else in Colorado, including trash dumps in the Sangre de Cristos. If you take a deer or elk, get it out of there fast. If you leave it overnight, you're just asking for it to become bear food.

Guy:

> A few years ago I went to that area dead set on getting a really large harem bull I had been watching all year. Unfortunately an "old timer" in the camp next to us got him first. It was a huge six by six. When I saw it, I hemmed and hawed, kicked the dirt around a little and congratulated him. After that, I moved to another spot but never did locate another large herd bull, only raghorns.

Spot 01: **BLM/National Forest Border.** Just past a hairpin turn before you enter the National Forest is some heavy scruboak on the left and right hand sides of the road. From there walk the drainages down to the creek beds. Stay on top of the ridges paralleling those drainages. You'll see deer down below you moving between clumps of scruboak or bedded on the hillsides. While driving in there one night we saw several huge bucks in our headlights. We also saw a few elk tracks down in there, but not as many as we saw up higher.

Spot 02: **Transition Zone.** As soon as you cross the National Forest borderline there's a couple of drainages about one mile to the southeast where the scruboak meets the aspen. Because you have to walk around private property borders to get there, this spot doesn't get a lot of hunting pressure.

Guy:

> I saw several nice elk in there - four or five points. Unfortunately they were too far off to shoot with my bow. I just couldn't get close enough. The scruboak leaves made a lot of noise when I tried to sneak through them, and the elk could see me if I entered the open areas. I would only recommend going to this spot during the first rifle season before the snows hit. The bulls may still be bugling a little so you can locate them in the thick foliage. And you won't have to worry about trying to get to within 30 yards like I did.

Spot 03: **Mt Welba.** About a mile and a half past where you enter the National Forest you will come to Road 138. If it's not gated, take it to the end where there is a little mound of bulldozed timber and dirt. From there walk north to Mt. Welba. There's a heavy concentration of elk in there because it's away from the roads. It should be easy to take a cow elk if you're after meat.

Spot 04: **West Pond Creek.** Drive up Road 110 through the Lost Park picnic ground. You will drop down the back side of the mountain. Going around the bend where you will continue to drop down, you will see an old road on the left which you want to take. Sometimes it's blocked off. Other times it's open. Walk back in toward West Pond Creek. Continue across West Pond Creek up the other side where there's a huge open meadow with a lot of beaver ponds (good fishing). Back in there in the early morning hours you will see elk literally by the tens and twenties. One time we saw close to 70 elk out in that meadow.

Hunt the fringes of the meadow keeping within the lodgepoles and the aspen. Don't walk across the open meadows or you'll spook the entire herd. There's a few old stumps you can use as cover if you have to stalk an animal that's out in the open.

Because the wind blows downhill in the morning, you should stalk a heard of elk like this from the left/below.

Spot 05: **Bear Scrape.** Take Trail 1144 down into the bottom of the valley. It's pretty easy walking. We saw a lot of bear sign along the trail. In addition to tracks, there was scat and claw scrapes on the trees. The trail will take you to a steep ridge. While we were hunting up there we got a big dumping of snow - probably around 30 inches. We were stranded for a week. In the snow we saw tracks from hundreds of elk, mostly cows.

Spot 06: **Stair Steps.** This spot is located directly to the north of the last spot. You can reach it either by going up the trail and walking back down the gullies to the north, or you can go down the road and walk up the gullies. This is a "stair step" mountain where steep slopes drop down several times to flat areas where the game congregates.

Guy:

I jumped bedded deer eight different times in those flat spots. I came down from above and spotted them feeding before they had even seen me.

Spot 07: **Harem Bull.** This spot is located about a half a mile north of the stair steps. It's flatter than the other spots we've profiled. You want to hunt the creek drainage (Sawtooth Creek) all the way down to where private land borders the National Forest land you're on. This is where the guy in the camp next to us took the big six by six bull. He spotted the bull out in the open meadows at first light. The elk were scraping away the snow trying to feed on the grass below.

Guy:

My uncle Phil Collier hunted the private land adjacent to this spot. He said it's the only time in his life when he has been standing in one spot and seen bull elk, cow elk, a buck deer, a doe deer and a regular "moo" cow all at the same time.

Spence:

Harem bulls are extremely difficult to hunt, especially with a bow. Remember, the herd has many eyes. I once tried sneaking up on a 6 X 6 down by Steamboat Springs. He was tearing up some scruboaks and snorting hard. When he put his head back to bugle, his antlers were so long they came all the way back and nearly touched his buttocks. But every time I tried to move in, I run into cow elk. I'd circle around but then ran into more. Everywhere I looked I saw big brown eyes. Eventually, one spotted me and spooked the entire herd. I had passed up three smaller satellite bulls and even more raghorns trying to get the master. I kicked myself later for not taking the shot my luck had dealt me.

Spot 08: **West Prong Creek.** This spot is located in a drainage on the north side of the Elkhead Mountains. Go back up Road 110 to Road 133 which runs north around a little peak. Take that road to the end or as far as you possibly can. There's a gate up there. If it's open you can take it all the way to Trail number 1144. But if it is closed you will stop at Unit marker 25 right along West Prong Creek. From there you will hike laterally to the northwest and go to the first wet drainage. It is bordered by dark timber and patches of aspen. The elk bed in the dark timber during the day. The creek doesn't make a lot of noise so you can still hear them if they answer your bugle. There's also a couple of wallows in the moist bottom. The wallows are in thick brush, so they're probably used during the day. They're great places to set up and wait.

Spot 09: **East Of Sawmill Creek Campground.** From the campground take the trail that goes back to the east 3/4 of a mile to the headwaters of Sawmill Creek. You'll know you're close when you see the beaver ponds. It's very open up in there and the meadows seem to have that "quiet" feeling. We've seen several groups of ten elk or less in there during the early morning hours. It doesn't make any sense, but hunters have overlooked this spot for years.

Spot 10: **Willow Creek Trail/Silent Bulls.** To get to this spot you are going to have to go back to Highway 13 which runs north out of Craig. Go approximately another 10 miles north up Forest Road 109 then drive until it ends just north of Sand Point. Take the Willow Creek Trail back. Less than 300 yards off the trail to the east we spotted several small herds of elk including several three and four pointers. We worked to them several times but couldn't get them to answer our bugles. We watched them lift their heads up to listen to our bugles, then go back to feeding without making a peep.

Spence:

Learning to hunt call shy elk like this is becoming a necessity as more and more hunters are picking up bugles. In the old days, we could get elk to come into calls that were nothing more than crude whistles. These days, they'll answer, but rarely come in. Try predictive still hunting and group driving tactics. Also, use cow calls to cover your sounds and calm the herd as you move in.

Spot 11: **Buck Point.** Continue on the trail from the previous spot about a mile to a mile and a half. You will get to a drainage called Cataract Creek. It's just to the west of Buck Point. Buck Point got its name for obvious reasons. We observed a high ratio of bucks to does up on the highest elevations of the point. There's no telling why the bucks prefer that hill, they just do. Try sitting in the saddle between Mt. Welba and Buck Point. It will pay off.

Spot 12: **Lower Beaver Ponds.** From the saddle between Buck Point and Mt. Welba, walk the Cataract Creek drainage all the way down until you get to some beaver ponds. The farther down you go the more ponds there will be. Elk trails crisscross through the willows that surround the ponds. This spot is best in the early season. The snow and hunting pressure will eventually push them down the drainage onto the adjacent private land. You are not legally permitted to hunt the private property without first obtaining permission. Some of the ranchers will let you in, but be prepared to pay a trespass fee.

Spot 13: **Beaver Creek Drainage.** This spot is located northwest of Cataract Creek. It's going to look almost identical to the Cataract Creek except there's a lot more water and as a result, more open meadows. There are a lot of stumps that you can use as stalking cover for elk you see out in the fields. They tend to follow the same pattern coming to this spot the same way at the same time of day until hunting pressure forces them to change their pattern. If you can be one of the first people in, it should be undisturbed.

There's also lot of BLM state land around this spot that provides some of the best antelope hunting in the state. The BLM land tends to be lower in elevation and more open than National Forest land.

Guy:

I've never seen so many antelope. This area is awesome. Drive the roads until you spot a herd. Then it's just a matter of planning your stalk using the gullies and changes in elevation as cover. If you have enough time to pattern them, you can set up an ambush where they cross underneath the fences or take water every day. If it's flat and there's no cover, dig a pit blind.

Another excellent way to get a buck antelope is to sneak as close as you possibly can to the herd, then raise a two dimensional decoy. Buck antelope are very territorial and it's highly likely one will either charge you outright, or at least come in for a snorting match. It's hard to believe this will work until you see it. When he comes in, stand up behind the decoy and shoot over its back. Even if you miss, they will sometimes keep coming. Remember, if you choose to make your decoy yourself, don't make it a dominant buck. If your decoy looks like a powerful herd buck, the real buck probably won't come in.

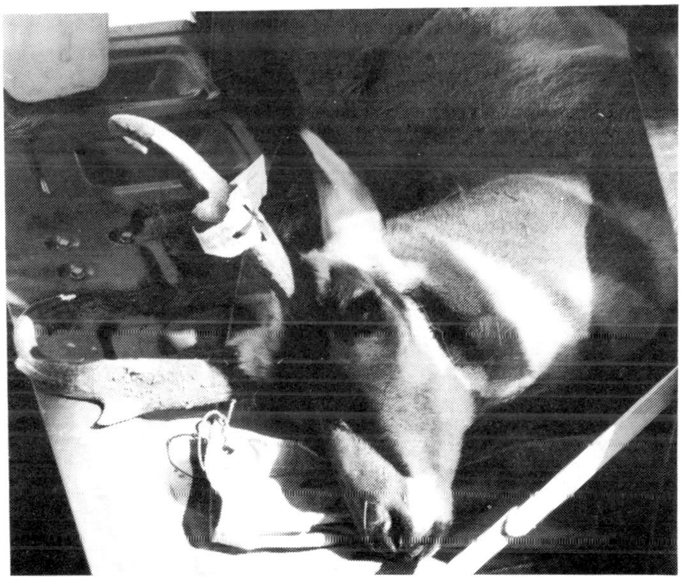

Spence:

Last season, I had a herd buck charge me on opening morning of the rifle season, and I didn't even have a decoy. These animals are extremely aggressive and territorial during the rut.

Remember, they rely on their eyesight more than anything else. After you spot them, plot your stalk so you'll come up as close as possible. You should only see the buck twice - once when you spot him and once when you've completed your stalk. The second time you see him you should be popping up within shooting range. The mistake hunters will often make is to keep sticking their heads up to figure out where the buck is. Hunters do this because they're afraid the buck is moving off and they're wasting a stalk. What happens when you keep sticking your head up is that they see you and do the very thing you're afraid they'll do, move off. So what if they move off while you're stalking. They won't go far. Be patient and keep stalking. Eventually they'll slow down and give you a shot. The best way to appease your fears is to watch them long enough to figure out which way they are heading. That way you can tailor your stalk to their pattern of movement.

Spence:

Last season I did not even take the buck that charged me on opening morning. I waited almost a week until I saw the trophy I wanted. It took me three hours of stalking through lung choking powdery dirt. And I still have the thorns in my forearms to show for my work. But when I popped up right on top of them, it was all worth it. They had moved exactly to the point I thought they would. At 200 yards I shot. After I shot I stood with my mouth open in disbelief as my buck chased his does across a flat bottom at 50 mph. He acted like nothing was the matter. A half second later I had the crosshairs back on him as he ran, but he suddenly stopped and fell straight over. I had taken a once in a lifetime 16" (green score) trophy antelope. The shot had clipped his dorsal aorta and part of a lung. I still can't believe that he ran 300 yards after I shot.

Elk Head Mountains

(Reprinted from Routt National Forest map)

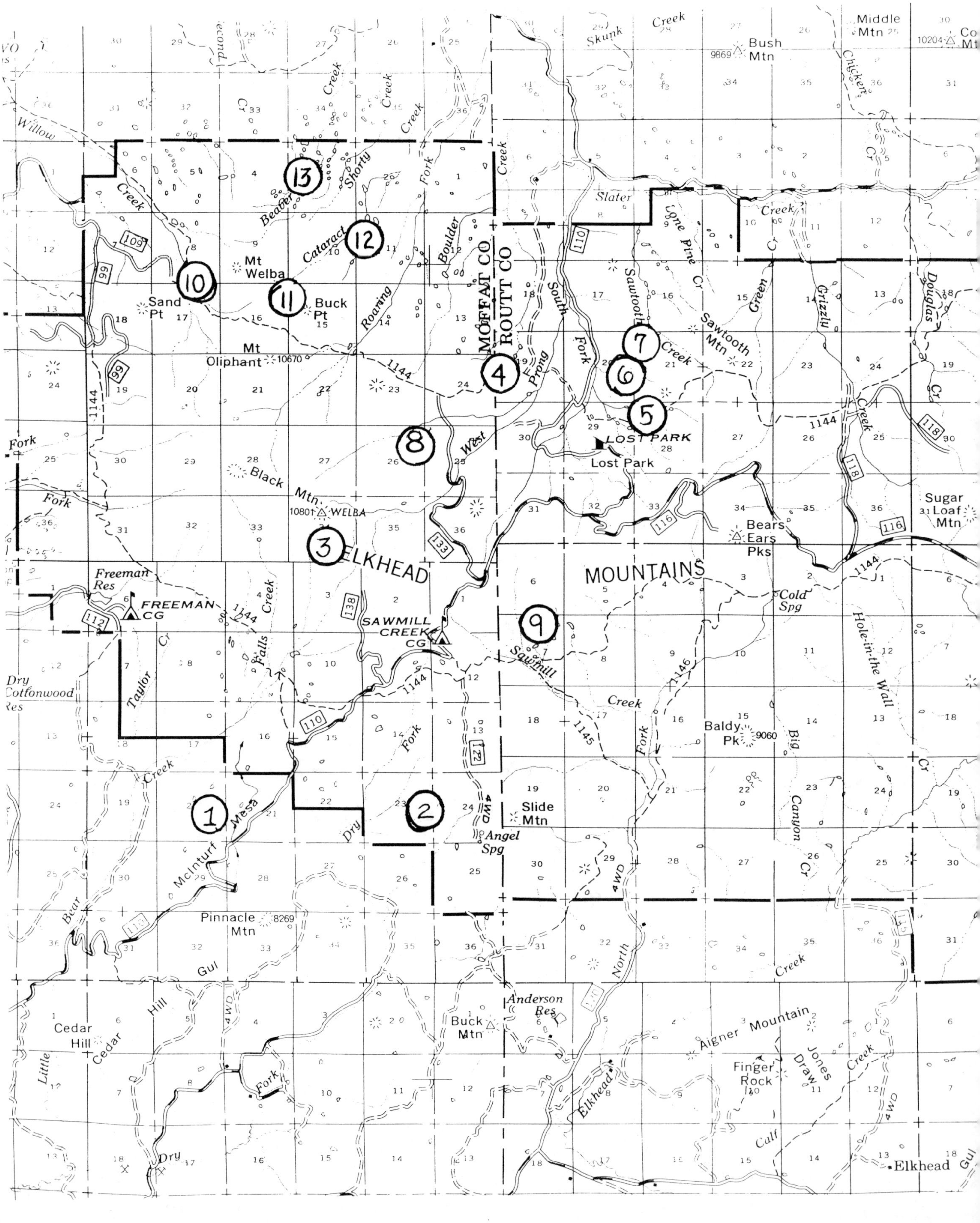

ELK HEAD MOUNTAINS 3-D MAP

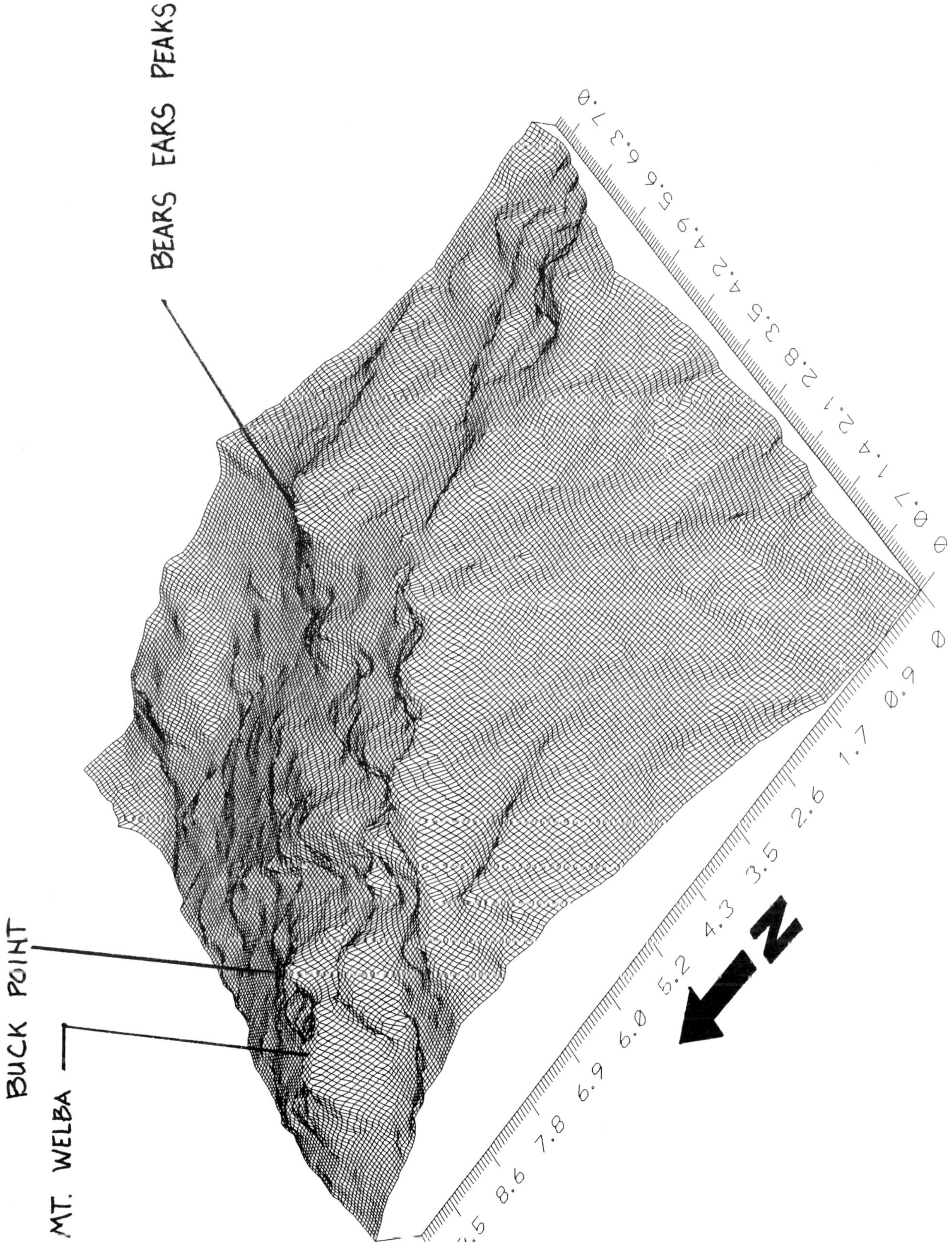

Elk Springs Ridge

How To Get There:

To get to this area from Denver take Interstate 70 west to Idaho Springs. Then take Highway 40 north out of Idaho Springs through the town of Empire. From there go through the small towns of Granby, Kremmling, Steamboat Springs, Hayden, Craig, Maybell and then down to Elk Springs, the whole time remaining on Highway 40. The good hunting spots are located directly southeast of the town of Elk Springs.

You can also get there by taking I-70 west from Denver until you get to the town of Rifle where you will take Highway 13 north to Meeker 90. From there take Highway 64 west along the White River to Blair Mesa then north on McKender's Gulch road and the spots we have marked on the map.

How To Hunt This Area:

The terrain in this area is similar to the Piceance Creek area in that it contains rolling sage brush covered hills with pockets of aspen, dark timber, pinion-juniper pines and scruboak. The elevation is not extremely high - between 6,000 and 8,000 feet. Like the rest of northwest Colorado, it produces big bucks and bulls. The elk in this area act differently than the high alpine meadow elk. They will not migrate from the high peaks to the lower valleys when the snows come. They are what we call "resident elk herds" because they stay in the same area year round.

We've had a lot of luck hunting areas like this during the pre-rut and full rut because the elk are easy to locate with an elk bugle. They've been known to bugle as late as December, but during the rut they bugle more often. Cow elk calls are also an excellent way to locate herds but they are not as loud as a bugle and you have to be a lot closer for them to work. One other good time to harvest big elk is when snow is on the ground. It's easy to follow their tracks and much easier to spot them as their chestnut colored coats stand out against the fresh snow.

Spence with a nice 3 X 4 taken at about 40 yards.

Spence:

I use an elk bugle as a "locator call" much like you might use an owl hooter to locate a turkey. But then when I move in I use cow calls. Just like owl hooting too close to a gobbler scares the bird off, bugling too close to a bull elk will often scare him off (unless the elk are in the peak of the rut). I bugle in close only when the elk has come in to me in which case I know he's hot from the rut and ready to fight.

Spence:

A problem can arise when I'm moving to a bull, I am not sure exactly where he is, and he won't answer my cow calls. Bugling in close may scare him off, while if I move in without pinpointing his position, I might stumble onto him and spook him as well. The best thing to do in this situation is to have one guy stay at a distance and bugle. As long as the bugler is far away, it's not intimidating to the bull. While the bull's answering my partner's bugles, I can move in close, covering the sound from my movement with cow calls.

When you're moving through scruboaks which are common to this area, you're going to make a lot of noise. There are always dry dead leaves under those trees (keep in mind it rarely rains in Colorado). Also, scruboaks are tightly packed and tear at your clothing as you walk by. After a day in that stuff, your legs will look like you have walked through a heavy briar patch. We believe that elk purposely hide out in scruboaks because they serve as an alarm system, warning of coming intruders. To effectively hunt scruboaks you need to get a "cover up" call like a cow call, deer grunt tube, hawk call, owl hooter or something that elk will recognize as a natural sound of their environment.

Guy:

This past year I watched one of Mike Lipinski's hunting videos called "Big Bulls." He was hunting in northwestern Colorado and the terrain was exactly the same as the stuff around Elk Springs. He would not say where he was hunting (because it was so good) but we think it was very close to our area. By watching this video you can really appreciate how thick the scruboaks can be, and how physically demanding it is to hunt in them.

Spence:

One time, at a ranch near Steamboat, Colorado, I walked back to my truck down a mountainside that was covered with thick scruboaks. I just wanted to get out of them, and wasn't worried about how much noise I was making. However, just as a precaution, I made occasional cow calls. I came into a clearing, and on the other side of a thick patch of scruboaks, I could make out the shape of a 5 point bull elk not 30 yards off. He assumed I was a cow elk and didn't even look up. Thirty seconds later, he got my scent, looked over to see a human and bolted. If I had been a little more on the ball, I could have ducked back into the patch of scruboaks I had just freed myself from, and waited for him to step out into the open. I didn't recognize the situation for what it was. I just assumed he had already seen me and would bolt any second. I spent over 4 hours trying to get back onto him and the cows he was with, but had no luck. All I saw were some timber bucks which I ignored.

Guy:

When Spence and I are elk hunting, it may start out leisurely, but once we hear our first elk bugle, the hunt turns into a mission. When you get elk fever nothing else in your life matters. We don't want to offend any whitetail hunters from back east, but once you get close to an elk, you'll throw deer hunting out the window. We have passed up easy shots at good sized mule deer because we were hot onto an elk herd. Once you're out here, you'll see why. Just imagine the excitement you felt when you saw the largest buck of your life, then multiply that rack size by 10 to get comparable elk size. Your heart just stops when you see an animal that massive.

While access is virtually unlimited in this area, don't let it fool you. Even though there are a lot of roads, it's easy to become lost, as our friend Derek can attest to. He got lost and spent an entire day sitting on the side of a road waiting for us to find him. He said that all the hills and roads looked the same.

Note: We owe credit to a friend of Guy's, Dave Bancroft, who introduced us to this area. Thanks Dave.

Spot 1: **Winter Valley Gulch**. This spot is located next to some windmill generated springs to the north of private land. You can hunt the ridge just to the east of Winter Valley Gulch. It has a couple of open areas that attract elk in the early morning.

There are several windmills throughout the valley that produce a lot of water and attract game. Also, the area gets a little bit more precipitation than the Piceance Creek drainage (30 miles to the south) so the vegetation is thicker and supports more game, especially more elk.

Guy:

This is the very first spot that I ever hunted in this valley. A friend and I bugled in three different bulls. They came from down along Cove Creek.

Spot 2. **Pinion Ridge**. To the west of the ridge is steep, densely timbered terrain where one morning we spotted several smaller bull elk. They were satellite bulls to a larger herd in the area. Over the years a friend of Guy's has killed several bulls around this spot.

Spot 3: **Open Bowl**. This spot is located in a big open basin between Pinion Ridge to the west and another ridge just to the east. Standing on the ridge you can bugle down into the valley and then pursue the animals that answer. There are several open meadows out in the sage flats at the bottom. Elk feed there early in the morning.

Spot 4: **Sagebrush Point**. This spot is located on a high point just south of Spot 3. From there you can look over an open valley that's full of sage and grass.

Guy:

From this point I once spotted 25 to 30 elk feeding on the north facing slope. But by the time I got down the gully and up the other side, the wind had shifted. They smelled me and were gone in an instant.

Spot 5: **Sagebrush Ridge**. This spot is located on a ridge from which you can look down into a huge open valley. Early in the season, when it's still warm, there will not be as many elk in the valley as there will be on the ridges. Later in the rifle season when the snows get deep the animals will migrate down to the valley. During warm periods, the trick is to look for areas that might provide the cool air elk like. For example, they are more likely to bed on a north facing slope than a south facing slope. Also, if it's windy, they will head to a ridge where they can enjoy the cool air and escape from the bugs.

Spot 6: **South Citadel Plateau**. This spot is located in a saddle just to the south of Citadel Plateau. There's also a timbered ridge sticking out into the flatter land to the south. We've seen quite a few cow elk and raghorns crossing through the saddle. The larger bulls which we didn't see were probably higher up on the ridges.

Spot 7: **Pinto Gulch**. (Note: This is a different gulch than the one profiled in the Rio Blanco area). In this area you can hunt next to a spring that begins in the top part of the gulch just off the edge of Citadel Plateau. Down in the gulch we spotted several bulls including one huge herd bull with a harem of about 15 cows. He was chasing off the competitors while eluding us for the better part of two days. Unfortunately when we returned on the third day the herd was gone. We figure they went up over the top of the plateau. It was extremely steep getting up there and we didn't pursue them.

Spot 8: **Central Citadel Plateau**. This spot is situated on a part of the plateau that sticks out to the south toward Deep Channel Creek. Up on top, in the distance we sighted several nice mule deer, including one four pointer accompanied by a five pointer. But we did not pursue. We were after a group of elk.

The terrain in this spot is open sage and grass dotted with thick stands of scruboak. The hillsides also have some dark timber where the elk bed.

Spot 9: **Long Arm**. On the map you can see several different fingers of the plateau sticking out to the south. Each one has elk on it. There is a little saddle at the extreme south tip of this area through which they cross instead of going up over the top of the plateau itself.

Guy checks out fresh elk sign he found in the dark timber.

Spot 10: **Coyote Basin Overlook**. This spot is situated along another finger of land that sticks out toward the south. It's wide open terrain - you can see for many miles. We saw where many elk had crossed an old four wheel drive trail, headed east across the next gully, and then farther east from there. But they were just passing through. Coyote Basin, where they went, is easy to walk to and has several ponds that are good ambush spots.

Spot 11: **Escarpment Peak**. Escarpment Peak is one of the tallest peaks in the area. It provides long views in every direction and consequently, the area's very best spotting opportunity. While sitting on this peak we've been able to spot numerous deer and elk in the early morning, and you will too. You will probably see game on top of the plateau, as well as off the sides. If you do spot game off the side, you need to keep in mind that you'll have to haul out whatever you shoot down there.

Spot 12: **Swan Draw**. This is one of the few spots where we recommend getting off the top of the plateau and walking the steep hillsides down into the valley. At the headwaters of Swan Draw is a little basin you can hunt that attracts a lot of game. It will be especially good when hunting pressure on the plateau gets intense.

Elk Springs Ridge

(Reprinted from USGS Meeker map)

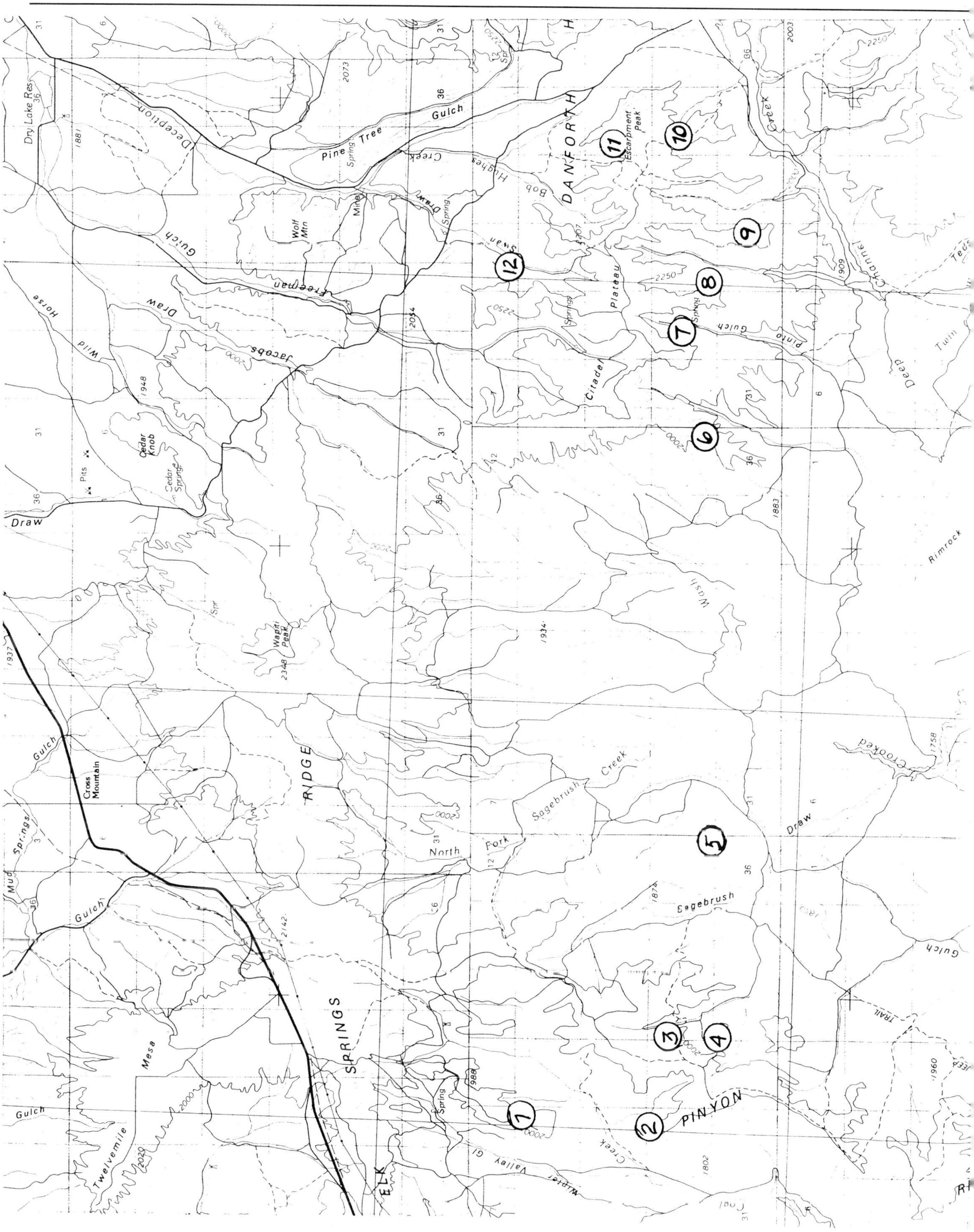

ELK SPRINGS RIDGE 3-D MAP

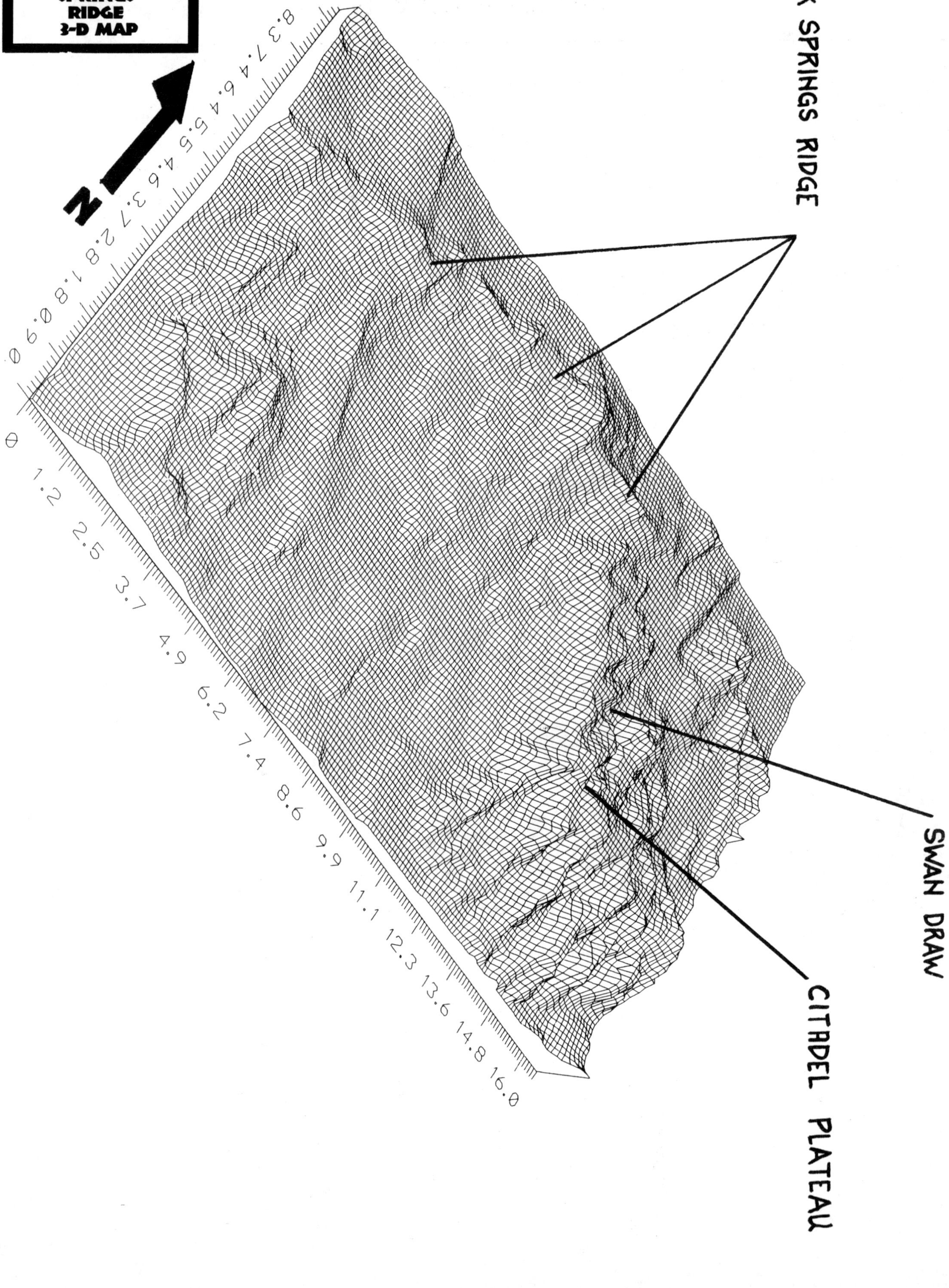

Flat Tops Wilderness

Big Game Hunting Unit(s): 24, 25, and 26.

How To Get There: The Flat Tops Wilderness covers an extremely large area. As a result, the spots we've profiled are widely dispersed, and there are four different routes to them.

To get to the first area take Interstate 70 west from Denver to Rifle (approx 150 miles). Then take Highway 13 north to Meeker. From Meeker take Road 8 through Buford driving along the White River up to Trapper's Lake.

To get to the second area you also take I-70 west to Rifle. From Rifle head north on Highway 13 to Meeker. Next take Road 8 to about a mile before the Buford exit. You will then turn and head southeast along the south fork of the White River. It will take you up into the Stillwater Valley.

To get to the third area take I-70 west to Dotsero (130 miles approx.), then turn north on Colorado River Road and drive to Burns. From there take road 10 northeast to the areas we've marked on the map.

In the old days you could drive your vehicle up on top of the Flat Tops. When it became a wilderness area, motorized vehicle travel was prohibited. Here, Guy's uncle Lloyd Carpenter poses with a beautiful 6 X 7.

To get to the fourth area take I-70 west to Highway 40 then north to the town of Kremmling. North of Kremmling you will turn left on Road 131 and drive over Gore Pass to Yampa and then on to Phippsburg. From there turn and head southwest on Road 15 and shortly thereafter turn left on Road 13. Follow Road 13 1.7 miles to a 4x4 road that will branch off to the left. This is the South Hunt Creek Road which you will follow until it ends.

How To Hunt This Area:

The Flat Tops were named for a particular typography where a steep high mountain flattens out on top, forming a large high altitude table. There are a few peaks rising out of the flat upper table, but generally, the land is very flat. A lot of the country does look the same which is why so many people get lost up there. To avoid that trauma, pick out a landmark from which you can always get your bearings.

This entire area is in its ninth year of four point or better bull elk hunting restriction. To take an animal it has to be at least four points on one side which could include a five inch or better brow tine. The result has been the development of a truly incredible trophy hunting opportunity. Plus, every year some real nice timber bucks are taken while people are up hunting elk.

This country provides some of the best close cover hunting anywhere. The vegetation consists of aspen and spruce stands, small parks, meadows, and heavy dark spruce pockets with a lot of blowdowns. The downed timber limits game travel to trails which makes them easy to locate and ambush. If a storm is coming in and barometric pressure is rising, you can hunt along game trails all day long. The animals will be moving about in anticipation of the storm, rather than bedding down like they usually do during the middle part of the day. Overall, the tremendous amount of precipitation this area gets contributes to heavy plant growth, and consequently supports a lot of game.

Note:

We're dedicating this section of the book to Guy's uncle, Phil Collier, who has hunted the Flat Tops extensively and has given us a lot of the spots we've profiled.

Spot 01: **Skinny Fish Lake Area**. To get to this spot, from Trapper's Lake take Trail 1812 to Trail 1813 (about one and one half miles) and Skinny Fish Lake. Just to the southwest, you can spot elk in the mornings and evenings in the open meadows surrounding McGinnis Lake. The elk are concentrated on the north side of this lake and are very responsive to both bugles and cow calls.

Spot 02: **Upper Skinny Fish Lake**. Above Skinny Fish Lake are some beaver ponds and open meadows which attract game. Hunt that drainage. The elk should be bugling in there quite heavily during the archery and muzzle loading seasons. Camp around the lake and get up in there at first light. If you are not seeing anything by the beaver ponds, try walking up a bit higher. Farther up there's a big meadow called Chinese Well which is situated just below the Lost Lakes Peaks.

Spot 03: **Lost Lakes**. Take Trail 1812 as it branches off the trail to Skinny Fish. The mountainside will become very steep. There are a couple of switchbacks as you walk up the side of what they call "the rim." Above the rim are the Deep Lakes. From there hunt over along East Lost Lake and West Lost Lake.

Once you get above the rim, travel is much easier, except for the areas that have a lot of downed timber. To the north is one such area which in spite of the difficult walking, is a very good spot. There are a lot of game trails through the fallen logs. Because the game is forced to walk those trails (rather than continuously jump over logs) they are great places to intercept deer and elk. A game drive may also work in this spot. Have a few people in your group push the elk and deer up the trails starting down in the lower valley around Lynx and Pinion Creeks.

Spot 04: **Between Lakes**. This spot is located in an open area between Deep Lake and Dynes Lake. There's heavy timber directly between the two, but if you walk to the south 400-500 yards it will open up at the base of the peak. Sit on the edge of the timber during the morning and evening and glass the fields for elk and deer.

Guy:

> Sometimes animals seem to just materialize out of nowhere. You have to stay alert. More than once I've looked away from a field I was glassing, then looked back a minute later and seen elk feeding in the field as if they had been there all day long.

Spot 05: **Round Lake**. This spot is located in the big open meadows by Round Lake just off of Trail 1119. Pay close attention to the dark timber that sticks out into the meadow to the south and east of Round Lake. You can walk through the timber heading south and push the animals out of the woods and into the open. Where the timber ends, you can sit on a hill and have good positioning on two large meadows and one hillside that has a creek running at its base.

Derrek Doolittle with a grouse he shot just at dusk.

Spot 06: **Upper Dead Mexican Gulch**. This spot is located at the upper headwaters of Dead Mexican Gulch on the northwest side of Devil's Causeway. Devil's Causeway is a narrow rock rim that rises 100 feet straight out of the Flat Tops. We've been told by several outfitters that the area around Causeway Lake is so remote that the elk don't even know what a human is. Because of this hunters can get really close to the elk. The spot we're showing on the map is actually in Dead Mexican Gulch on the opposite side of the rim from Causeway Lake. You can walk a trail over through a small passage in the causeway and drop down into the gulch (8 mile walk). In the past, the dark timber at the top of the gulch has produced world-class bull elk.

Spot 07: **Stump Park**. This spot is located in the southeast part of the Flattops Wilderness Area. You get there by driving to the town of Dotsero then on to Burns. Drive Road 510 (four wheel drive only) to the Stump Park trailhead. From there you will take Trail 1859 to the northwest.

You'll be hunting the northeast side of a ridge overlooking the north fork of Derby Valley. In the upper portion of the valley is a lot of lodgepole pine and open meadows. Down at the very bottom are some aspen stands. We've seen herds of two to three hundred elk feeding along the bottom and we've picked up five and six point sheds there in the spring. You can also find elk in the lodgepole pine stands.

Spot 08: **Keener Lake And Hooper Lake**. To get to this spot take FSR 610 to Trail 1860 and walk up to the lakes. You can hunt the grassy areas surrounding the lakes (bring your pack rod for extracurricular fishing) and the area to the southwest down by Derby Peak. The elk are going to be thick in there, especially during the first rifle season, and sometimes the second too, depending on the weather. During the third rifle season, hunt as high as the snow permits. As long as the snow is not too deep, they'll stick to the higher altitudes. So should you.

Spot 09: **Middle Derby Creek.** This spot is located along the middle fork of Derby Creek. Take the trail along the bottom of the gully just past McMillan Lake. To the north are some expansive meadows. To the north is a small ridgeline running northwest, and a larger one paralleling that. Stay on top of the larger one where you get a good view of the wide open country below.

Guy:

This is probably one of the top places in North America to harvest a trophy bull elk. I've seen a picture of a hunter who last year shot a huge five point bull right on the side of the Derby Peak. There are a couple of outfitters working this area. In their advertising they have said "We are into the elk every day." If you go there, there's no reason you couldn't see elk every day too.

Spot 10: **Upper Derby Creek**. As you continue up the middle fork of Derby creek along Trail 1858, just above timberline you will come to a couple of lakes that attract game. There are also a lot of shale rockslides up there. The deer and elk don't like being out on the rocks, and consequently, they will be concentrated in the pockets of timber between the rockslides.

Guy:

Walk from ridgeline to ridgeline covering as much ground as you can. Bugle down every ravine and hollow until you get a bull to answer. They'll answer more readily earlier in the season when they haven't been pressured by too many hunters. Once you get a response from a bull, move in as close as possible, cow calling to cover the sound of your movements. Listen for the rustling and bumping noises they often make when feeding in thick woods.

Many times Spence and I have moved in close only to have the bull shut up and move away. Sometimes this happens because the bull just isn't looking for a fight. But we have seen an increase in this type of behavior over the years, and attribute this to excessive and bad bugling by hunters.

Spence:

Of course, a bull in the peak of the rut will answer any call and come in. I even heard about a guy who had a bull elk come in to the sound of his chainsaw. It wouldn't leave him alone. But other than those few days when they're fighting mad, getting them in is going to be hard. It takes good calling.

Anyone can quickly pick up the basic calls. But to be successful, you have to have the ear to pick up on the nuances of elk language. I tell people that the basics will give you an unnatural call that to elk sounds much like a computer generated voice sounds to us. Only the stupid, the hard up and the very young will come in. But with practice, you can put out a sultry cow call, a heart wrenching calf call, and an entire range of bugles from sassy little upstart raghorn to enraged herd bull.

How do you learn their language? That's easy, just listen to as much of it and imitate as much of it as you possibly can. You should live and breathe elk calls. Start out with the tapes of calls and call strategies put out by the pros. But then, as you get better, you'll want to get tapes with real/live elk sounds on them so you can listen for voice intonations the professional caller on the tape might have left out. One thing that I've found to be very effective is to listen to those live tapes on low volume just as I'm going to sleep. I firmly believe that your subconscious will pick up on things your conscious mind may have missed. You'll know when you're really getting close to elk language fluency when you start dreaming about it. It's just like learning a second language. When you start dreaming in that language you will become truly fluent.

Do elk in different areas or herds have different accents? I really think they do. There's no telling how much of their language is learned, and how much is instinctual. I've never heard two elk call the same way. I think it's important to closely imitate the voice of the animal you're hunting. Much like a telephone salesman will develop rapport with a prospect by matching his voice to theirs, your elk will bond to you when you sound just like him. Plus, just like sales, you can steer the elk through your conversation to your ultimate goal. You can slowly build the intensity of your exchange with the bull and bring out the fighting instinct in him. The most important thing you should remember about elk calling is this - <u>The object of your practice calls is not to learn to call, but rather to learn to listen to a real elk call and imitate it exactly.</u>

Using these methods, you can develop highly effective elk calling in as little as a month. Most of the people who reach this level, get comfortable and settle for the results it brings. They're in the top 2%, so they see no reason to get better. But going from the "effective" level to the "truly exceptional" will put you in a league where you can call in once-in-a-lifetime bulls. What's required is that you abandon the rote planned calling responses and "feel" the elk. The only way I can describe it is that you abandon all thought, and it seems like each response you make is coming from someone else. You feel like you're "playing above your game." If you shoot clays, you'll notice you shoot better when you react and don't think. This is the same way. You're basically letting yourself be as good as you could be if you believed more in yourself. You're approaching perfection, and your calls are devastating on the elk. You'll know you're getting there when inside you feel like maybe you're becoming the elk you hunt. Native American cultures used to perform rituals in which they imitated the animal they hunted in order to become part of the spirit of that animal, and because they were thinking like that animal, they could effectively hunt it.

It works because you only consciously remember a portion of what you see. The rest is stored with perfect accuracy in your subconscious from the time of your birth to the time of your death. Your mind picks up a lot more information about the game you hunt than you remember. If you trust in yourself and go with your feelings, you will have all that stored knowledge at your disposal. It works just as well for tracking. Sometimes you just have to let it go and follow where you feel the elk have gone, because they haven't left enough sign to follow with your sight.

Guy:

At some point in your hunt, you may find yourself right in the middle of a herd. <u>Do not bugle then.</u> Once Spence and I were right in the middle of a large herd. There were cows 360° around us. Plus, a big herd bull was farther downhill confronting a lesser bull. The cows were just too easy to shoot (one was only 15 yards away) and we decided to pass. We were trying to figure out a way to get at the herd bull. Spence and I were whispering back and forth and got into a disagreement over what to do. He wanted to bugle. He said it would enrage the herd bull because he'd think another bull had gotten into his harem. I whispered, "No, you'll scare all the cows off." He said, "I'm going to bugle." I kept whispering, "Don't" and he kept whispering back, "Yeah, I'm going to." Well, his persistence paid off and he got to bugle.

When Spence bugled, the whole side of the hill just exploded with elk - branches breaking, hooves hammering the ground, while turf and terds were actually flying through the air in every direction.

Spence:

I remember actually moving behind a big pile of brush to make sure I didn't get trampled by the stampeding herd. I know my perceptions are warped, but looking back I could swear that I was sitting on the ground and getting bumped around.

Guy:

One last thing I want to mention - while the open country allows you to easily spot game, it also makes it harder to get close to the game. Deer and elk have good eyesight as everyone knows. They also have a great sense of smell, so you always have to hunt from downwind. The only real advantage you have is that you know you're a hunter, while they don't know what you are. When you make sounds that are natural to them, like cover calls, you push this advantage to its limits.

Spot 11: **Mcmillan Lake**. Don't be fooled because this spot is so close to the road. All the outfitters take their clients up higher in the backcountry and neglect this spot. This means, there's more unspooked game. Plus, when the weather gets bad the elk are even more concentrated around the lake. We call this a "sleeper area." Last year Guy harvested a nice deer out of what a game warden told us was a "sleeper area." So give it a shot.

Spot 12: **Mackinaw And Crescent Lakes**. This high elevation spot is located up around Mackinaw Lake and Crescent Lake to the southwest of Sheep Mountain. There's a small bottleneck of timber to the north. If your hunting party consists of four or five guys you can drive game into the bottleneck because they will stay in the timber when driven unless you get right on top of them and force them out into the open.

Spot 13: **Bull Lake**. This spot is located up around Bull Lake in a drainage off the south fork of Derby Ditch. There is a nice big pocket of timber back in there. Work the pocket thoroughly always keeping the wind in your face. If you don't spook the elk, you can hunt that timber a long time. If you do alarm them, they'll run right up the side of some big steep mountain where you can't follow, and you'll never see them again. There are also some low lying seeps and marshy areas where you'll find wallows.

Guy:

Once again, this is a trophy spot that grows huge elk and mule deer. The deer are not as concentrated as the elk, so it's best to go up for elk, and if you see a deer while you're up there, tag it. My uncle shot quite a few big animals back in there during the years he was hunting hard. He doesn't hunt this area anymore because for him it's too much work to get back in without a horse. He has had reconstructive surgery on his foot which was damaged in a road construction accident, and has not been able to get around like he used to.

Spot 14: **Stillwater Valley**. This spot is located just southeast of Buford. As you drive up the Stillwater Valley most of the land along the bottom is private. However, at the end of the valley you will see a sign for Hill Creek Trail. Follow that trail up the side of the flat top. This is extremely rough country due to the steepness and the amount of downed timber. You are going to have to do some climbing to get up above the thick stuff and into the open meadows above.

The trick to hunting this spot is to get up high (you can sit on the rock rim) very early and let other hunters push the game to you. Come daylight all the other hunters (locals from Denver) are going to park along the bottom of the South Fork of the White River and hunt up toward the rim.

Spot 15: **Fowler Creek**. This spot is located at the headwaters of Fowler Creek. Take Trail 2256 up. The trail breaks off of Trail 2255 or Trail 1826. It will take you past Spot 14. Up toward the headwaters of Fowler Creek the hills are completely timbered and you will be at about 10,500 to 11,000 feet in elevation. There are a few open meadows up there, but the area you want to concentrate on is along the creek bed. Look for tracks and frequently used wallows. If you have a light treestand it's a good idea to set it up above one of the wallows provided the wallow is not out in the open. They only use wallows that are unprotected at night.

Spot 16: **Upper Stillwater Valley**. This spot is located at the top of Stillwater Valley at the beginning of Trail 1827/Lost Solar Creek Trail. At the top of the valley there is a big open meadow with a finger of woods sticking out into the middle where an elk herd resides. This is one place where you won't have to go very far to get a crack at a bull. Farther up, the South Fork of the White River flows through a steep canyon. On the north side of the canyon is a big meadow, while the south side is heavily timbered. You'll find good hunting all through that area.

Spot 17: **Far Up Stillwater Valley**. You get to this spot by walking farther up Trail 1828 from Spot 16. You will cross about four different drainages on your left, then come to a high spot that overlooks a decent sized meadow just to the north. You will be at about 10,000 feet. It's a good place to sit and watch the edge of the timber for big animals moving around early in the morning and late in the evening.

Spot 18: **Mid Solar Creek.** As you continue farther up Solar Creek you will cut across another two drainages into some open parks. Right there a forest bottleneck crosses the trail from the north to the south. In addition, the bottleneck is located in a saddle which gets an inordinate amount of game activity. On a number of occasions we've seen animals crossing through. The animals in that area didn't seem to bed down much. They were out feeding all day long which may have been the result of an impending storm.

Spot 19: **Lost Solar Park**. This spot is located a half mile past the last one on the far side of Horseshoe Lake. You'll be hunting the fringe of a huge meadow that elk frequent. Field glasses work well there.

Spot 20: **Upper Doe Creek.** This spot is located where the flat tops really start opening up. The terrain gets very flat and you will be able to look over a huge expanse of grass meadows. Those meadows support Colorado's largest elk herd.

Guy:

> Several years ago Bugle Magazine put out a special issue on Colorado elk that included a photo of over 200 elk. That picture was taken from an plane flying right over this area around Twin Lakes. That picture alone is enough to make me want to hunt there the rest of my life... No kidding.

Spence:

> Some people wonder why the magazines give Colorado elk hunting so much attention. The reason (which most people are not aware of) is that Colorado has North America's largest elk herd (210,000). In fact, Colorado has twice as many elk as any other state. Plus, Colorado does not limit the amount of licenses that can be purchased, while most other states do.

Spot 21: **Buck Creek - The Meadows**. Drive Road 600 north until you can drive no farther, being careful that you don't go to the Wagon Wheel Creek area. Then take Trail 1827 up along Meadows Creek. On your right will be Elk Knob just off of Trail 1838. All around Elk Knob, (it was named that because it looks like an elk) we've seen many elk, especially on the east side where there are a lot of beaver ponds and a creek drainage. The creek bottom is a great place to look for fresh tracks and gauge recent elk activity in the area.

Guy packing out a 6 Pt.

Spot 22: **SW Trappers Peak.** Four miles above the meadows (it's a heck of a hike back there) you'll find a lot more water as the area becomes flatter. All around the water you are going to see an incredible amount of elk sign. You should plan to spend the entire day hunting up there. You can get your bearings from Trappers Peak so you'll always know about where you are.

Spot 23: **Upper South Fork Of The White River**. This spot is located farther up White River. You will notice that all the north facing slopes of the drainage are heavily timbered with spruce. The elk will be in the spruce during the day, and in the bottoms and fields in the mornings and the evenings.

If you find a place right along the river where they're crossing back and forth you might want to sit there early morning and late evening. You can also follow tracks up from the crossings and sometimes catch them where they bed.

Spot 24: **Saddle Of The 1830 Trail**. This spot is situated in the area just to the west of the south fork of the White River. You get there by walking up Trail 1830. You can hunt a saddle that goes from the Park Creek side to the White River side. This is the best place to sit and catch the local herd moving from one side of the drainage to the other. You will be positioned between two knolls on which are several watering ponds that attract game.

Spot 25: **Rainbow Lake**. Just off the north fork of the White River, near Rainbow Lake, to the south of Paradise Creek is a gully that a herd of elk frequents. You are going to be hunting the steep side of the Flat Tops in thick, wet, dark timber. There are some good sized bulls in there.

Spot 26: **Paradise Creek Gully**. This gully will take you all the way to the top of the basin if you're motivated to really walk. A local outfitter told us his clients had good luck up there.

Spot 27: **Open Meadows**. This spot is located in a big open meadow on the side of the Flat Tops. While the top of the Flat Tops is level, the sides are very steep and wet. All the water comes from springs formed by melting snow that seeps through the flat table above. This meadow is completely surrounded by dark timber and is hard to find. The bulls can feed in there and avoid the big open areas up top where they are more vulnerable to hunters. This spot tends to get overlooked by hunters who prefer the more picturesque area above.

Spot 28: **Mirror Lake**. Mirror Lake is a drop off point for a lot of the local outfitters. They put their hunters in camps not too far from there, then hunt below Mirror Lake and Sable Point.

Spot 29: **Sable Point**. This spot is a favorite of the locals. You'll be hunting above timberline. Once above timberline hunters gain an advantage in that they are able to see elk at quite some distance. You can plan a stalk and gather information about where the game is holing up for the day. As you move closer, be sure to remain downwind and use available cover to conceal your movements.

Spot 30: **Sable Lake Area**. This spot is not completely on top, but rather is located on a shoulder off the side of the Flat Tops. To get there take Trail 1820 up. This trail is called the Big Pack Trail because it goes all the way from the Marvin Creek side over the top and down to Mirror Creek. The shoulder you'll be hunting is wider and more level than surrounding terrain, which attracts wildlife and makes it easier for you to hunt.

Spot 31: **Wild Cow Park**. This spot is located right near the rim. You can't drive in there. But if you willing to walk a mile into the wilderness area, you'll be in a place that's known for its elk hunting. You'll come to several ponds and creeks where you should concentrate your search for the freshest sign. Plus, there is a huge open flat up there, probably one mile wide by three or four miles long where you can use your spotting and stalking tactics.

Spot 32: **East Wild Cow Park**. This spot is located right up along the rim of the Flat Tops directly to the east of Wild Cow Park. You'll be hunting in a big patch of timber between the rim and Wild Cow Park. The vegetation there supports a large number of animals. Hunters from both the top and bottom push game into those woods.

Flat Tops Wilderness

(Reprinted from White River National Forest map)

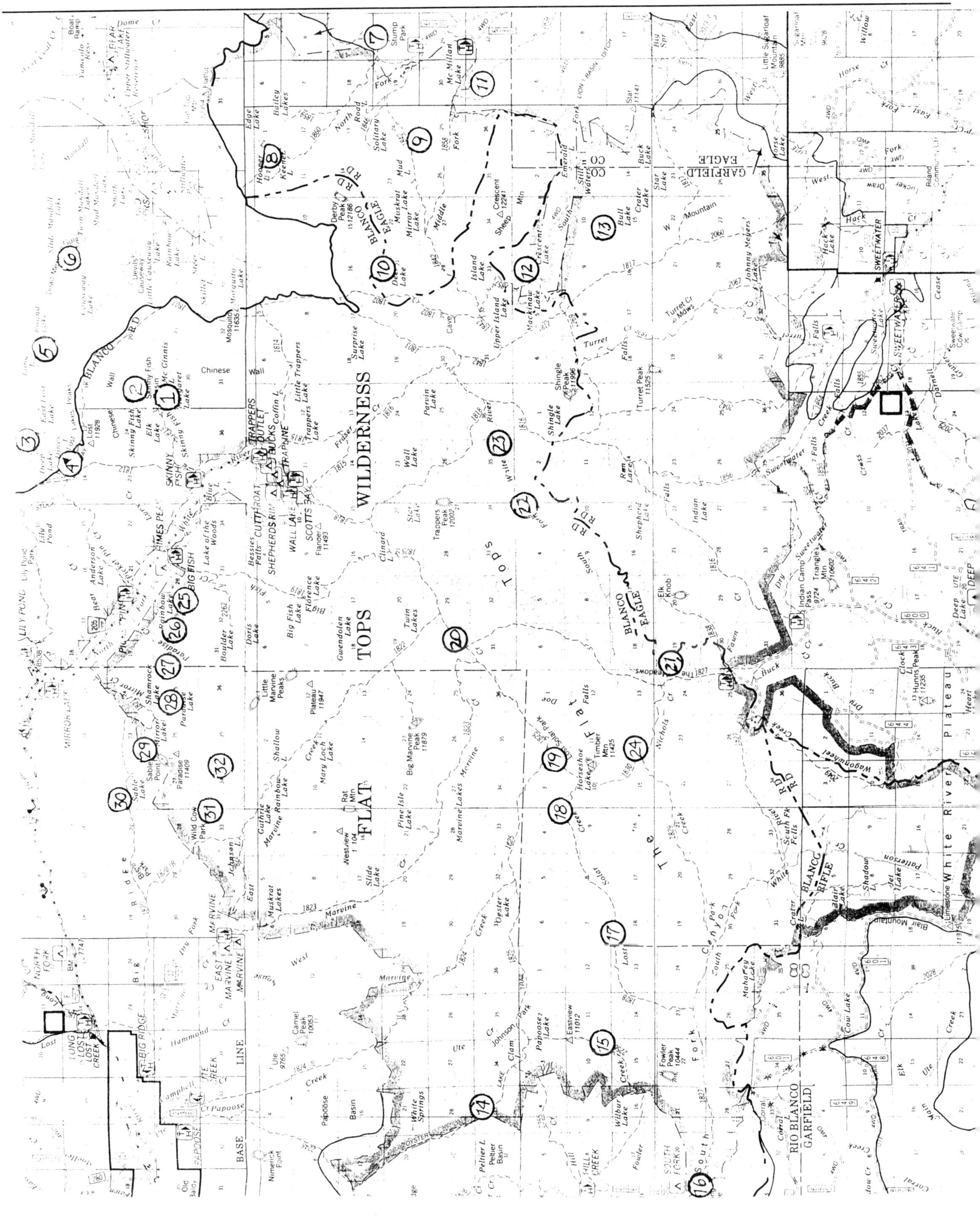

FLAT TOPS WILDERNESS 3-D MAP

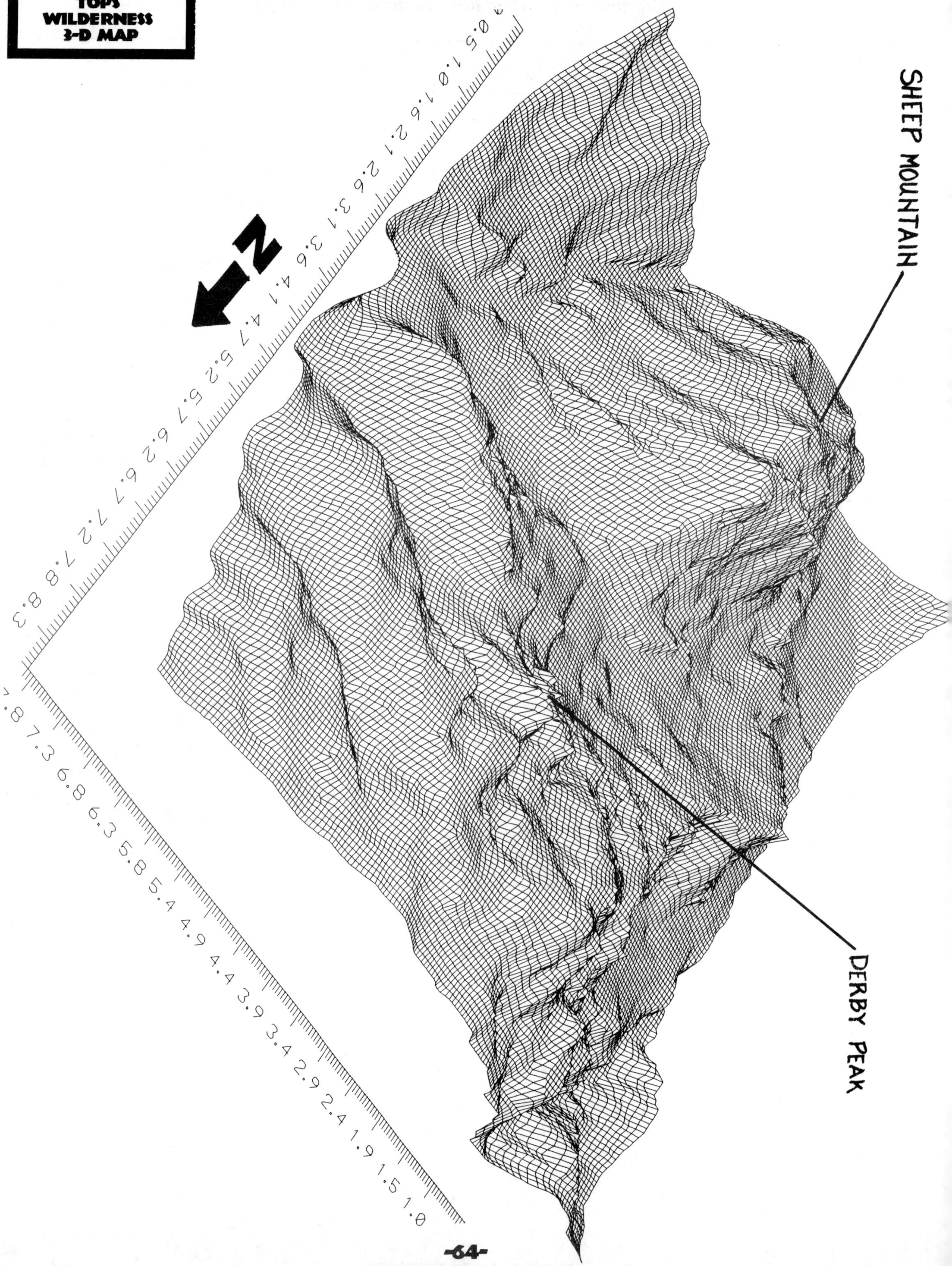

FLAT TOPS WILDERNESS 3-D MAP

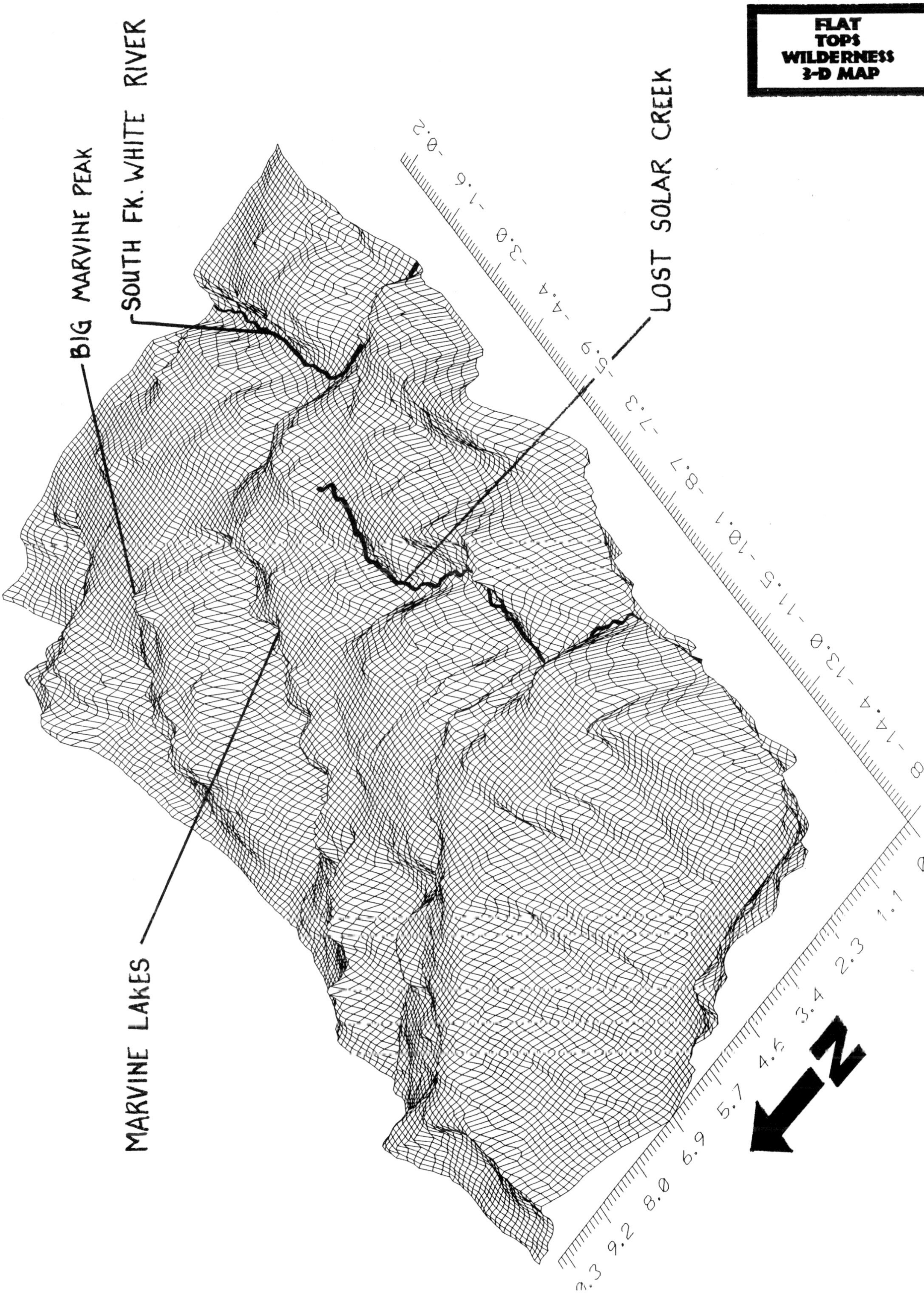

FLAT TOPS WILDERNESS 3-D MAP

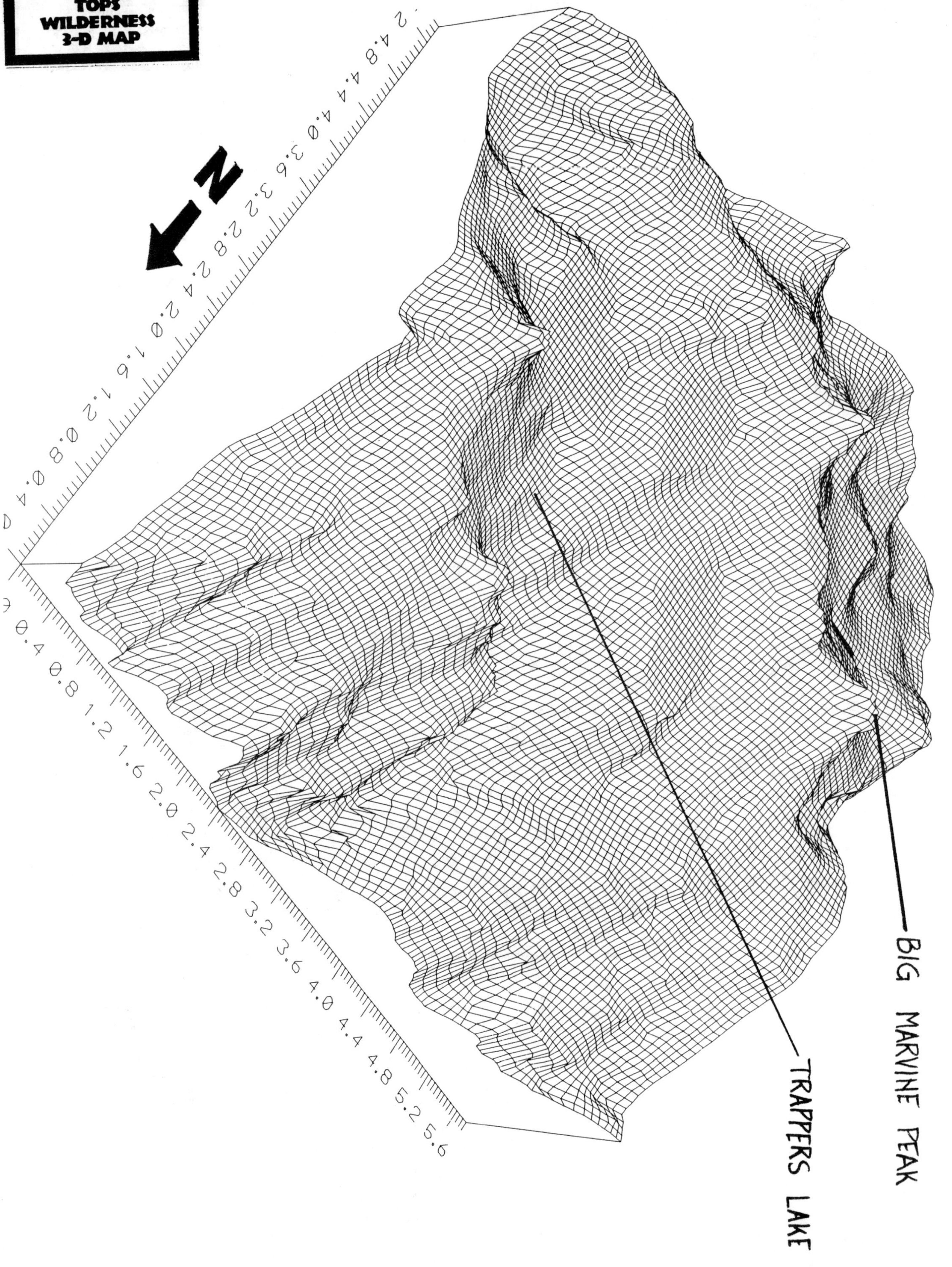

FLAT TOPS WILDERNESS 3-D MAP

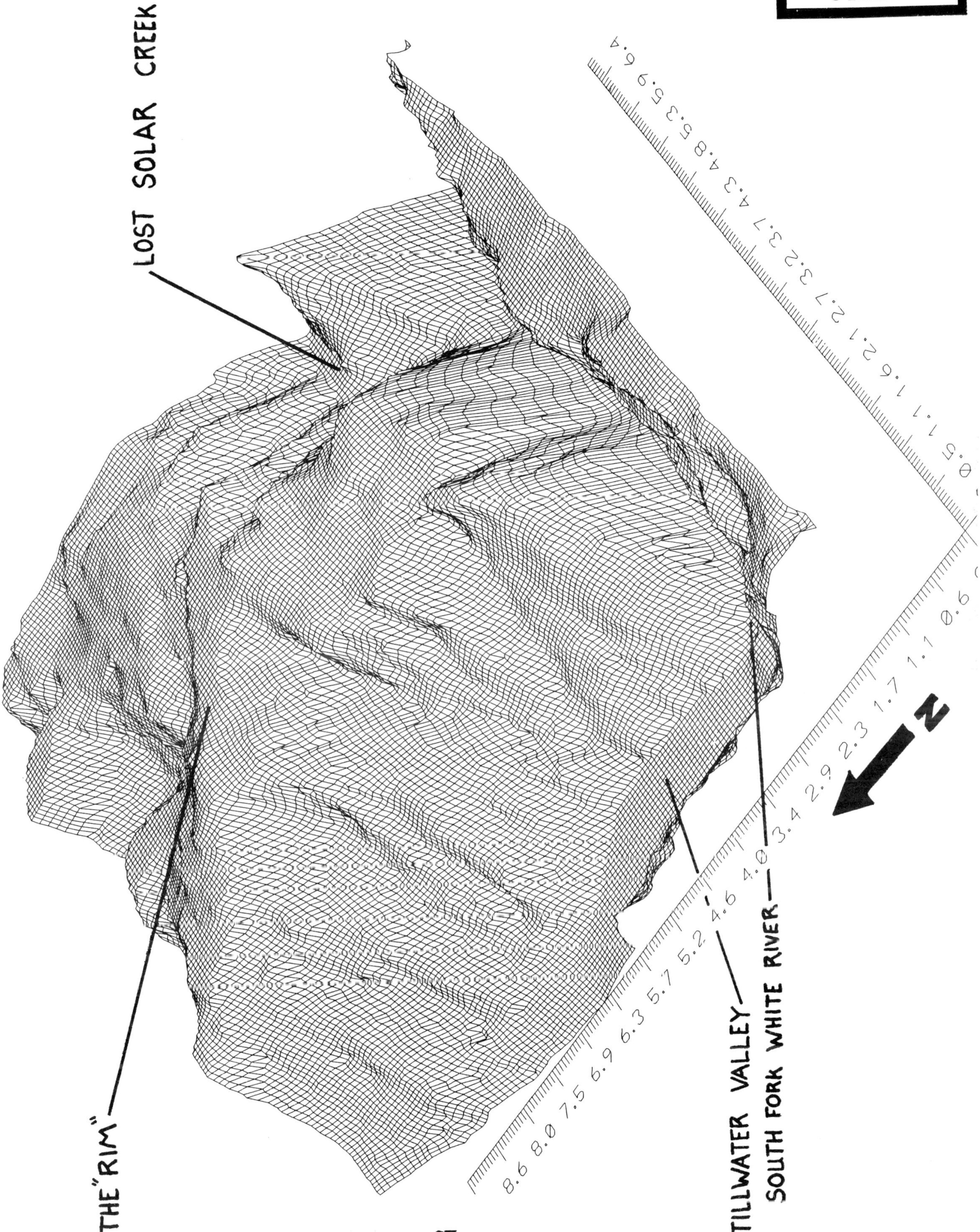

FLAT TOPS WILDERNESS 3-D MAP

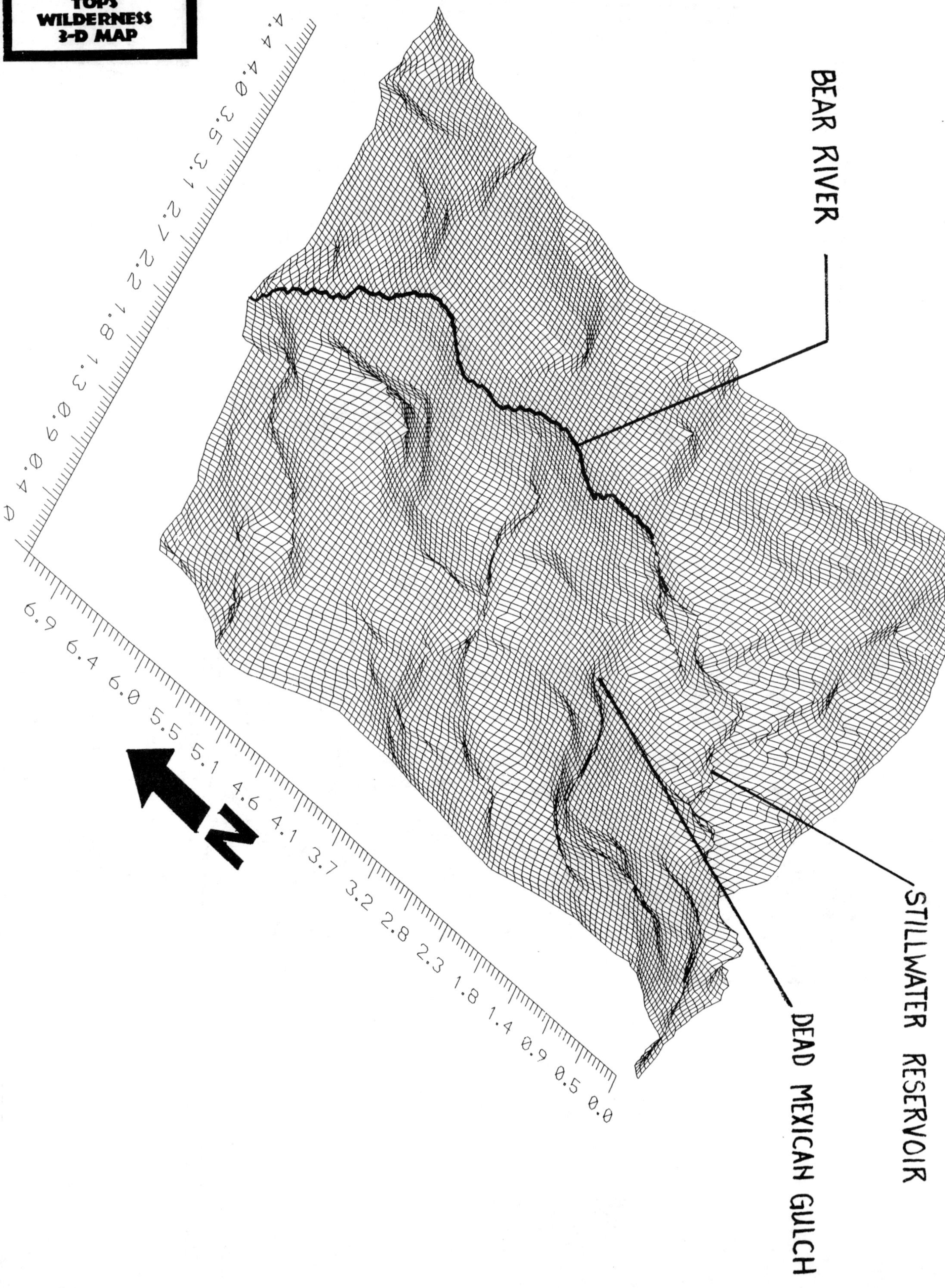

FLAT TOPS WILDERNESS 3-D MAP

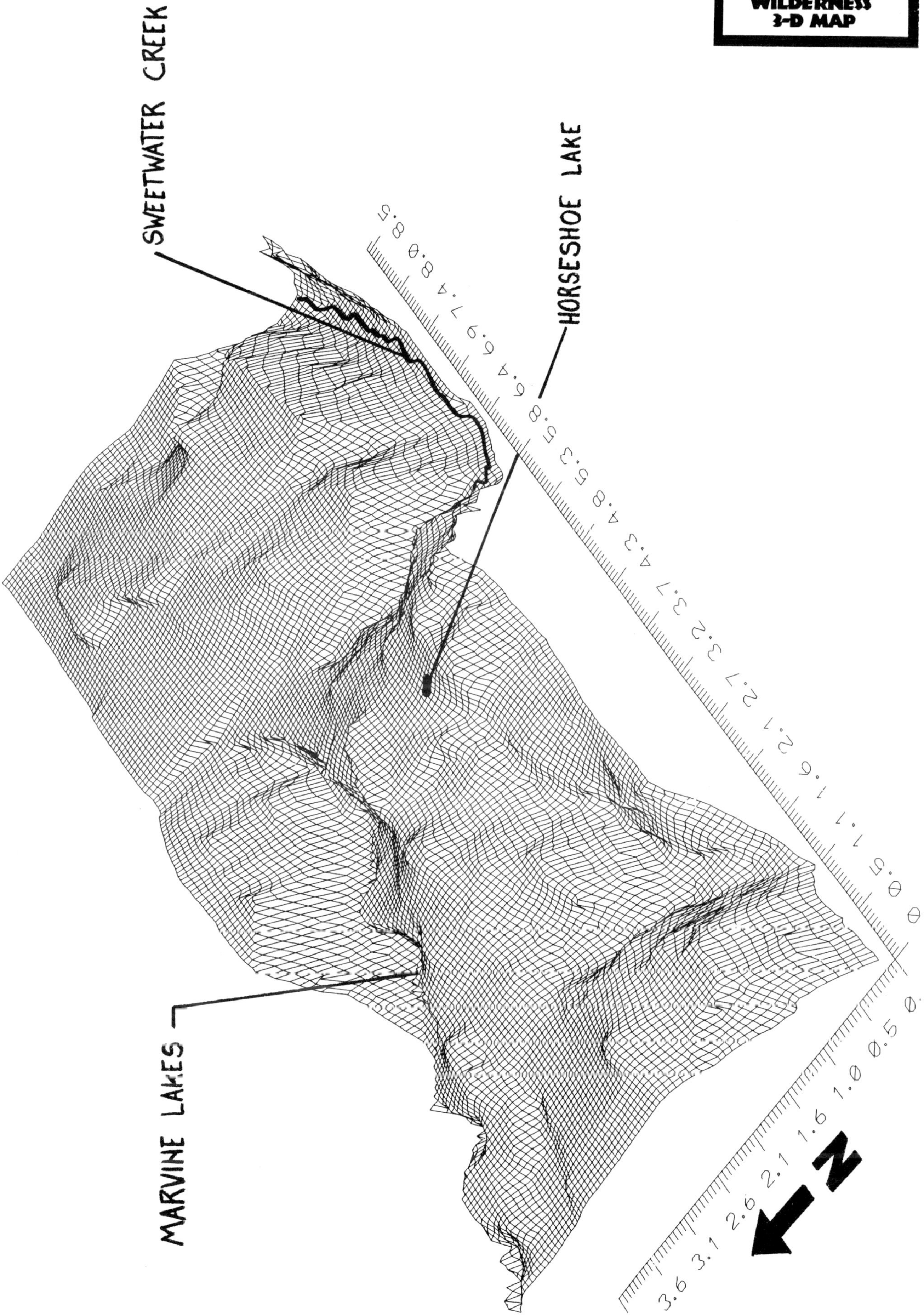

Gold Camp Road Area

Big Game Management Unit(s): 581, 511, 59

How To Get There:

All of these spots lie just off the road between Colorado Springs and Cripple Creek. The Gold Camp Road was originally built to get gold out of Cripple Creek. It's an amazing road. It's hard to believe they could have built a road through such rugged terrain way back in the 1800's.

How to Hunt This Area:

Driving down Gold Camp Road you will cross numerous gullies. You can either hunt up or down them. In the lower areas you'll find more deer, while up on the mountain tops above treeline you'll mostly see elk. The best way to zero in on the elk is to glass the bald mountain tops in the early morning and late evening. The deer in the lower meadows are more numerous and easier to hunt, but the deer up high in the dark timber ("timber bucks") are more likely to be trophy size.

Spence:

> I had a college roommate who hunted the back side of Cheyenne Mountain (which is an area discussed below). His tactic for timber bucks, and a tactic you should employ, is to hike through the thick timber looking for deer trails between small openings. What's difficult about hunting this terrain is that you have to keep your concentration for hours on end while hiking big wooded mountains that provide few or no breaks in terrain. People tend to get into the rhythm of walking and breathing and lose their concentration. What happens is that they "zone out" and end up stumbling onto the deer and never getting a shot off. It takes an extreme hunter to be successful in this type of terrain, but when you do have success you are sure to take a big trophy. My roommate was a distance runner and I think it helped him develop the ability to stay concentrated for long periods of time. The huge trophy mounts on his wall were proof enough.

Spot 1: **Bison Creek**. Along the creek on the north side of the road are flat meadows with large rock outcroppings rising straight out of the bottom. You need to drive a little east of the creek to get to the public land. You can parallel the creek, walking to the northwest, then cut back to it farther up where the creek bottom is public land. It's a good spot for deer year round and elk later in the season. Most of the game comes out into the meadows in the morning and evenings, and then sits up in the rocks watching the meadows during the day.

Spot 2: **Cathedral Park**. We're not quite sure how this place got its name but we imagine it's from the cathedral-like rocks you'll notice on the left hand side of the road. There's a gully in Cathedral Park that parallels Bison Creek. Walk that gully up and you'll find yourself in some very good deer habitat.

Spot 3: **Tunnel Hump**. Just on the east side of Gold Camp Road Tunnel, on the north side of the road, is a short gully which parallels the Cathedral Park gully. There's a road part way in that's been backhoed at the bottom, and is therefore impassable. But you can walk up it and move very quickly through some good deer habitat.

Spot 4: **Deer Park/Elk Park**. Take Road 3769 up Beaver Creek toward McReynolds Reservoir but then take the Road 379 southeast. In this area game is concentrated by hunting pressure from below.

Spot 5: **Mount Big Chief/Gould Creek**. Follow the creek bed up. There is a resident elk herd on the side of Mount Big Chief that comes down into the aspens and meadows along the creek to feed at night.

Spot 6: **Fire Road 379 And West Side Of Mount Rosa**. Drive north on Road 379 and hunt the gullies to the left. This spot gets game that is being pushed from Deer Park and Mount Big Chief. From this spot you can also hunt the back side of Mount Big Chief. You can also hunt along the creek to the east that goes up the side of Mount Rosa where you are sure to see elk.

Spot 7: **Mount Rosa East/Stove Mountain West**. Drive Road 381 north to the east side of Mt. Rosa and the west side of Stove Mountain. There is no other access into this area. Because it is high and isolated, it's a decent elk spot. Use your field glasses to spot elk above timberline.

Spot 8: **Emerald Valley**. This spot is very similar to the Cheyenne Mountain spot discussed below. Driving down Gold Camp Road you will come to an overlook from which (facing east) you can head to the left or the right. Take the right turn where you will begin to drop down Old Stage Road. Farther down, on the right is a road up a little valley going up to Emerald Valley Ranch. If you take this up the creek bottom there are a lot of willows which provide good deer and elk habitat.

Spot 9: **Cheyenne Mountain**. From Old Stage Road drive up the Cheyenne Mountain Road toward the Radio Towers. As we discussed previously it's supposed to be a good area for trophy timber bucks, but it's quite difficult to hunt.

Gold Camp Road Area

(Reprinted from Pike National Forest map)

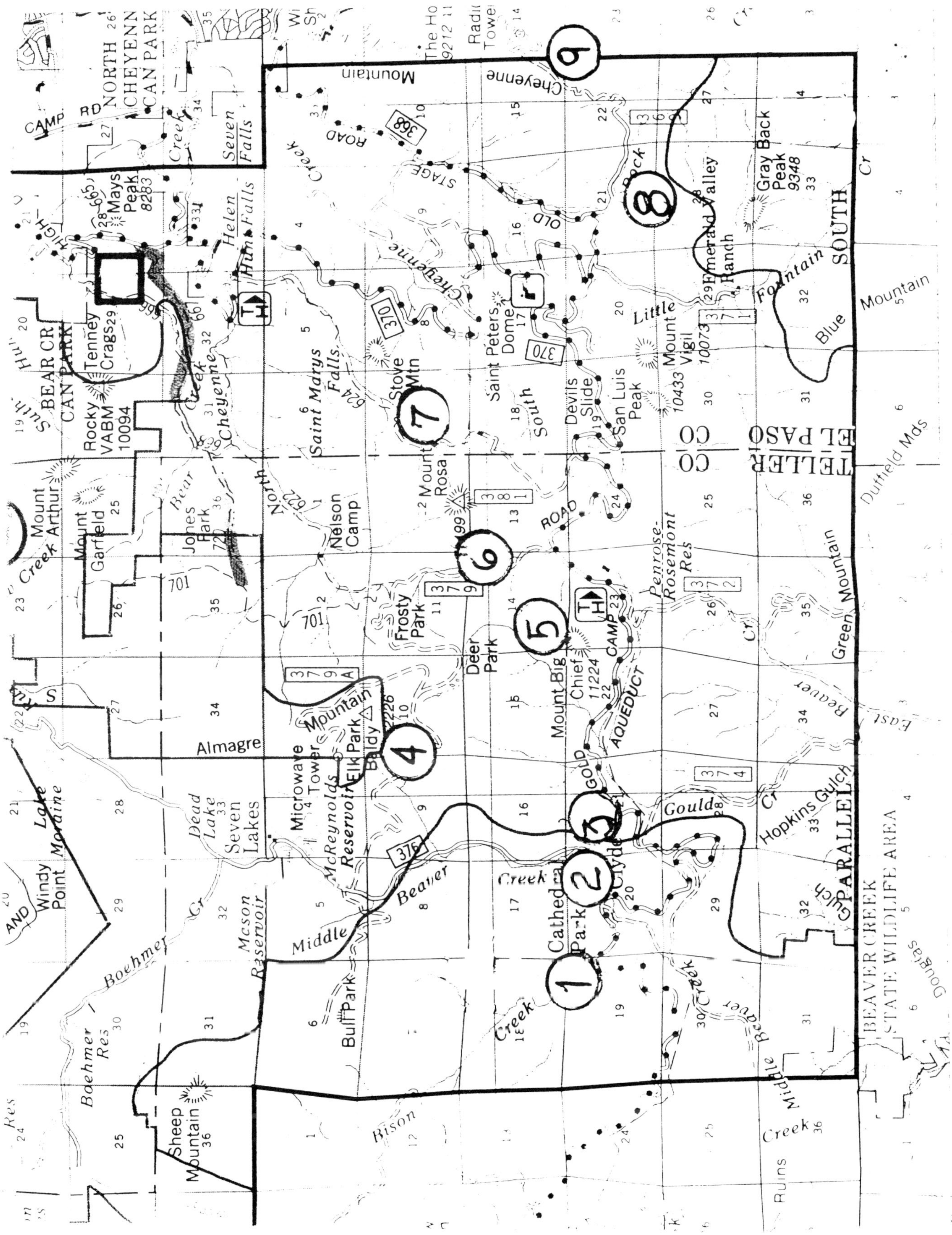

GOLD CAMP ROAD 3-D MAP

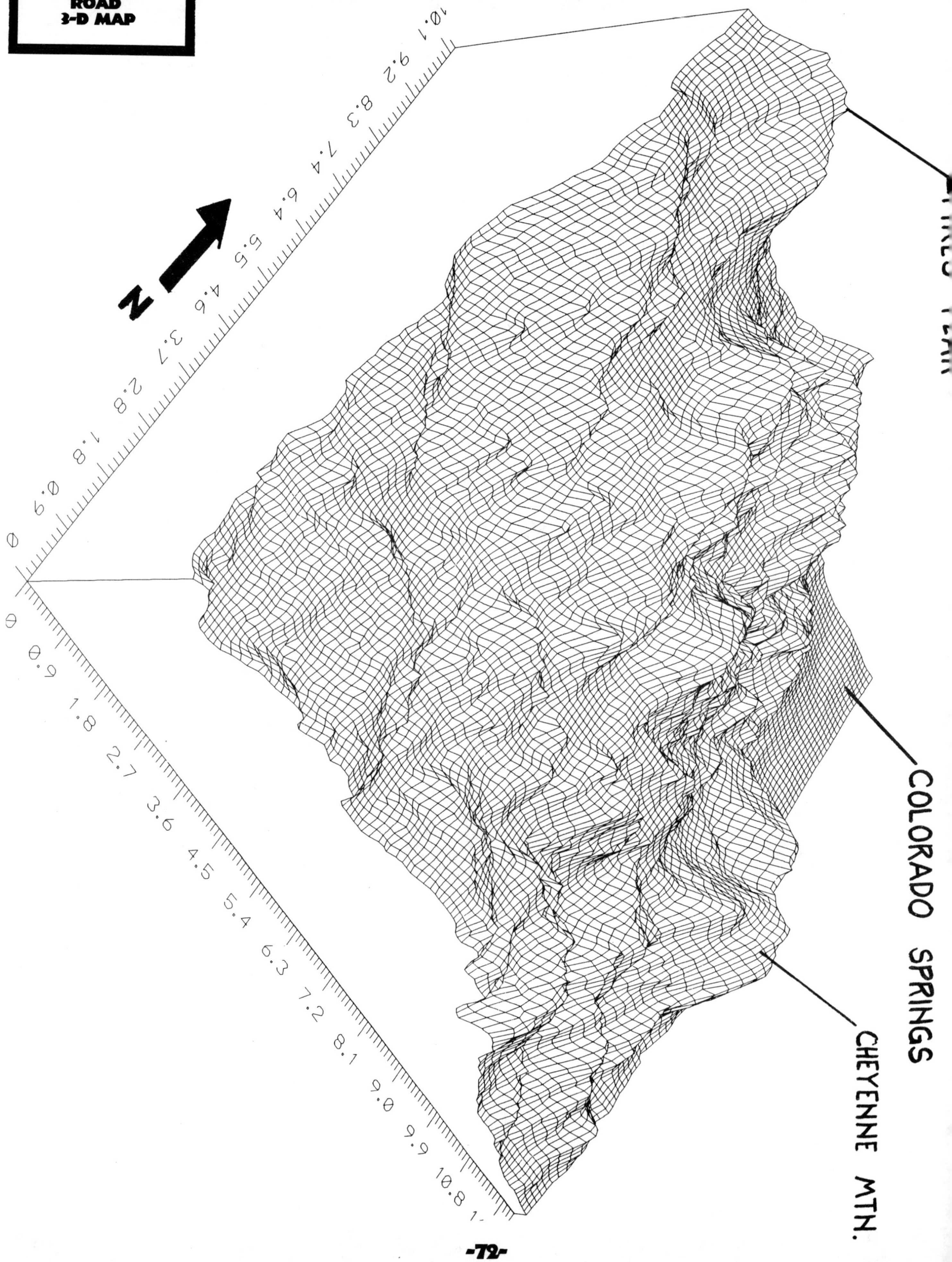

Gore Pass/Lynx Pass

Big Game Hunting Unit(s): 15

How To Get There:

From Denver take I-70 west to Highway 40, then take 40 north to Kremmling. Approximately seven miles north of Kremling, turn left on Highway 34. Go up over Gore Pass, drive 8 miles to Road 270 then head north. Some of the spots are up on Lynx pass, while the others are above Tepee Creek (take Road 263 from just below the pass to where it ends).

How To Hunt This Area:

The way to hunt this area is going to vary depending on which particular spot you are hunting and in which season you are hunting. When you are up on top you'll find there are a lot of open meadows. If you are rifle hunting the obvious way to hunt would be to sit on the edges of the meadows in the mornings and evenings as the elk come out to graze. The deer will also be among the elk as they too have similar feeding patterns.

The large meadows are located on top of the mountain while the sides of the mountains are steep and heavily timbered. There are some old logging areas on the sides that attract game and also make excellent spots to ambush the animals. There are a lot of old logging roads that have been blocked off to motorized vehicles but remain accessible to foot travel. This makes for very easy walking and consequently, you can penetrate deep into the backcountry quickly and quietly.

Should you decide to walk across the open meadows you will find them to be very marshy. So make sure to have waterproof boots. The water is the result of seepage from on top of the peaks up by the end of the forest road.

There are downed timber areas on some of the hillsides that are difficult to travel through. You can do it provided the weather has been dry. If there's snow on the logs, it will be much too slick to walk on top of them and the area will become impenetrable. The result is that the elk will go into the downed timber during the second and third rifle seasons and effectively evade hunters.

Spence:

> Because we now only archery hunt, we haven't run into this problem in a long time. But if I were to hunt a downed timber area in the snow again, I would get some type of spiked boots that let me walk on slick logs. That way I could get into heavy concentrations of elk and deer where other hunters couldn't go.

Spot 01: **High Rock Creek**. Once you get to Lynx Pass take Forest Road 263 until you come to the fork. From there continue on Road 263 until it dead ends at the top of the mountain. You'll be in a spot that's fairly flat and sparsely timbered. To the northeast is a huge meadow where the deer and elk come out to feed. You'll see a lot of them if there hasn't been much hunting pressure. It's a good place to hit on opening morning.

Guy:

> I once saw 40 to 50 elk out in that meadow on opening morning. But once the other hunters got in there they moved up toward the side of the mountain where it's hard to walk.

Spot 02: **West Rock Creek**. This spot is located opposite of Spot 01, on the west side of the road. The mountain slopes away to the south and west. On that slope, the timber is thicker and less penetrable by humans. After opening morning you'll find the elk and deer there as they flee hunters.

Guy:

> Last year toward the end of the archery season my friend Mike Neelis and I hunted up there. While we didn't get any answers to our bugles from Spot 01, we got a lot of return bugles from Spot 02.

Spot 03. **Guy's Drainage**. This is Guy's favorite spot to hunt in the Lynx Pass area. As you are coming up Road 263 there are several alternative roads veering off to the left that are closed to vehicle travel. They are marked with signs that say "non-vehicle travel, foot travel only." Approximately 3/4 of a mile before you get to the top of the first road you will see a road forking off to the left. Park there and walk past the first couple of drainages. Hunt the third drainage.

The easiest way to hunt this spot would be to drop one person off along the road and let him cross over into the drainage while the other party takes Road 263 back to Lynx Pass. Next turn and go back north to the private property line that lies at the bottom of the drainage. Park the vehicle there and either hunt up the drainage or wait for the other hunter to push game down to you. You will be able to see this much more clearly when you look at the map.

Guy:

> Back in this spot is where I've seen the most elk in the entire area. Right in there I took a shot at a nice four point last year while bugling at a six point and his herd of cows. Unfortunately the harem bull was not willing to leave his cows. I happened to notice out of the corner of my eye that a satellite bull was sneaking around in response to my cow calls. I then became the silent cow as I could see him steadily coming toward me. Although I was quiet the bull kept coming which led him to my left, broadside and quartering away. A perfect text book shot. The only problem was that my equipment let me down. My bow sight had been knocked off by some branches while I was crawling up on the herd bull. As I released the arrow it took a nose dive and passed completely through the lower rear left flank. I sat in disbelief. I looked for the bull for eight hours to no avail. My hunting season was over. I'm sure he recovered and never came in to a bugle or cow call again.

He'll probably live to become the biggest bull on the mountain.

Spot 04: **North Lynx Pass**. The drainages you cross in order to get to Spot 03 are also very good. They were full of sign last year. However, they are very steep and there is quite a bit of downed timber in there which makes for rough walking. The elk bed in the downed timber because they know it's hard for anybody to get close to them.

Guy:

Two years ago while hunting those drainages I bugled heavily and got several responses. There were three of us in the drainage and I thought it was my hunting buddy Greg Sheets doing the return bugles. I sat there and waited for him for a half an hour as I kept hearing bugles from the drainage below. A few minutes passed before Greg finally made his way to me. Then I realized he came from the side of the mountain opposite where I was hearing the elk bugling. I turned to Greg and said, "Have you been bugling to me for the last half hour?" He said, "Heck no. I just came from this side." I bugled again. There was an immediate response 150 yards away. We collected our gear and moved to intercept the bull. As we got closer I let Greg slip down toward the elk while I set up to do some more bugling. From my position I could see Greg fifty yards below me. He notified me by hand signals that he could see twelve animals including one with antlers (that was actually a spike). As Greg slipped to within 50 yards of him I remained up on the hill, and continued to bugle. I then picked up a large branch and began raking a tree simulating a big bull " showing his stuff." As I was doing this the spike frantically herded up the cows and moved them to the next county. The sounds of a big bull had frightened him off. This whole sequence had taken place in a timespan of about 2 minutes. Had I known all this was going on I would have stopped bugling and started cow calling. This might have brought the spike closer in for a look and Greg could have had a crack at him.

Spence:

Anymore, I take several calls with me, including spike diaphragm calls and medium bull calls. Too many times I've moved in on a bugling elk only to have him move off because he thought I was too big of a bull for him to handle in a fight. I learned this the hard way one morning in South Park when I spooked off 6 different lesser bulls in a 4 hour period.

Spot 05: **Aspen Ridge**. This spot is located directly southwest of Spot 03 on the south side of Morrison Creek right next to private property. There are a lot of beaver ponds down in that area where the elk go in the evenings to feed. As you look from the south side of the road up onto the north face of the mountain, you'll notice an area where the aspens and dark timber are thick. Up there is where we found sign for massive numbers of elk.

Spot 06: **French Creek**. This spot is located south of Black Tail Creek Campground in the southernmost portion of the Routt National Forest. Head four miles south of Highway 134 on Road 212. You'll be hunting next to private property bordering French Creek. The terrain changes from rolling hills to steep timbered mountains. Ranchers have cleared lanes through the forest to put up fences. Walking along those lanes allows you to cover a lot of ground with minimum exertion. Your general strategy should be to intercept elk that are moving from meadows and aspen back into dark timber in the late morning. You can spot their routes by looking for places where they've torn down the fences put up by the ranchers.

Spot 07: **Ammons Creek**. This spot is located at the base of Ammons Creek along Road 212. The vegetation consists of black timber with intermittent aspens. Park at the bottom and hike up the creek bed. Look for fresh tracks cutting across the creek and up the hillside. Also don't overlook Black Tail Creek which comes up through the same area. In addition there are also a lot of beaver ponds right off the side of the road where elk have been known to wallow.

Spence:

If you're going to work your way up a creek bed like this, I can't stress enough the need to be extremely cautious when you come to an open meadow. Just like deer, elk sit back and watch meadows. You have to treat every meadow as if it is being watched, and then figure out where to walk so you are not seen, but you can see the game.

Last year I carelessly stumbled into a meadow that was full of elk tracks. I was tired and didn't bother to work it properly. On a small hillside to my right I heard a noise and immediately knew I'd been spotted. I went up and investigated. I found the beds of several cow elk and one big bull elk that had recently rubbed a good sized tree. They had bedded down in a spot where they had a perfect view of the meadow and me.

Spot 08: **East Fork Creek**. This spot is located at the headwaters of East Fork Creek. You can't walk the creek bed up from the road to get there because you would have to cross private property. The private property restricts access and causes the spot to get overlooked by most hunters. However you can park on the west side and hike one mile to the east and be there within 40 minutes. In this spot you'll find the animals in among the aspens and black timber.

Spot 09: **Blacktail Creek**. Continue on Road 212 out of the National Forest and onto the surrounding BLM and State land. You will notice a sign saying " Leaving National Forest." Past that you will see a hairpin turn which is where you want to park. You'll hunt the lower drainage of Blacktail Creek. Most people don't hunt this spot. They stay up in the National Forest. You'll see a lot of big deer down in that drainage, as well as elk in the late season, provided there has been enough snow to push them down.

Gore Pass - Lynx Pass Area

(Reprinted from Routt National Forest map)

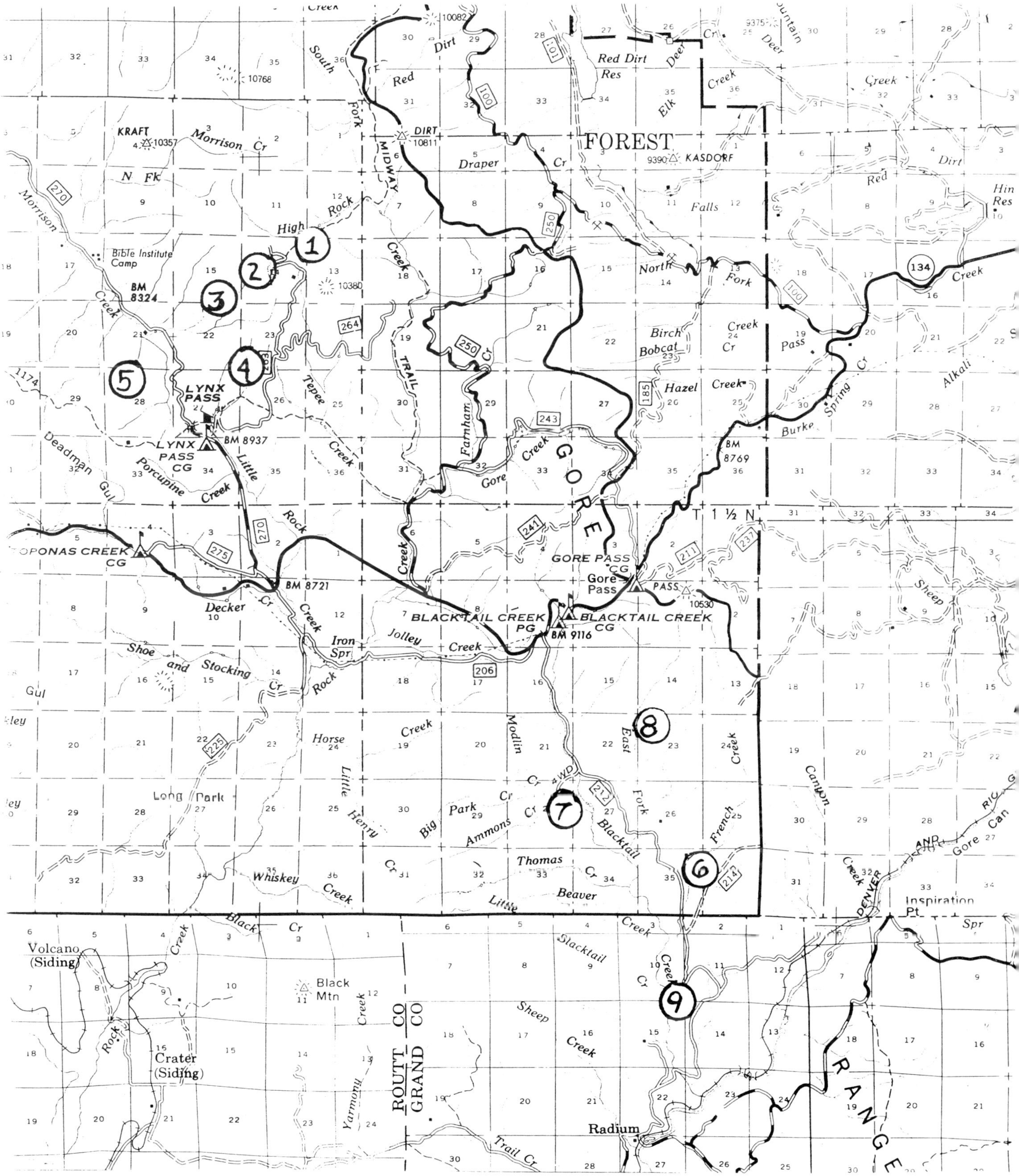

**GORE PASS/
LYNX PASS
3-D MAP**

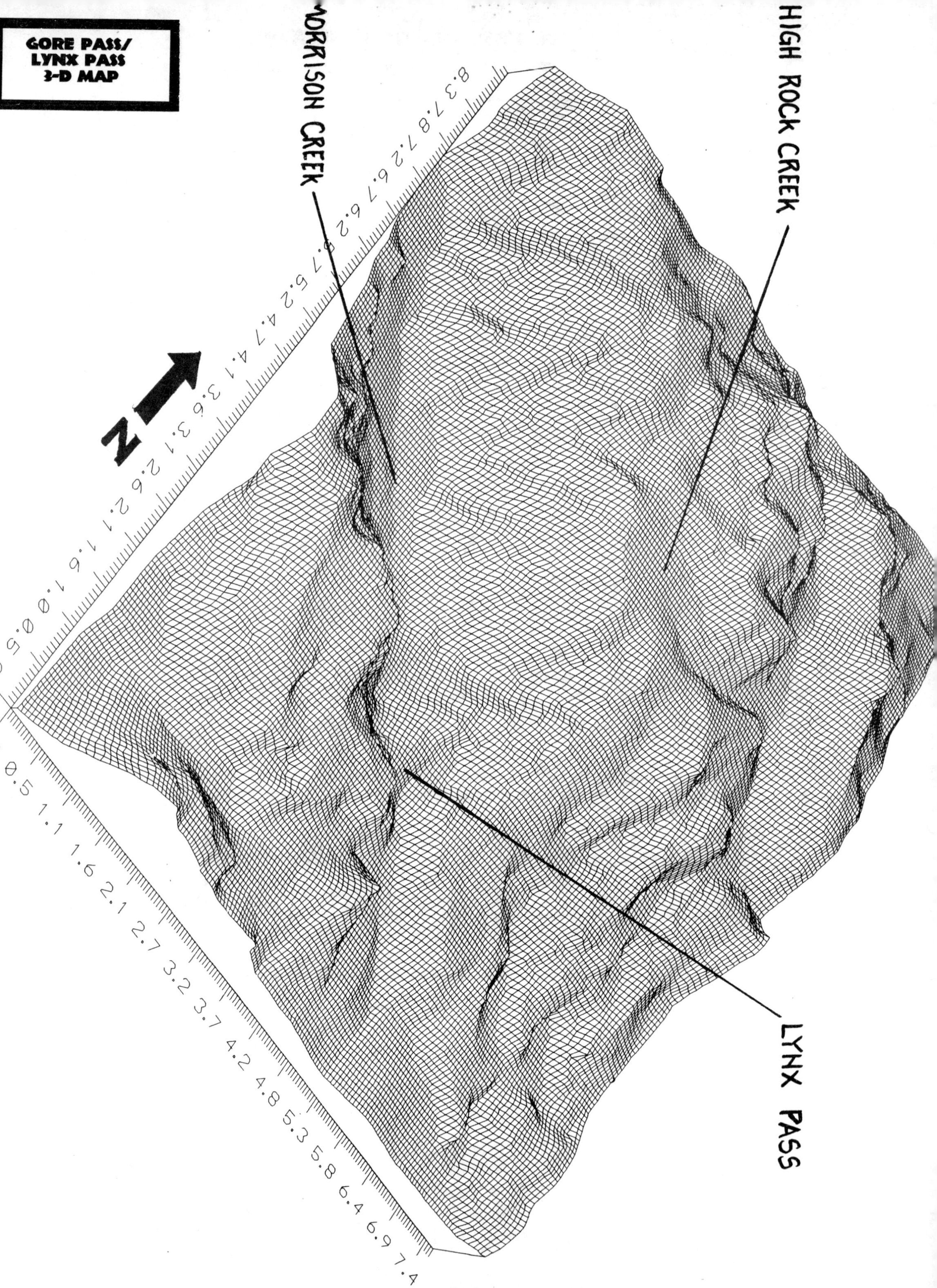

GORE PASS/ LYNX PASS 3-D MAP

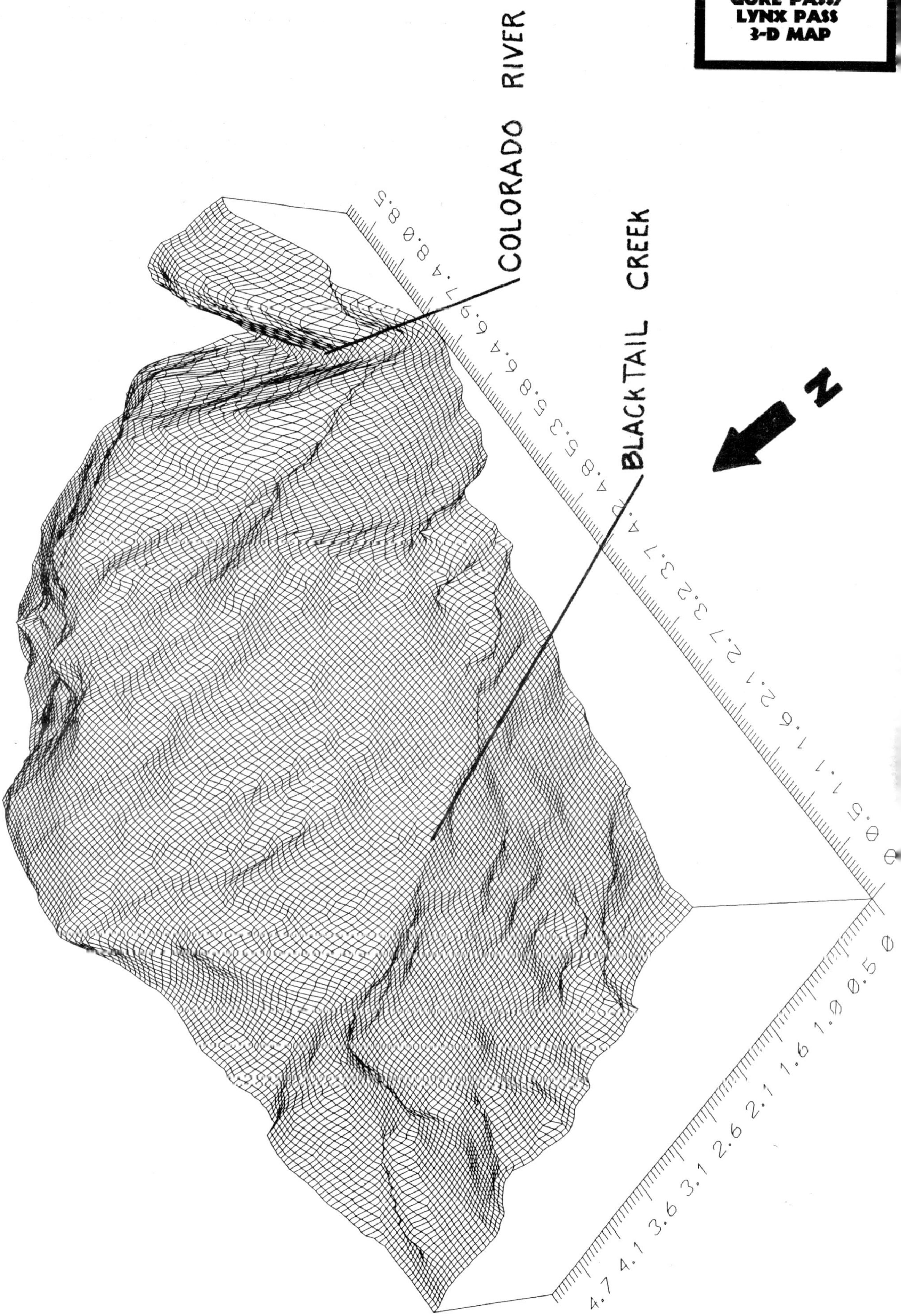

Grizzly Creek Area

Big Game Hunting Unit(s): 16

How To Get There:
This area is located to the south of the Zirkel Wilderness. To get there take I-70 west out of Denver to Highway 40. Go north through Granby to Kremmling. From Kremmling continue on Highway 40 to Highway 14 at Muddy Pass. Head north on Highway 14 toward Walden. As soon as you cross a set of railroad tracks turn left and follow the signs to Grizzly Creek. Once you get inside the National Forest boundary you'll come to Grizzly Lake where there is a public campground. From there you can drive about three miles farther in right up to the wilderness boundary.

Spot 01: **Grizzly Creek.**

Guy:

During the first two hours of opening morning, my uncle shot a nice five point bull just north of Road 626. He didn't find it until three days later because it was snowing very heavily the day he shot it. Fortunately, the snow preserved the meat. Anywhere you hunt in this area will produce trophy size animals. But we could only point out one spot because my uncle lucked out and got one at the first place he hunted.

Remote Zirkel Wilderness Area lakes like this one and their surrounding meadows attract multitudes of elk.

Grizzley Creek Area

(Reprinted from Routt National Forest map)

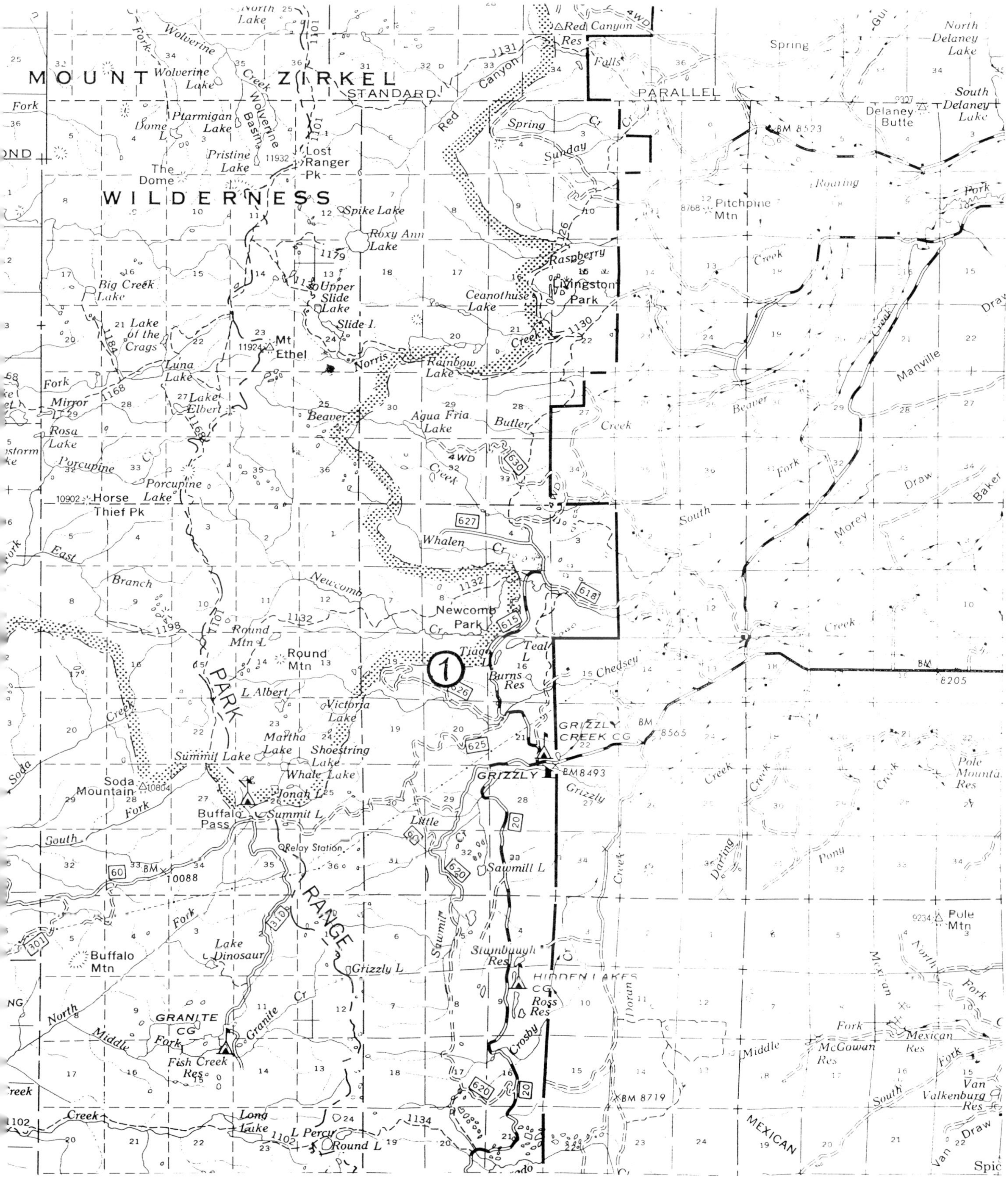

GRIZZLY CREEK 3-D MAP

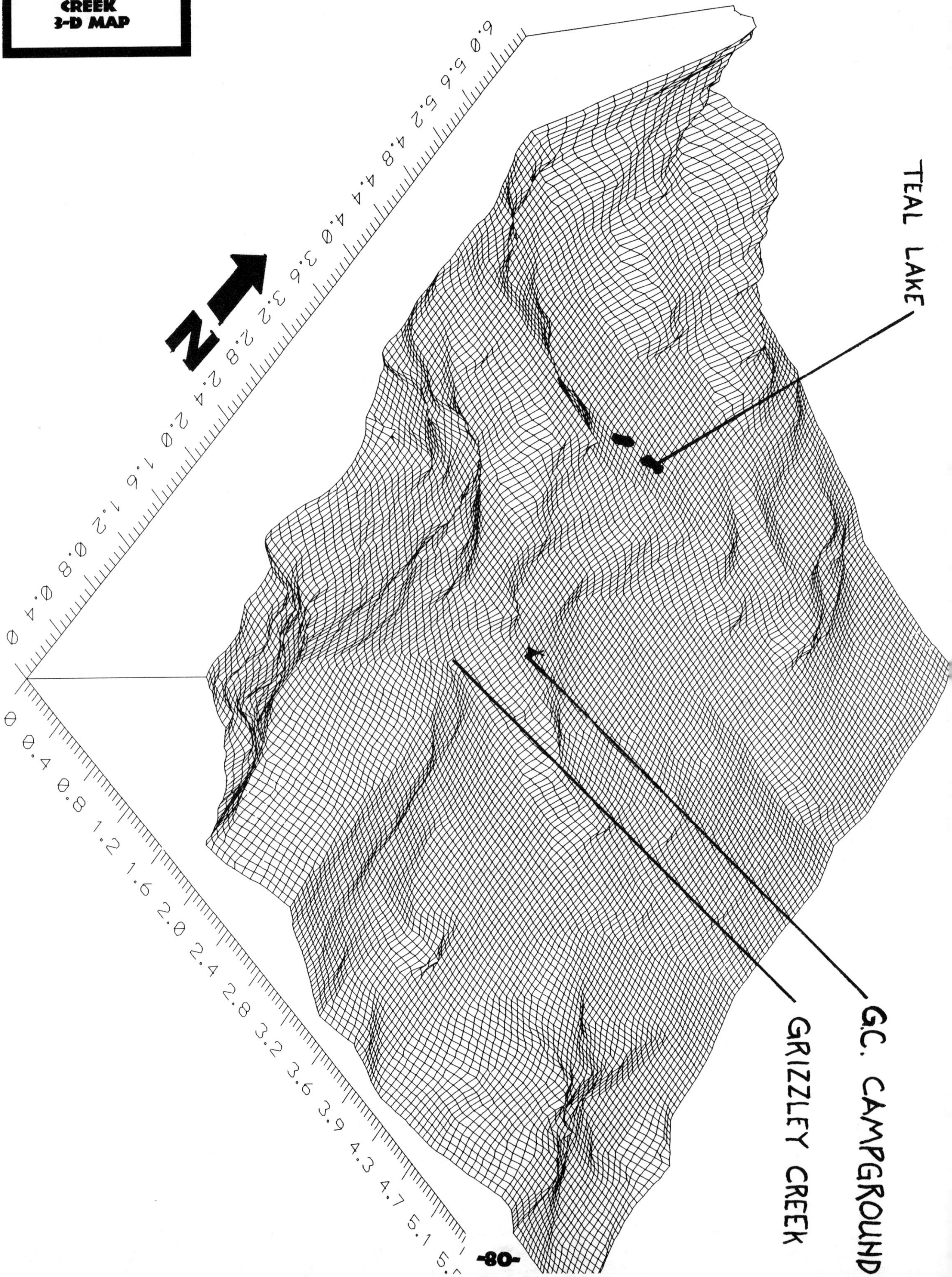

Hahns Peak

Big Game Hunting Unit(s): 14

How To Get There:

Take Road 129 north out of Steamboat Springs to Steamboat Lake. About three miles past the lake, around the town of Columbine, take the Forest Service road east toward Hahns Peak.

How to Hunt This Area:

The vegetation in this area is primarily dark pines and aspens on the hillsides, with open grassy areas in the valley bottoms and above timberline. Occasionally you'll find deep gullies that are bare on one side and timbered on the facing slope. You can walk the ridges between those gullies and find trails crossing from one side to the other. Many times, the trails will take you from an aspen stand, to a waterhole and then move into dark timber a few gullies over where the game has bedded down. Bachelor bulls stay higher up in the timber and traverse the mountain sides. They stay close to rockslides where it is hard for hunters to walk.

You are probably not going to be able to spot from your vehicle. The game there gets enough hunting pressure to know to run at the sound of cars. The bulls are also a little bit call shy. We saw them during the archery season, but rarely got them to answer a bugle.

Spot 01. **East Hahns Peak.** There's a road that goes up by the top of Hahns Peak. The road flattens out before it makes its final steep ascent of the peak. Right where it flattens out, another road comes in from the north. Don't take either road. Instead, keep going straight down the steep hillside to the east. 300 yards down the hill, we found heavily used elk trails traversing the hillside staying just below and between both roads.

Spot 02. **East Hahns Peak Springs.** As you head down the east side of Hahns Peak, farther down from the previous spot, you will find springs just below a big rockslide area. You'll know you're close because the grass gets much thicker and greener. If it's been very dry, there may not be any water, but it will still be much greener than surrounding vegetation. All the game trails in the area lead to that little spring. We only found one spring. But on the map, it appears there are more. The others should be at about the same level. Once you find one, walk (staying level) around the mountainside looking for more. More than likely, the game trails will lead you to the next one anyway.

Spence:

> They are not springs as you might know them back east. They're better termed "seeps." A small amount of water flows from them at certain times of the year. They attract a lot of game because they are usually in remote areas. The animals can avoid man but still get the water they need. Because those areas concentrate game, and the ground is muddy, you'll see more tracks here than anywhere else.

Spot 03. **Follow The Seep.** From the seep or spring mentioned in the previous spot, follow the narrow gully down to where it flattens out heading southeast before joining with Beaver Creek. The trees on the hillside to the west are big and mature. You can see 150 yds to 200 yds through them. Numerous elk trails run through those trees paralleling the meadow in the flat bottom. They watch the meadow using the big woods as cover. We got one elk to bugle to us from one of the trails when we stood at the seep above, but he was only passing through and had moved off by the time we got down there.

Spot 04. **Between The Seeps.** The previous spots we profiled dealt with the middle seep on the east side of Hahns Peak. Between that seep and the northernmost one, is a bench that on the lower portions is covered with aspen, then open grass as you move farther uphill to the northwest. All along the ridgetop we found elk tracks where they had moved from one gully to another. At dawn and dusk, a hunter could sit on that ridge and probably pick out an animal moving between gullies.

Spot 05. **The Forks.** Several jeep trails come together around this spot (1155 and 409 are the main ones). To the northeast are some open fields where we saw a number of large mule deer standing under lone pine trees.

Spot 06. **Lower Farwell/Beaver Creek Tributary.** A forked gully runs northeast on the west side of Farwell Mountain. It joins the lower part of Beaver Creek about a mile from Pearl Lake. You want to hunt the west side of that gully. Elk move between the gully and upper Beaver Creek.

Guy:

> I was walking in there when all of a sudden, a group of eleven elk stood up about 100 yards out. They were bedded down on the edge of a small field in some dark timber. At first they weren't sure what I was and just stood staring. Then the wind shifted blowing my scent to them and they ran. They were all cows. The bull must have been farther back in the timber.

Spot 07. **Lester Creek.** Just to the northeast of Pearl Lake is Lester Creek. A group of hunters from upstate New York told us that there had been a large herd of elk in the timber right where Lester creek flows into Pearl Lake. Those elk had mysteriously vanished on the first day of the muzzle loading season.

Spot 08. **Willow Creek.** Take Road 400 northeast out of Glen Eden toward Hinman Park. About a mile past Willow Creek you will be on Forest Service land. Walk northwest to the top of the hill. There's a small elk herd of about twenty animals that feeds in that area. Two years ago their early morning pattern was to head down the southeast side of the main gully feeding along Willow Creek which is about one mile southeast of the spot where Lester Creek leaves Pearl Lake. Then they would feed around the south side of the hill overlooking Elk Creek.

Spot 09. **Upper Lester & Coulton Creeks.** Take Road 409 around to the east side of Farwell Mountain. Walk southeast to Farwell Lake, then farther down to upper Lester & Coulton Creeks. This will be the hardest part of the walk. It's very steep. Where the terrain first starts to flatten out, the creeks run parallel and very close together. Elk move between the two creeks. You'll be hunting in a large 25 square mile roadless area. If you have two vehicles in your group, park one along Elk Creek and walk the 5 miles south to it.

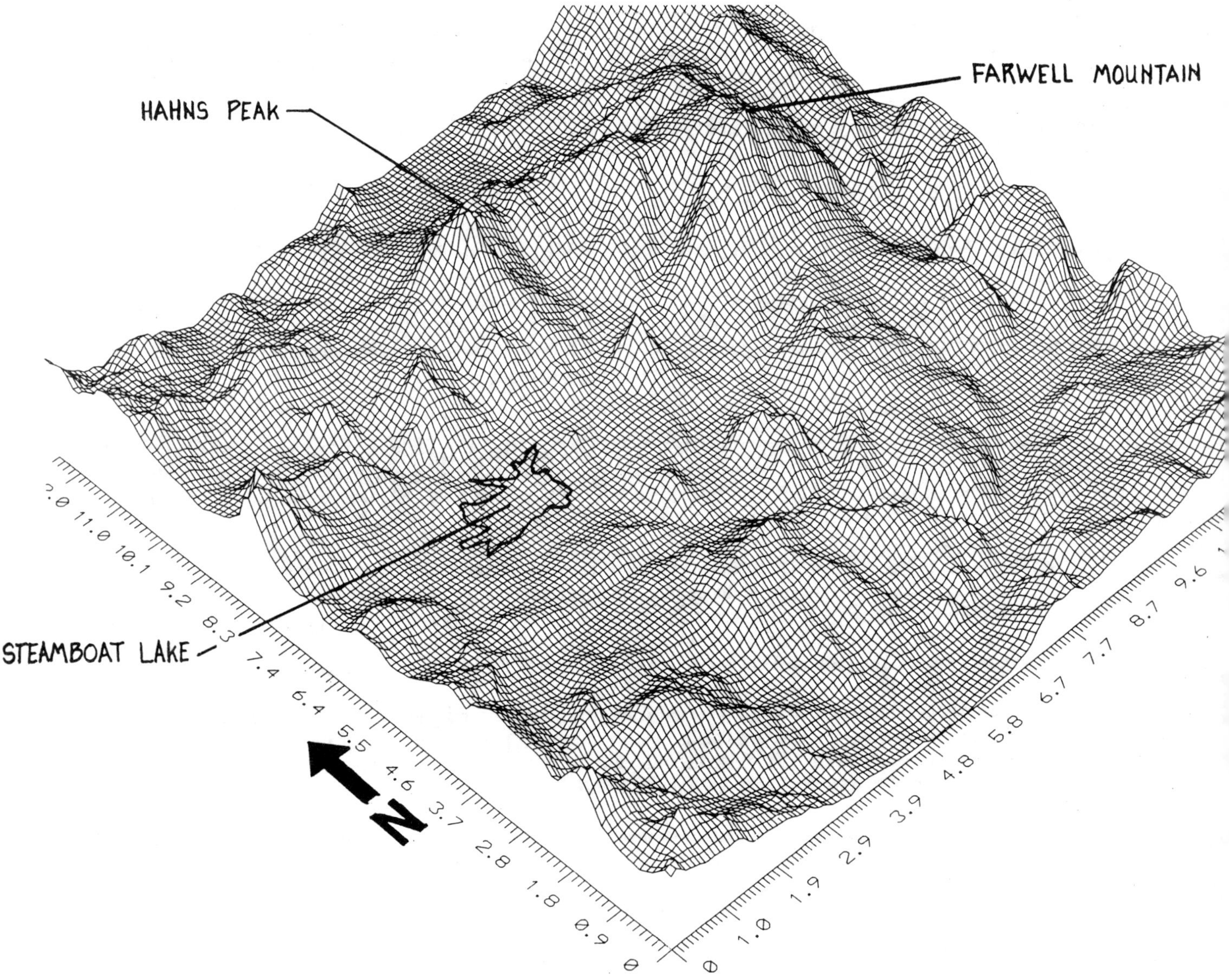

HAHNS PEAK 3-D MAP

Hahns Peak

(Reprinted from Routt National Forest map)

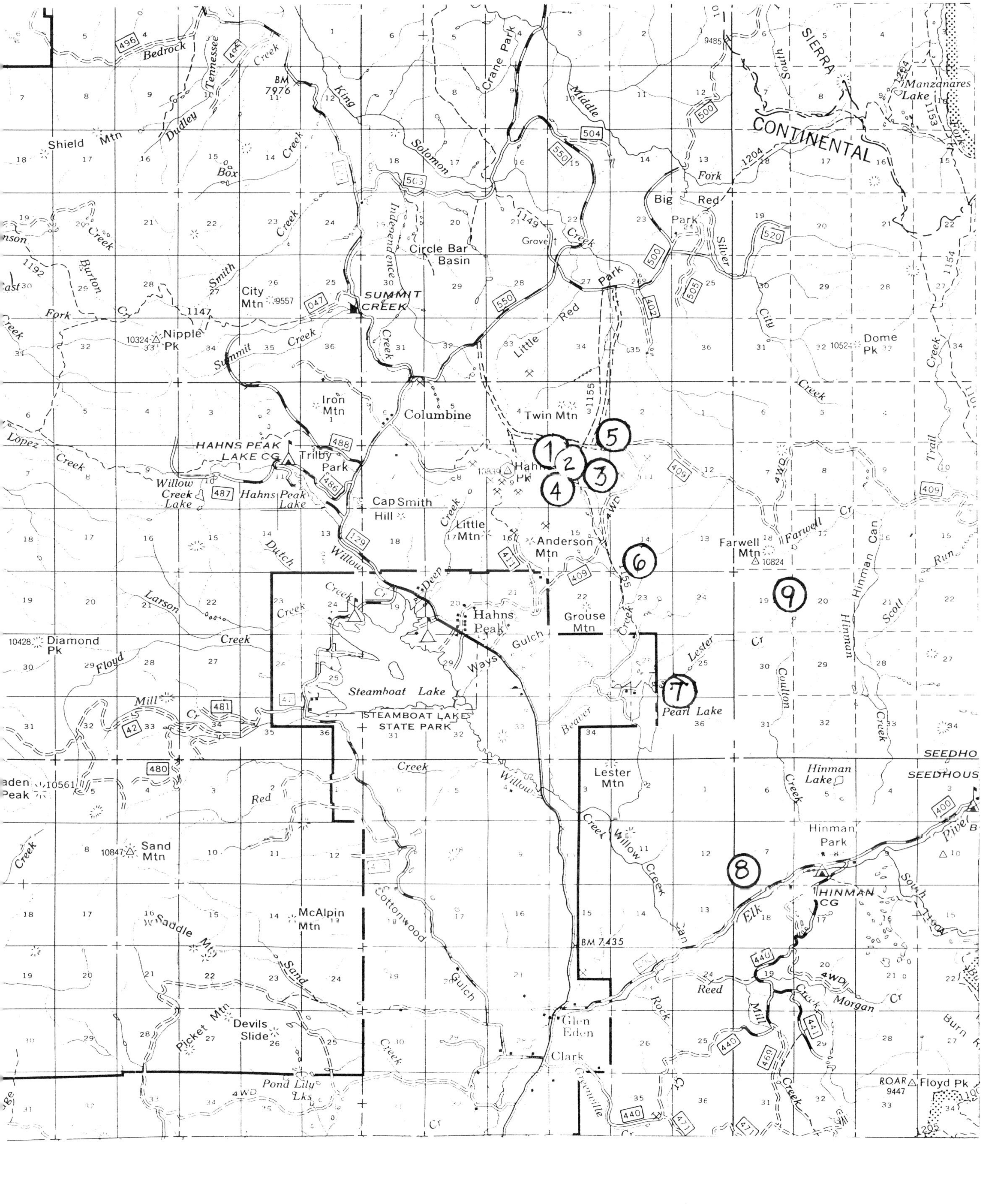

Independence Mountain, North Park and Walden Area

Big Game Hunting Unit(s): 161

How To Get There:

There are several ways to get to this area. We'll start first with Independence Mountain itself. From Denver drive west on I-70 to Highway 40. Take Highway 40 north over Berthoud pass through the towns of Winter Park and Granby. After you've gone through the town of Granby there will be a Highway 125 turnoff to the north which will take you over Willow Creek Pass. Remain on that highway through the towns of Walden and Cowdry. Independence Mountain is located approximately ten miles west of Cowdry on Jackson County Road 6 just to the north of the road. There is a great deal of access to the mountain. You will be able to get your four wheel drive virtually anywhere in there. There is a circular drive that goes all the way around, as well as one that goes through the middle.

How To Hunt This Area:

The first access road off of JCR 6 heading north is Road 35. This will lead you up a fairly steep face but don't let its appearance fool you. You can make it in with a two wheel drive. Once you get up on top the access is virtually unlimited. The vegetation is mostly thick pines with groves of aspen and south facing slopes covered with sage. During the early morning hours the elk will come out into the sage. They like to graze on the grass that grows along the edges. The deer can be found anywhere on the mountain but there is a concentration of them along the access road as you drive in. The terrain there is very hilly with a lot of sage. The best strategy is to get on a hill that provides a good vantage point and use spot and stalk tactics.

Guy:

> Three years ago, while coming back from Steamboat Springs where I had been skiing, I decided to stop in there and take a look around (March 20th or so). I was driving up the access road and lo and behold there was a herd of probably 75 elk which seemed to be following my truck. No matter which way I went they came toward my vehicle. I imagine somebody had been in there feeding them. Because it was mid-March there were no racks on the animals. Nevertheless there were a number of bulls that had impressive mass.

If you are going to be hunting in there during the archery or muzzle loading seasons, the best way to locate big bull elk is by bugling and then listening. You are not necessarily trying to get them to come to you. Instead, just by getting them to bugle back you can locate them, move into position, and then use cow calls to lure them closer.

During the rifle seasons the best way to hunt this area is to get on a good vantage point or in a saddle where you have an expansive view of the surrounding terrain. Get there before first light and scan with your binoculars. Don't expect to see them come in. It's more like they just appear out of nowhere.

Spence:

Many good hunters who learned to hunt back east fail to effectively use binocular spotting tactics when they hunt out west. They expect to get a lot of clues before the animal appears, especially if they've hunted white tails. Back there, you often hear the pad of feet or rustling in the brush before you see the animal. In Colorado, you always see the animal way before you hear him. Also, I've seen guys from back east scan and pass on terrain that actually had a lot of animals in it. To them it looked barren and they figured there was no way they wouldn't see an animal if it were out there. The great distances and lack of perspective fooled them into thinking the animals would be much larger in their binoculars, when actually, they were only tawny colored dots.

Lack of perspective when spotting game in the mountains can cause hunters to overlook animals. The white specks circled in this picture are really a herd of 100 elk.

Around Lake John you'll find big sage covered hills where trophy antelope (14 inches plus) live. Get up there the day before the season starts and try to locate a decent size herd. That time of year the bucks will be herding up the does. They will be in good numbers and easy to locate. They will be busy watching the does rather than hunters. Watch them until they bed down in the last hour of light. If you can do this your work is pretty much done. They do not often move around at night. When the sun comes up, your buck should be right where you saw him bed down the night before. Once the shooting starts in this area, it will become much harder to take a buck.

Hunting antelope around Lake John is not physically demanding. A lot of the time you can hunt very close to your vehicle. Jeep trails crisscross over the entire area. But a four wheel drive is not a necessity unless it has been raining and the trails become slick.

Spot 01: **Alkali Lake**. Directly east of Lake John across Road 7 there is a jeep trail that goes up toward Alkali Lake. There are a lot of antelope around the lake. If they are not visible when you get there, wait a couple of hours and you'll see some. We've seen as many as 120 around the lake at one time.

Spot 02: **Monahan Draw**. About five miles north of Alkali Lake there is another trail going off Road 7 to the east. It will take you to Monahan Draw. There is a small creek running through the draw and a small lake that in the summer dries out quite a bit, leaving a very small waterhole. The antelope do not have many of choices as to where to drink, so if there has not been any rain this is a great place to hunt from a pit blind.

Spot 03: **California Gulch**. This spot is located east of Road 7, south of 6 West Road, and two miles north of Spot 02. Heavily hunted antelope as well as large numbers of mule deer tend to hole up in there because of the coulee it lies within. It has a lot of deep ravines which provide excellent cover. If you walk the tops quietly you will see lots of mule deer down in there. You'll also find several roads crisscrossing California Gulch that are not labeled or named on the available maps.

Spot 04: **Mansfield Draw**. This spot is located north or JCR 6 West along Road 35 (the road that goes to Independence Mountain). In that one draw you can run across antelope, plus deer and elk that are working their way up to the top of Independence Mountain.

Guy:

In 1987 my buddy Fish and I hunted this particular area quite extensively. While driving on JCR 6 West we happened to notice some hunters down in a ravine. They were pushing a herd of five bucks they didn't even know existed. They couldn't see them from where they were. We then decided to take JCR 35 up to the top of the ravine and walk down to intercept the deer. As we looked down the gully I was amazed to see the deer were still coming. Looking through my scope to the spot where we were going to have the best shot, as well as surveying the size of their racks, I could see a nice buck approaching. At the exact moment I whispered to Fish, "It's a good buck" I heard his gun fire. Fish had dropped a nice 4 X 4 right in his tracks.

Spot 05: **Placer Creek**. If you follow Road 35 to the top you have a choice to either turn and go back to the east or go to the northwest. If you turn right to go back to the east, you'll come to the area where Guy saw the herd of elk while coming back from skiing (see "How To Hunt This Area" above). Nearby Fisher Draw also holds a lot of elk. This spot would probably be best for hunting during the late rifle season. The snows up high will push the elk down into those open valleys.

Spot 06: **Parson Draw**. If you continue on Road 35 from Placer Creek, the road branches off to the right and goes approximately five or six miles back to Parson Draw. In that area you'll find a lot of lower valleys that are covered with nothing but sage and grass, while the sides of the ridges have aspen and dark timber. This is an excellent spot to sit and ambush both elk and deer as they pass through the draw.

Guy:

While hunting there in 1987 we were slowly working through the draw when we heard several gunshots up above. We went up to investigate and ran into a guy who had a nice six point bull down in a grove of aspens. He said he had been sitting there on a rock for an hour and a half waiting for the elk to come out into the open. After it passed through some aspens he could finally get a clear shot, and dropped it.

Spot 07: **Three Mile Reservoir**. This spot is located four miles to the north of Parson Draw Creek. It's a separate valley that contains a little pond called Three Mile Reservoir. To the north is Spring Creek. This draw is exactly like Parson's Draw. It's very productive, and of course the farther you get away from the roads the better your success should be. If you're hunting this area in the archery and muzzle loading season there won't be any pressure whatsoever.

Spot 08: **North Wheeler Creek**. Road 35 completely circles Independence Mountain. Travel up around to the north by the Wyoming border and hunt the gulch along Wheeler Creek. This particular area is known for producing great sized bulls. There are even a couple of outfitters up in the Big Creek area who take people down onto Independence Mountain to cash in on the good hunting.

Guy:

In 1985, we camped in this spot. We were driving one morning to get to another area when we saw four big branched antler bulls completely in velvet trotting along the bottom of the creek. They bolted when they saw our truck. They were not fully developed yet, but I guarantee they became big trophy five and six pointers the next year.

Spot 09: **Republic Gulch**. Our buddy Craig Fishel ("Fish") hunted this spot a lot. It's located three miles north of Republic Creek and directly to the east of the South Fork of Big Creek. You'll be hunting along the border of BLM land and Routt National Forest.

Guy:

Fish, and another friend of ours, Gary Ives once hunted the west side of Road 35 where the timber opens up into an expanse of sagebrush. While walking up the road they came upon a giant mule deer buck with at least a thirty inch spread and a base of six to seven inches in circumference. They had elk tags only, no deer tags. Fish said one of the hardest things he has ever had to do was just watch that deer bound away. Needless to say, whenever Fish comes to town, this is where he always wants to hunt.

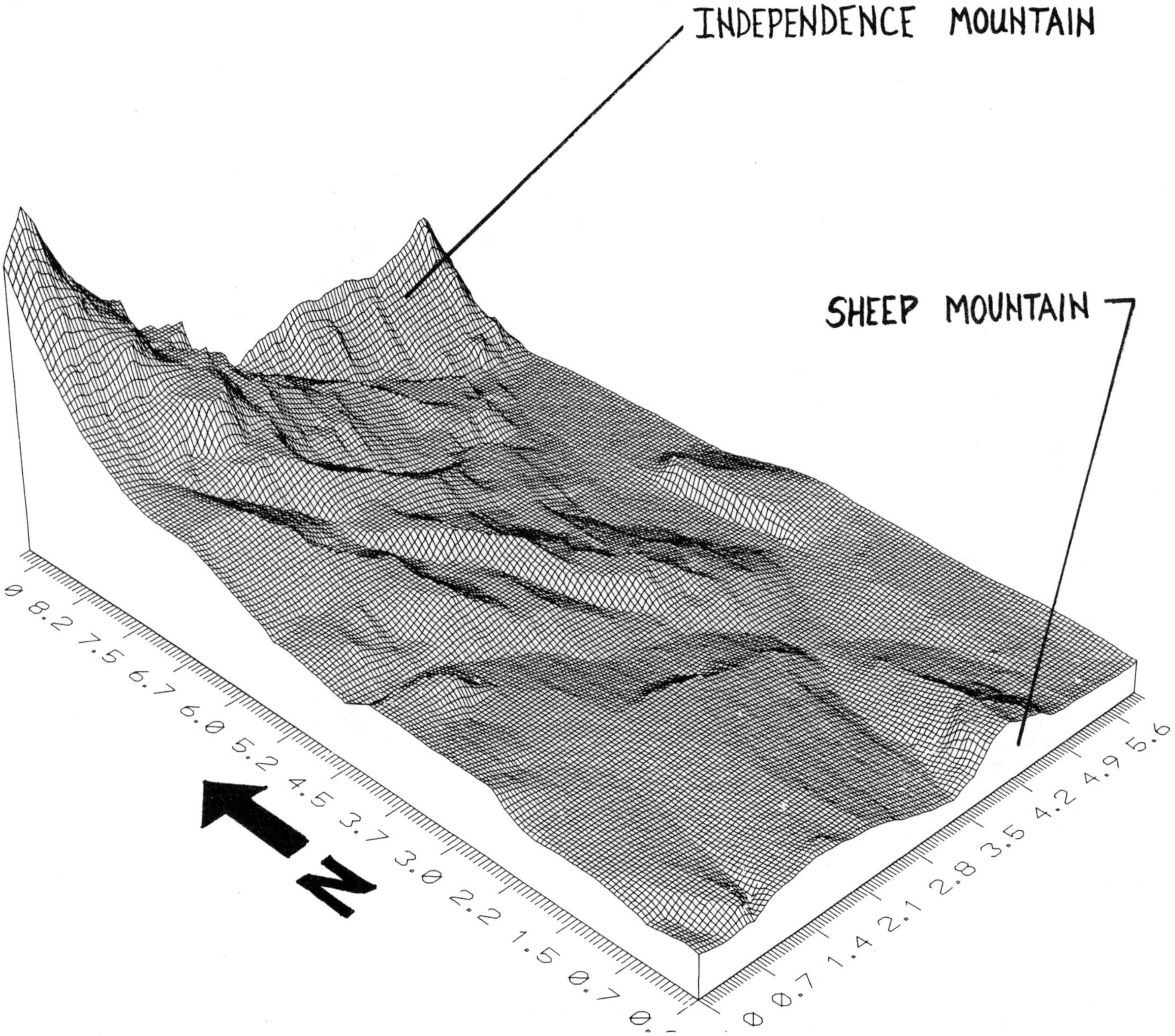

INDEPENDENCE MOUNTAIN, NORTH PARK... 3-D MAP

INDEPENDENCE MOUNTAIN, NORTH PARK... 3-D MAP

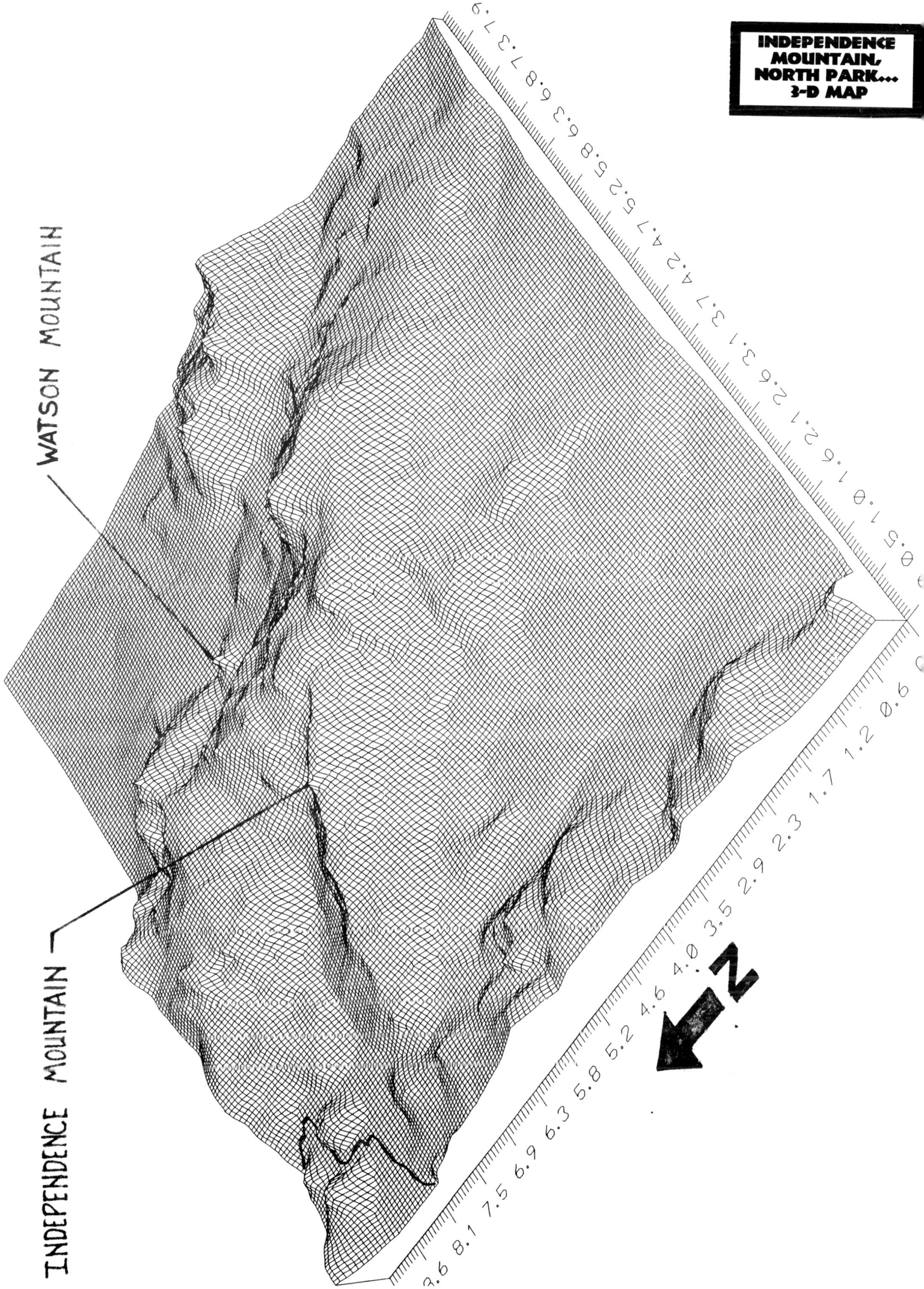

Independence Mountain, North Park and Walden Area

(Reprinted from Routt National Forest map)

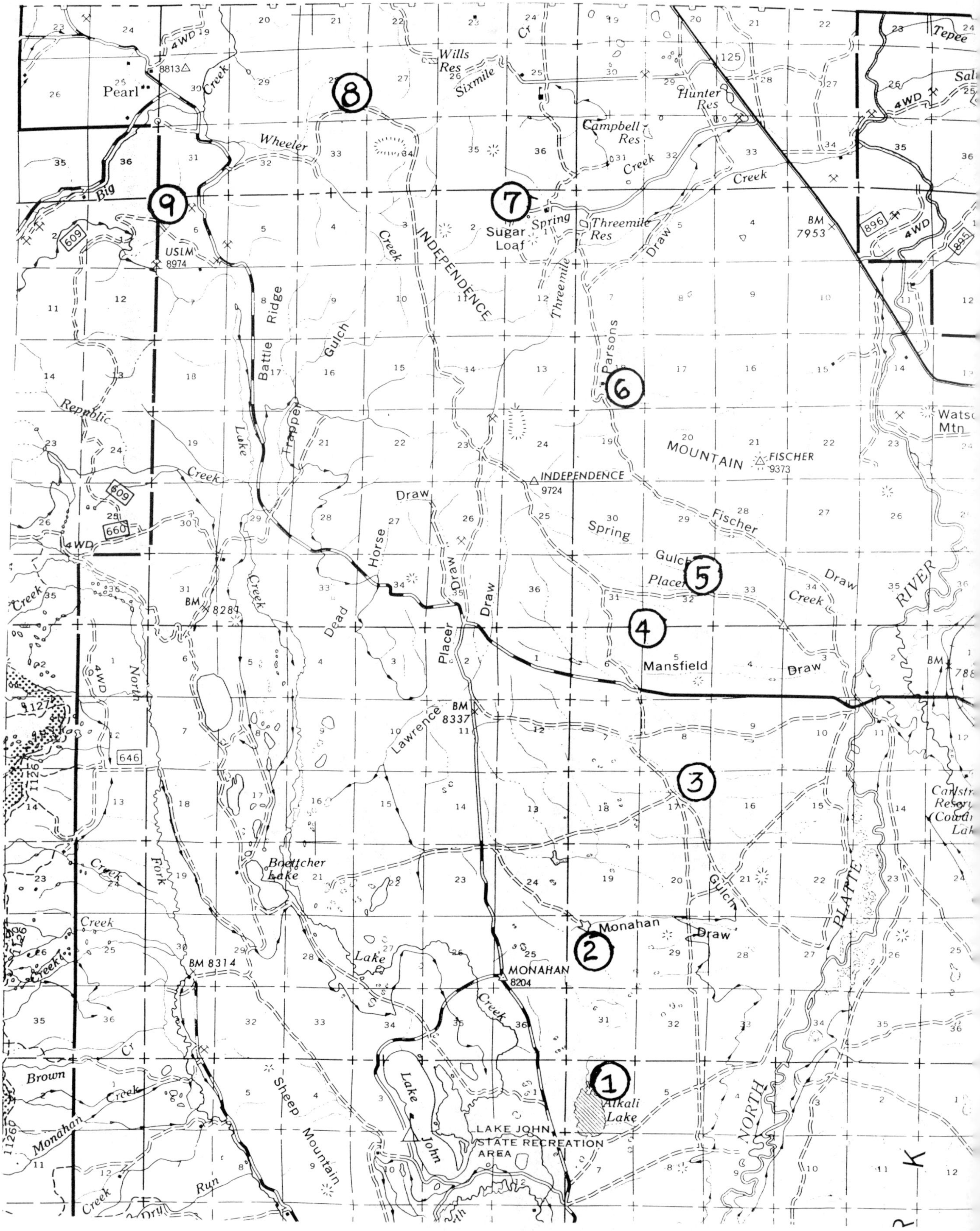

Monarch Lake Area

Big Game Hunting Unit(s): 18, 28

How To Get There:

To get to this area take Highway 40 north from I-70 past the town of Granby. There you will turn and go north on Highway 34 to Lake Granby. At the first possible place to turn go east to the head of the lake following the signs to Arapaho National Recreational Area.

How To Hunt This Area:

Monarch lake at dawn when the air is completely still.

The type of game found in this area is primarily mule deer, elk and some moose. The best time of year to hunt is during the archery and muzzle loading seasons, first rifle season and possibly the beginning of the second rifle season. This area sits in a very high valley. The elevation starts at 8,500 feet and the access road may close during the third rifle season. Access around the sides will be difficult if not impossible because the sides of the valleys are very steep and densely forested.

The most effective way to hunt this area is to slowly work through the timbered areas and small meadows that the deer and elk frequent. The heavy timber around waterholes and springs on the north facing slopes attract the most game. Look for tracks around the waterholes, and work your way up the small tributary waterways looking for elk crossings. Once you get up on top it flattens out which means easier walking for both you and the elk. You may see black bears in there as well. There are always a few sneaking around Monarch Lake which has both excellent fishing and campgrounds with trash cans.

Keep in mind that you can probably use the local horse rental company (located at Arapaho Bay on Lake Granby) for getting in and for packing your game out. It's worth looking into.

Spot 01: **The Roaring Fork Creek**. This spot is located just south of Rocky Mountain National Park. It holds an extremely large number of elk, but it's difficult to get to. To get there you can either walk around the edge of the campground all the way to where the creek comes down, or walk the bottom of the creek up. There are a lot of aspens on the south facing slopes that attract the elk from the park.

Spot 02: **Hells Canyon**. Hike around the north end of Monarch Lake and walk up Buchanan Creek until you get to Hells Canyon. The area around Long Lake is going to be good hunting during the archery and muzzle loading seasons as well as the first combined rifle season. It's a hell of a hike which is why it was probably named Hells Canyon. Once you get up around Long Lake it's all relatively flat. You'll see a lot of elk as well as very large timber bucks up there.

Guy:

> I've been up in that area fishing in the summer before the hunting season started and seen hundreds of elk. I've never gone up there actually hunting but I know that they are in there. I wasn't willing to make the hike up the canyon. But if you are looking for a trophy and have a lot a time, it can very well be taken right out of that spot.

Spot 03: **Buchanan Creek**. Continuing farther up Canyon Creek you will come to Trail 2 which will take you up toward Buchanan Pass. The terrain in this spot is similar to that in the previous one. You will see sign for elk, deer and bear plus bighorn sheep. You can't go wrong if you are willing to do a little work and pack back in.

Spot 04: **Strawberry Bench**. This spot is located south of Monarch Lake. There are several trails you can take up or you can hike due south of Monarch Lake up the hillside. It's quite a steep hike but once you get up on top you will be on a flat bench. The bench is kind of damp and there is a little creek that runs right through the middle of it. You will also notice a high mountain peak directly to the south of the bench. It's called Lonesome Peak. It's 10,580 feet elevation. Anywhere around that peak is all going to be very productive for elk hunters. Try to get midway up on the peak and traverse it at the same altitude all the way around. Walking that way will save you a lot of muscle aches that night.

This spot is also a calving area for the elk during the spring. You will see a lot of them in there starting in late May until the heavy snows hit.

Monarch lake at 9:00 AM. Notice the wind has picked up and distorted the reflections in the lake.

Guy:

I hunted this spot last year. I didn't shoot anything but I did see quite a few cows, calves and four points. It was quite early in the season and they were just starting to bugle. I was holding off for something much larger.

Spot 05: **Strawberry Lake**. This spot is located right below Strawberry Lake. You'll be hunting in a little gully where a stream runs all the way down into Lake Granby. Elk use that gully to travel from the high area down to the big lake and the grasses that grow along it. We worked that area quite a bit last year and saw elk sign everywhere we went. Also if you have a sling shot or are not afraid to waste a few arrows it's always a good place to take some blue grouse. We saw quite a few of them up there. They make great table fare in hunting camp.

Spot 06: **Arapaho National Recreation Area**. In this spot you'll be hunting the flat area between Monarch Lake and Lake Granby's Arapaho Bay.

Guy:

Last year, after hunting some of the upper spots, I drove down the road between the lakes and noticed some fresh elk tracks cutting across the road. I decided to park the truck, and follow them through the meadow. The ground was completely torn up by elk which wasn't surprising. I can't begin to tell you how many times during the summer I've been night fishing in the river between the lakes and heard elk just bugle all night long.

The area around Monarch Lake is a spring calving area for elk. This bull we found feeding among the cows already had a good sized rack growing. Notice the partially remaining winter coat on his hind quarters.

Guy (continued):

When we hunted that area last year, the same thing happened while we camped in the Arapaho Bay Campground. We must have heard 30 to 40 bugles that night. There were so many bugles that campers became annoyed and started yelling at the elk trying to get them to shut up. The next morning I made my best guess as to where the elk had gone which led me to Strawberry Lake.

Monarch Lake Area

(Reprinted from Arapahoe National Forest map)

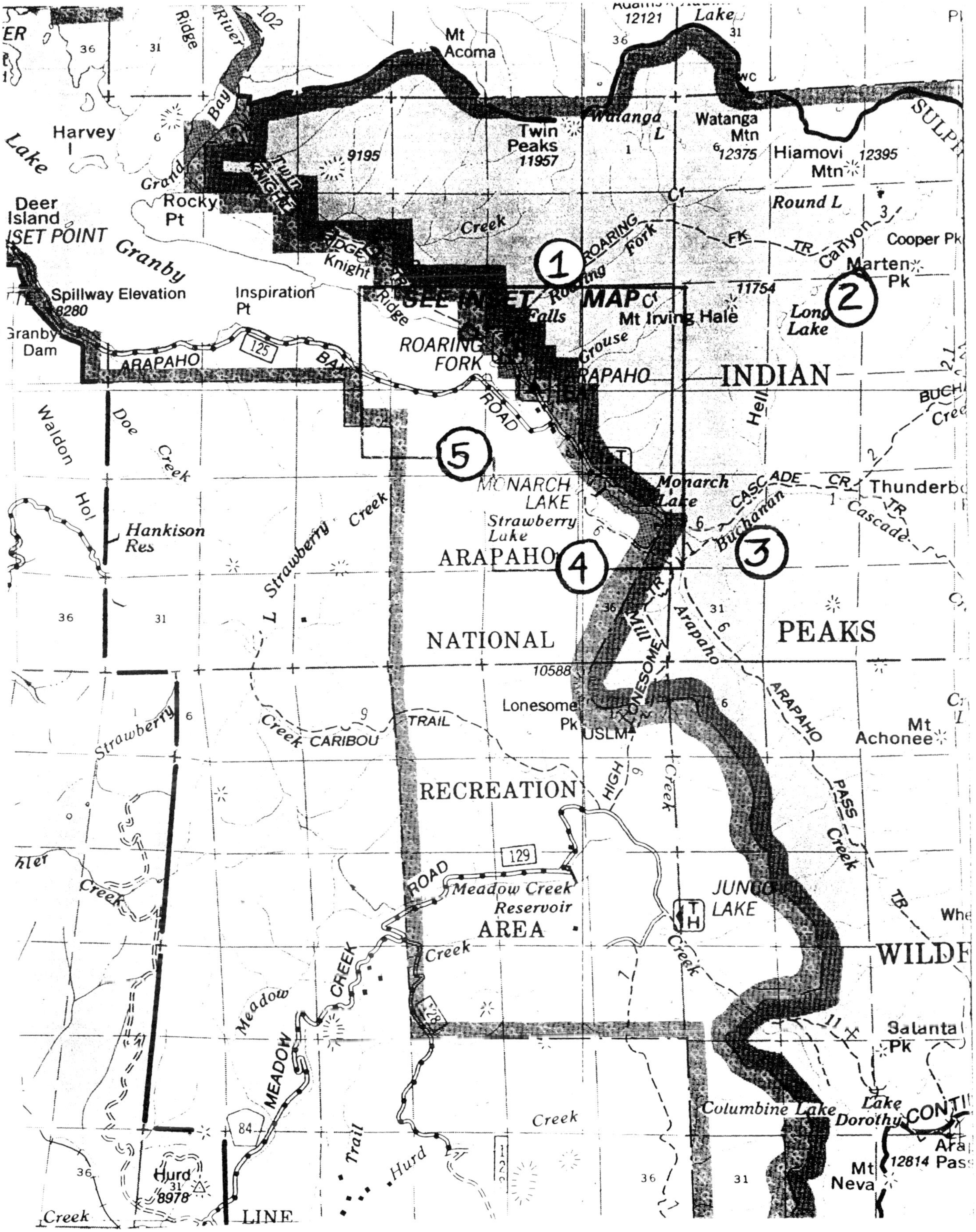

MONARCH LAKE 3-D MAP

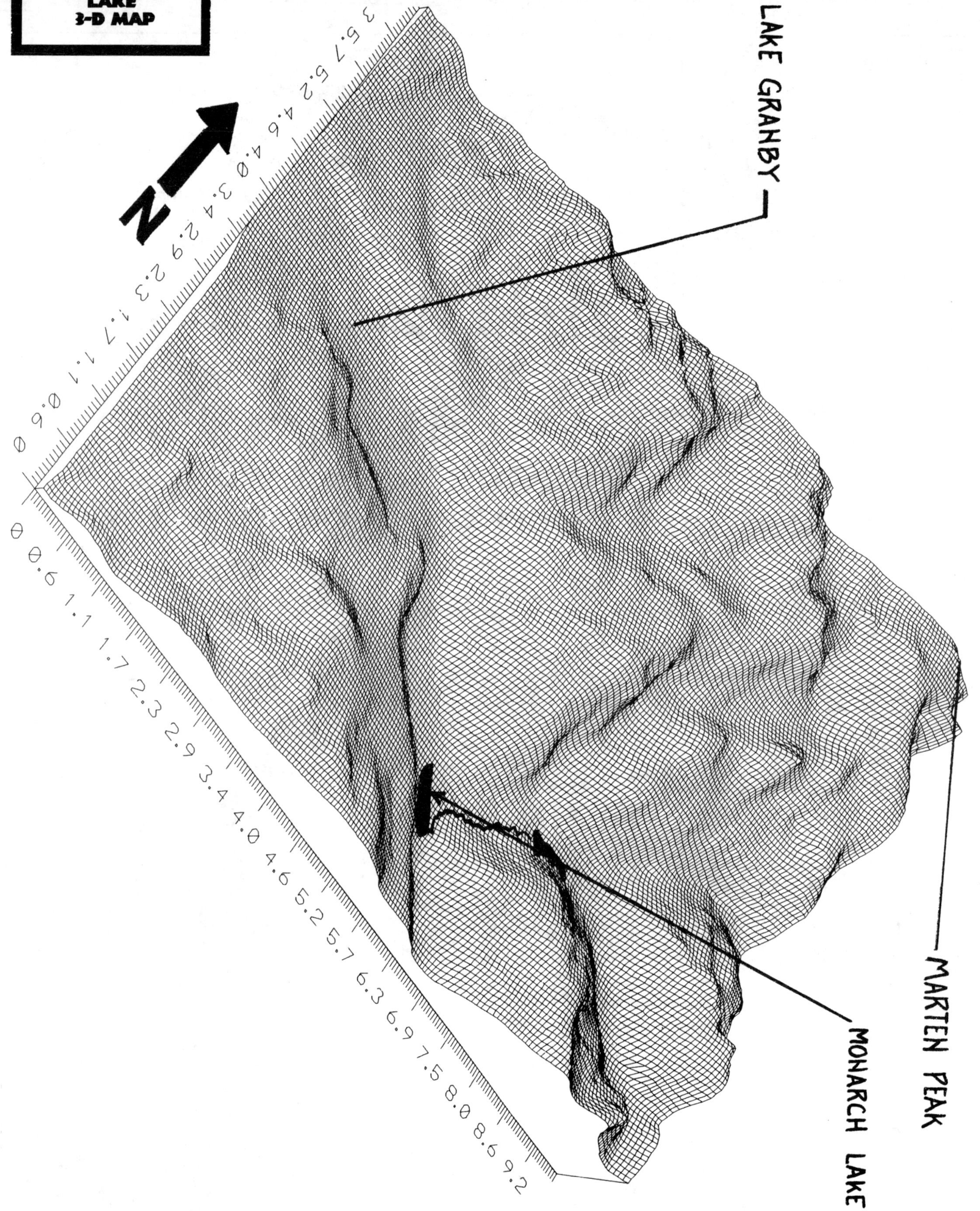

Mosquito Mountains

Big Game Hunting Unit(s): 500, 501

How To Get There:

Take Highway 285 out of Denver through Grant and over Kenosha Pass. Right before you get to Fairplay you will turn off on Road 412 heading north. There are also some other areas just off of Highway 285 on Kenosha Pass that are discussed below. This area is one of the most diverse in terms of game types. In addition to elk and mule deer there are big horn sheep, mountain goat, bear and mountain lion.

How To Hunt This Area:

How you hunt this area is going to vary greatly depending on which particular spot you are going to. Some of the spots are heavily timbered which means you will not be able to use spot and stalk methods. You're going to have to find a place the deer and elk have been using. Then you either set up a tree stand or move slowly through the woods one step at a time, scanning the area ahead of you intensely. Try to pick out silhouettes and shapes among the trees. If you are not sure what you're looking at, pull out your field glasses for a better look. You'll be amazed at how much game you'll see this way.

Guy Collier, Derek Doolittle and Phil Collier hunting the alpine tundra by Baldy Saddle.

On the other hand, if you go down in the Mosquito Mountains just north of Fairplay you are going be hunting a lot at timberline. There you'll be using spotting and stalking tactics. The elk in this area can be patterned. We have seen them come out at the same spot above timberline every day of the week at the exact same time. And that's not just one or two spots that we patterned. We were able to accurately predict elk movements in five different spots.

You will need four wheel drive to get back into some of the spots. The ridges are very steep and there is a lot of exposed rock where you'll need extra ground clearance. Put your front tires on those big rocks and just crawl up at a snail's pace. You can get back there, but it might take an hour or two. The good thing is that those rough roads keep most of the other hunters out. Once you get there, you'll be in a truly phenomenal hunting spot. We have glassed over 150 elk in one day in this area. The DOW has done a great job turning this into a true trophy area. Many of the spots are "draw only," so be sure to check with the most recent DOW publications for restrictions.

Spot 01: **Hall Creek valley.** Just a few miles west of Grant, take Road 120 west from Highway 285. Go up to Burning Bear Creek Trail. There is actually a road that goes back in and you can camp between the peaks. This is going to be a good area for archery, muzzle loading and any of the rifle seasons. There are a few water troughs set up to help out cattle during dry spells. Elk like them too so they're going to be your best places to set up.

Guy:

Years ago, I used to see bear tree stands up in this area. At the time it was legal to bait bears with cow carcasses, or anything else for that matter. Once I found several cow carcasses that had been worked on by bears. It's an intense experience to find fresh bear sign. At first I'm just surprised. I say to myself "What - here?" Then I'm awe struck by the sheer size of the tracks and the power those paws must have. Then I'm a little spooked, wondering if he's still around - maybe watching me from hiding.

Guy:

My very first experience with an elk was up in this area. My uncle Phil Collier told me to sit in a saddle and wait for something to come through. I was very inexperienced at the time, and was shocked to hear a snap behind me. I turned around and honestly, I was not more then 10 feet from a cow elk. She could not smell me and didn't know what I was. We sat there and looked eye to eye for what seemed like ten minutes, but was probably only about 15 or 20 seconds. Finally she bolted.

Spence:

We have a saying about "stare downs" - the first one who moves loses. If you get into this situation, don't even move a finger, and don't make eye contact. There's a big difference between remaining still and remaining motionless. You want to be completely motionless. If you wait long enough, and the wind doesn't blow your scent to them, lots of times they will look away long enough for you to draw, or at least begin your draw.

Spot 02: **Lininger Lake.** Turn north from Highway 285 at Hoosier Creek Road and then turn right on the four wheel drive trail that runs north of Lininger Lake. The hills are not steep so you can cover a lot of ground in a short period of time. There are going to be a few little open meadows to hunt. You might be able to catch deer and elk in them in the early morning. But generally speaking you are going to just have to move slowly, spotting and walking, spotting and walking. One of Phil Collier's buddies shot a nice five point bull in there a couple of years back.

Spot 03: **Before Kenosha Pass.** Right before the pass top, on the east side of Highway 285, there will be a little place you can pull off at and drive up. There are no signs marking it so you want to keep a sharp eye out. There's a gate you can open and drive through (be sure to close it so the cattle don't get out). This road circles the mountain next to Kenosha Pass campground. As you go up the road you will pass several meadows that support small herds of elk. Early in the morning you will find them feeding there. Before this became a restricted area it used to get a lot of hunting pressure. But that's not the case anymore. Hunting pressure has dropped off at least 75%. We've only seen one other hunter in there during the last couple of years. Although it's restricted for elk hunting, you can still hunt for deer without a special permit.

Spot 04: **Kenosha Campground.** Pull into the Kenosha Pass Campground off of Highway 285. Walk the trail that crosses the mountain to the south. There are several good aspen groves to hunt in the early morning and late evening. Once full daylight hits, the game moves out of this spot and into the dark timber. The vegetation opens up to the huge pastures of South Park. You will be able to see them from the south side of the hill. It may happen that you will be positioned between elk that have moved down into the big open pastures at night, and the dark timber they seek for day cover. Be prepared for a moving shot. In addition to being wintering ground for elk, South Park holds some sizeable antelope herds.

Spot 05: **Church Camp.** Turn off highway 285 and head north through Como. Then turn left on Road 838. You will drive through a private church camp to get to the Forest Service property. Once you get to the top of the road it will turn and go back down to the south. You can park anywhere in there. Take the Tin Pan Trail to the back side of Mt. Baldy. It's marked by little pie tins nailed to the trees. The trail is flat until you get to the base of the mountain. It's easy hunting along the base.

You can also hunt to the south of the trail which opens up into some big meadows. A few years back we had been sitting watching the first meadow to the south for about 20 minutes when all of a sudden deer just started popping up out of nowhere. Apparently they were bedded down and were waiting for us to move on. When we didn't, eventually one couldn't stand the suspense anymore and stood up. This set the others off like a chain reaction. The wind was blowing, so we couldn't hear any sound. Our only sensory input was the optical illusion of deer popping up out of the ground. Just when you thought you'd seen them all, another would pop up. We counted a total of 12 pop-up deer. Unfortunately, the largest was only a three point basket rack. After they ran, we paced the distance. They were only 27 yards away. Hopefully, by now there's some bigger ones in the bunch. It's at least worth checking out.

Guy:

One hard lesson we learned in this area is that elk often come in silently. So if you're calling, you need to keep an eye out even if they're not answering you.

We walked the tin pan trail the last day of the archery hunting season one year. We were bugling and expecting elk to answer us way up on Mt. Baldy. Suddenly, one went off not more than 50 yards away. We were hidden by some very thick brush so he didn't see us. We could only see his antlers whipping back and forth as he raked a small pine. That started a cat and mouse game that lasted an hour and a half. At first, he would not come in. Spence tried moving away and bugling while I stayed put. The bull followed him keeping the exact same distance which brought him to less than 30 yards from my position. There were just too many branches for a clean shot and eventually he moved off. We repositioned and using the same tactic, called him back to within 40 yards. But again, I could barely see him through the brush. He moved off down the hill this time and completely stopped answering Spence's calls. Twenty minutes later, Spence came back to my position and made one last frustrated bugle. We heard nothing and began talking about what we would do next. Suddenly we heard a big snort and the sound of bushes being uprooted as he tore a new trail through the brush. He had come in silently from another direction and watched us from a position exactly 22 yards off. If we had been set up, we could have easily taken him.

Spence:

You don't always think of these things until after you've made the mistake. But the correct tactic would have been to move back a little ways to a spot that provided a more open shot. When I figured out that the bull was distancing my calls, I should have known that he was a younger bull and probably without cows. It wasn't likely that he was going to move a harem off to keep it away from another bull. He was just not looking for a fight. I was using a trophy bull call and there was no way he was coming in to that. I should have switched to a young bull reed that was less intimidating to him. Although he came close to Guy, he never was close to coming in to my calls. He was always 100 yards away from me until the very last call.

The church camp people are very hospitable. Last we checked, they would let a hunter rent one of their cabins for $20 per night. They have hot and cold running showers and commodes. They showed us a rack of a bull that they had found dead on their property. Evidently a hunter had shot it but it ran and he did not find it. That rack is every bit a 375.

Spence:

I don't know the circumstances surrounding this bull that was shot and never found. But I've heard of hunters who shoot an animal, hardly even look for it, then go out and continue to hunt. As far as I'm concerned, if you shoot an animal and don't find it, your hunt is over. Your legal limit is out there somewhere slowly dying as a result of your poor shooting. In response to my opinions on this subject, someone once told me that animals are too dumb to feel pain because they don't really understand it. That is a the most bogus rationalization I've ever heard.

Spot 06: **Little Baldy Mountain.** If you follow the Tin Pan Trail all the way up you will come out right about timberline. Up in there we saw a three point buck. Now a three point does not impress a lot of people. However this buck had a spread that was the better part of 36 inches. It was huge. We were surprised that was all the points we could count. There were several other deer feeding a half mile away. We probably could have put a stalk on them but we were hot on some fresh elk sign and didn't want to fool with deer.

Spence:

Around 1984 we both came down with what we call "the elk fever." It has caused us to do things other hunters, especially those back east, would consider crazy. Every season we've passed up numerous easy shots at good sized deer just on the chance we might get close to an elk.

What really got us hooked on elk was the bugling. When they come in, it's just like a wild turkey coming in gobbling, only 10 times louder. Plus, they stomp, snort and rake the bushes with all the power of a full sized 1,200 pound horse that has also grown huge antlers. I've seen them completely uproot small scruboaks with their antlers. When they get really close, you smell the muskiest musk you can imagine. They're like a totally out of control animal with a year's worth of hormones pumping through their veins all at once. While your heart is pounding through your chest, and your hands are shaking with adrenaline, you always wonder if they're going to charge you. And in fact, we watched a hunting video where one did charge a camera man. But that's very rare, and it was more funny than it was dangerous.

Spot 07: **Mt. Silver Heels/Little Baldy.** To get to this spot you are going to have to go almost all the way to Fairplay. Turn off on Road 412 just past a small pond. Drive west to Road 194 through the gate and stay on the main road. You don't want to go up to Crooked Creek. You want to stay to the right and go up Road 194. It will parallel some private property. The road will make a 90° turn to the right, another one to the left, and then go up Little Trout Creek. You can take the road all the way up between Mount Silver Heels and Little Baldy Mountain.

We camped right where the Little Trout Creek originates. It comes out of a few springs right at timberline. From there we could see 30 to 40 elk come over the top of the mountain every night. Unfortunately we didn't have a spotting scope with us and couldn't count points. With our binoculars we could see one big bull among the cows as well as several satellite bulls off in the distance. If the satellite bulls got too close to the cows, the big bull would push them off. As long as they stayed on the herd's perimeter, the big bull didn't seem to be too bothered by this. If you can get up there late in the evening, and not be afraid to walk back in the dark, you will have a great set up.

Spot 08: **Silver Heels - Baldy Saddle.** Take the road all the way up to the saddle between Mt. Silver Heels and Little Baldy Mountain. There's an old burn up there that supports a lot of game. It's best to sit above the burn and scope the fields for elk.

Guy:

Late one evening, I set up a spotting scope on a hill overlooking the burned out area. I bugled a couple of times which seemed to cause some movement down in the valley. I zeroed in on the movement with the spotting scope and brought a 4 point bull into focus, with a 3 point bull standing just behind him. Our friend Derek Doolittle was with me and decided to stalk the larger bull. However, he had to make a big circle to stay downwind and he was quickly running out of light. I watched him move in while I kept the bull bugling. He got to within 90 yards of the bull before it got dark. We came back the next morning and evening, but the elk had relocated farther down the valley.

In addition to hunting the saddle, you can walk down Australia Gulch. We have found some big rubs down there. Trees that were ten inches in diameter had been completely stripped of bark.

Spot 09: **Elk Fight.** Take the 1 X 1 trail over to Mt. Silver Heels then walk west until you reach a rockslide. It's extremely steep back in there. Walk the trails that cut back in toward the old mines.

Four years ago, a buddy of Phil Collier killed a five point bull back there. He had been going down to the gulch bottom every day and not seeing much. On his last day out he was coming back up the trail and heard two elk fighting. They were so busy with one another that he was able to get within 40 yards. He shot the bigger one when they broke away from clinching. Both elk ran about 40 or 50 yards and then one fell over. The elk didn't even know he was hit. He probably thought the other elk had gored him slightly.

Spot 10. **Bald Knob.** Located to the northwest of Mt. Silver Heels in Baldy Saddle is a bald knob just above timberline. To get to it you will have to walk down into a steep gully to the north and up the other side, which will take about an hour and a half. Up by the knob we've always seen a large elk herd at first light. Unfortunately, we have never made it over to the knob early enough. By the time we've gotten over there, they've already moved down into the timber where it's thick and difficult to hunt.

Guy:

I can't count the times I've looked over to this spot and seen 90 or more elk, including at least 10 bulls. There's one really big one in the bunch (6 X 6). With the spotting scope I've watched him put his head back and bugle so loud I could hear it all the way across the valley. Once I even saw steam coming out of his mouth.

Spot 11: **Palmer Peak Backside.** Drive to the end of FSR 413. There are a number of trails through there that don't appear on any maps. At the end of the road take the trail heading southeast on the west side of the valley. It will take you to a saddle where the elk cross over to Trout Creek drainage. Driving into this spot, we saw several cow elk standing along the road in the middle of the afternoon. Also, about a mile from the saddle we stumbled on a small 4 pt bull elk that stood on a larger game trail above us (about 45 yards). We were surprised to come upon him in the middle of the afternoon. We tracked him to the saddle which was heavily used by the local game. If we see 4 groups of elk like that in the middle of the day, we can't imagine what it would be like in the early morning.

Taken from the Baldy Saddle burn area, the valley at the base of Mt Silverheels is pictured below.

Spot 12: **Palmer Peak Base.** Take FSR 412 to FSR 194 and then drive 6 miles back. Cross the creek and work your way through the beaver ponds. On the other side you'll find a lot of thick aspen between large rockslide areas. Walking parallel to the ridges above, and sticking to the aspens, we've jumped many elk. Also, just at timberline, we've found heavy elk sign where elk were paralleling the open area above in the early morning. It may not be possible to get up there by first light because the walking is so rough. However, you can get into the aspen right away and hunt. Hunting at timberline will require at least a 1/2 hour uphill walk.

Spot 13: **Base Of Mount Silver Heels.** Take FSR 194 all the way up to the base of Mt. Silver Heels where Trout Creek starts. Use your field glasses to view the areas just at timberline, and the meadows below. You can see both deer and elk moving through the open spaces in the early morning. Many times they will go into a clump of trees and bed down. You can then plan a stalk that's sure to get you close. Snow in the later hunting seasons will push them farther down the valley.

Spot 14: **Crooked Creek Drainage.** This drainage is somewhat steep at the bottom becoming flat toward the top. The gully is narrow all the way up but opens up at the top. Sit toward the top early in the morning to catch elk in transition.

Spot 15: **Beaver Ridge.** Take Highway 285 to Highway 9 then take FSR 659 northeast to the areas indicated. You will need a four wheel drive to get past a couple of the steep places. We scouted this spot the day before the season opened. On the private property about a quarter mile before the National Forest boundary, we saw a 6 X 6 bull elk we named "Big Balls" for the huge appendage hanging down between his legs. He and about 20 cows just stood in the middle of the road looking at us. We had to honk the car horn to get him out of the way. He moved off into the woods and stood about 30 yards away looking back at us. We knew that the minute the hunting season opened, he would disappear.

Heading about a mile to the north, we popped up over the horizon and jumped two more 4 X 5 bulls. They ran to about 150 yards, stopped and turned around to stare at us before heading into the dark timber.

Spot 16: **Spike Herd.** About a mile up the road from the previous spot is a small untimbered hill to your right. Just past that is a small drainage that runs back down into the timber between the base of Mt. Silver Heels and the hill. We counted 75 head of elk down in here. About half were cows and the rest were spikes and raghorns. We've never seen so many young male elk. The entire herd ran right in front of our truck in single file not more than 100 yards off. Now, a year later, those spikes have probably matured into good sized bulls.

Spot 17: **South Of Boreas Pass.** Take Como Road up Boreas Pass then walk southwest toward Tarryall creek. We found this spot by standing up on the back side of Mt. Silverheels and glassing the terrain below. Down on the hills above the mines we saw numerous herds of elk moving between clumps of trees. Also, one herd was walking along the power line that cuts through those mountains. The game down in there is undisturbed because there is no access from the mine, and the walk from Boreas Pass road can be tough.

Mosquito Mountains

(Reprinted from Pike National Forest map)

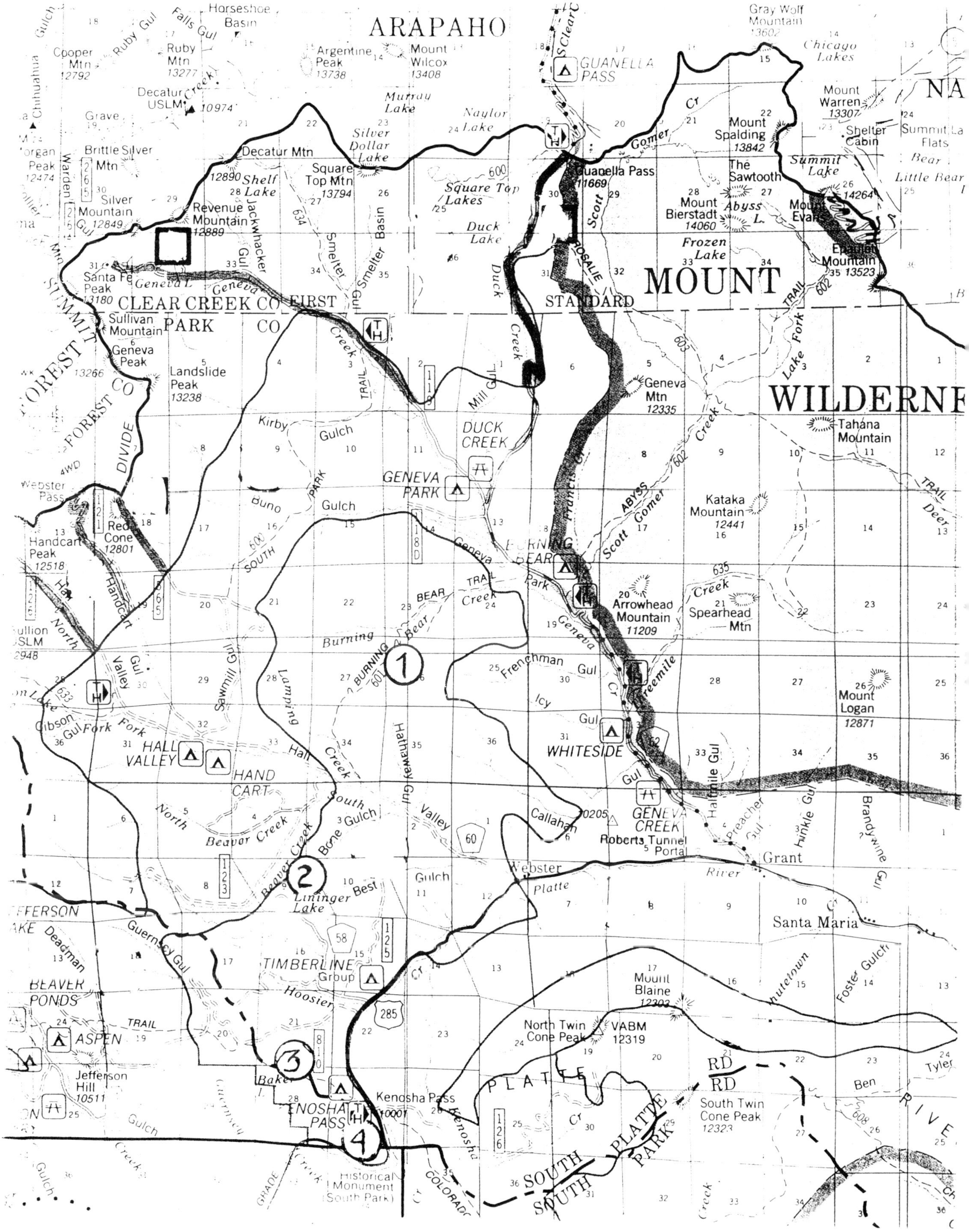

Mosquito Mountains

(Reprinted from Pike National Forest map)

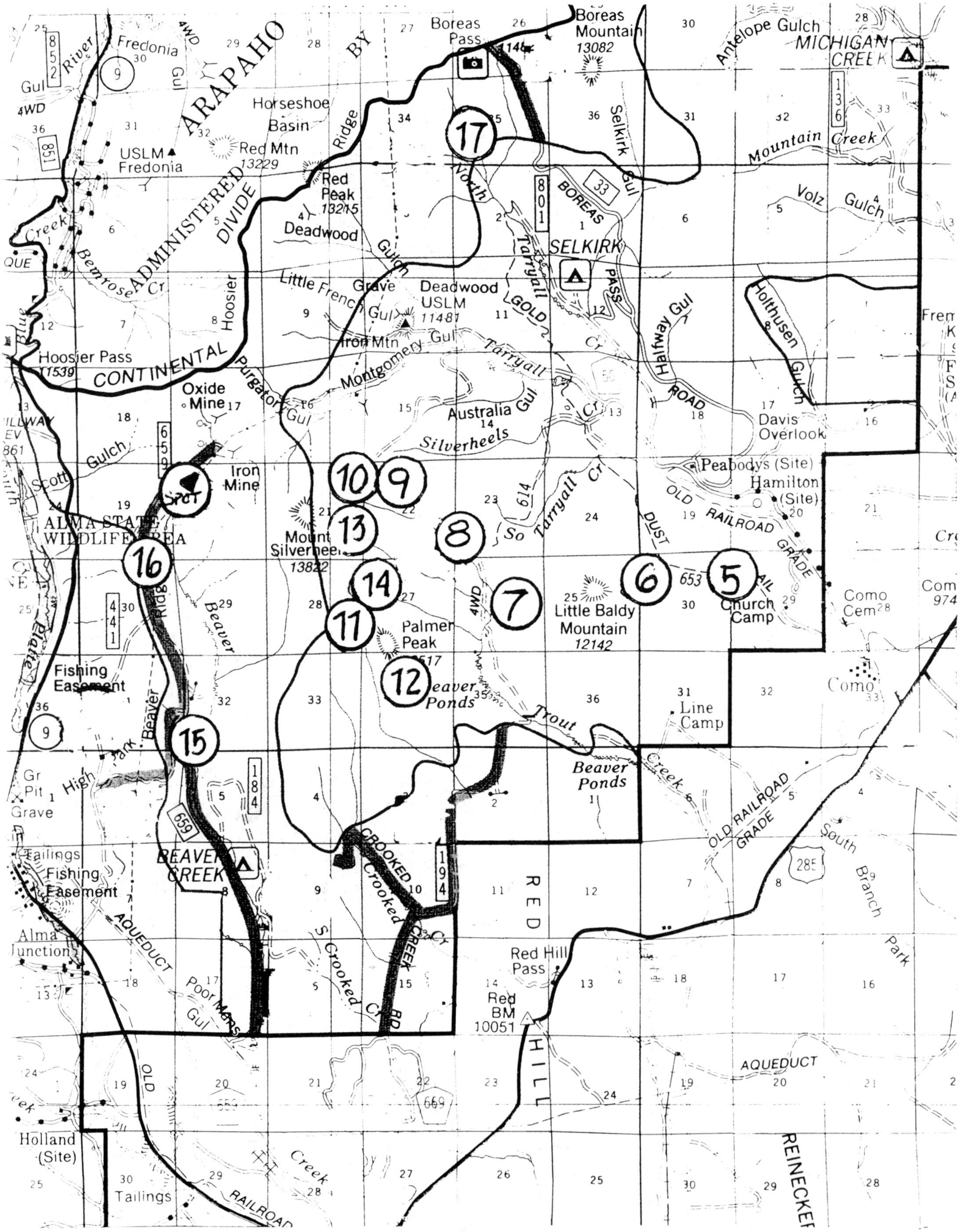

MOSQUITO MOUNTAINS 3-D MAP

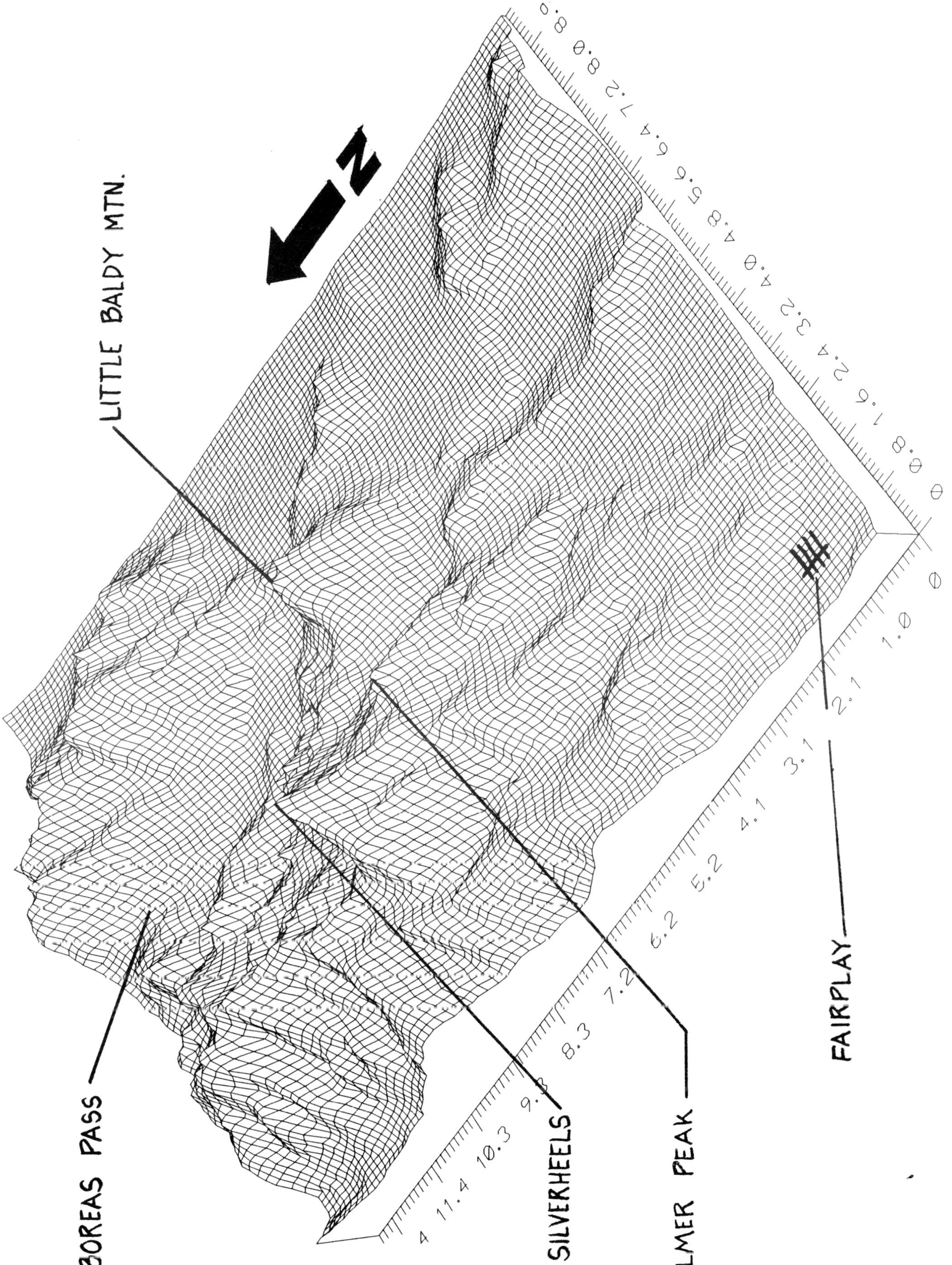

MOSQUITO MOUNTAINS 3-D MAP

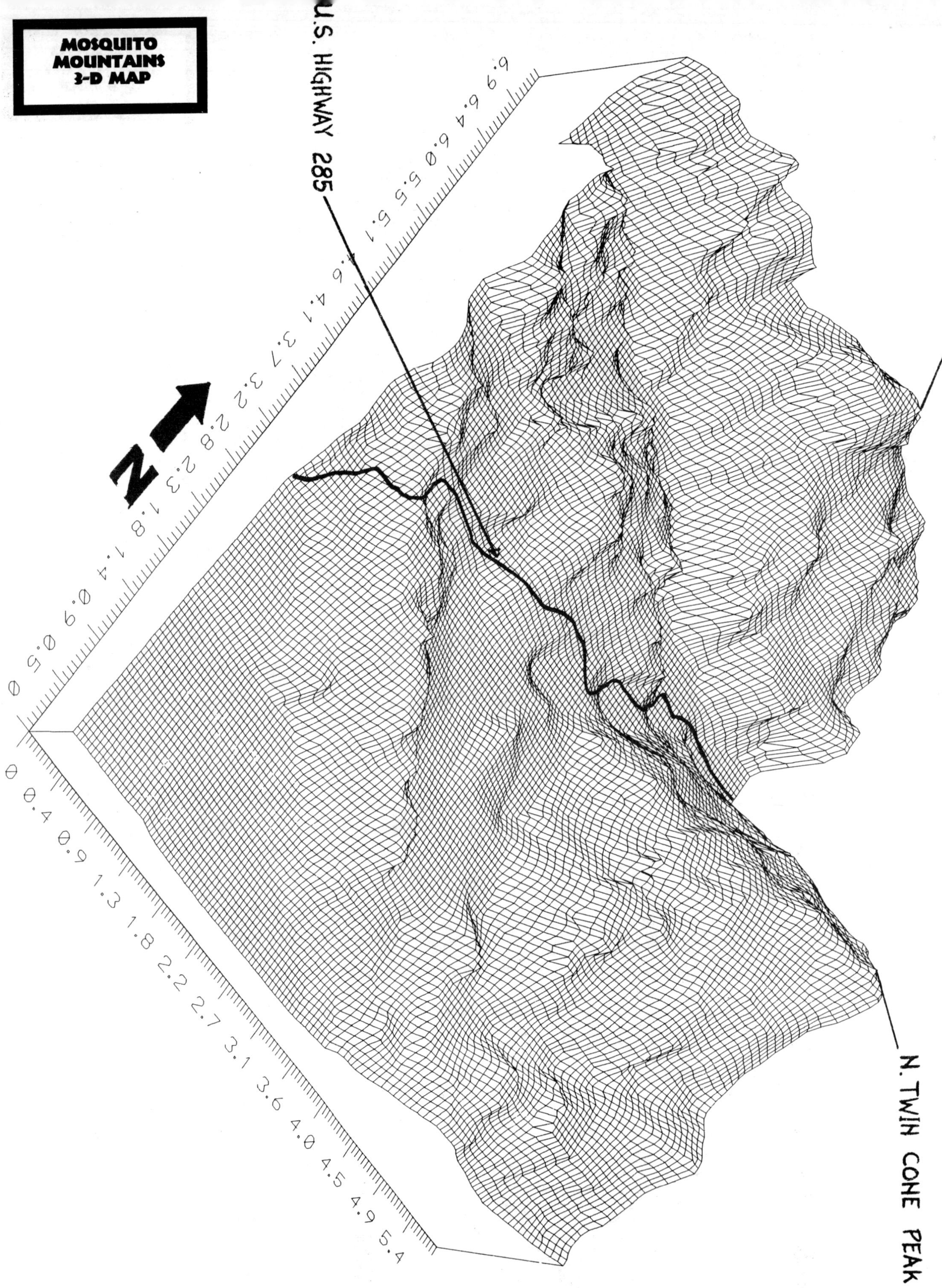

Oak Creek & Dunckley Pass

Big Game Hunting Unit(s): 231, 12

How To Get There:
From Kremmling go west on Highway 134 across Gore Pass. On the other side take Highway 131 to the town of Yampa. Then take Fire Road 17 west to the spots indicated on the map.

How To Hunt This Area: Much of this area can best be described as "wet." There is a lot of water on the hillsides below the flat top cliffs, and in the creek bottoms. Those spots are so wet, that when a tree reaches a certain size, it can't support its own weight and falls over. The result is a lot of lush green vegetation with thick mosses and ferns growing between downed timber. The ridges above the wet spots are drier. However, all of the game activity focuses on the wet spots and the food they provide.

It will be obvious when you are getting into a good elk spot. They cannot move through the thick undergrowth without leaving a trail. Their hooves kick away chunks of rotting wood as they jump over logs. When you see this, follow. The elk like to bed down between the logs. Don't be surprised if you see a set of antlers sticking up behind a log, and nothing else. Your tendency will be to walk on top of the logs, rather than continuously lifting your legs over each one. It's easier. However, when you're up that high, you're in full view of the game you pursue.

Spence with a little 3 X 4 mule deer he took along Oak Creek when he was 19 yrs old.

Spot 01: **Upper West Branch Of Oak Creek.** Just to the east of the spot where the west branch of upper Oak Creek intersects the road is a patch of dark timber 50 yards off the road. There are actually elk in there even though it's right next to the road. They cross the road and feed in the meadows along Oak Creek at night, then return to the timber by morning. There's also a black bear that prowls this hillside.

Spence:

> The year after we were married, my wife Becky and I camped along Oak Creek. When we got up in the morning, we found bear tracks right next to our tent. We never heard it. I tried to tell her that they were some old tracks from someone walking barefoot around their campsite. I wanted her to keep going out with me and I was afraid this would scare her off. She wasn't fooled by me and to this day, she's paranoid about bears. She's actually become very good at recognizing bear sign.

Spot 02: **Crossroads Waterhole.** Take Road 940 south toward Dunns Peak. There will be some logging roads branching off this road to the west which you can walk up. The very last logging road will take you toward the base of Sands Peak. Walking up the road you'll come to a place where several other old logging roads intersect. Right at the intersection is a waterhole that is full part of the year. Unlike the valleys below, the ridge you're on is dry except for that waterhole. Elk moving down from Sands Peak water there.

Spence:

> When I was new to elk hunting, I had a pretty frustrating experience there. I got an elk to answer my call up on Sands Peak. I hiked up there, only to hear a return bugle from the ridge below by the waterhole. When I got down there, I bugled again. To my frustration, one answered me back up on Sands Peak where I had just been. I couldn't get any return bugle down by the waterhole. But there were tracks to it from every direction. In retrospect, I was just moving in too loud and too fast putting out lousy bugles. When I got close, they knew I was a human and shut up. From far away, I sounded halfway real.

Spot 03: **Downhill Springs.** Drive up Road 940 south toward Dunns Peak. Take the second gated road to your right, and walk west. On the downhill side of the road are springs that support a lot of green foliage, while the surrounding foliage is pretty dry. Look for elk in those spots. Keep an eye out for fresh tracks crossing the road and heading down to the springs.

Spence:

> I hunted this spot back when I was an inexperienced elk hunter. I made the mistake of not nocking an arrow when I came across fresh elk tracks crossing the road and heading down to one of those springs. Twenty yards down the road a cow elk came into view standing not 30 yards below the road. This was right around noon. I guess I just wasn't expecting to see anything. The fact that I had luck in that area can be attributed mostly to the sheer number of animals found there, and not any great hunting skill I possessed at the time.

Spot 04: **Sand Point.** Directly below Sand Point to the north is a flat spot that runs east and west along the base of the point. Elk move along the base preferring the flat thoroughfare to the steeper slope above. One bull elk appears to stay right in the area most of the time, bedding and dusting right behind a small rock outcropping that forms one side of the flat thoroughfare.

Spot 05: **Deer Trails.** Follow the west branch of Oak Creek up from where it crosses Fire Road 16. You'll find dark pines to your right crisscrossed with large deer trails. In some spots, the deer trails are at least 4 ft. wide and heavily used. Farther up, the terrain will open to a very large meadow.

Spence:

> Years ago I was walking up that trail and spotted three mule deer feeding in the big meadow. I crawled to within 25 yards of them and shot from behind a bush. Somehow, my bow sight had been knocked off and my first arrow was low and to the left. They perked up but didn't move. I put the bead high and to the right of the closest buck and shot again. It went right over his back. They ran to the top of a mound and looked back at me. They still didn't know what I was. I abandoned the sight and shot on instinct. The arrow arcked up and came down right on top of a three by two. In retrospect, I would never shoot at that distance (65 yards) again. At the time, I was only 19 and hadn't yet seen the results of a poorly placed archery shot. Fortunately, the shot hit a major artery and the buck didn't run very far. I tracked him into a gully to the west where I found him laying in a creek bottom.

Spot 06: **Marshy Hillsides.** Directly below Sand Point and above the meadow mentioned in the previous spot are a lot of very marshy meadows and lakes which form the headwaters of the upper west branch of Oak Creek. To get there walk up from the spot where the west branch of Oak Creek crosses Road 16. All the thick underbrush severely limits visibility but supports many many elk. In years past, we've always seen elk in there.

Spot 07: **Between Oak & Trout Creeks.** Walk the fields north of Fire Road 16 between Oak and Trout Creeks. According to locals, they're good places to hunt during the late rifle season provided the snow has pushed the elk down.

Spot 08: **Southwest Of Dunckley Flat Tops.** This place is not very easy to get to, but it is great for deer. Unfortunately the easiest access has been blocked off because a couple of hundred yards of it crosses private property. To get there cross Dunckley Pass heading west. One mile before the road makes a sharp U-turn and heads downhill, park where you can. There are no pulloffs. Start from the top. You will have to cut down through some small cliffs. The woods below are full of deer.

Spence:

> My friend Craig Fishel "Fish" and I walked this area one evening a few years ago. It seemed that every time we came into an open meadow, we ran into deer. The total deer count for a two hour walk was over 70. It's well worth the tough walk down.

Oak Creek & Dunckley Pass

(Reprinted from Routt National Forest map)

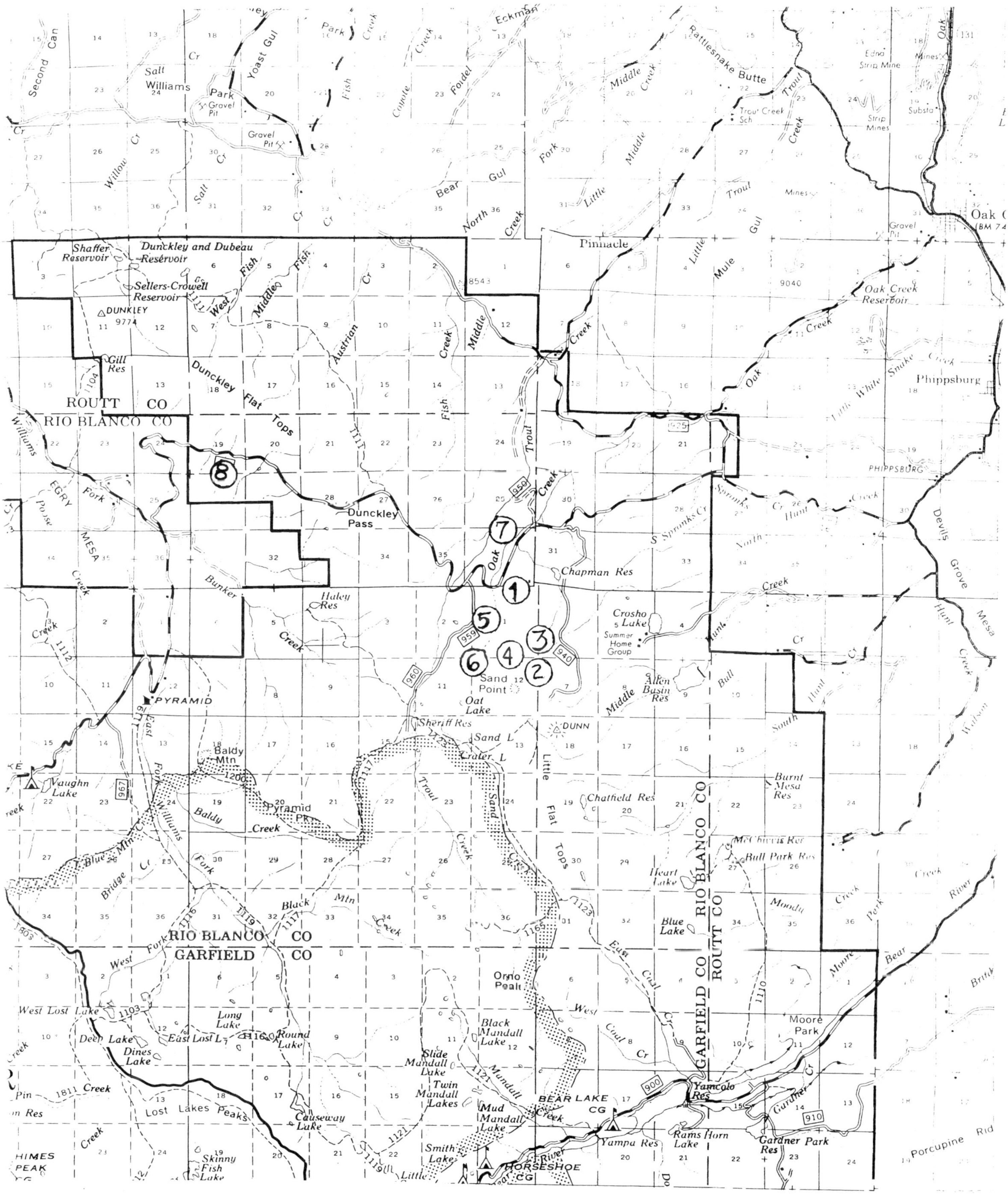

OAK CREEK/ DUNCKLEY PASS 3-D MAP

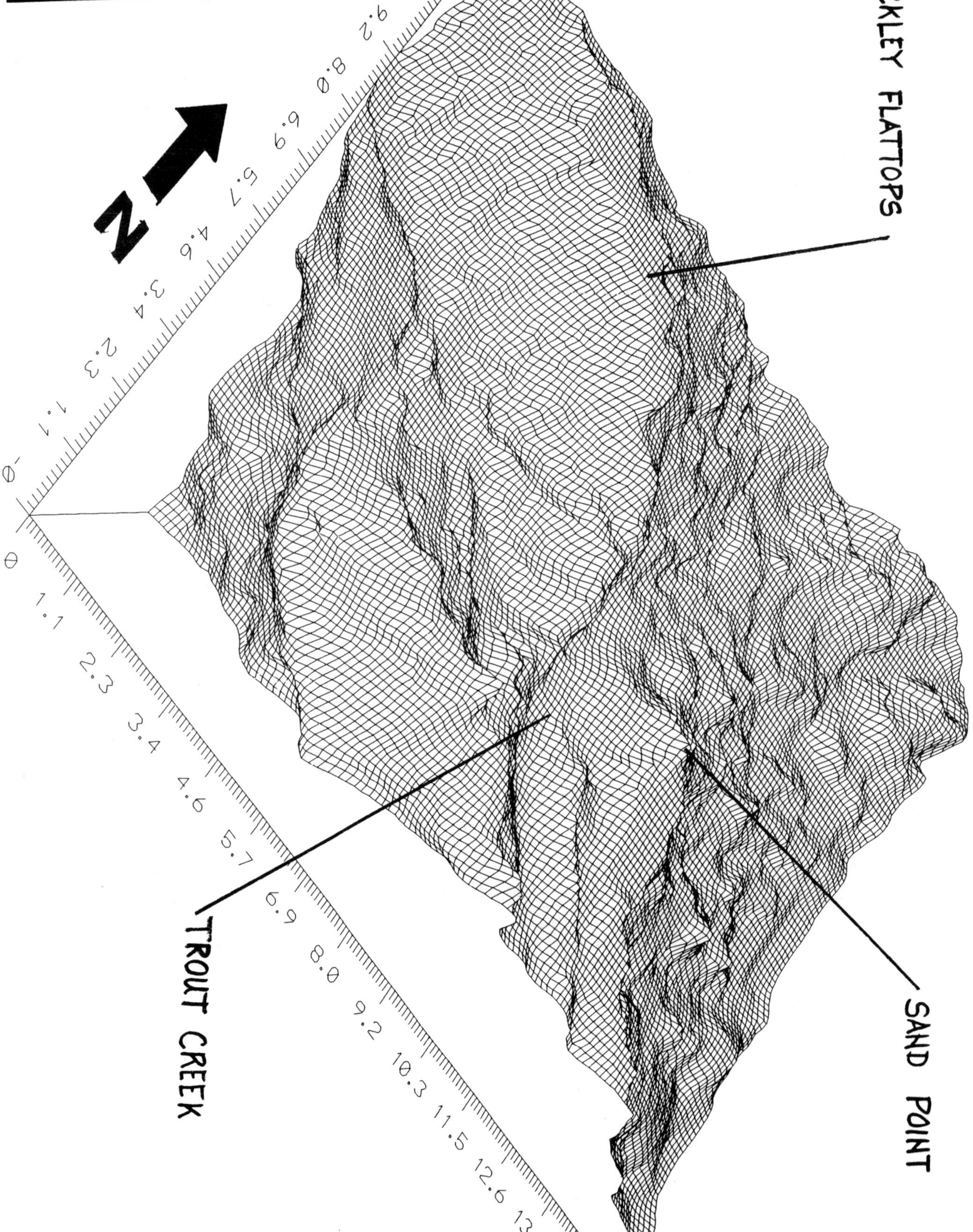

Pawnee National Grasslands

Big Game Hunting Unit(s): 87 and 88.

How To Get There:

Take I-25 north of Fort Collins to Highway 14. Driving east on Highway 14 you'll come to the little town of Ault. From there you will turn left on Highway 85 and drive through the town of Nunn. Approximately seven miles from there you will see our hunting areas located on the right (east).

How To Hunt This Area:

Pawnee Grasslands is a vast prairie with rolling hills and dramatic bluffs. It has draws and washes cut out of the earth by seasonal rains. Some of the washes and river beds are filled with cottonwood trees, ground shrubs and various grasses. Around the bluffs and some of the higher hill areas you are going to run into pine forests. How you hunt this area depends largely on what type of game you are after.

Although it looks barren, the Colorado prairie holds a surprising amount of game. Old farmhouses like this, and the adjacent creek bed (notice the trees along the bottom) attract both deer and antelope.

Antelope hunting: If there has been a lot of rain, we recommend that you use the spot and stalk method to hunt antelope. Last year, due to heavy rains, it was impossible to pattern the antelope because they could get water anywhere. There was no concentration of game around any one waterhole. In hot dry years (which is usually the case), all antelope activity centers around what water can be found.

Once you spot an antelope herd, try using an antelope decoy (bow season only). Sneak in as close as possible to the herd, then raise the decoy. Hopefully you have remained undetected. As the decoy is raised the attention of the dominant buck will be immediately focused on the decoy. The buck will most likely charge the decoy (and you) to chase the intruder away from his harem. This is when you take your shot. He'll more than likely come to within 30 yards and stop. The decoy will work best in the last weeks of August through September (pre-rut and rut). Most of the good antelope spots are along high ridges or the saddles between them where the antelope cross. We have seen animals in every one of the spots indicated on our maps. As always we do recommend getting a great pair of binoculars because the antelope have binocular type vision themselves and can see you from a long way off.

Whitetail Hunting: Hunting the whitetail deer is going to require a bit different strategy. You will find them in the bottom lands where the cottonwood trees and the thick tangle brush grows. They are easier to pattern than mule deer. They make scrapes and rubs, and do all the other things you would expect the whitetail deer to do back east. The nice thing about Pawnee Grasslands is that the whitetails are concentrated along the creek bed bottoms where they are easy to find. You can go in there and either hang a stand, or organize small drives.

One trait of eastern Colorado is that it does not receive a lot of water after July. However, there will be small pockets of water remaining along the creek beds which the deer will use. Last year was an exception to the rule. We had water everywhere. But in normal years you will find waterholes randomly. If it is dry, try setting up a tree stand above one of the waterholes. The whitetail need water every day and will come in regularly, usually in the mornings and evenings if they are undisturbed. Once they are disturbed they will become nocturnal and much harder to hunt.

Mule Deer: Mule deer hunting requires different tactics. They will be on the plains, down in the washes, and also heavily concentrated around the bluffs. The bluffs in this area rise straight up out of the relatively flat rolling hills and usually have cliffs on one side. They are flat on top where you will often find pine trees. They provide great vantage points for spotting game. The deer like the views they provide as well. We've seen herds of 30 to 40 mule deer up by the chalk bluffs. They watch the plain below for intruders, and move off at the sight of any hunters or predators approaching. That's why it's important to get up there under cover of darkness.

Guy:

Last year while antelope hunting I saw several nice mule deer bucks (probably about a 25 inch spread with four points on each side) up there. But I was hunting antelope and didn't pursue. This year I am going to hunt the eastern archery deer season in hopes of bagging a big whitetail out there.

The spots we describe in the Pawnee National Grasslands are all areas where we have spotted game. It is a general tendency of the game to move from valley to valley. Use the higher ground to scope the sides of the hills facing your position. Once you spot a moving animal, try to figure out where it is going and plan your stalk accordingly.

Spot 1: **Lone Tree Creek Drainage**. This spot is located approximately eight miles north and due east of Highway 85 and the town of Nunn. It's just below a small ridgeline along a creek bed. The creek bed holds a lot of animals, especially during the heat of the day. It provides great forage as well as a place to escape the elements during inclement weather.

Spot 2: **South Lone Creek Drainage**. This spot is located directly south of the previous spot, across the gully and on the north facing slope. This is where some of the antelope and deer will bed to escape the hot sun. They bed in the intermittent yucca and sagebrush you'll see.

Although the terrain appears very flat and sparsely vegetated, Spence was able to stalk to within 200 yards of this 16" (green score) antelope by keeping the sun at his back.

Spot 3: **Upper Little Owl Creek**. This spot is located approximately three miles south of the previously described spots and two miles east of Highway 85. Like the other spots, it's on a high point from which you can look over two little gullies. There is also a narrow saddle just to the northwest. You'll notice several small watering holes below you that are frequented both by antelope and mule deer. They feed on the grassy hillsides overlooking the waterholes.

Spot 4: **Upper Cow Creek**. This spot is located three miles directly east of Rockport and is completely surrounded by private property. Exactly one half mile north of Rockport is a road that will take you across two miles of private property. Go through the gates and the road will take you to a deep draw. This spot, like the others, provides a good vantage point. You can look down into a gully and out over the flats to the east. The gully holds several big mule deer as well as a nice herd of antelope.

Spot 5: **East Fork Cow Creek**. This spot is located directly south of the previous spot. It's also situated in a small drainage that holds both mule deer and antelope.

Spot 6: **Owl Creek**. In this spot, while out varmint hunting we've seen several game species including prairie dogs, badgers, coyotes, and fox. Early on in the year it's fantastic for dove hunting. The creek bed is completely wooded, so it's going to provide a lot of cover. There is an old farmstead along the creek where we've jumped both mule deer and whitetails. Directly to the west of the old farm we have often seen a big herd of antelope that stays there year round. There are some big rocks you can use to break up your silhouette when moving in on those antelope.

Guy:

You may want to try deer drives in this spot. Put a couple of people upwind of the deer. Their scent will travel down the creek bottom and push the deer to whoever you have waiting at the other end.

Spence:

The deer will almost always stay in the trees when they are pushed. They know better than to move up the treeless hillsides. They will also stop at the edge of any open areas they have to cross. This makes it very easy for the blocker to get a good shot, provided he picks the right spot.

Spot 7: **Middle Owl Creek**. This spot is located directly south of the previously described spot. However it is on the south side of the creek up in some of the deep ravines and steep hills.

Guy:

While dove hunting there, we jumped several nice bucks, all of which used the same escape route - running southwest up the hill and into the deep gullies. Unfortunately, when we saw the deer we were not deer hunting. We concentrated most of our deer hunting efforts to the west of I-25. But eastern deer hunting is definitely catching on in Colorado. I'm doing it this year.

Spence:

This is another good drive and block spot. The trick is to get the deer that are running through the gullies to stop so you can get a clean shot. They will stop if they hear a whistle, deer call, predator call or cow elk call.

Spot 8: **Lower Owl Creek**. This spot is located farther down Owl Creek and just to the southwest. Over on the side of the big hill you will see more and more antelope sign as you get away from the creek bed. Antelope like to be out where they can see for great distances and this hill is just that type of spot. Up there we saw several big antelope bucks among a large herd of does. This would be a great place to spot and stalk. You can use all the hills and ravines as cover to get up close.

Spot 9: **Pond Ridge**. This spot is located approximately seven miles north and about three miles east of the town of Nunn. The closest road is about 3/4 of a mile away. You'll be hunting next to a big tract of private land. Hunt to the south of that along the barb wire fence. The exact spot we have marked on the map is a hilltop overlooking a pond that is wet most of the year. From there you can either wait for the game to come to you, or stalk any antelope herds you spot through your binoculars.

Spot 10: **1650 Ridge**. This spot is located one half mile directly to the south of the spot just described. You will be on a point overlooking a waterhole that antelope frequent.

Spot 11: **Head Waters Of Robinson Creek**. This spot is located about one mile northeast of Spot 10. It is directly north of state land and less than a quarter of a mile walking distance from the road. You'll be in a saddle running from the northeast to the southwest. You can sit in a blind or spot and stalk. It is a great place to catch animals traveling back and forth from one waterhole to the next. It is mainly an antelope spot.

Spot 12: **East Fork Eastman Creek**. This spot is located 3½ miles east and one mile south of the original Owl Creek Spot 6. You will need to walk about a quarter of a mile from the road. There you'll find a road separating the highest point in the area from a waterhole. If you sit on the high point, you can catch the antelope going back and forth across the road to the water.

Guy:

Another interesting characteristic of antelope is that they will not jump fences. They will always find a place to crawl underneath the fence. So if you can find a place in the fence where the antelope crawl underneath, you'll have a great place to build a pit blind. Dig it within about 30 yards of the crawl. This can be very effective as antelope are territorial and therefore patternable. Like whitetail deer, when they like a particular area they will stay there until they are pushed out.

Spot 13: **Chalk Pond**. This spot tends to get a lot of use from people with motorcycles and horses. Ranchers also graze a lot of free-ranging cattle in the area. You'll be hunting around a waterhole that's positioned up against a hillside. It's a great ambush spot for both antelope and for deer coming down from the bluff areas. It's exceptionally good if the weather has been very dry. If it has been wet, seasonal springs in the Chalk Bluffs will serve as their source of water.

Spot 14: **Upper Coal Creek Wells**. This spot is located one mile south of the previous spot. It's accessible from the grasslands road. You'll hunt right next to a well and water tower.

Guy:

One advantage to hunting around windmills is that you can use them like treestands. Hunters have built platforms on them. The antelope become accustomed to the noise and movement associated with a clanky windmill. This hides the motion and sound of a bow or rifle being drawn. This particular windmill already has a hunting platform on it. So if you get up in there before anybody else does, it's yours for the day. Feel free to use it. It's all public land.

Spot 15. **West Fork Coal Creek**. This spot is located approximately eight miles east of Highway 85 and six miles north of Nunn. It's surrounded on three sides by private land which limits hunting access and pressure. You will be on a point overlooking a big valley and creek bed providing a great opportunity for spotting game and planning good stalks. To your east will be a large chunk of public land you can hunt.

Spot 16: **Elbow Point**. This spot is located approximately five miles south of spot 15. You'll be hunting in a little gully that tends to hold a lot of animals when the weather gets bad or if the wind starts blowing. There's a high point you can sit on that allows you to overlook the land directly to the west. There is also some tall sagebrush where the animals hole up if it's really hot.

Spot 17: **Coyote Ridge**. This spot is located a mile southwest of spot 16. It's an open area surrounded on three sides by private property. Spots like this are excellent because being adjacent to private property causes them to get overlooked by hunters.

Guy:

If you are out there during the archery or muzzle loading season, you will rarely see another person. I hunted for almost a week out there, drove 150 to 175 miles a day, and never saw another hunter.

Spot 18: **Three Point Ridge**. This spot is located directly north of Spot 17. There are three saddles and three ridges from which you can overlook a huge valley. This is a great place to set up your spotting scope or good binoculars and scan the valley below. You can watch the antelope coming to you as they make their way up the saddles.

Spot 19: **Lower Eastman Creek Gully**. This spot is located directly north of spot 18. You'll be on a high point that allows you to overlook a good gully. You will not be very far from Eastman Creek.

Spot 20: **Coal Creek Pond**. This spot is located right off the side of the road. We have seen antelope in there many times. The property on the south side of the road is private, but virtually everything else is public. It's a great place to set up a pit blind and wait for the antelope to come in to water.

Spot 21: **North Pit**. This spot is located north of an area we call the "pit." The pit, like I've mentioned earlier, gets some motorcycle use. The noise they make doesn't seem to bother the antelope. They've been conditioned to it and don't run away when they hear motorcycles. There's also an old abandoned farm to the north of the pit that deer go to. Old farmhouses seem to attract a lot of game.

Spot 22: **Middle Willow Creek**. We have seen several big antelope back in there. They move from one hill to the other, never really leaving the area.

Spot 23: **West Willow Creek**. This spot is located farther down the creek bed of the pit mentioned in Spot 21. We've seen a lot of tracks left by deer coming down from the bluffs to the creek. This part of the creek bed is usually dry, so they are not going there for the water. Mostly it's used as a travel route. There is also a lot of small game along the creek bed you can hunt during the day if it gets a little slow.

Spot 24: **McGrew Reservoir**. This spot is located ten miles directly to the east of Nunn. Around the reservoir, a lot of antelope can be found. Walk around the edges of the southeastern side of the reservoir and look for places where they go to water.

Spot 25: **Purcell**. This spot is located approximately two miles south of Spot 24 and is surrounded by private property on all sides. You will be positioned on a high point looking down into a valley from the southwest. This is a great place to spot from and plan a stalk on the animals you see. We have not hunted there, but have seen a lot of nice bucks in the area.

Fence rows in the agricultural lands surrounding Pawnee Grasslands attract a lot of game. Here Fish (left) and Guy hunt for pheasants.

Guy:

These spots should all be productive. It just depends on whether you catch them passing through there at the right time. This entire area is a vast open prairie. If you are not seeing them in one spot, just move over to the next hill and scan the adjacent valleys. Sooner or later you'll spot game.

Spot 26: **Grassland Ridge**. From the top of this hill you overlook valleys to the east and to the west. It's a great vantage point. You are only about a half mile from the road so it's really not that difficult to get to.

Guy:

Last year on the 20th of August I saw 45 antelope in the second gully. The bucks were constantly chasing the does around, so it's a great place to use one of those antelope decoys.

Spot 27: **Difficult Draw**. This spot is located approximately 12 miles east of Rockport. It's very secluded, and has a lot of antelope. It's situated on a small piece of public land surrounded by private land. There's a little gully that sometimes holds water which should be productive. You will not be far from the bluffs.

Note:

All of the spots in this area are surrounded by private land, but you do have access. You will almost always have to go through a couple of gates and drive across private land to get there. But access to public land is guaranteed by law. If you are denied access, you can call the Division Of Wildlife who are good about following up on those types of complaints.

Guy:

We have ridden our motorcycles back over to this area and seen several dozen antelope wandering about. We've ridden to within about two or three hundred yards before they spooked. That's a little too close for their comfort. Generally speaking, vehicles don't bother them at distances farther away than 300 yards.

Spot 28: **Double Wells**. This spot is located about seven miles to the south of Spot 27. There's a windmill that pumps out water for the cattle, which the game also use. You'll see a platform up in the windmill which you can sit on and wait to see what comes in. This spot is especially good if it has been a dry season.

Spot 29: **Point Lake**. This spot is located about a quarter of a mile directly to the east of spot 28. There's a nice hill and little saddle you can sit in to watch the pond below.

Guy:

In this spot I attempted to stalk an antelope buck during the archery season. He was with about 16 does and there were also a couple of lesser bucks in the group. I could have cursed myself. I got to within 75 yards when the wind shifted. He started snorting and moved off, even though he had not seen me. I learned that antelope possess the same sense of smell as elk and deer.

Spot 30: **Willow Creek Pond**. This spot is located about two miles to the north of Spot 29. Once again, you will be hunting around a pond. We have always seen a lot of tracks around the pond. Late in the year the pond shrivels up to just a small watering hole. The smaller the better because it concentrates the antelope and you will know exactly where they are going to be. A blind would work well around the pond. Unless the blind is inconspicuous, it's best to build early. That way the animals can get used to it.

Spot 31: **North Fork Willow Creek Draw**. This spot is located about four miles to the southeast of Spot 30. You'll be hunting up above the creek bed in a saddle antelope pass through to get to the creek and the little pockets of water found there.

Spot 32: **Coal Creek Well**. This spot is located approximately 14 miles east of the town of Pierce. You'll be hunting around a well. There's actually a hill between the well and a pond. This is a great spot to sit and glass the surrounding landscape. This spot should be very productive for antelope.

Spot 33: **Wildhorse Creek Well**. In this spot, you'll be hunting around yet another well. An alternative is to sit up on the hill and look for stalking opportunities. There is an open valley between Spot 33 and Spot 32 you can glass for game.

Guy:

If you are going to be hunting in this area, you may want to try some of the new lines of lighter colored camouflage. Something in a sage or light brown that breaks up the patterns works well. Desert Storm camo is an inexpensive alternative to the high dollar stuff, and does the job just as well.

Spot 34: **West Geary Creek**. This spot is located on a hill approximately two miles east of Spot 31. It's in the southwest corner of the grasslands plot you'll see on the map. The hill has a lot of grass on it where we've seen antelope each year. Also, directly to the east is some state land you can hunt.

Guy:

Last year, on the other side of the road, I stalked a herd of about 15 antelope. As I mentioned before, water was everywhere along the sides of roads and low lying areas. Unfortunately, where you find water you'll also find mosquitos. I was nearly eaten alive. By the time I realized what was happening I was within 70 yards of the antelope I was after. It was too late to turn back and retreat. I had to continue with my stalk. I believe those little menaces were the downfall of my perfectly executed plan. As I swatted at them I looked up to see the herd buck staring at me. I'd blown it! Don't let this happen to you. Bring insect repellent. You don't have to be miserable like I was.

Spence:

History shows that insects and bad weather have brought down more armies than actual battles. The mosquitos out on the prairie are especially bad because they rarely get water. Their window of opportunity is so short that they have to swarm in order to perpetuate their species. The only place I've seen it worse is northern Minnesota. Up there mosquitos look more like birds of prey than insects.

Spot 35: **Grassland Corner**. This spot is located two miles to the southeast of Spot 34. We have yet to drive through the big open valleys in the area and not see antelope feeding in the distance. Just pull out your binoculars and scan the flats.

Spot 36: **Willow Creek Lake**. This spot is located two miles to the southeast of spot 35 between two waterholes. The smallest waterhole will dry up in the summer. Therefore the larger waterhole will attract all the antelope. In addition, there's another well to the northeast. The antelope will definitely be moving through the area.

Spot 37: **Little Crow Creek Spring**. This spot is located around a little spring. It doesn't produce a lot of water, but there's enough to attract quite a bit of wildlife. We thought it would be worth mentioning because we've been up there several times and seen a lot of small game. We did not see any big animals come in but there was sign indicating they had.

Spot 38: **South Little Crow Creek Spring**. This spot is located up higher from Spot 37 overlooking some private land as well as the Pawnee National Grassland. You are somewhat isolated in this spot, as there's quite a bit of private land to the north, east and south. This allows you to get away from any hunting pressure that does occur. You can pursue animals that are undisturbed.

Spot 39: **Twin Ponds**. Once again, this is a spot located between two ponds. When you're positioned by water you are definitely going to see animals. We found antelope and deer tracks all the way around the ponds. We're not exactly sure what time of day they use the ponds, but we recommend that you at least check them out. If you can establish a game pattern, you'll definitely have luck.

Spot 40: **North of Crow Valley Park**. This spot is also located next to a water source. The north side of the property is privately owned, but the rest is open to hunting. Because it is remote, it will likely get overlooked by other hunters. Check the waterholes for recent activity. It will definitely pay off. There are also some campgrounds just to the south. This area was frequented by the Pawnee Indians in the latter part of the nineteenth century.

Spot 41: **West Keota**. This spot is located farther to the east from the original grassland's hunting spots we described. It's separated from those spots by a big parcel of private land. More public land becomes available the farther east you go, but a lot of people do not even know that land can be hunted. In this spot there's a water source at the base of a big hill. You can position yourself on the hill overlooking the waterhole. In addition, there are several large valleys below which you can watch for movement.

Spot 42: **Highway 14**. This spot is located approximately six miles southwest of the little town of Keota. Once again we are putting you on the side of a hill next to a waterhole. Use your binoculars. You just can't go wrong. Antelope are thick in this area.

Spot 43: **Ridgeland Saddle**. In this spot you will be hunting in a saddle between a couple of little ridges (hence the name). This saddle will be especially productive because you are starting to get into pine trees. The pines provide more cover and as a result, attract more mule deer. Once you get up on top you'll have quick access to other hunting spots. This is especially beneficial in the event you spot animals moving down an adjacent ridgeline.

Spot 44: **Central Chalk Bluff**. This spot is located on a small plot of grasslands up against the side of the Chalk Bluffs. It is completely surrounded by private land. It definitely produces "book class " mule deer. We saw a herd of about 40 deer by the bluffs. At least 15 were bucks. We were there in December, so the bucks and does were still hanging out together. If you are lucky enough to draw an eastern plains deer license, you definitely should take a look at this spot. It's less than half a square mile in size, which is small, but then again, it will more than likely get overlooked by other hunters.

Spot 45: **South Keota**. This spot is located on a ridge about two miles south of the town of Keota. Like most of the other antelope areas we have profiled, it is situated next to a water source. Sitting on the ridge you get a great view of several valleys to the northwest and northeast. There's also another water source to the south. Look for antelope moving between the waterholes.

Spot 46: **Highpoint**. In this spot you'll be hunting in a group of ravines adjacent to jagged bluffs which are covered with pine trees. This is an excellent place to bag a trophy buck. There is a rocky outcropping directly to the east you can sit on. From there you'll have a view all the ravines. In the past we've spotted numerous deer moving through the ravines.

Spot 47: **Wyoming Line**. This is a very isolated spot up near the Wyoming/Nebraska border. We've often seen deer and antelope in the area. People will overlook it because it's just a little spot on the map. If they do notice it at all, they will figure it's too small of a spot to drive that far for. That's why it's so good.

Spot 48: **Mesa Ponds**. This spot is located about two miles south of Spot 47. You'll be hunting up on top of a large bluff between two water sources. There are a few trees scattered throughout the sagebrush up there. We've seen several large racked mule deer by those trees.

Spot 49: **Deep Ravine**. This spot is located on the south side of the bluff area profiled in the previous spot. You'll be hunting in a deep gully next to some private property which has a few springs. The deer typically follow the ravine down from the bluffs to the springs. When we visited this spot, several deer that were on their way to the springs crossed the road in front of our vehicle. The biggest of the bunch was only a three by four, but it was definitely respectable.

Spot 50: **West Wolf Spring**. This spot is located just to the southwest of Pawnee Buttes. The buttes dramatically rise straight up out of the flat plain. On the back side of the buttes are some steep gullies where pine trees grow. In and around the trees we've seen several herds of mule deer. We've also jumped a lot of deer in the gullies.

Spot 51: **Pawnee Buttes Basin**. In this spot you'll be hunting between the buttes and the Pawnee Creek Basin. The creek has a lot of trees along it where you'll find mule deer, whitetail deer, and antelope. The deer bed down on the sides of the buttes during the day, and feed down by the creek in the morning, evening and at night. Find a trail they are using as they come down from the buttes, and set up an ambush.

Guy:

Pawnee Buttes are extremely picturesque. They look like something out of the movie "Dances With Wolves." People actually go up to the Buttes to hike, which is rare for the Colorado Eastern Plains (most people hike in the mountains west of Interstate 25).

Spot 52: **Hill Side Well**. This spot is located about six miles south of the Pawnee Buttes. It's completely surrounded by private property. Hunt the hills around the well. They attract a lot of antelope. You may also catch a few mule deer coming in to the well.

Note:

Roads crisscross this entire area. All you have to do is park along the road or drive any of the trails marked with "Grassland Trails" arrows. There's an incredible amount of open space to hunt.

Spot 53: **North Elizabeth Spring**. This spot is located on an odd shaped tract of land surrounded by private property. You will be hunting in rolling hills where you'll find "pockets" of game. By moving from one hill to another, you will spot game you were unable to see from the hill you were just on.

Spence:

At first glance, the prairie looks flat and barren. But this is very deceiving. There is a lot of game out there. Just a slight change in elevation can hide an entire herd of animals. In old frontier accounts I've read, the calvary was always complaining about how deceiving the prairie was. In one account, a soldier complained that the Indians could hide an entire army behind what appeared to be just a low lying hill. The way to hunt the prairie is to move from one high point to another, and keep glassing. Only a slight change in your position provides a completely different perspective of the landscape you just glassed.

Spot 54: **South Of Igo Creek**. This is another good antelope hunting spot. You will be on a high spot overlooking several miles of public land mixed with tracts of private land. There are a few seasonal waterholes in the area that attract wildlife. Watch for antelope going to and from the waterholes.

Spot 55: **Wild Horse Creek**. In this spot you'll be hunting around a pond that's close to the creek bottom. There are some more hills just to the south which also attract game. Throughout the area are intermittent trees which you can use as cover for stalking.

Spence:

Remember, if the tree you're using as cover in a stalk is closer to you than half way between you and the animal, your perspective is incorrect. You may not be hidden at all because the closer you or the animal gets to a tree, the steeper the angle of view around the tree.

Spot 56: **Saddle 56**. In this spot you'll be hunting on a big saddle between two wide valleys. Each valley has a creek bed in it. Plan your strategy according to where in each creek bed the animals are watering. We've seen several nice herds of antelope moving across the saddle.

Spot 57: **North Sidney Draw**. This spot is located right up on the Nebraska border just north of Sidney Draw. Once again, this area has a big bluff with steep rocky outcroppings and intermittent pine trees. From the top we spotted several mule deer bucks below us. We weren't hunting at the time but we did mark it on the map. This is another spot that tends to get overlooked because it's small and surrounded by private property.

Spence:

Consider a pined bluff area to be like an oasis in the middle of the desert. The surrounding landscape is usually waterless, doesn't have a lot of cover, and has a lot less food. The bluffs on the other hand have everything the game needs to sustain life. They are going to gravitate toward the bluffs.

Spot 58: **NEB Well**. This spot is located two miles east of Spot 57 on the Nebraska border. Like Spot 57, it has steep rocky cliffs. It also has a good man-made well that concentrates game into a small area. A few years ago we visited this spot and swore we would go back. The vegetation around the well was completely beaten down by all the antelope and deer that watered there.

Spot 59: **Pawnee Delta**. This spot is located south of North Pawnee Creek and Igo Creek and is surrounded by private property. From the southwest corner of the plot a little road runs back to a well. You are free to take the gate down and drive in. Drive back as far as you can without spooking any of the game, and set up a platform on the windmill. It can be very productive, especially in hot weather.

Spot 60: **The Gravel Pit**. This spot is surrounded on all sides by private land but there is plenty of access. Your walk in will be less than 3/4 of a mile. The creek bed that runs through the public land is usually dry, but we've always seen both deer and antelope around it. They bed down there during the heat of the day in the yuccas and sage. Glass under each tree and bush, looking for the outline of a deer or antelope. You'll be surprised by how many you can spot this way.

Spot 61: **No Name**. This is another good antelope hunting spot. It is located along Highway 14 about four miles northwest of the little town of Stoneham. You will be hunting two to three miles south of Pawnee Creek. To the north you'll notice a big drainage which is on private property. You'll be standing on a ridge from which you can see a long way in every direction. The antelope move from the drainage to the ridgeline you will be hunting on.

Spot 62: **North Pawnee Creek**. In this spot you'll be hunting along high ridges that parallel North Pawnee Creek. There is less than half a square mile of public land to hunt. But by law you must be permitted access to public lands. There's an outcropping you can sit on from which you can look up several gullies and over an expansive valley down below. You'll see a lot of game in that valley.

Spot 63 (and Spot 64). **Avalo Wells**. This spot is located two miles south of Avalo. There are two wells in there that attract antelope. Somewhere between the two would be an excellent spot to ambush game. We made the area around the wells into two separate spots because there were two different herds watering at them. We spotted them at 11 o'clock in the morning in the early part of August. It was probably 90 degrees and the animals were using the water supply regularly. Unfortunately it wasn't yet hunting season. Too bad....

Spot 65: **Mid Spring Creek**. This spot is located on another section of public land along Spring Creek. It is completely surrounded by private land. Spring Creek will hold water, but by mid-September the water will be found only in small isolated pools. Find those pools and you've found your "honey hole." There's an outcropping you can sit on that allows you to look over several miles of land. Some of those miles are private so you might have to wait until the antelope come through to the public land. You may want to use a decoy to pull them off of the private land.

Spot 66: **Jackknife Ridge**. In this spot you can hunt a good size chunk of public land totaling nine square miles. Hunt the saddle. It gets used by antelope going from the northeast to the southwest.

Guy:

This spot produces several nice bucks each year. As a reminder, if you want to hunt antelope in Pawnee Grasslands during the rifle season, it does take a few preference points to get a permit. Because there is so much public land there, many people want to hunt in that area, and the competition is stiff for the limited antelope licenses available. However, archery hunters may purchase licenses over the counter and no preference points are required.

Spot 67: **Two Mile Creek**. This is another spot where the terrain gets steep and pine trees become more prevalent. You will be hunting right along Two Mile Creek. The farther north you go the more rugged the terrain becomes. There are many more gullies and steep draws in this spot than in the valleys below. The rugged terrain provides excellent hideouts for deer and thus is a more productive hunting spot.

Guy:

In 1984, while we were still in college, we went to this spot to hunt coyotes. We didn't see any coyotes, but we did see hundreds of deer. We promised ourselves that we would go back. But unfortunately, this area is so big and remote that we always ended up hunting somewhere else. As I was looking over my notes I remembered how good it was. I've decided to go back there this year. I may even put up my tree stands in a couple of spots.

Spence:

Unless you want to limit your hunting hours only to the early mornings and evenings, you need to hunt the gullies where the deer bed. Your chances of success increase dramatically when you hunt the entire day. The middle of the day is just as good as any other time if you modify your tactics to the deer's mid-day habits.

Spot 68: **R Tr Well**. This spot is located close to the Nebraska border. Again, the terrain is "chopped up" with a lot of bluffs and trees. It's going to produce deer and a few antelope. The whitetails will tend to stick to the lower areas along the creek while the mule deer will be up in the rocks. You want to watch the valley below and the watering holes we have circled on the map.

Guy:

It's to the hunter's advantage to do a stalk while the animals are still sleeping. I've caught them in their beds several times. During the off season I've practiced stalking them for fun, which really helped to sharpen my stalking skills. I like to see how close I can get to the animals without them knowing I'm there.

Spence:
Many hunters blow their first few opportunities of the season because they're too hyped up, become impatient and blow an opportunity. Sometimes, you never get another chance. I suggest you get out and engage your hunting skills before the season. Practice spotting, tracking and especially stalking. That way, on opening morning you'll hunt as well as you normally would on the last day of the season.

Guy shows off his bird. Notice the low ridge to the back and left. We spotted both deer and antelope right there.

Spot 69: **Isolated Ridge**. This spot is located directly to the north of Spot 68 three miles south of the Nebraska-Colorado border. Once again you will hunt a wide rocky area with ridges to your left and right. Work the ridges, remembering to stay downwind of the deer that bed on the sides of the hills.

Guy:

This entire area can produce huge mule deer. It's just a matter of catching them on public land. One day Craig Fishel (alias "Fish") and I were heading out Highway 14 to do some pheasant hunting. Just as we crossed Pawnee Pass west of the town of Sterling and about a mile from Pawnee Grasslands, I spotted some huge animals in a wheat field to the north. I couldn't believe my eyes. I yelled to Fish, "Holy cow, what are elk doing way out here!" There were antlers sticking up everywhere. We immediately pulled over and put the binoculars on those massive heads. I then said, "You're not going to believe this. Those are mulies." "No way," he said. So I handed him the bino's and he gasped in amazement.

A few minutes later, as we turned up the road just to take a better look at the deer, we were forced to a screeching halt so we wouldn't run over a herd of antelope darting across the road. Ignoring the antelope, I glassed a mule deer out in the field and honest to God, I think it would have been a new world record. I can't prove it (Fish is my only witness and he didn't get his nickname for telling "small" stories), but his rack was enormous. It was nontypical and must have had 40 points on it. And I guarantee it was every bit 40 inches wide. There were several other deer in there that would be world class, but that one in particular was just unbelievable. Although this particular animal was on private land, I thought it worth mentioning. Deer are migratory, and more than likely, he spends some of his time on public land. If nothing else, his genes are spread out in the herd. You might get lucky and bag one of his overgrown offspring.

Pawnee National Grasslands

(Reprinted from Pawnee National Grasslands map)

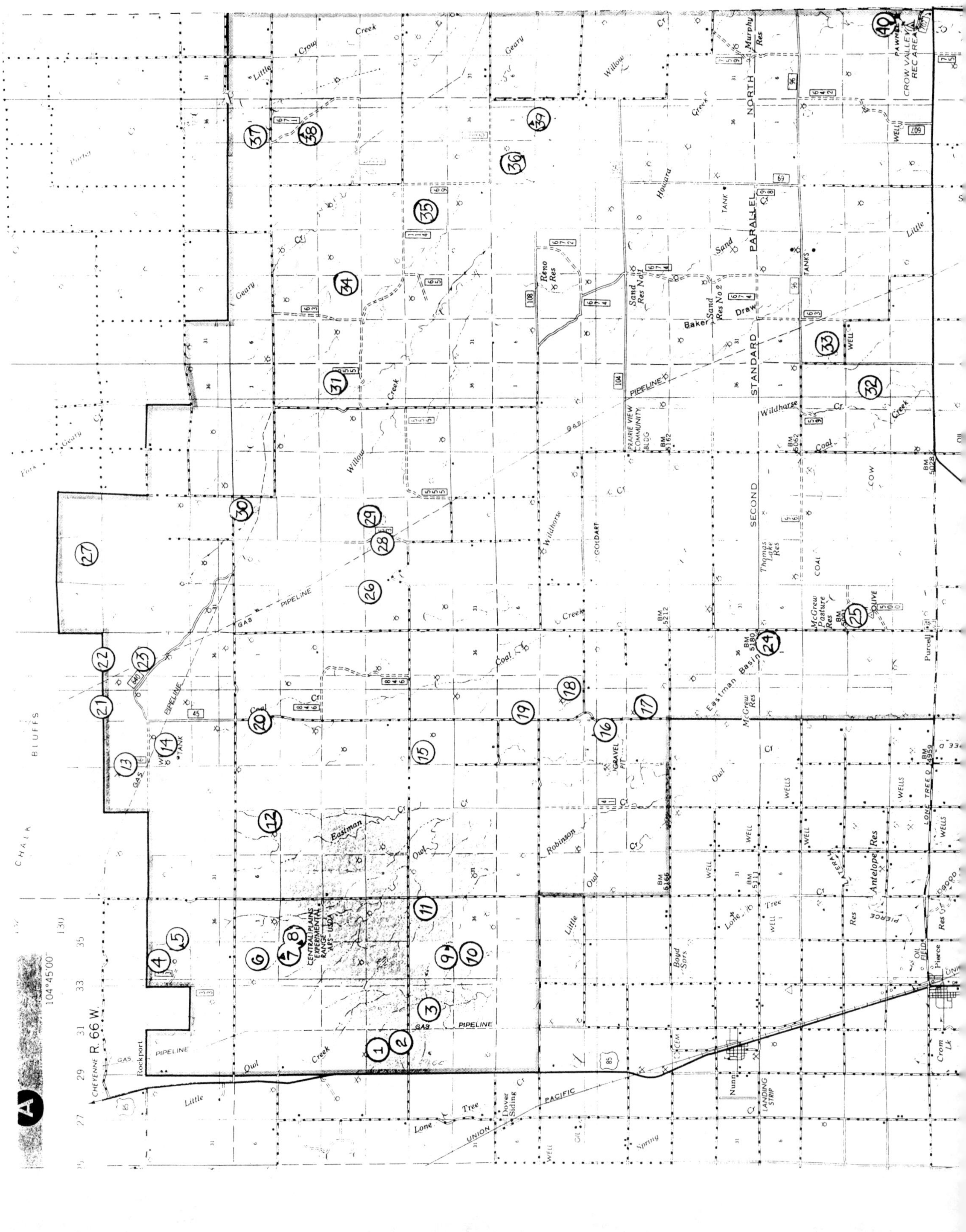

Pawnee National Grasslands

(Reprinted from Pawnee National Grasslands map)

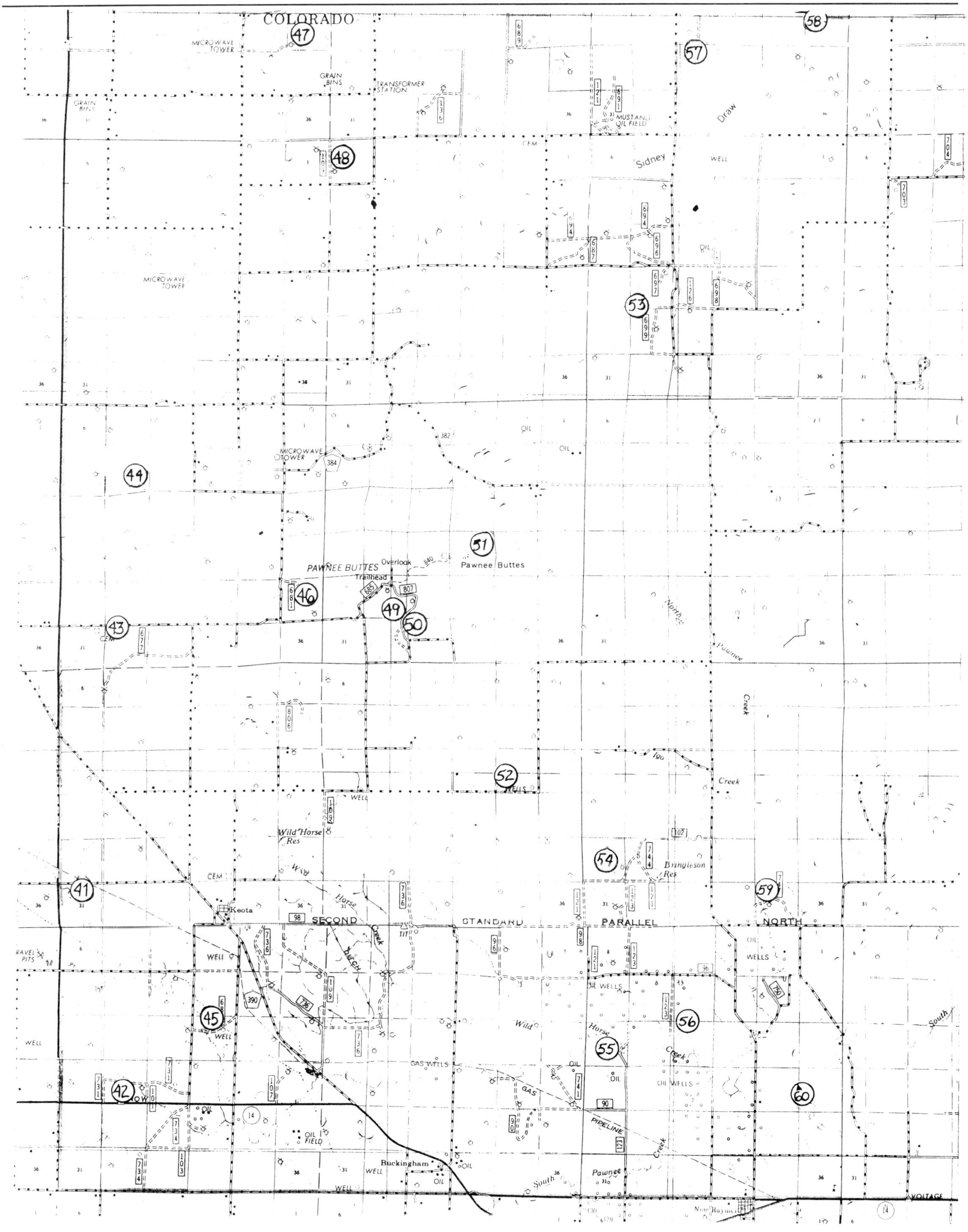

Pawnee National Grasslands

(Reprinted from Pawnee National Grasslands map)

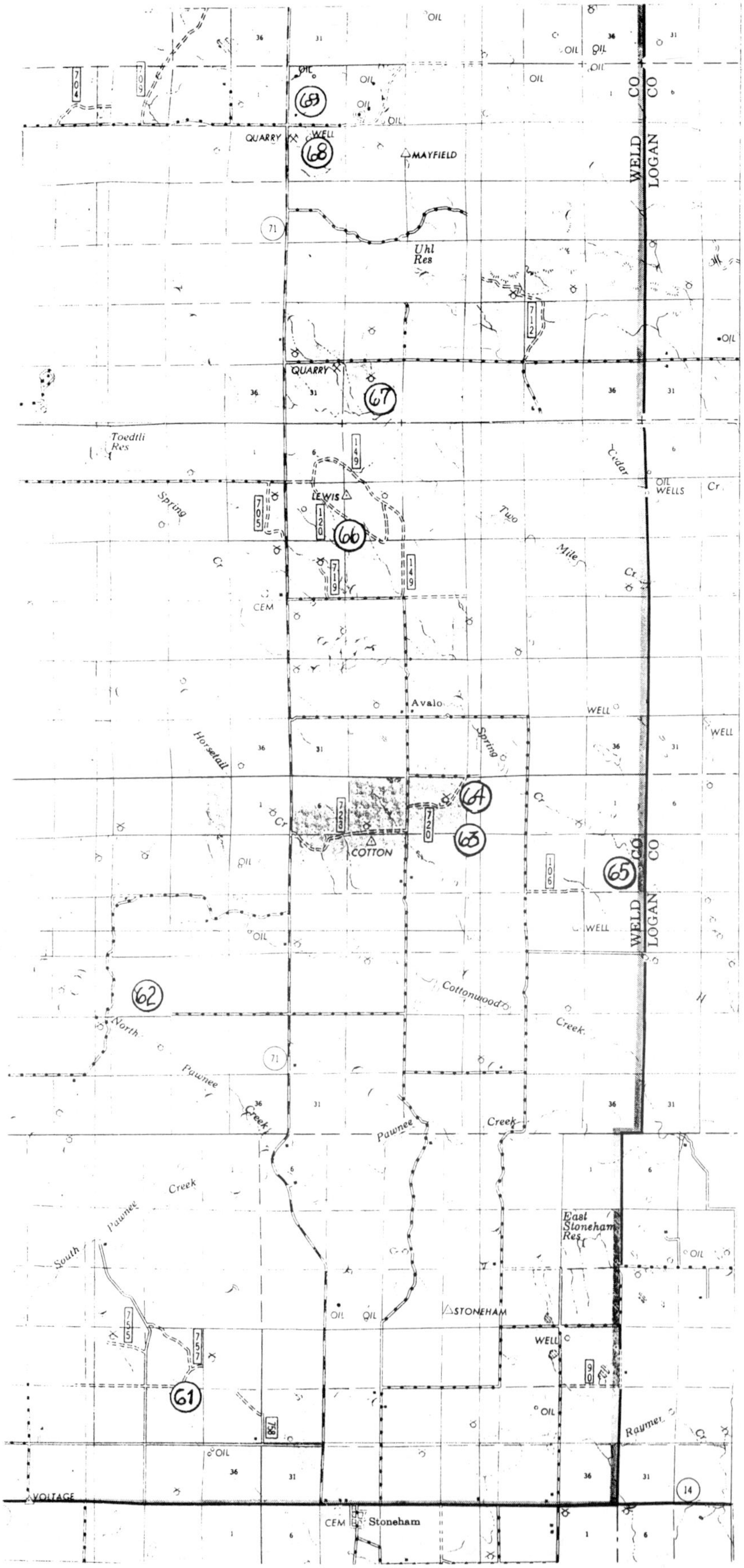

Pennock Pass

Big Game Hunting Unit (s): 19

How To Get There:

Head west out of Fort Collins around Horsetooth Reservoir, through Masonville, then up Buckhorn Canyon. Stay on the Buckhorn Canyon road until you get about two miles before the top of Pennock Pass. This area is located right between West Pine Mountain and East White Pine Mountain.

How To Hunt This Area:

We spent a lot of time 4 wheeling into this area one summer. We didn't do a lot of hunting in there, but probably should have. It's pretty high in elevation, around 10,000 feet. There are a lot of lodge pole pines and some intermittent aspen stands. Because the country's so rough, stick to the old logging roads where you can cover more ground. If you keep your eyes open, you'll be surprised at how many deer you'll spot in the thick brush. The bottoms of the hollows have a lot of water and lush green vegetation. Small groups of elk hang out there. Walk along the logging roads and listen down each hollow for elk bugling or cow calls. There's hundreds of hollows and elk could be in any one of them. If you do hear them, move down along the ridge, making sure the wind is not blowing to them. They seem to pick out one spot where there's water and feed there for weeks or even months. If you get on them, they're not likely to move off very far.

Because deer and elk see in black and white, the use of shadows as cover is extremely important. Notice how the hunter in the bottom right side of this picture blends in with the trees by staying in the shadows.

Spot 01: **South Face Of West Pine Mt**. Turn off Buckhorn Canyon Road and take Road 100 to the end. Driving down that four wheel drive road we nearly ran over two extremely nice trophy mule deer with very black looking racks.

Spot 02: **West White Pine Mountain Saddle.** After hunting most of the day for the deer mentioned in the previous spot, we returned to this area to set up a camp. Right there we spotted a herd of eight to ten elk. There was at least one four pointer and a raghorn with them. They moved off when we got close. We tried to move in on them but to no avail. We think they moved to the north side of the mountain which was very steep. We didn't want to walk down into that big canyon because we didn't have much time to hunt. Nevertheless this is a good "sleeper" area. Some day, someone will pull a big trophy out of there and it will become famous and the next season it will be full of hunters .

Pennock Pass

(Reprinted from Roosevelt National Forest map)

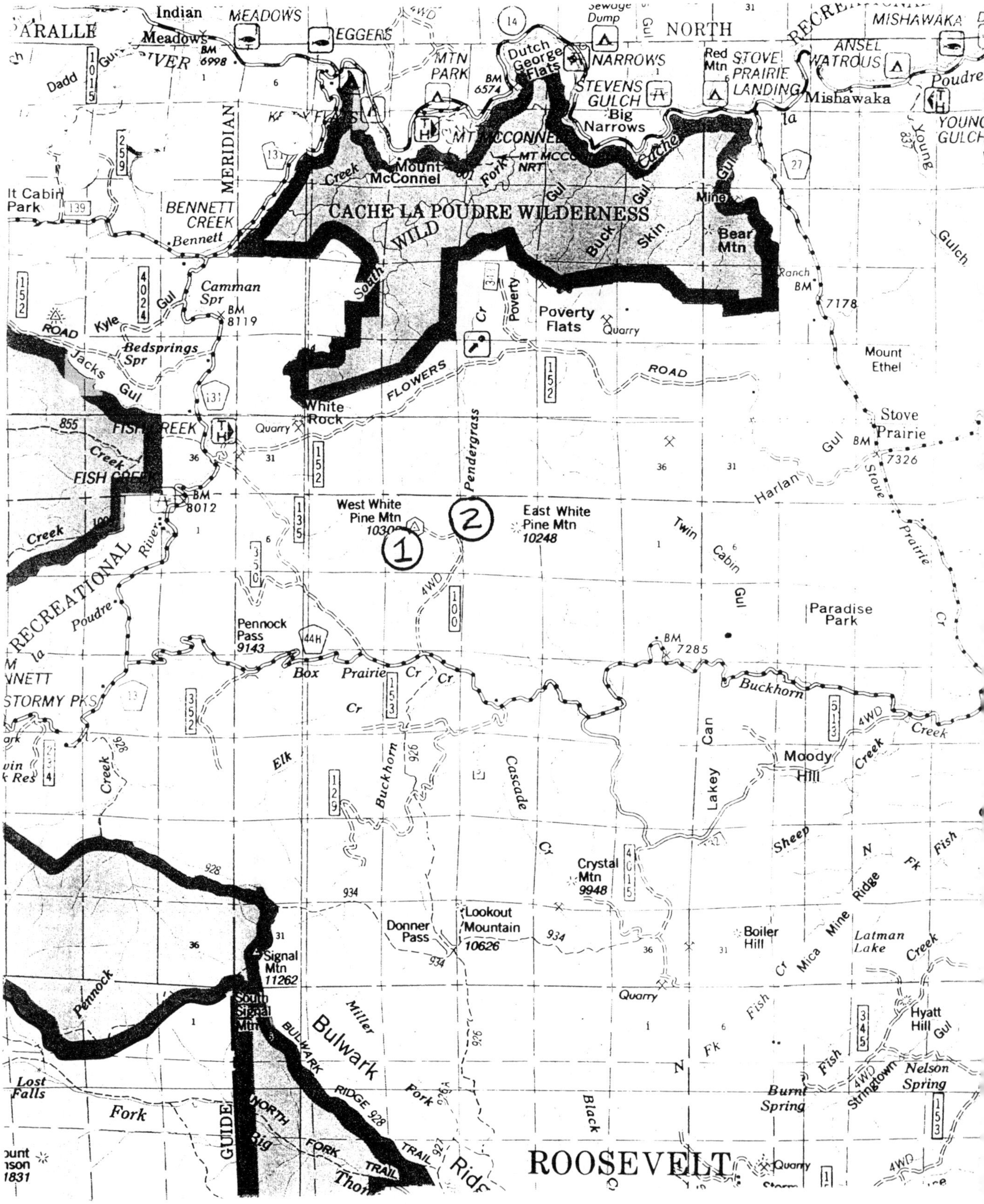

PENNOCK PASS 3-D MAP

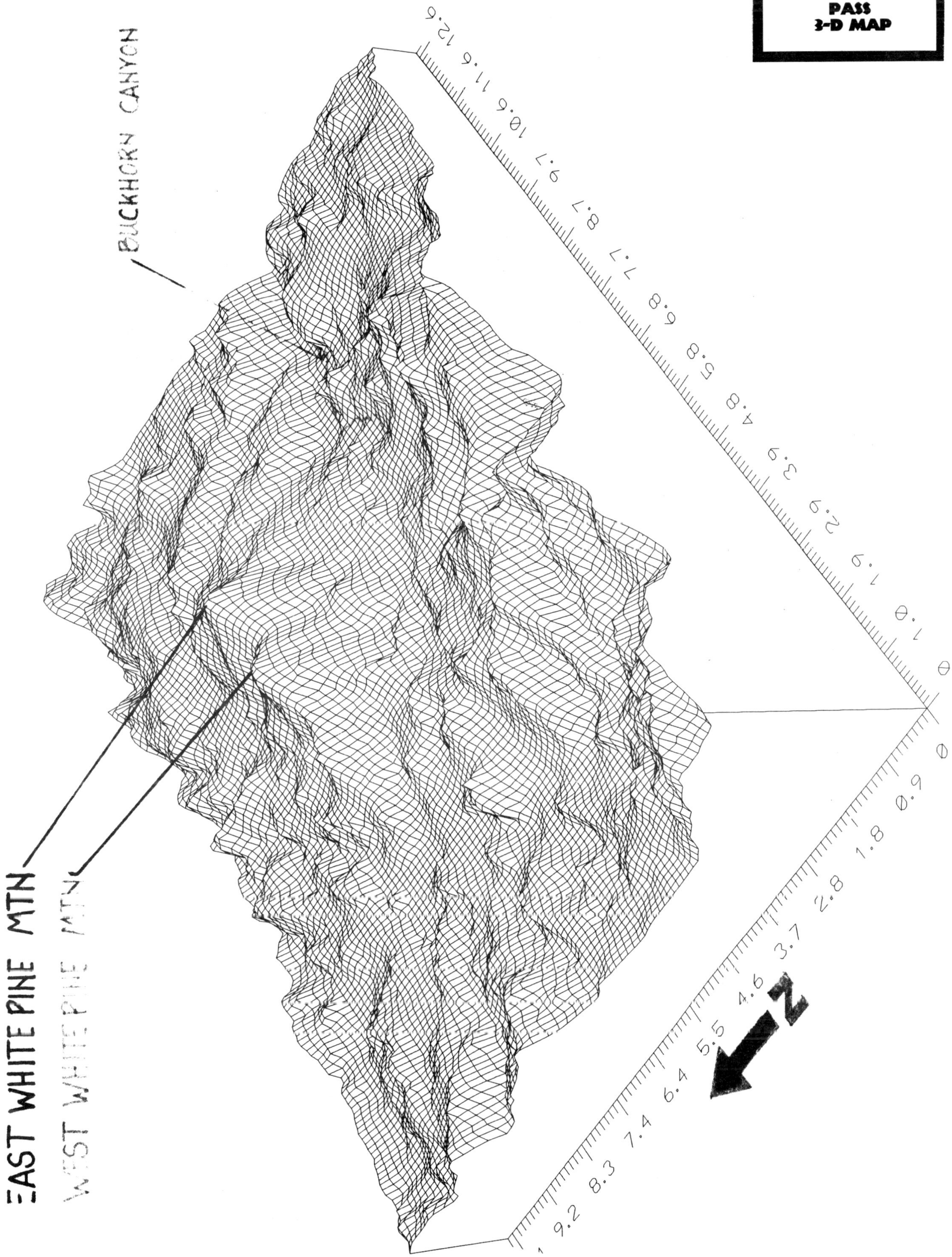

Phantom Canyon

Big Game Management Unit(s): 59, 581

How To Get There:

Just east of Canon City, take Road 67 north from Highway 50. The road runs along the bottom of the canyon all the way to Cripple Creek.

How to Hunt this Area:

Note:

A word of caution. In this area it's difficult to tell when you are on public land and when you are on private land. Observe all signs and keep a good map handy.

Deer in the Pinion-Juniper of lower Phantom Canyon.

At the bottom of the canyon the vegetation consists mostly of pinion and juniper trees. Deer are the primary game species down there. As you get farther up, on the ridges you will find more aspen and dark pines which is better elk habitat. The lower parts of the canyon are extremely dry and very steep. We've run into hunters over at Beaver Creek who complained that although lower Phantom Canyon was good hunting, it was too steep for them to hunt. Unfortunately, in Colorado, if you are willing to hike longer and harder and hunt areas other people don't want to hunt, you are going to see more game and get more game. Just get into shape if you want to hunt Phantom Canyon.

The tactics of hunting Phantom Canyon are quite simple. Along Eight Mile Creek which runs in the canyon bottom, are meadows. When they are undisturbed, you can find deer in the meadows in the early morning and late evening. They move back up the hillside into the brush at first light. As hunting season comes into full swing, they only come to water at night or find alternative waterholes up in the gullies. You either need to find a waterhole up there, or pattern the deer as they come back from the creek, and set up an ambush.

The deer will often sit on a ridge overlooking the creek and watch for hunters coming up the gullies. If you can walk a ridgeline and come from behind or above, you may catch them bedded down and get a shot as they run down the side of the gully.

Higher up the canyon there are good spots for elk. Up there, your tactic should be to walk the ridgeline above the canyon and wait for game to be pushed up to you by hunters who come in late.

Spot 1: **Switchback**. Driving up Road 67, before the first tunnel and right after a sharp switchback, you'll see a gully to your left. Walk northwest up that gully. It will drop back down into another creek known as either Six Mile Creek or Four Mile Creek. It's labeled differently, depending on the map. It's a good spot that gets very little hunting pressure.

Spence:

There's a funny story to go with that sharp switchback. You can't really tell that it's a switchback as you are driving up. It just appears that a little ridge is blocking water running down from a gorge on the other side. I got out of my truck and looked at it, thinking that if water was running down and being blocked up, it would be a good place for hunting. I saw some people getting ready to hike up there and I thought they must know what was behind the ridge. So I asked, "Do you know what's up there?" A short, fat balding man answered me really belligerently by saying, "I guess what's up there's up there." I thought, "What a jerk!" I looked at his license plates and saw that he was from Indiana.

Anyway I ignored him, jumped the creek, and headed for the tip of the ridge. I was in pretty good shape but it still took me ten minutes and I was breathing heavily when I topped the ridge. I looked over the side and there was the road circling back around right below me. You never would have known.

I hurried back down off of the hill to my truck. The guy from Indiana was finally ready to hike. He had a walking stick he had pulled out of the bushes and was carrying a pretty big backpack. I figured he was planning on spending the entire day hiking up that gorge on the other side of the ridge. I thought of telling him he was wasting his time, but didn't. I figured he deserved the hike considering the "attitude" I got from him. I watched him hike up, huffing and puffing, and through my binoculars could see this look of bewilderment on his face as he looked back down on the road.

Spot 2: **Pretunnel Dry Creek**. Before you drive through the first tunnel on the right hand side you'll notice a dry gully going up the eastern side of the canyon. There is a little spot where you can pull off. You will have to cross the creek to hunt. But if you walk up that gully, you will see deer.

Spot 3: **Post Tunnel Wet Creek**. On the other side of the first tunnel on the left hand side is a pulloff at the mouth of a gully that has water in the bottom. You can walk the gully northwest paralleling Eight Mile Creek. It's brushy in the bottom with a lot of big rocks, but it's a great spot for deer. They'll go there to escape hunting pressure in Phantom Canyon.

Spot 4: **Holbert Mountain**. Driving up the road you will see a bridge that looks like a trestle. The bridge forms part of a steep switchback that goes farther up Phantom Canyon. Right at the base of the hill going up to the bridge and the turnoff to Holbert Trail, on your right is a little gully that heads up to the base of Holbert Mountain. It goes all the way up to the saddle that divides this gully from West Mill Creek. This is an excellent deer spot. You'll be hunting in the saddle we talked about in the section of this book on Beaver Creek. If you don't remember, a group of soldiers from the Fort Carson Army Base saw over 500 deer a day by that saddle. The reason there are so many deer up there is that they get pushed up from Beaver Creek, Phantom Canyon and East Fork.

Spot 5: **Holbert Canyon And Holbert Trail**. Right before the switchback in the road and the trestle-like bridge is a gate on the right hand side of the road. Go through the gate and down into the creek bottom to the trailhead. Walking up the trail you are almost assured to see numerous deer.

Spot 6: **East Fork Creek**. From the previous spot, continue walking up Holbert Canyon along the bottom of the creek. It's great for deer and elk hunting.

Spot 7: **East Fork West Side**. From Holbert head straight north along the creek bottom. When you get to the fork take the left tributary up the mountainside. You will come out by the top of the mountain where you are almost assured to see deer and elk.

Spot 8: **Nipple Mountain View**. Walking up the east fork you will come to a fork in the trail. Take the gully to the right. Walking this route will really get you up to the isolated areas on top. You'll be hunting an area that is bordered by private property and consequently, access by other hunters will be extremely limited. You should be able to see Nipple Mountain to the northwest.

Spot 9: **Trestle Creek Bottom**. Where the road crosses East Creek by the trestle-like bridge are some meadows along the bottom of the creek. Just to the west on the hillside are a number of deer trails and winter elk trails coming right down to the creek. They probably won't be in there during the day, but you can trace the trails back up into the mountains and set up ambush spots.

Spot 10: **Glenbrook East**. Driving up the road you will see a sign that says "Glenbrook Elevation 8,059 Feet." To the right is a ridge that provides good hunting for deer, and for elk in the late season. There are game trails all over the hillside through the scruboak and bushes. Work your way up the ridge at first light and look for game moving up from below you. Later in the day, walk the ridge and look for bedded animals that will be watching the gullies below.

Spot 11: **Phantom Canyon West Gullies**. As you are going up the canyon on the right hand side are a number of gullies heading straight up to the ridgetop. A good strategy is to get up on the ridge and let the other hunters who are hunting in the bottom of the canyon push the game up to you. When you get up there you are going to be a few miles west of Holbert East. Anywhere up there is good hunting. The ridge still has snow late in the spring so it's going to have lush vegetation which really attracts a lot of game.

Spot 12: **Glenbrook West**. One hundred yards up from the Glenbrook sign is a gully going up to the left among rolling hills of scruboak and pine. Park at the bottom. We got stuck on the hill going up, bottomed out on a rock, tore up the bottom of our truck and only saved ourselves a 50 yard walk. Aside from our bad luck, this spot is great for deer and late season elk. The only problem is it's hard to tell if it's private or public land. On the map it looks like there's a little of both. We even asked a local, and he said he didn't know, that it was impossible to tell up there. It's not posted so use your own judgment.

Spot 13: **South Nipple Mountain**. Part of this mountain is privately owned, specifically the north side. But the south side is BLM land and there is a spot where you can park just past mile marker 20. If you head straight west along the base of the mountain you can walk all the way to East Fork Creek and North Fork Creek (make sure you stay in BLM land). That walk will take you into a really remote area. You can walk for four hours straight west before you hit a major road. There are a lot of elk and deer in there and they won't be used to seeing humans.

Phantom Canyon

(Reprinted from USGS Pikes Peak map)

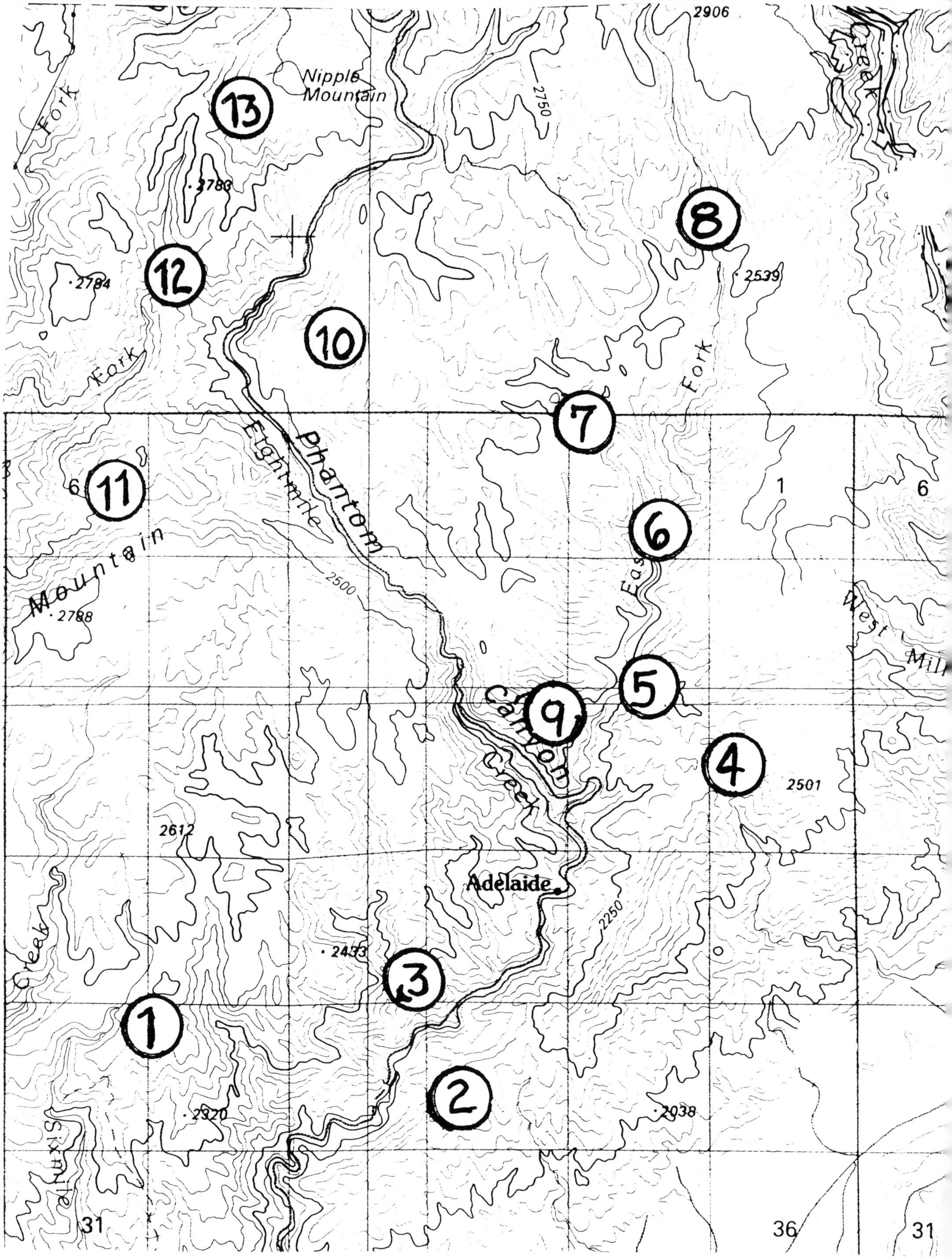

PHANTOM CANYON 3-D MAP

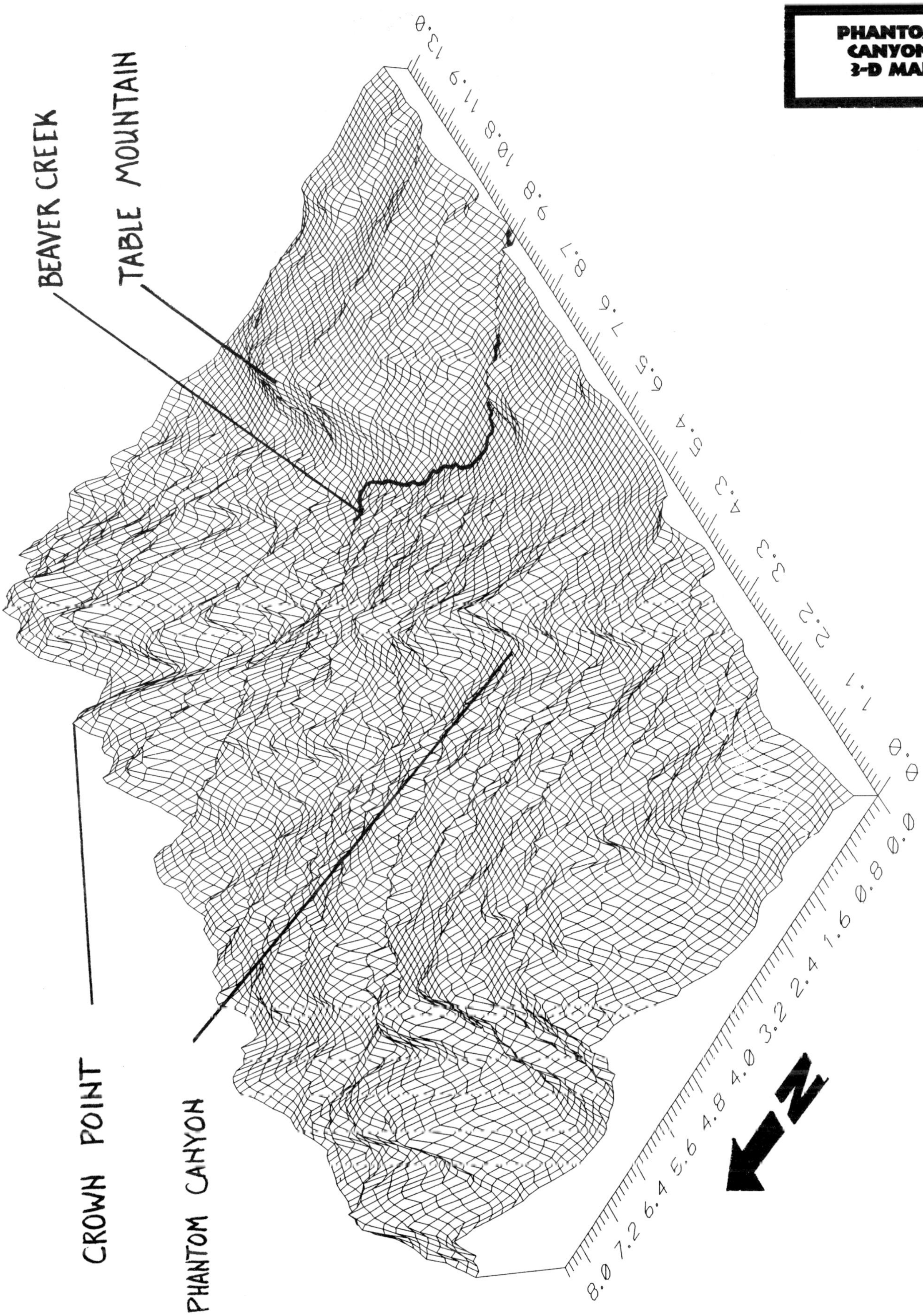

Pingree Park

Big Game Hunting Unit(s): 19, 8, 191

How To Get There:

Take Highway 287 northwest out of Ft. Collins. Then take the Highway 14 exit west up the Poudre Canyon. Just past Kelly Flats take Road 131 west toward Bennet Creek.

How To Hunt This Area:

Although you may find elk in this area, it's primarily a trophy deer area. The terrain consists of dark timber broken by grassy meadows where game feeds at night. It's heavily hunted and your tactics should be adjusted accordingly. Sit in saddles where game can be pushed past you by other hunters. Also, find areas that are hard to get to and you will find pockets of deer that have been pushed there by the hunting pressure. Most important, don't walk in the open fields. The deer watch the fields all day long sitting about 50 yards back in the woods. Walk a little bit farther in than them with the wind always in your face. Also, as the season progresses you will find more and more deer on the bluffs overlooking the Poudre River where they are pushed by heavy hunting pressure.

Spotting with binoculars works somewhat. But by far the best tactic is to walk along the established deer trails. They move through the thick pines from one meadow to the next. Keep in mind that by imitating the movements of deer versus the movements of humans, you can get close to the deer despite the heavy hunting pressure.

Spot 01: **Deer Crossing.** Just before Bennet Creek Campground, Road 131 makes a sharp turn along the base of a steep hillside. Right at dusk, from the road we've frequently seen large mule deer running up that hillside to the meadow above.

Spot 02: **East Ridge Gullies.** Take Road 139 past Salt Cabin. Just past the forested hill to the right the terrain will open into fields. Take the first small (unmarked) road going up the hill to the north. You will park along a flat spot at the base of the ridge to the north. A little way up the side of the ridge you'll find open fields which were formed as a result of a forest fire. That burned out area and the excellent forage it provides is what draws all the game to this spot. Walking along the base of the ridge heading to the east, you will cross the mouth of three small gullies running up the side of the ridge. The middle one, which is the largest, is the one you should take. Stay on the east side of the gully until you reach a small rocky outcropping where the hill levels off for about 100 yards. A major deer trail comes right past the rock then heads down into the gully. Sit on the rock and wait. If any deer are coming through there, they'll come right past you.

Spence:

> I've seen deer on that knob every time I've walked up the gully, and I've been there spring, summer and fall. Years ago, a buddy of mine was sitting there when several deer came down the trail and stopped right in front of him. The reason they stopped was that they were looking down into the gully and across to the other side for hunters before they headed down. He actually had time to rest his 30-30 on the rock to shoot a beautiful 4 X 5 mule deer.

Spot 03: **The Rock.** Instead of heading east along the flat area discussed in the previous spot, head northwest up the hill to the open field above. A little farther up you'll see a huge rock knob where you can sit and get a good view of the entire valley. It's an excellent spot from which you can watch deer movements.

Spence:

> I saw a guy sit up on that rock for three straight days, from dawn to dusk. It paid off. Three bucks crossed over from Mineral Spring Gulch one evening and came right past his position. He took a huge 5 X 5 buck while his partner took a 3 X 4. He jumped up and down yelling "a five pointer, I got a five pointer." His reaction was more the release of a lot of tension than anything else. He had come up with an ambitious hunting strategy that after a while, he was beginning to question. He had to go back to camp every night and listen to the other guys talk about the deer they had seen while walk hunting. The only story he could tell was that he sat on a big rock all day and saw nothing. But he came out with a trophy of a lifetime.

Guy:

> There's always someone who's going to tell you you're doing something the wrong way, or that you can't do it at all. Don't listen to them. First of all, hot new hunting methods start with someone doing something that other people were too conservative to try. Second, don't listen to the voices of doubt, including the ones in your own head. If we had listened to all the "cannot" people in our lives, we would never have gotten as much game as we have.
>
> There's one really good example of this I can think of. Last turkey season we were working a heavily hunted wildlife area down by Canon City. From the hill above the spot where all the hunters parked, we watched most of them leave the woods way before they should have and return to their cars. We kept hunting and went on to blow a few chances at gobblers. But at least we were still trying. When we returned to the parking lot, they were all standing around telling the typical "belly aching" stories of people who can't stick with it. They said the turkeys were too elusive, that too many people hunted the area, that the peak gobbling had already

passed: that there had been a big die-off over the winter....etc., etc., etc. We have a saying for those types of hunters, "miserable attitudes love company."

Unlike them, we stuck with it. Spence practiced his hen calls all week. The next weekend we came back and he whipped 4 big toms into a gobbling frenzy. Plus, he got two more toms down in the field below us going at the same time. Positioned between Spence and the flock, I shot an old 9 inch double beard as all 4 gobblers came running in.

Spence:

This goes to show you, that with the right attitude, a hunter can score, even in a poor spot.

Spot 04: **Springs Gulch Bottom.** We've seen a lot of deer come in and out of that gully. By walking the bottom toward the Poudre River, you can find trails crossing from one side to the other which you can follow until you find them bedded down.

Spot 05: **Springs Gulch Pass.** Sit up there and wait for deer to cross. One morning, we heard shots from the saddle as we moved up the side of the hill. A hunter was up there before the sun came up and capitalized on a deer we had pushed to him. We've also seen elk cross back and forth through there but it isn't considered to be very good elk hunting.

Spot 06: **Crown Point Gulch.** To get to this spot, walk directly west of Springs Gulch. The gulch has historically produced big bucks. Walk the ridge on the west side of the gulch.

Spot 07: **Sheep Gulch/Sheep Creek.** Head directly west of Crown Point Gulch to this spot. It is named for the bighorn sheep that live in the area, but it also has a lot of deer. It is rough walking, but worth the effort. This spot gets less hunting pressure than the gullies to the east, and is probably the best spot in the area during the third rifle season.

Spot 08: **Salts Cabin.** Hunt the wooded gully to the west of Salts Cabin. By moving very slowly and staying hidden, we got close to a herd of 28 mule deer down in there. We saw a whole group of hunters working the same gulch. But they were using very poor hunting tactics. They were walking right through the middle of fields instead of working the fringes. We saw them later and they told us they hadn't seen a deer all day long. It's no wonder.

Persistence is the name of the game in Colorado Hunting. Here spence displays a big tom he called in for Guy down by Canon City. All the other hunters had given up on the area. Although this turkey was not taken in the Pingree Park area, we have seen turkeys there as well.

Spence:

When hunting game that's really being pushed, work the area just like you're being hunted yourself. When you move across the terrain the way the deer move, you'll see more deer.

Spot 09: **North Dadds Gulch.** Head north past the ridge that parallels Road 139. The top flattens out. On the west side of Dadds gulch you'll find some wide open meadows bordered by dark pines. The closer you get to the bluffs overlooking the Poudre River, the more game you will see. Hunting pressure from below and from Road 139 really packs them in there. The deer sit about 50 yards back in the woods and watch the meadows during the day. By staying about 75 yards back in the woods we were able to sneak up behind numerous deer. They were always looking toward the meadow, expecting hunters to come from that direction.

Spot 10: **The Forks.** To the southwest of the fork in the road where Dadds Gulch Road and Salt Cabin Road meet is a little rocky ridge. The deer sit up there and watch the road below.

Spence:

One time, by staying hidden and moving slowly, I came to within 20 yards of a group of does that were bedded on the ridge. By moving just like them, I fooled them into thinking I was just another deer coming up the ridge. Suddenly, I saw them all tense up and point their ears toward the road below. A few minutes later, a hunter came up the road walking right out in the open. He never knew he had passed a group of deer, and probably unwittingly passed deer all day long.

Deer like these sit 50 yards back in the woods during the late morning and early afternoon watching the fields for approaching hunters.

Spot 11: **Big Hill Rockslide.** Head northeast from where Road 259 intersects Road 139 (the road east of Salts Cabin Road). On the west side of the big hill is a small rockslide area. On the northeast side of the rockslide is a rocky knob. Sit up there. A deer trail comes from farther up on the hill and heads west along the ridge and the fringe of the rockslide.

Spence:

While sitting there, a small group of deer came by me, including a three point buck. He was grunting like a mule, chasing a couple of does.

Spot 12: **Big Hill Top.** Walk northeast from where Road 259 intersects Road 139 (the road east of Salts Cabin Road). Circumvent the hilltop, looking for tracks heading down any of the numerous gullies. There are a lot of open areas up there with deer trails running from meadow to meadow. It is where the deer go when pushed from below.

Spot 13: **Upper Dadds Gulch.** At the end of Road 259, head northeast along the trail that drops down into Dadds Gulch. There are some large open grassy meadows to the west of the road. Sitting on a large rock in the evening, we watched herds of deer browsing in those meadows. They came from all different directions, moving from one clump of trees to another.

Spot 14: **Lower Dadds Gulch.** At the end of Road 259, take the trail down into the gulch toward the Poudre River. On both sides of the trail (actually an old logging road) thin slits of meadow branch off. They are the result of very limited woodcutting in the area and support a lot of deer.

Spence:

In 1982 I shot a three point buck down there. I was walking up one of the old cuts that branched out from the road. The deer were out there feeding in the middle of the afternoon. I don't think he expected to run into a hunter that far back.

Spot 15: **Seven Mile Creek.** From Rustic which is found along Highway 14 in the Poudre Canyon, head north on Road 69. One half mile up, take Road 225 heading west. The locals told us to hunt the ridge directly to the south of Road 225. They said deer are pushed there from all the other areas. One guy claimed that herds of deer even cross the highway to go to this spot when they were pushed by hunters in Dadds Gulch, Mineral Gulch, Crown Point Gulch and Sheep Gulch. We tried this spot and saw a lot of fresh tracks on the eastern hillside. We were walking west from the spot where Road 69 and Road 225 intersect. Unfortunately, it was snowing pretty hard and our field of vision was very limited.

Spot 16: **Manhattan Cemetery.** Drive up Road 69 from Rustic, then head west along Road 68C into the Forest Service land. Work the hill to the south toward Seven Mile Creek Road. This is another spot where deer are concentrated by hunting pressure along the roads.

Pingree Park

(Reprinted from Roosevelt National Forest map)

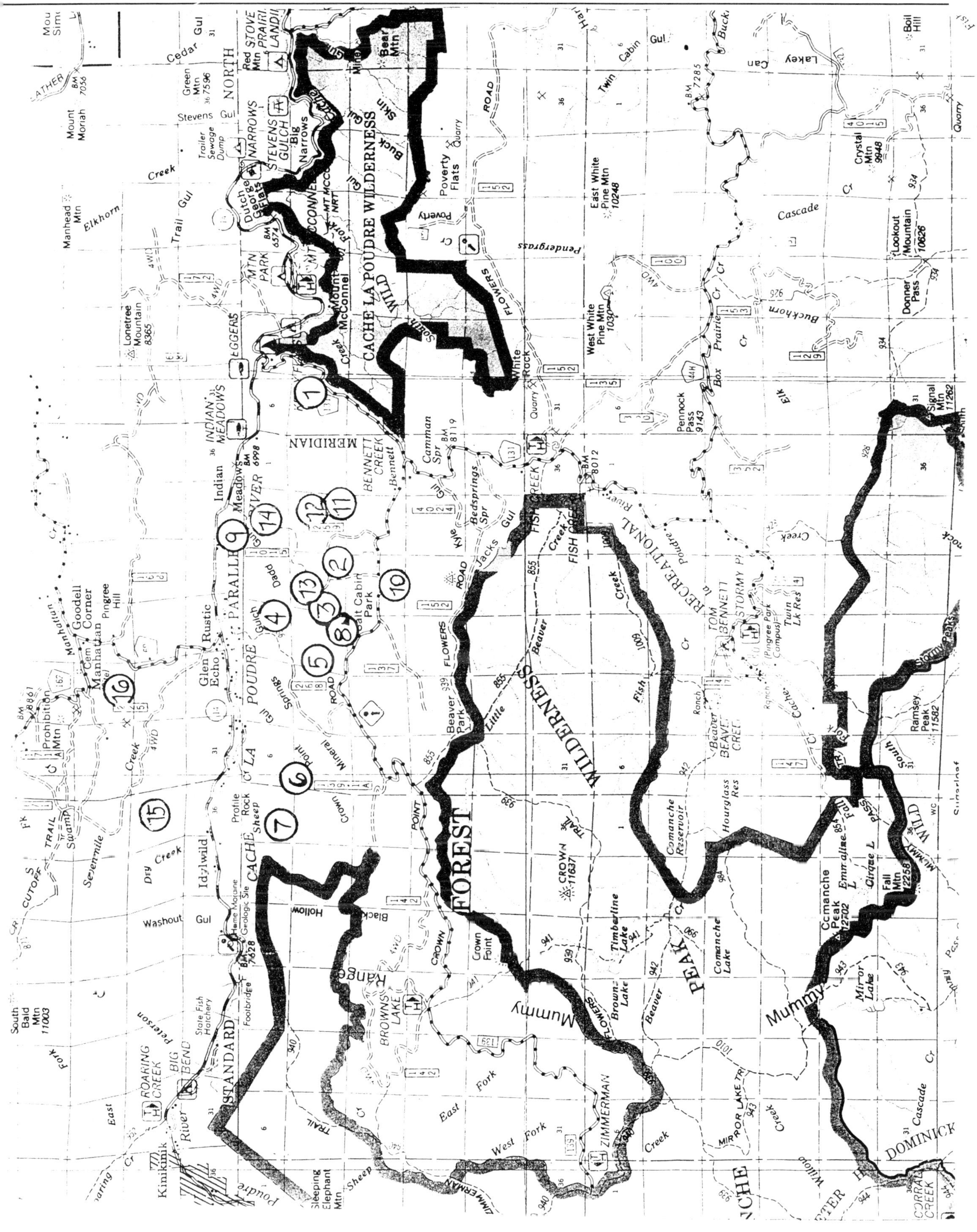

PINGREE PARK 3-D MAP

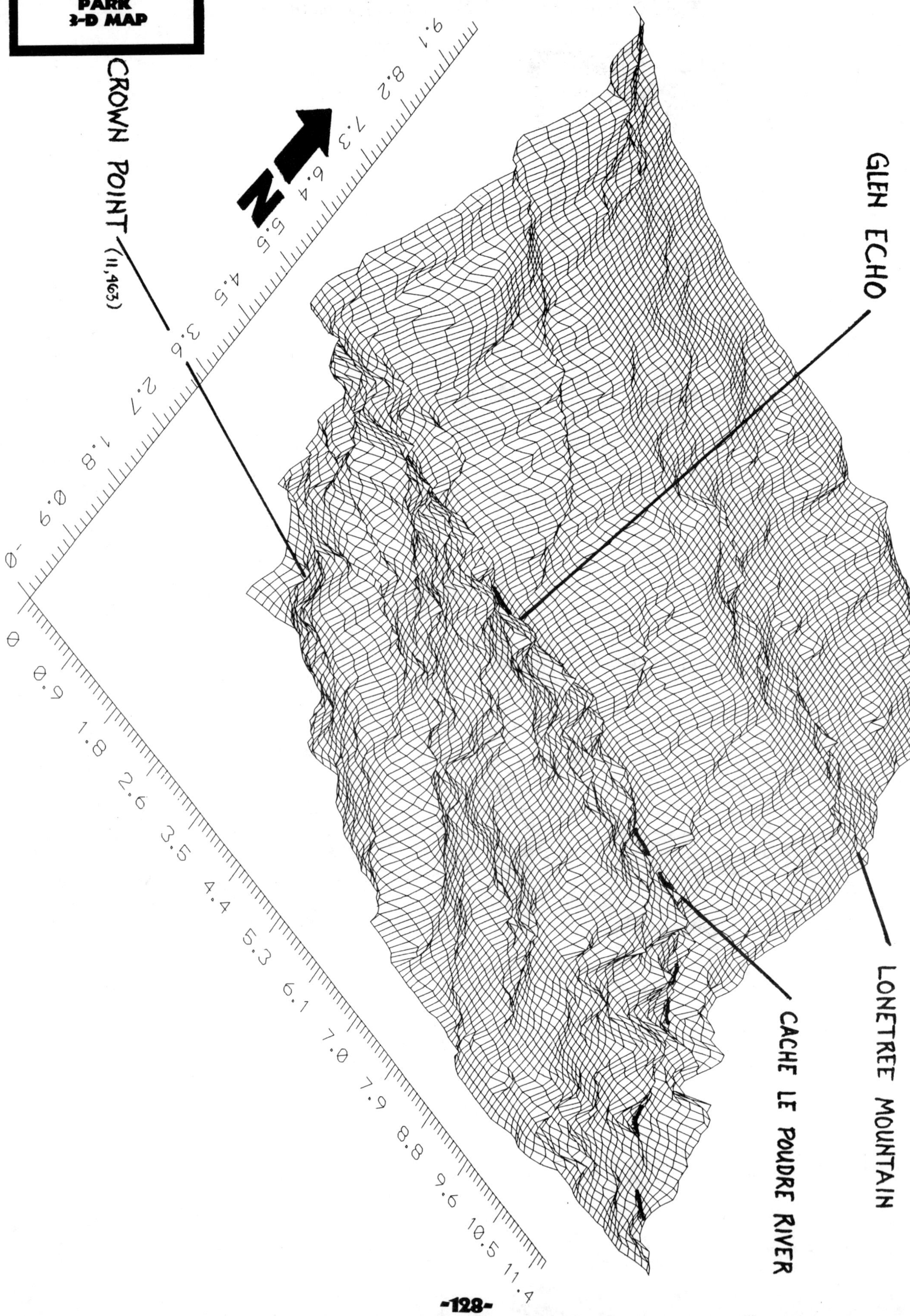

Powderhorn Primitive Area & Surrounding Areas

Big Game Hunting Unit(s): 66
How To Get There:

From Denver take Highway 285 to the town of Salida. Then take Highway 50 west to the town of Gunnison. Just west of Gunnison turn off Highway 50 and head south on Highway 149 to the town of Powderhorn.

How To Hunt This Area:

This area has several different types of terrain. In the lower elevations you will find wide open grassland. The hunting on the grassland is good during the winter or late rifle season when elk are moving out of the higher mountains that have gotten heavy snow. Those areas provide good viewing distances and very long shots.

As you move up in elevation you get into sage mixed with patches of aspen. The hunting in those areas is good in the second and third rifle seasons. The elk feed on the lush grasses among the aspen, moving from one clump to another. Look for trails between clumps of aspen.

Higher up you will hit grassy areas mixed with aspen and widely dispersed ponderosa pines. Those areas are good year round for deer hunting. We have often seen mule deer hanging around right underneath big ponderosas. They seem to like them. You may also find elk up in that type of terrain during the second and third rifle seasons.

Still farther up in elevation you hit the big forests of dark pine mixed with aspen. The dark timber and aspen which stretches all the way to timberline is where you will find the most elk. There are also some deer up there, but they generally prefer the lower sage areas.

Powderhorn has more accessible thick timber areas than it does areas above timberline. Therefore tracking and forest hunting is mostly what you are going to do. There are a lot of low lying hills and ridgetops which you can climb in less than one hour. There are good areas to hunt above timberline, but they are very difficult to get to. We have only hunted the big forests down lower. But with that much heavy forest, there are likely to be many elk on the higher mountains too.

Trophy mule deer like this one can be taken in the lower portions of the Powderhorn area.

In this area, one side of a ridge can be completely devoid of sign, while the other side is covered with tracks. Your most effective tactic would be to walk until you cut a fresh set of tracks, and follow them. More than likely, they will lead you straight to a spot that has even more elk. Then it's just a matter of working the area at the right time of day.

Spot 01: **Kelso Gulch**. As you are coming down Road 3034, about 4 miles south of the town of Powderhorn, the road makes a quick turn to the right. On the left you will notice a hunting camp right next to some aspens. There's a lot of open sagebrush dotted with clumps of aspen in there. Right by the camp we spotted a small herd of elk that were feeding from clump of aspen to clump of aspen. They were down pretty low considering it was September. A little farther up the road, the hill to the west gets steep, dropping down to the east fork of the Powderhorn River. Right where it gets really steep, we spotted a herd of deer on the left feeding among the ponderosa and sage.

Spot 02: **Ten Mile Springs**. Road 3034 ends at the entrance to Powderhorn Primitive Area. Take the trail down and walk along the creek next to the beaver ponds. We did not see any elk down there but there were a number of large buck mule deer which came down in the evenings for water. The elk only feed in there at night, and move back up onto the ridges before first light.

Spence:

> I ran into another hunter who swore he saw a 7 point buck down there. The buck was 130 yards out and he was hunting with a muzzle loader. He knew he probably wouldn't hit it, but shot anyway, figuring he might never see one that big again. He missed, and now his "one that got away" story has made it into our book. What was more amazing than his story was the fact that his beautiful girlfriend was out hunting with him, and she was more into it than he was. Where do you guys find these women?

Spot 03: **West Dempsey Gulch.** There is a trail that goes up the east hill away from Ten Mile Springs which doesn't appear on any maps. Take that up to the top. On top, a shallow creek runs north along the ridgetop forming a small bowl. That's Dempsey Gulch. Go straight into the woods to the east of the gulch and down the hillside.

Spence:

> While Guy bugled, I stalked to within 50 yards of a 5 point bull elk in this spot. The bull was raking the bushes up and down, stomping and snorting to every call Guy made. However, his body was hidden behind thick brush. I couldn't get closer because between me and the elk were large mounds of pine cones left by squirrels. They caused me to make too much noise when I tried to move in. The elk got tired of strutting

around and moved off before I could circle around for a shot.

Spot 04: **Dempsey Parks.** Head South up West Dempsey Gulch into the thick pines. To the east of the pines are some rockslides. You'll find many elk trails through the thick brush that borders the rockslides. Farther down the hill from the rockslides are elk trails crisscrossing the entire hillside. Down there we found some "smoking warm" elk dung. We were able to get one elk to answer our bugle down along one of the trails, but he was just passing through the area and kept going farther to the South.

Spence:

> I'm pretty experienced at finding my way around in heavy woods because I did a lot of turkey hunting in the Missouri Ozarks as a kid. But I actually got lost in this place for the first time in my life. The pines were so thick that it was impossible for me to get my bearings from surrounding mountains. After about an hour of stumbling around making a conscious effort not to panic, I was able to recognize an oddly shaped aspen I had seen coming in. I found the trail a few minutes later. After that, I started carrying a compass.

Spot 05: **Fish Canyon Ridge.** We ran into some ranchers who had been rounding up summer cattle back along Fish Canyon Ridge. They told us that there are a lot of elk back there. They took their horses up and got several elk to bugle back to them. But they were very reluctant to tell us anything else about that spot. This probably means that it's a lot better than they led us to believe. However, it's a remote area and hard to get to. If you are willing to hike you can get into some unspoiled territory back there. Horses would really be the way to go.

Spot 06: **Burnt Creek.** The upper part of the mountain west of Ten Mile Springs Campground is a very good area if you are willing to take about a 4 hour hike uphill to get to it. Right at the top there is a large high altitude pan-shaped valley (extremely remote) which is full of aspens. We heard a colossal elk fight up there - two bulls really going at it. But it was on the last evening we were hunting Powderhorn and we really didn't have the time to make the climb before it got dark.

Spence:

> There are instances in a hunter's life that leave an incredibly intense impression on your mind, one that you'll never quite shake. This was one of them. It had been raining most of the day (miserable hunting), but just as the sun went down red, it broke through the clouds. Looking up to Burnt Creek, we could see aspens that had just turned fall golden glistening bright and wet in the sun. They stood out against freshly fallen snow on the Calf Creek Plateau behind. At that instant, a lone elk bugled up in that remote valley, and another answered. More kicked in. They kept bugling, and bugling and bugling. Something in my head said, "That's the secret valley of the elk, go there and you'll never come back."
>
> But the sun went down and the moment passed. It wouldn't have been the same if I had gone there the next morning.

Spot 07: **Lower West Dempsey Gulch.** Take Road 3119 up to a point where you are just to the east and below West Dempsey Gulch. From there you can get out and walk directly to the west to hit the lower part of the gulch. The gulch is deep there and as you walk north it gets deeper. The bottom has thick foliage and undergrowth which is great feeding habitat for elk. We found elk trails crisscrossing from both sides. The terrain gets increasingly rugged as you walk north. Eventually you can walk no farther. Before the gully becomes impassable, on the last major rocky outcropping to the right we spotted a herd of deer that watched us walk past.

Guy:

> The one thing about hunting this spot is that you can't hear very well. Once you are down in that gully you will hear nothing.

Spot 08: **Above Cebolla Creek Campground.** When you go up Road 3119 to Spot 7, instead of going into West Dempsey Gulch, hunt the area directly to the east for deer. It's very open and grassy. We saw deer sign everywhere.

Spence:

> While getting ready to hunt there, Guy was reaching into the back of the truck to get his bow out when a chipmunk sprung straight up out of his backpack. Then it ran right over Guy to get out. This caused Guy to jump up and hit his head against a beam in the topper and roll around in the back of the truck as it ran across him. The chipmunk then scurried out of the truck and climbed a very tall ponderosa. This was kind of poetic justice because earlier I told Guy that I thought a chipmunk had crawled into the back of the truck at Ten Mile Springs. While I was in the back getting something, thinking any minute I was going to run across that chipmunk, Guy sneaked up, grabbed my foot and screeched loudly. This caused me to jump up and hit my head on the topper. It really served him right when the real chipmunk nearly attacked him.

Spot 09: **Rudolph Hill.** This area is open and grassy with widely spaced ponderosa dotting the hillside. There's a lot of very heavy deer sign on the hill. One way to hunt up there is to walk up the gully bottoms where there's very thick brush and green vegetation the deer like to browse. Or, you can get up on the ridge and look down into the gullies. It's probably best to place one person on each side of a gully and walk up the ridge parallel to one another until you kick something out. Be prepared to take a running shot.

Spot 10: **Swine Heart Ridge.** This is one of the most dramatic pieces of scenery in the area. The ridge looks like Half Dome at Yosemite National Park. There is a trail up the side that takes you through some very good deer habitat. It's supposed to be good on top as well, and from where we stood, it looked great for deer. It appeared to be level walking. Walk right along the edge and you'll see game.

Spot 11: **Back Rudolph Hill.** Going into the back side of Rudolph Hill (the road up Beaver Creek) the trail to your right will take you all the way up to the top of Rudolph Hill. This is also a good place to find deer.

Powderhorn Primitive Area & Surrounding Areas

(Reprinted from Gunnison National Forest map)

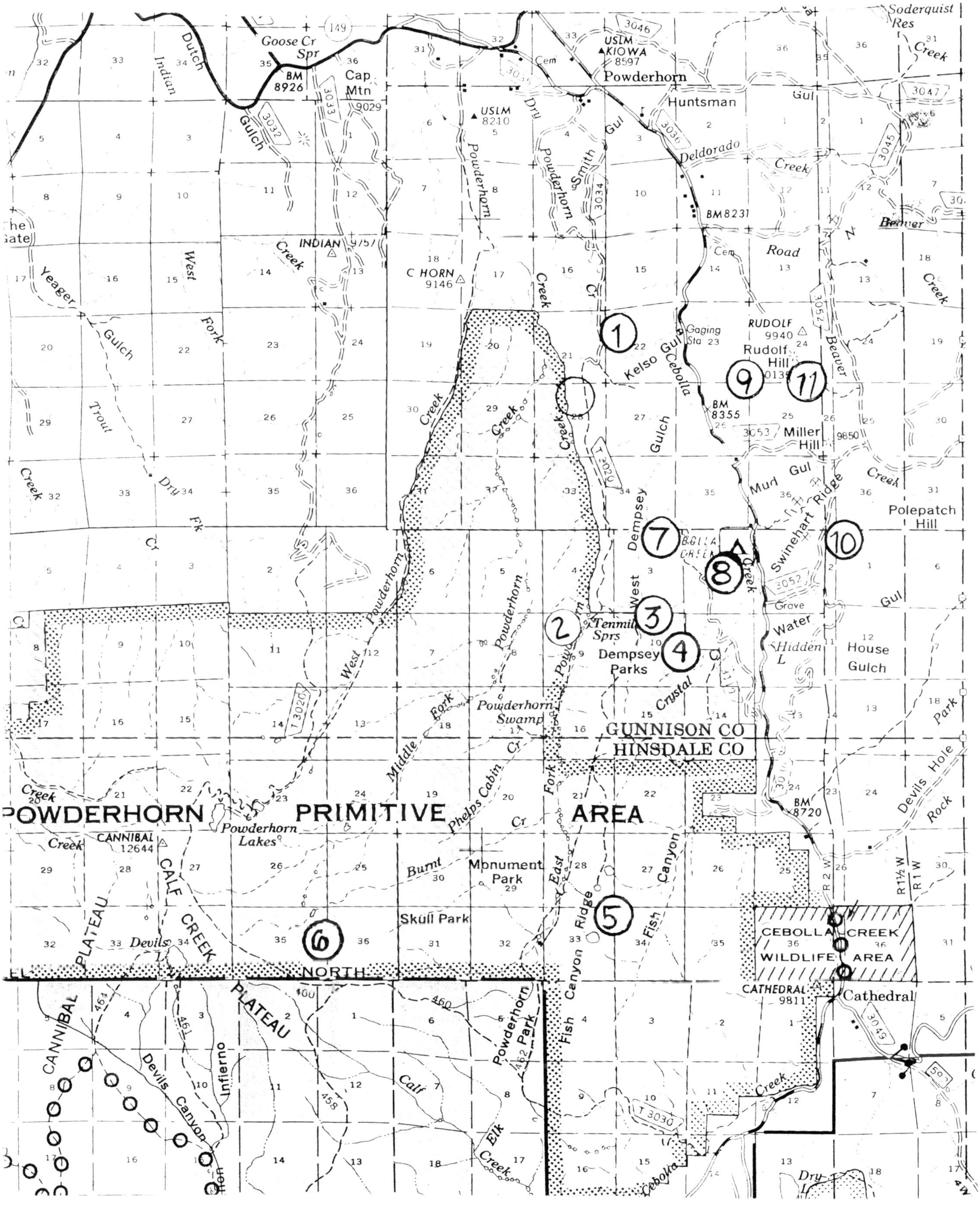

POWDERHORN PRIMITIVE AREA 3-D MAP

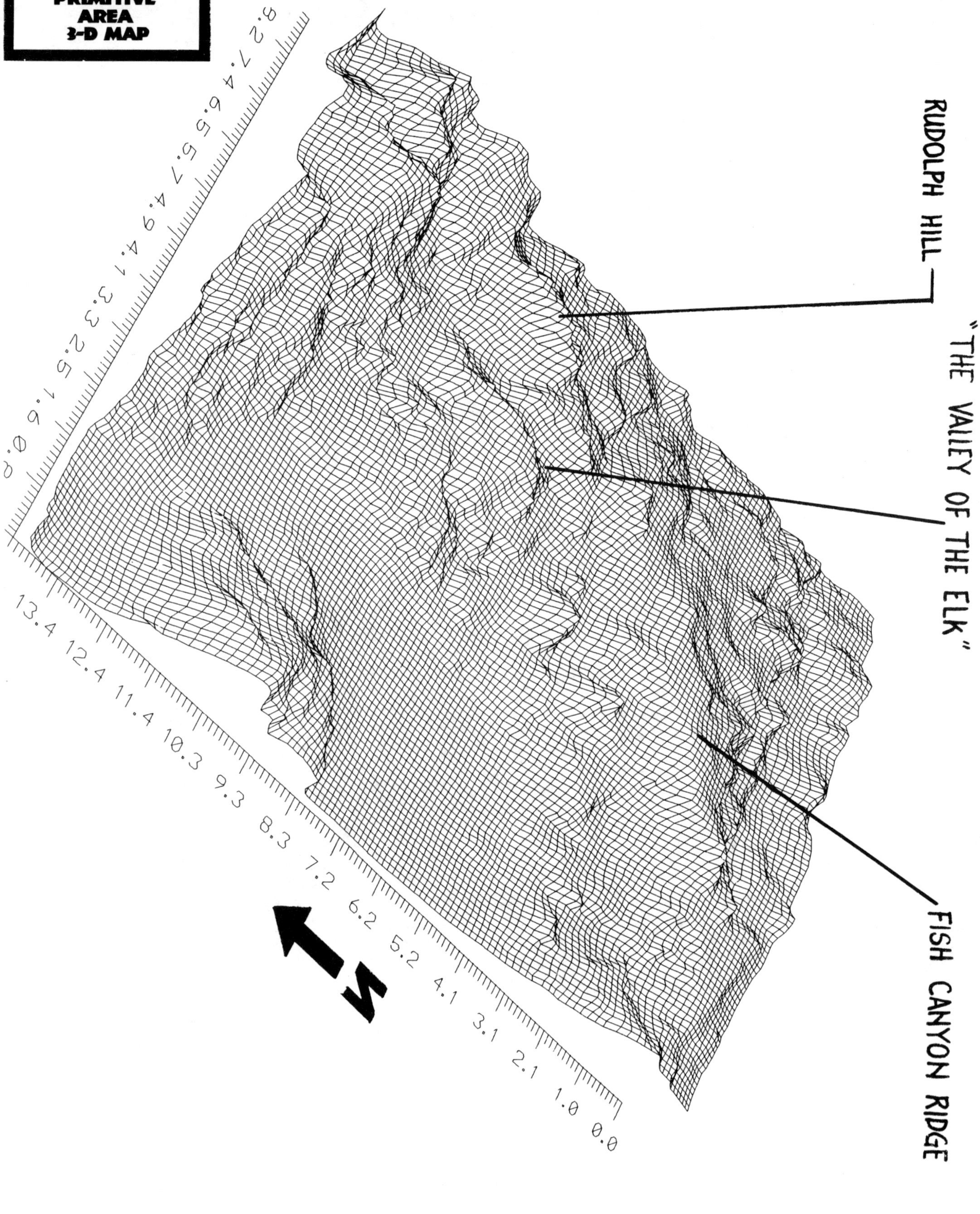

Rio Blanco/Piceance Basin

Big Game Hunting Unit(s): 22

How To Get There:

To get there take I-70 west from Denver to Rifle, Colorado. From Rifle go north on Highway 13 to Rio Blanco. From Rio Blanco head west up the Piceance Creek Drainage. Most of the areas profiled are to the south of Piceance Creek on the Roan Plateau.

Thick brush like this found in the Piceance Basin supports North America's largest deer herd.

How To Hunt This Area:

The Roan Plateau terrain is mostly rolling hills with steep gullies in between. Most of the hills are covered with sagebrush and scruboaks, except for the north faces where there are pockets of dark timber and aspen trees. Due to the wide open views this area affords, spotting and then stalking is by far the most effective method of hunting.

This area is home to the largest migratory deer herd in North America. It is known to Coloradans as "the deer factory." It produces sheer numbers as well as quality trophy bucks. If we had to rate it on a scale of 1-10, it would definitely be a 12. When we hunted there, we saw 150 to 250 deer a day depending on weather conditions.

Guy:

Spence and I had several arguments over whether or not we should put these spots in the book. It's Spence's favorite deer hunting area. I told him we had to, that we had to pull out all the stops if we wanted this book to be successful. I reasoned with him that because the area is so vast, and there are so many animals, it would not be affected if other people came in and hunted. This area will support thousands of hunters, I said. He finally said, "OK, I hope people appreciate just how good the area is they're getting."

Spence:

Hunting deer in this area is really more like hunting rabbits than deer. When we walked the hills, deer would pop up and run out ahead of us just like cottontails do back east. It happened all day long, from sunrise to sunset.

The way you successfully hunt this area depends upon the time of day you are hunting and the season that you are hunting in. Earlier in the year when it's very hot and dry, you'll have a lot of luck sitting in the saddles during the early morning and late evening. The animals will cross from one side of a ridge to another as they move from feed and watering areas to late morning bedding spots.

You can also road hunt in the early morning. While driving along the roads just at sunrise, we have often seen deer standing literally ten feet off the side of the road watching us drive by. Sometimes we stopped and the deer would just stand there, providing easy targets. However, we didn't see any real " wall-hangers " that close to the road during legal hunting hours.

During the hot part of the day, the deer will bed down underneath the scruboaks or underneath trees where they can see for a long way.

Guy:

Last year we found hunting to be very productive in the mid-afternoon. To hunt at that time of the day you'll need at least two people. Place your partner on a hill facing yours, and walk parallel to each other down a draw. As you move through the thick scrub, the deer on your side of the hill will sense danger and move from their bedding sites out ahead of you before you even see them. It's so thick that you usually can't see more than 30 to 50 yards ahead. Although you can't see the deer, your partner on the other hillside can see them as plain as day. You'll also see deer moving out ahead of him that he doesn't know are there. You can then signal each other to the deer. We used previously devised hand signals to put each other on the deer, but a hand held radio would also work. Try to signal your partner to where you anticipate the deer will go.

One time I really blew it on a monster buck when we were hunting this way. I was watching Spence walk through an area we call the "Backward Seven" (it's Spot 15 below). I literally saw the side of the hill explode with deer moving out ahead of Spence in every direction. I was directing Spence with hand signals to where several big bucks had run. There were also several other lesser bucks just standing still on the side of the hill trying to figure out what Spence was.

I then noticed one doe staring at something below her that I could not make out. I dismissed it as a large tree stump. But the way this deer kept looking down really got my attention. After further investigation and plenty of patience the "stump" moved its head. This massive buck was bedded less than 75 yards from Spence's location. Spence never saw this deer as I attempted to guide him to it because the scruboak was extremely thick. I guided him to within 20 yards, but the buck remained completely motionless. He was just sitting underneath a bush in complete shade, hoping to be overlooked. Obviously the buck knew Spencer was there but he was going to hold as tight as he could until the last possible moment. When I got Spencer to within about 10 yards the buck exploded, ran directly down the hill and up the side of the hill I was on. I ran down hill 50 or 60 yards trying to intercept the buck. I stopped and listened for the sound of the deer running up my side of the ridge. I moved a little farther down hill trying to see through the thick brush, looking to my right for legs sticking down from the bushes, or any other movement.

Spence:

Meanwhile, Guy's looking down at the bushes and I'm frantically trying to signal him. The deer had switched paths and was coming straight to him from the left rather than crossing the opening to his right. What happened next was a scene that had I brought a video camera, you would have surely seen the next week on one of those shows that pays for funny home movies. Guy came downhill around one side of a bush and the deer ran uphill around the same side. They nearly ran into each other. As I watched through my binoculars, the deer jumped straight up in the air with fright, and so did Guy. The deer ran so fast he looked like someone who has just jumped into freezing cold water and is trying to get out quickly. I fell down on the ground laughing. I laughed so hard my sides hurt.

Guy:

That deer came to within 3 yards of me. He was a 6 X 6 with about a 36 inch spread. I saw him coming an instant before he recognized me to be a human. He just kept coming and I thought I was being charged by some red eyed devil of a monster deer. I started to raise my muzzle loader more to avert the coming attack than to take a trophy deer. At that moment, he realized I was a human and jumped straight up in the air, twisted around and disappeared into the brush. It seemed like it happened in slow motion. I remember hearing a big snort as he twisted, feeling the wind on my face as he brushed extremely close, and smelling the strong smell of a big animal. An instant later, before my gun had even reached my shoulder, he was gone.

Many times while driving along small 4x4 roads in this area we have spotted bucks bedded on the sides of the hills. Those deer always provided exciting stalking opportunities when everything else was "slow". Last year, over the course of a week's hunt, we took numerous shots at deer this way. A lot of things can go wrong in archery hunting - namely arrows deflect off of tree branches, brushes and sage brush, even at close range. Eventually though, this paid off for us.

The elevation in this area is relatively high. As the season progresses the snow gets deeper up high which pushes the animals down to lower areas along the Piceance Creek drainage and other lower drainages. When the snow comes, you'll see far fewer deer up high, but many more elk. The elk will be the last ones to come out because they have long legs which allow them to walk through deep snow.

Guy:

I drove up there two years ago in the third rifle season and saw lots of nice elk racks coming out. I was up in there by myself and just was not comfortable with the whole idea of a coming snow storm, so I stayed only one day. Of course, I only had a deer tag, and saw hoards of elk. They were moving along the gully bottoms right out in the open. Just sitting up on a hill overlooking a drainage, I could have taken any one of a number of good sized bulls.

Spence:

An old timer down at Rio Blanco told me there are elk up on the plateau even in the summer. He told me to find the deepest "hole" I could that has water in it, and I'd find the summer elk. What he means by "hole" is the size of the drainage. Some are small cuts that drop down maybe 200 feet in elevation. Others are huge and drop down 500 feet or more. I tried hunting one of the deep holes. It was difficult to get down to the bottom, but I did find a lot of elk tracks down there around a waterhole.

Spot 1: **Little Creek**. As you come up the Piceance Creek road approximately 12 miles from Rio Blanco you will see a sign that says "Sprague Gulch." There's a ranch house on the left. You will cross the creek and follow the dirt road back approximately 18 miles to a cluster of hunting spots we have profiled. Last year, toward the end of the archery season, we drove in and hunted along Little Creek.

Guy:

While I circled around to the south side of Little Creek, my buddy Derek Doolittle went up Bear Run Creek and sat in an ambush spot. While Derek saw several big bucks, I encountered several does and lots of fawns which were bleating and making all kinds of noises. I was able to bleat to them and bring them to within about five yards of me. But I never saw the big bucks that Derek did from the other hillside.

Note:

We let Derek put in a little piece below regarding his encounter with some deer. Derek lives in North Carolina and comes out to hunt with us every year. He likes it so much that now he's planning on moving out to Colorado right after he gets married.

Derek:

I knew this was a hot spot when I began walking the area and saw deer in literally every bush. I selected a horseshoe shaped pile of brush as an ambush spot. I was on the side of a ridge among some aspen trees. When I first set up I nocked an arrow knowing I would see some game shortly. It was not long after that when I heard some branches crack behind me. Hoping it was not the does we spotted earlier, I moved my head slowly so I would not spook whatever was behind me. My heart nearly pounded out of my chest when I saw three bucks. One was a 3x4, one was a forked horn, and one looked like all the big trophy bucks I'd seen in magazines about hunting out west. This monster was a 5x5, easily Pope & Young. Hoping to get a shot off I did not move - feeling if I moved the bucks would be spooked and I would not have a chance at them later. I never got the chance to draw my bow that afternoon as I watched the bucks disappear over the ridge. The season was coming to a close in two days. I never saw those bucks again.

Spot 2: **Derek's "U" Shape**. We've marked the spot where Derek sat when he saw the big bucks. He said they came down off of Jack Rabbit Ridge and crossed a little road. The map indicates the road runs along a creek bed. It is not really a creek bed, or if it is, it's all dried up. Despite this, it's a great place to sit in the mornings or evenings or just walk through during the middle of the day.

Spot 3: **Middle Fork Boundary**. In this spot a trail/crossroad goes up around Bear Run Falls. Up there, the deer move on top of the ridge to cross between the saddles. We also found an abundance of elk sign in the area, and heard a few elk bugles coming from the private property to the south. Unfortunately, we couldn't lure them over to our side.

Spot 4: **East Middle Fork Point**. This spot is located just to the east of the Middle Fork right by the campground marker shown on the map. You'll be hunting in a steep little draw where a grove of aspen grows.

Guy:

Last year in this spot, Derek sat at the bottom and took a little nap as I circled up above and pushed about five or six deer down to him. The biggest buck was about a three by two. Derek woke up in time to take a shot but he didn't connect. That little pocket has quite a few deer.

Spot 5: **Upper Davis Point**. This spot is situated directly above Spot 2. You'll be hunting on the ridge where the big deer came from that passed so close to Derek. We have never hunted the ridge, but we've seen deer come off of it more than once. The ridge has a lot of scruboak growing on it. Falling acorns from scruboaks are one of the staple food sources for deer, especially in the fall. We've also heard there are turkeys in there.

Spot 6: **East Upper Davis Point**. This spot is located at the very top of a ridge right above where we camped last year. At the very top the vegetation opens up. There is no cover up there. From there the deer walk up through several saddles which provide them the shortest route from one valley to the other.

Guy:

From the opposite side of the valley we saw Spence down at camp shooting a muzzle loader at targets. He was killing time because he had already gotten his deer the previous morning. Each time he shot, deer would run out of the woods and up into the saddles above and behind him. They were far enough up that he couldn't hear them running. He just kept shooting.

Spot 7: **Roan Plateau Border**. This spot is located just across the gully from Davis Point. Hunters driving along the road on top of the plateau will push deer down into this gully. There is a road along the bottom you can drive or walk up. This spot gets overlooked due to its remote location.

Spot 8: **Camp Hill Saddle**

Guy:

This is a saddle where I sat several years ago and saw several deer crossing from one side to the other. The only problem was I had set up on the northwest side of the saddle and the deer crossed on the southeast side. They were just out of bow range. Had I set up 30 yards closer, I would have had my choice of several deer.

It's quite amazing. In this area deer just seem to materialize out of nowhere, or what seems to be nowhere. As the sun sets deer rise. One evening I was watching a hillside as deer began to stand up all over the place. What looked to be barren land was actually tall sage brush and small scruboaks that allowed the deer to blend in and remain unnoticed.

Spot 9: **East Shuttle Creek.** This spot is located on the east side of Shuttle Creek. We have walked this ridge several times during the day, and jumped many deer. There are a couple of pockets of spruce and aspen where the deer like to hide.

Guy:

As a general rule, if you are walking through there in the middle of the day, the deer will be bedded down or chewing on brush while laying down. If you can move slowly enough through those pockets, many times you will get a shot at an unsuspecting deer. The key is to wait for the afternoon winds to begin blowing thereby covering the sounds of your movement and also blowing away your scent. I have eased in on many animals this way. This is time well spent for hunters who are coming to Colorado from out of state who want to make use of every hunting hour.

Spot 10: **"Stump Spot."** This is the spot opposite the side of Shuttle Creek where Guy mistook the big mule deer for a stump (see "How To Hunt This Area" above). Sit there and scour the side of the hill with your binoculars, or pick it apart with a spotting scope. Concentrate on picking out deer shapes in the shadows at the base of trees or bushes. What they will do is paw an area free of sharp rocks or sticks and then bed down.

Spence:

Up above this spot I found at least 20 deer beds pawed out of the side of the hill. The ground provided them a flat place to sit with cool dirt below them. This type of deer bed looks like a little amphitheater cut out of the side of the hill.

Spot 11: **Campsite**. This spot is located right where we camped years ago. At the very bottom is some dark spruce and aspen with several large trees in which you can hang game. You may also hunt this pocket during the day. Several times we sat there in the middle of the afternoon to eat lunch and saw deer run around the point from Shuttle Creek. Some does walked to within 30 yards of camp while we were just sitting there in the open talking and making a lot of noise. It's obvious that the deer in this area can be found just about anywhere, including in your camp.

Spot 12: **Top of McCarthy Gulch**. This spot is located in the area to the east and just north of the Naval Oil Shale Reserve. You are not allowed to hunt on the reserve. You will see a fence there that you can hunt along as you walk down the drainage.

Spence:

I walked this drainage just as it was getting dark. I could hear deer moving all around me, but couldn't see any because it was so dark. I could even hear deer jumping over a fence. When I came around a hillside, the remaining light silhouetted two fawns chasing each other on the ridge above.

Spot 13: **Eagle Perch**. This spot is located in a thick grove of aspens you can work as you come down from the top of the hill to the east. Hunt there during the middle part of the day, preferably placing a blocker near the open areas where the deer have to cross to evade you.

Guy:

I have walked through this spot several times. One time I got a lucky break because there was a screeching golden eagle up in one of the trees. It was making so much "diversionary" noise that I was able to sneak to within 20 yards of three does. I was still in search of a bigger buck than the previous year's harvest, so I passed on the does.

Spot 14: **Scrub Bush Acres**. This is a good spot to start hunting from when you walk the Shuttle Creek drainage.

Guy:

I've parked my truck back in the scruboaks on the east facing slope of this spot. I did that to keep the chrome from reflecting sunlight and alerting the deer to the presence of a hunter. There are a lot of thick scruboaks in there where deer bed. You should drop hunting partners off and have them push game down to the creek where you have hunters waiting in ambush. You could just move through there slowly yourself during the day. In the early morning and evening you'll have better luck up in one of the saddles.

Spot 15: **The Backwards Seven**. We call this spot the "Backwards Seven" because when you look at it from the opposite side of the gulch, the thick vegetation forms the shape of a backwards 7.

Guy:

This is the spot we described in the beginning of this chapter where we first began using hand signals to direct each other to the deer. Right in this "backwards seven" at any one time, I could see 35 to 40 deer through my binoculars. Spencer asked that I at least leave this spot off of our maps so he could have it to himself. But I went ahead and put it in too. I figure that we now have more spots than we could hunt in 10 years (we spend a lot of time in the field), so there's no need to hold back.

Spot 16: **90 Degree Turn**. In this spot we saw a huge buck right after legal hunting hours. We were driving down the road on our way back to camp when our truck's headlights caught this deer up on the side of the hill. He was a five by five, with probably close to a 30 inch spread. He was slowly grazing. He didn't seem to be too distracted by the headlights of the pickup. We sat watching him and wishing we could see him that close during the daylight hours.

Spot 17: **Porcupine Saddle**. In this spot you'll be hunting in a saddle that goes from Davis Point Ridge down to the valley where we camped. We saw a lot of deer up there, but none were trophy size. If you just want shooting opportunities, especially if you are taking your kids out for the first time, this is a great place to sit. We probably saw 15-20 deer a night just in that one little saddle.

Spot 18: **First Shot Grove**.

Guy:

This is where I took one of my very first archery shots at a mule deer. I had been still hunting earlier in the morning. It was starting to get late so I decided to get up and move slowly through the area. While walking through some heavy aspens, I noticed some movement down below me. When I got in for a closer look I could see it was a nice three by three mule deer. He was a decent sized animal, especially for me at the time (I was such a novice). As he browsed, I moved into range. Unfortunately he was standing at a steep angle below me. When I put the pin on his vitals, and let the arrow fly, the arrow went through the top of his rack. I didn't compensate for shooting at such a steep angle downhill. Had I done so it would have been a nice harvest.

Spence:

We have a lot of opportunities like the one Guy just described that don't pan out. But you have to remember, we've spent the past 10 years mostly archery hunting. When we used to hunt with guns, we would take 500 yard shots to fill our tags. With archery hunting, we have taken most of our animals at 30 yards, and sometimes even closer. Due to the limited range of bows, and the wide open western terrain where it's difficult to hide, just getting to within 30 yards is a major feat itself. But at that point, you're only half way there. Making a killing shot through wind or thick brush is also extremely difficult. Every season we get something, but usually only after seeing hundreds of good animals that are easily within gun range, but out of bow range. If you go to our spots with a rifle, and see the animals we do, it will be virtually impossible to not fill your tag.

Spot 19: **Twin Buck Point**. Last year in the mornings and evenings, we consistently saw deer bedded down in this spot. One time while driving out of camp to hunt the surrounding gullies, two nice bucks jumped up from their beds in that gully. We later went up and looked at the spot where they had been and found 15 or 20 different beds. You can pick out their beds because they look like small oval shaped dirt cushions. The deer have pawed all debris away to make it more comfortable. One tip: if urination is within the bed itself, it's being used by a buck. If it's outside it's a doe's bed.

Spot 20: **Grouse Ridge**. This spot is located just to the north of Spot 19. You'll be hunting on the side of a mountain. You can get there by walking downhill from the main road on top. Several times, while driving this road in the evening, we spotted deer grazing all over the hillside. The only problem with this spot is that it may get dark before you have an opportunity to shoot.

Spot 21: **Grouse Saddle Ridge**. Several years ago we spotted deer that were using the saddle every evening. This spot remains good as long as the road on top doesn't get too much use. If it does, the deer will move on to less disturbed areas.

Guy:

Hunting this spot one evening, I lost a battle for light. I was stalking two bucks. It got dark quickly and all I could see was their silhouettes on the ridge above. The two bucks were rearing up and sparring for the better part of ten minutes. I could hear them grunting and kicking around. That was frustrating!

Spot 22: **Crouch Spring**. This spot is located at the bottom of Middle Fork Gulch toward the plateau. Down there you'll come across a holding tank that cattle use as well as wild game. One thing we should mention is that this area lacks water, especially late in the archery season or early in the gun season. Anywhere you find a source of water will be a great place to set up a tree stand, provided you can find a tree big enough to support it. This is definitely a very effective way to hunt deer. Unlike eastern deer, western deer rarely look up in the trees for danger. They have not been conditioned to look up by generations of tree stand hunters. Very few people hunt from tree stands in Colorado.

Spot 23: **Lower Crouch Spring**. In this spot you'll be hunting at a local deer watering hole. In addition to the spring marked on the map, there is another spring one quarter mile to the northwest that attracts game year round. Late in the season the water freezes up, but ranchers will sometimes break up the ice for their cattle. If the deer are not going to one spring, chances are, they will be using the other. Deer for some reason will visit the same water source to the exclusion of other closer ones. Who knows, maybe the water in one tastes better at certain times of the year.

Spence:

I really believe that deer in this type of area will go to the freshest water they can find. I witnessed this firsthand when I found a big buck that drowned in a tank of water. The tank was half in and half out of the ground. It was left open so a helicopter could get water out to fight a fire in Mesa Verde National Park. Although there were other muddy holes to water at, the buck chose the water tank. It was the cleanest water in the area. The buck jumped in for a drink and broke two legs. It was unable to keep its head above the water and drowned. I was on the local helitack (helicopter fire fighting) crew. We found the deer when we flew back to get more water. Brother, talk about heavy. It took three of us to lift that water-logged deer out of there.

Spot 24: **East Fork Steward Gulch**. This spot is great because it is located on a high point in the bottom of a gully where two drainages meet. Anywhere you have two drainages meeting you have the ability to glass twice as much prime habitat.

Spot 25: **Williams Gully**. This spot contains a lot of thick scruboaks and aspen with scattered clumps of dark timber. During the hot part of the day deer drives work well in this terrain. The plan should be to have somebody circle down below this little gully and walk slowly up through it allowing the breeze to carry human scent through the pocket. This will push the animals up and hopefully into the sights of awaiting hunters. This method can produce when others fail. Mark, a friend of Guy's, took a nice 3x4 in this spot thanks to a deer drive.

Spot 26: **Headwaters Of McCarthy Gulch**. A lot of the bottom lands along the Piceance Creek drainage and some of the gulches are private property. It's only private for the first two or three miles in. Ranchers usually permit access to the public lands on the other side of their property. However, this spot does not have any access from below so you will have to get there by taking the roads back on top of the plateau then walking down. There is one road that leads right down to the headwaters of McCarthy Gulch which offers some pretty good hunting. You'll notice a little timbered point where deer bed down during the day. There are also some frequently used saddles up there where you can set up in the mornings and the evenings.

Spot 27: **West McCarthy Gulch**. This spot is located right along the road. You'll be hunting in a saddle that connects McCarthy Gulch to the east fork of Story Gulch. In this saddle we've seen a lot of deer tracks left by deer in the early morning (not evening). Find a place to sit where you can see for a long way, and wait.

Spot 28: **Middle Fork Of Story Gulch**. This spot is located at the top of a saddle. It's one of the very rare saddles that gets activity all day long - morning, noon and night. For some reason, even though it's right off the road, it just does not get much pressure. The only people we saw up there were grouse hunters.

Guy:

If you have a slingshot or you are not afraid to take a shot with your bow, or even your rifle, the whole month of September is grouse season. Bring plenty of blunt tips or judo points as well as a small game license. We did and we kept our skillets full.

Spence:

Grouse are very good if you cook them the right way. I've seen some guys try what we call the "Conan The Barbarian" grouse cooking method. They pierce the grouse breast with a stick and roast it over the fire. What they get is a piece of meat too tough for a dog to chew. The best way to cook them is to fry them in butter and garlic with a lid over the skillet to keep the meat moist. When cooked this way, grouse breasts are the most tender fowl you'll ever eat.

Spot 29: **West Fork Story Gulch**. This spot is located right along the main road. Hunt the saddle between the east fork of Stuart Gulch and the west fork of Story gulch. The gulch serves as a major deer passageway. There is a lot of scruboak up there that can be used as cover for an ambush.

Guy:

I set up in this spot one morning and watched several deer go through the saddle. The largest I saw was a fork horn which I didn't want to shoot. There were also a lot of does meandering through the bottom. Although I didn't see anything I was going to shoot, I still enjoyed watching the animals interacting and moving about naturally. Every time I have the opportunity to view wildlife I learn something new. This is the kind of hunting education you can't get from a magazine or hunting video.

Spot 30: **Middle Fork Of Stuart Gulch**. Like a lot of other spots we've profiled in this area, this spot is located where two separate drainages come together. You can sit on a high point that provides an excellent view of the surrounding area. The drainages won't have any water in them. Rather, this spot is located in an area that the game only passes through on their way to other areas.

Spot 31: **East Willow Creek**. As you get farther to the west on the Roan Plateau, you will see fewer trees and more sage. This spot is located on top of a hill overlooking a sage covered saddle. It's somewhat isolated from all the other spots which means it will see an influx of game when the other spots are getting a lot of hunting pressure. We did not see a lot of animals while walking up from the bottom of Scandard Gulch. But once we got farther back, the density of game increased.

Don't get discouraged if you are not seeing game on your way in. Sometimes it takes time for nature to "calm down" after man enters an area. So be patient and sit down for a while. You are always going to see more if you are willing to get out and walk.

Spot 32: **Original Campsite**. This spot is located back off the Sprague Gulch road by a place where we camped several years ago. Many times as we came back into camp from our morning hunt, we found deer tracks all over the top of the tire tracks that we made driving out a few hours earlier. We even found tracks going right through camp. It goes to show that you can harvest deer just sitting in your tent and using it as a blind. The deer don't seem to be afraid of tents.

Our hunting camp up Sprague Gulch. Every morning deer came down out of the Aspen to the right and ran between the truck and the tent.

Spot 33: **Bear Cliff**. This spot is located just to the north of Spot 32 where we camped. Walk the trail that drops down off the side of the road. The hill you'll be descending is fairly steep. The west side of the gully is covered with extremely thick scruboak. It's difficult walking, but provides an excellent view of the west facing slope. We spooked several deer out of that gully. Once spooked, the deer were impossible to locate in the thick brush. We also found an abundance of bear sign down in there.

Spot 34: **Opposite Bear Cliff**. This spot is located adjacent to Spot 33 on the opposite side of the valley. In there Spence saw two nice three by three bucks jump up in front of him and run up the hillside. The term "jump" comes from the animal leaping from its bed and running away to escape danger. Unfortunately this generally means the stalk is over for that particular animal. That's just one of the hazards of hunting with bow and arrow. Had it been rifle season he probably would have filled his tag with one of those deer.

Spot 35: **Deer Hillside**. This spot is located in an area we noticed while driving down from Sprague Gulch Road. We had seen some movement so we decided to park and use our spotting scope to scan the hillside. We picked out several deer feeding. Unfortunately this was the last day of our hunt and we were heading home. We were worn out, dirty and sunburned. We just didn't feel like hiking across the gully and up the opposite side in pursuit of those two bucks. Besides Spencer had already harvested his deer the day before.

Spot 36: **Piceance Valley**. This spot is located next to some of the private land in the lower valley. During September the lower valleys are green with alfalfa and hay. The deer literally pour out of the hills in the evening to feed in the fields. The farther you get down in the valley the more pinion and juniper trees you will find on the hillsides. The combination of pinion-juniper forest, pine forest, aspen, sage and alfalfa all in one area creates one of the best deer spots we've seen.

Spence:

> Last season I left camp to get some ice for packing a buck I shot that morning with my bow. On the way back as it was getting toward evening, I saw over 250 deer in the fields outside of Rio Blanco. Just to the south of the last hill you cross before coming into Rio Blanco, I stopped to watch five big bucks sparring in a field to the west.
>
> Around Rio Blanco, the fields were dotted with groups of deer. This was the first time I saw deer "hurry." They were moving out of the hills walking much faster than they normally do. They looked like they were moving to the action and didn't want to miss out on one minute of the deer socialization.

Spot 37: **Barn Spring**. This spot is located up the middle fork of Stuart Gulch. Once again it's one of those areas where the top of the ridge is completely dry and treeless while the valley below is green from a spring. Any time you have conditions like that, the deer are going to pour out of the timbered hillsides in the early evening to water at the springs.

Spot 38: **East Fawn Creek**. From Spot 37 jump over a few gulches to this spot which is located at the headwaters of Little Dry Gulch. Some of the land along the bottom portions of those gulches is privately owned, but you still have access across the private property. Just make sure you close the gates behind you after you drive through so the ranchers' cattle don't get out.

As you come to the end of the Hunter Creek Road you will find yourself between the headwaters of West Hunter Creek and East Fawn Creek. You'll be driving a road that requires four wheel drive in some spots, especially if it's wet, because the roads become very slick from just a little precipitation. Directly to the north there is a big open area on a bit higher ground. It's a great place to set up with binoculars. An alternative hunting method would be to look along the sides of the road for fresh tracks and follow any you see.

Spot 39: **Upper West Hunter Creek**. This spot is located right along the road in a saddle going from West Hunter Creek to Dry Gulch. We saw a lot of deer crossing the saddle, but no bucks.

Spot 40: **Upper West Hunter Creek II**. Just to the north of Spot 39, along Hunter Creek, is a heavily wooded point of land protruding to the north. We once chased a couple of deer out of there. They ran up into the saddle above.

Spot 41: **Mid West Hunter Creek**. This spot is a lot like Spot 40 in that you can hunt a little ravine which cuts back and forms a low pass. You can only walk to this spot from the top because the bottom is private property.

Spot 42: **West Hunter Creek Inlet**. This spot is located north of spot 41. You'll hunt a hollow just off the main gulch. There's not much cover except for some brush up on the sides of the hill. Look for deer bedded there.

Spot 43: **Hunter Creek**. This spot is also located along Hunter Creek right above where a rancher has built a holding tank for his cattle. When the weather is dry, the deer go there to water. There's a little hollow above the holding tank through which the deer have beaten a good sized trail going to and from the tank.

Guy:

> I remember a few years back, while driving up there early one morning, we looked off to the side of the road and saw deer tracks everywhere. We hadn't yet seen the pond, and were wondering why the deer were so concentrated in that area. After further investigation we found the water tank.

Spot 44: **Lower Hunter Creek**. This spot is located right on top of the ridge to the north of the lower Hunter Creek. It's fairly flat up there and the access is relatively easy. It's wide open so it's an excellent place to hunt with a muzzle loader or high powered rifle. You'll be hunting along a migratory route where the deer pass through on their way down from the higher country to the lower valleys. This spot will produce better in the later seasons.

Spot 45: **Piceance/Hunter Creek Intersection**. This spot is located along a route deer use to get down to some lush valleys and feed. Sit at the upper end of the hollow above any deer trail and pick out the deer you want. It can be that easy.

Spot 46: **Black Sulphur Creek Drainage**. This spot is unique in that it's located in an open park completely enclosed by scruboak and trees. The park area is from three or four hundred yards across. If you are hunting with a flat-shooting rifle, you will definitely have an advantage there.

Spot 47: **Ryan Gulch Ranch**. This spot is located on a ridge between Black Sulphur Creek and Ryan Gulch. Below will be some private land and a ranch that sits back in Ryan Gulch. The ridge is extremely narrow, and consequently, you can watch two gullies at one time.

Spot 48: **Ryan Gulch 1**. Like spot 47, this spot is located across from Ryan Gulch. You will be hunting a transition zone where vegetation changes from open sage flats to hills covered with scruboaks. Walk the line where the vegetation changes. Animals are concentrated along it.

Spot 49: **Ryan Gulch 2**. This is another spot where a timbered ridge juts out into surrounding sage flats. While sitting a little higher and watching this ridge, we have seen both deer and elk later in the season. Below the ridge are other pockets of timber you can also watch. In this spot, coordinated drives work well for pushing deer off of the timbered ridge and onto the open flats where other hunters can get clear shots.

Spot 50: **Ryan Gulch 3**. This spot is located along a dried up creek bed directly to the east of Spot 49. It's easy walking along the bottom of the wash. It's easy for the game too, which is why you'll see so many tracks in the bottom.

Spot 51: **Ryan Gulch 4**. This spot is located at the top of a big drainage. It's very open and surrounded by higher ground on three sides. You can sit on the higher ground and view several thousand yards of good deer habitat. This is a perfect spot to sit if you have a high powered rifle.

Spot 52: **Meeting Trails**. This spot is located where the access road turns from four wheel drive to a two wheel drive road. From the top you have an excellent view of the Piceance Creek Valley below, and three different gullies. Also, to the west there is a saddle joining the hollow you will be hunting in with Black Sulphur Creek. In addition, right up on top there are a couple open parks that attract game. This spot has it all.

Spot 53: **Gardenhive Gulch**. This spot is located north of the Piceance Creek drainage. In this area are a few landing strips, old mines and gravel pits. The land is public, owned by the BLM. Due to the variety of vegetation that grows around abandoned man-made structures, you will find an excess of deer. You'll be hunting in a saddle which further concentrates game that is passing through. This is a good place for rifle hunting. It is exceptionally productive during the late rifle season when the snow pushes even more deer down.

Spot 54: **Collins Gulch**. In this spot you'll be hunting in a very narrow saddle. This is a great place to set up with a bow not only because it offers "close in" shooting, but because it is located along a vegetative transition zone with numerous small gullies feeding it.

Spot 55: **Jones Gulch**. This is another spot where you'll be hunting in a saddle. Once again anywhere you find a low crossing you're going to find greater numbers of deer. Although we haven't seen any extremely large animals in there, we've seen enough sign to warrant a closer look.

Spot 56: **Dry Prong Creek Drainage**. This spot is more remote than others we've profiled, which means that as hunting pressure increases, you'll find more and more animals there. The vegetation includes sagebrush in the bottoms and heavier timber pockets on the hillsides. You can hunt in the timber pockets almost all the way down to the dry fork of Piceance Creek.

Spot 57: **Dark Canyon Spring**. This spot is located less than half a mile off the road. It's a great place to sit over in the evenings and catch deer coming to water. In this area, anywhere you find water, you'll find many deer.

Spot 58: **Post Gulch Spring**. In this spot, you'll be hunting around a spring at the top of a gully which farther down joins the dry fork of Piceance Creek. Unless the weather has been very wet, the water does not run for any great distance. Keeping in mind that the spring is one of the only water sources in the vicinity, it's no wonder it attracts so many deer. From the road above the spring you can scan over the entire gully with a pair of binoculars or a spotting scope. You'll see the most deer in there during the early morning.

Spot 59: **Segar Mountain**. On the north side of the dry fork of Piceance Creek there are a couple of saddles where you can hunt. They are located away from the hunting pressure of Piceance Creek below. The best saddle to hunt leads from a drainage on the dry fork side to a drainage on the Segar Gulch side. In there we've seen sign for some very large animals.

Spot 60: **Upper Segar Gulch**. Like most of the good spots in this area, this spot is located in a saddle between thick timber and open sage to the northwest. Set up on the downwind side, and wait for the animals to cross through.

Spot 61: **Middle Segar Gulch**. This spot is located in a highly defined saddle between Sager Gulch and Hay Gulch.

Guy:

Several years ago while walking through that saddle I jumped 30 or 35 deer. I did not see any extremely large bucks. But there were several bucks that would have been respectable bow kills. Anywhere you hunt in that basin you are going to find animals. But there are certain spots where your chances are improved greatly. If you hunt this area, I guarantee you will see overwhelming sign from animals, if not the animals themselves.

Spot 62: **Middle Hay Gulch**. This spot is located in a treeless saddle not far from the road. Because the saddle is treeless, you will find it easy to spot deer passing through. The animals normally feed in the saddle in the evening. There is not much water around the gulch, so if you can find a seep or spring you'll have an excellent hunting spot.

Spot 63: **Dark Canyon**. This spot is located along a transition zone where open flat terrain joins hilly sagebrush and timber. Within this area is also another saddle that has been known to produce big bucks in past years. We have marked the saddle on the map.

Guy:

Three years ago we talked to a group of hunters who set up camp within a quarter of a mile of that spot. Every single one of them had a buck hanging up. The largest buck they took was a respectable four by five. It was an absolutely gorgeous animal. I would love to have had a chance to hunt that particular deer. They said they took it up in the saddle.

Spot 64: **Little Coral Gulch**. You can get to this gulch from the access road we have marked on the map. Hunt up by where the road forks. The animals we saw going through the saddle all headed down into Greasewood Gulch in the early morning.

Guy:

Undisturbed deer will always use the route that is easiest to walk. As hunting pressure increases, they stick to the cover which usually means they travel a harder route.

Spence:

Several years ago I discovered a very effective method of hunting deer that have become extremely wary from excessive hunting pressure. Look at the terrain ahead of you and try to figure out where you would go if you were being hunted. It sounds simple, but many hunters continue to hunt deer like they're out trying to jump rabbits. They walk out in the open and are easily spotted. To hunt spooked deer (and trophy deer that act spooked even when there's no hunting pressure) you need to stay hidden. Walk the brush. Walk it slowly.

Spot 65: **Greasewood Gulch**. This spot is located on the flat terrain right before the hills get very steep as they drop down to the bottom of Piceance Creek. In this area you'll find many small saddles where pinion and juniper trees grow intermittently. Deer spend their days up in those flat spots looking down on the creek bed where they go to feed at night.

Spot 66: **Ranch Creek**. The thing that's unique about this spot is that you can stand on an outcropping above the canyon and view a great deal of land below. There is not any water up where you will be standing. But there is water below flowing through Piceance Creek. You can spot deer down there in the evening and morning. The land along the creek is privately owned. However, from this spot you can see exactly where the deer are going after they leave the fields by the creek and enter public land. Pick out a big buck. If he is moving, intercept him. Even if you don't get a chance at him the first day, the second day you'll know exactly what route he's going to take when he leaves the fields. Also, if you can figure out where the deer are bedding down, plan a stalk.

Spot 67: **Upper Ranch Creek**. This spot is situated right along the road. Driving past it several years ago we saw two big bucks after legal shooting time. We've never really hunted there and we didn't talk to anyone who did. But every time we drove past we saw deer.

Spot 68: **Open Flats**. The north facing slope of this spot is relatively open. There are several pockets of timber on the hillsides where deer bed later in the day. Also, there is one high point that you can climb to from which you have an uninterrupted three mile view. Early in the morning you can spot deer and set up for stalks after they bed down.

Guy:

Spotting and stalking can be frustrating because mule deer possess excellent eyesight and hearing. If the deer remain in the open you will have to crawl on your hands and knees through the sagebrush to get to them.

Spence:

When I know I'm going to be doing a lot of stalking, I bring special equipment. Usually, this includes knee pads, elbow pads and thick gloves (in case I have to move any thorny brush out of my way). With this equipment, you won't burn out on stalking and will be able to do a lot more stalks in one day. Last year I used it to make a 3 hour stalk and take a 16" (green score) antelope.

Spot 69: **Middle Yellow Creek**. This little spot is situated in one of the offshoots of Yellow Creek. There's a gully we've marked on the map where we spotted deer bedded down during the day. Several times while on the ridge we spotted deer in the valley below. We didn't see any bucks larger than fork horns, but there were definitely a large number of deer in there.

Spot 70: **Yellow Ranch**. This spot is located up above the Yellow Creek Ranch. You'll be hunting on a hill overlooking a timbered area to the north and east. Yellow Creek should have water. The timber that is just above the creek serves as a bedding area for deer that frequent the private land below. Watch for deer coming out of the timber to the creek. Work the boundary lines.

Spot 71: **Upper Duck Creek**. In this spot you'll be hunting on top of some hills overlooking a creek bed. The high land attracts deer like magnets. Every time we've walked this spot, we have seen deer. None were extremely large. But there were three or four bucks in the 2½ year old range with spreads around 20 inches.

Spot 72: **Middle Duck Creek**. This spot, like a lot of the other spots in the area, is located in a basin above a creek bed. There are also a number of saddles up there through which deer cross. Sit down and pick apart the landscape with your binoculars. Watch for movement.

Spot 73: **Upper Middle Yellow Creek**. We decided to put this spot on the map due to its optimal hunting topography. Timber sticks out into the flat terrain forming a bottleneck. When deer can stay in cover they generally will, which forces them into bottlenecks and makes it easy to hunt them. This specific bottleneck goes from a pocket of timber just to the north to another timber stand in the valley below.

Spot 74: **Middle Pinto Gulch**. This spot is situated on the open sage flats above Yellow Creek about a half mile from the road. Early in the morning you can find deer out on those flats. It was obvious there had been quite a bit of hunting pressure in the area, because the deer ran at the sound of our vehicle without stopping to look back.

Spot 75: **East Yellow Creek**. This spot is situated in a flat sage saddle by East Pinto Gulch. We spotted several points along the saddle where deer herds cross over to the back side of Pinto Gulch.

Spot 76: **Alkali Flat**. Even though this spot is situated above the Alkali Flat, there is one pocket that doesn't get the hunting pressure typical of this area. The reason for this is that the road only comes to within a half a mile, and the way the high ground sticks out to the northwest, the spot is hidden from view. The lay of the land has created a safe haven for deer. We originally found this spot using our "map reading intuition."

Spence:

If you know what to look for, you can find a good hunting spot just by looking at a map. The best possible spot you could find would be rugged and roadless, at least 16 square miles (4 miles X 4 miles) that is surrounded on all sides by other easier to hunt areas which get a lot of hunting pressure. Most hunters stick to the flatter easy hunting spots which forces game into the rough terrain.

Another piece to the puzzle is water. Many of the maps show hillside seeps which flow up high, but dry up before they get to the valleys below. In Colorado the rivers and creeks usually have roads along them. Due to the human disturbance in the area, the game will only water at the rivers and creeks at night. But the high seeps allow game to water and feed undisturbed. They are animal magnets.

The last element to a good spot is cover. If the map shows the area to be over 11,000 feet, it will be treeless and won't have a place for the game to hide. High flat spots below timberline (even small ones) with ravines on either side are what you look for. Once you get to the spot, begin looking for vegetation traits you can't see on the map, like transition zones and forage. If the flat spots have meadows on them, you're in for a very good hunt.

Spot 77: **Lower Yellow Creek**. Because this spot is a half mile from the creek it will hold a lot of deer. You will be sitting on a high piece of ground which allows you to view the deer moving between the public land and the private property below. You'll also have a good view of a saddle which adds even more desirable traits to an already good spot. This is definitely a place that will produce deer. We can't guarantee the deer will be big, but if you are looking for numbers, this is the spot.

Spot 78: **North Pinto Gulch**. This is another spot where deer numbers are almost guaranteed. You will be hunting along a transition zone between sage flats, pinion-juniper and pockets of aspen. The saddle you'll hunt is deep and provides deer the easiest route over to Pinto Gulch and to Yellow Creek.

Spot 79: **North Upper Pinto Gulch**. Once you get up on top, this spot is flat and open. Climb up the northwest hillside in the early morning and glass the flats above for deer. You may catch them out away from cover and get an opportunity for a good stalk.

Spot 80: **Upper Pinto Gulch**. In this spot, there are two higher points up on a ridge and a low point between them which you can watch. Up there we spotted several deer moving from lower Barkus Creek over to the Pinto Gulch side. Later in the day, they bedded in the timber along Pinto Gulch. This is definitely a great place to go mid-afternoon. Walk some of the pockets of aspen, and see if you can't push deer to your buddies down below.

Spot 81: **The Pit**. This, like the last spot, is located on a high point giving you the same advantages as Spot 80. You'll be hunting along a saddle at the headwaters of Barkus Creek. The combination of the saddle where they cross in the morning, and the aspen pockets where they bed down to escape the heat, gives you the opportunity to hunt the entire day.

Spot 82: **Middle Barkus Creek**. In this spot you'll be positioned on a point of high ground that sticks out into the sage flats like a dock protrudes into water. From there you can see a long way down the valley to the northeast (Barkus Creek valley) or up the ridge toward the Pinto Mesa windmill area. There are some grassy areas out in the sage where you should focus your binoculars. You can spot deer in those spots in the early morning.

Guy:

If you are trying to save money on equipment, optics are one thing you do not want to scrimp on. They are a necessity in the west where long views give game an advantage over you. Also, the density of game per square mile is much less than in the east. If you're not spotting game, you may end up walking all day in the completely wrong direction. Buy the very best pair of binoculars you can (10 X 50 or better).

Spot 83: **Trail Canyon**. In this spot you'll be hunting above Trail Canyon. Because the canyon is steep, the deer will stick to the ridgetop and the saddles. However, as hunting pressure increases, you may find them in the steeper terrain to the west. Work the ridge, scanning the terrain to the north and south with your binoculars.

Spot 84: **Spring At East Fork Of Greasewood Creek**. This spot is located next to a spring at the headwaters of the east fork of Greasewood Creek. In the late rifle season, the deer will only go to this spot at night. But earlier in the season, it's good in the daytime.

Spence:

Even if the deer have become nocturnal, you still should check out spots like this one. I go to them to gauge deer density in the area, and to look for the tracks of trophy sized animals. If the water is muddy, I know animals have been there a few hours previously. If I find the tracks from a big buck, I take my time and follow them, step by step away from the waterhole. Once I figure out which trail the buck has taken, I follow at a faster pace. I check each trail branching from the main one that he might get off on. It usually takes 3 hours to track a buck to his bed. Sometimes however, I track the buck to a spot where he's doubled back up on a ridge and watched the trail he came up. If a buck is that smart, I never even see him. He sees me following and moves away. However, I do establish a pattern that he may hold to the next day, provided I haven't spooked him entirely.

Spot 85: **The Base Of Calamity Ridge**. The road you drive to this spot cuts through a saddle next to a steep ridge just to the west and a small highspot just to the east. Hunt the open areas south and north of the saddle. We've seen a lot of does in there (no bucks). But then, where there are does, there are also bucks. The bucks are just more elusive.

Spence:

A lot of times you'll see does in the fields, but no bucks. If you're hunting during the rut, the bucks won't be far away. By remaining patient and scanning the surrounding terrain, you can spot the bucks farther back in the brush, or just over a small hill. It's important that you don't spook the herd, even if they're moving off. When they move off, try to keep them in view, but don't move yourself. Wait for the buck to follow. If no buck follows, reposition yourself and stay on the herd. The buck may join them later. You can hunt them all day this way. The does will act like a buck attractant that's better than any scent you can buy.

Spot 86: **Mid Barkus Creek**. This tiny spot is located up a draw that branches off of Barkus Creek. As you go up the draw there is one outcropping of land coming from the northeast, and another point of land running directly to the west. Between the two high spots is a saddle from which you can see down the entire Barkus Creek valley. In the morning deer move from north to south through the saddle.

Spot 87: **Molar Mountain**. This mountain gets its name from its shape which looks like a giant molar tooth. Between Molar Mountain and the ridgeline that separates Greasewood and Barkus Creeks is a wide saddle where we spotted some does in the company of one small buck.

Spot 88: **Lower Greasewood Creek - East Fork**. In this spot a ridgeline protrudes into an open valley to the northwest. Farther to the northwest is another highpoint. Deer are constantly moving through the saddle located between the two.

Spot 89: **North Of East Greasewood Creek**. In this spot, the land is steep on one side of the valley, while the other side is more level. Coordinated deer drives work well in there.

Guy:

Sometimes while participating in a drive I've seen the entire side of a mountain come alive with deer. The best way I can describe this phenomenon is if you were up in an airplane looking down at a generic landscape, then all of the sudden things that looked stationary begin to move. At first it doesn't register in your mind, then you realize that things are not as they appeared a few minutes ago.

Spence:

I've learned a lot by watching animals that are being driven. It's funny to watch them react to the other hunters and imagine that that is the same way they react to you as you move through their territory. I've observed that driving works well not only because it pushes game, but also because it creates a diversion and an opportunity for the blocker to get in closer than usual. The trick is for the drivers to move slowly and make enough noise so the deer get up way out ahead, moving off at the same pace as the drivers. The blocker on the other hand moves in quickly from downwind.

The benefit to creating diversions was most apparent when I kicked that monster buck to Guy up by the backwards seven (see "How To Hunt This Area" above). The deer was so focused on getting away from me (I was on the same hillside as it) that it was oblivious to Guy who stood on the facing hill. If it had not have been for me, that deer would have been focused on Guy and we could have never spotted it.

Spot 90: **Trail Gulch**. The terrain gets much steeper the closer you get to Calamity Ridge. The steeper the sides of the ridge, the more deer you'll find on top where it's flatter. You can also find deer on the steep stuff, but it's much more difficult to hunt there. There's a spring on top that holds water almost year round. If it's an extremely hot day, and there hasn't been much hunting pressure, sometimes the deer will even go to the spring during the middle of the day.

Spot 91: **Radio Tower South**. A half mile to the north of the road that goes to the Radio Tower is a huge saddle. There is no timber in the saddle and therefore it's easy to see whatever comes through. Due to the long shots you'll have to take, this spot is best during the rifle season. The sagebrush there is about four feet tall which can cause you to shoot higher on the animal than you should. Beware of shoulder shots.

Spot 92: **Blair Mountain**. In this spot, animals move between the White River basin and the Blair Mountain ridgeline. Hunt between the two. The terrain will change from an arid plateau on top to a moist green valley below.

Guy:

There is plenty of access to this spot which causes it to get quite a bit of hunting pressure. I've seen one really nice trophy head come out of there. Most of the hunters I talked to as they came out would not tell me where they got their animals. But the guy who shot the big trophy told me he took it just to the northeast of Blair Mountain. He even showed me the spot on the map.

Spot 93 and 94: **Hay Canyon Saddle To Little Spring Creek**. This spot is comprised of several saddles lined up in a row. You are going to have to find the one that has been getting the most use, and hunt in it. The deer in the area tend to change saddles every year. When one food source plays out, they move to the next.

Rio Blanco

(Reprinted from USGS Douglass Pass map)

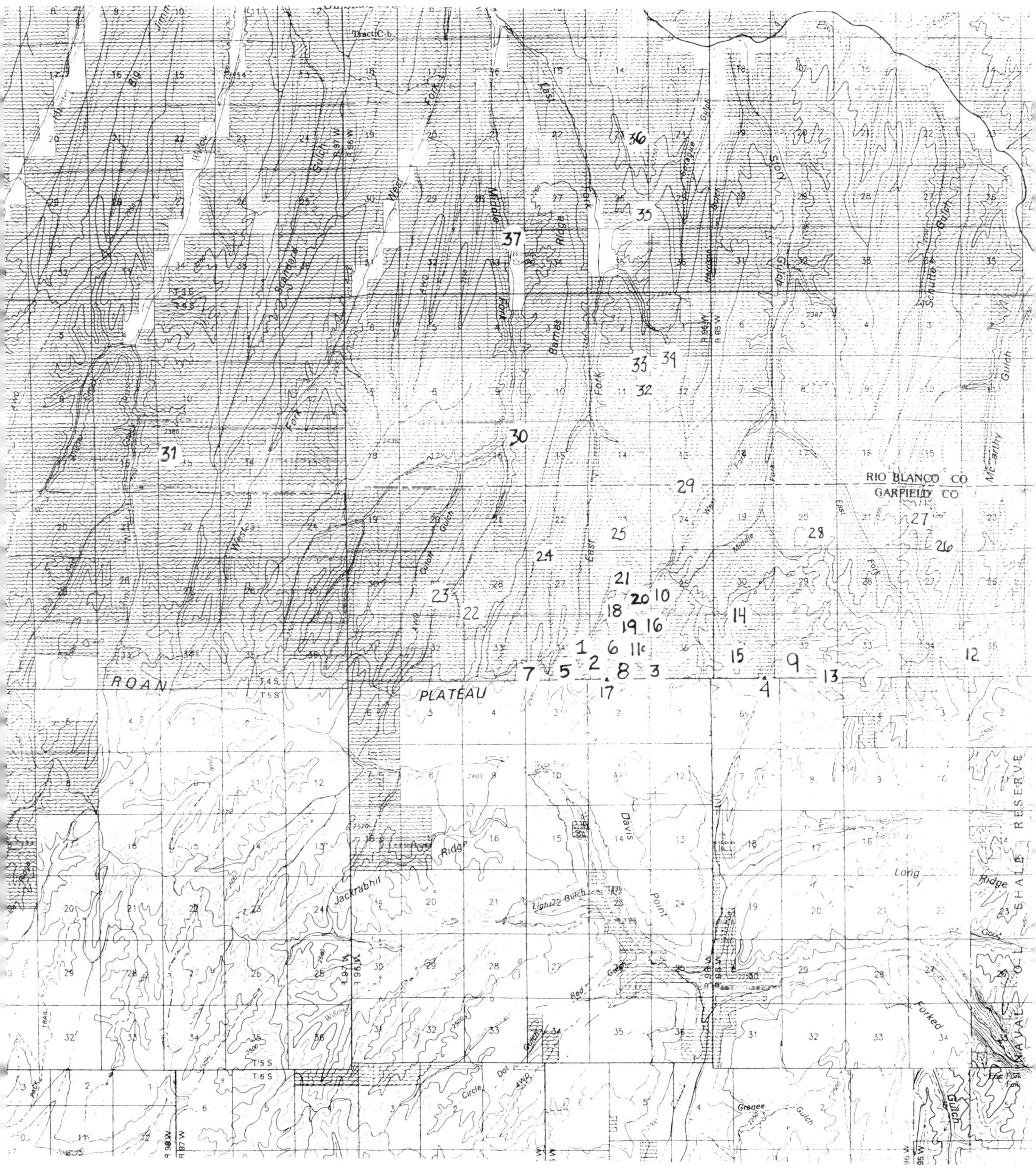

**RIO BLANCO
PICEANCE BASIN
3-D MAP**

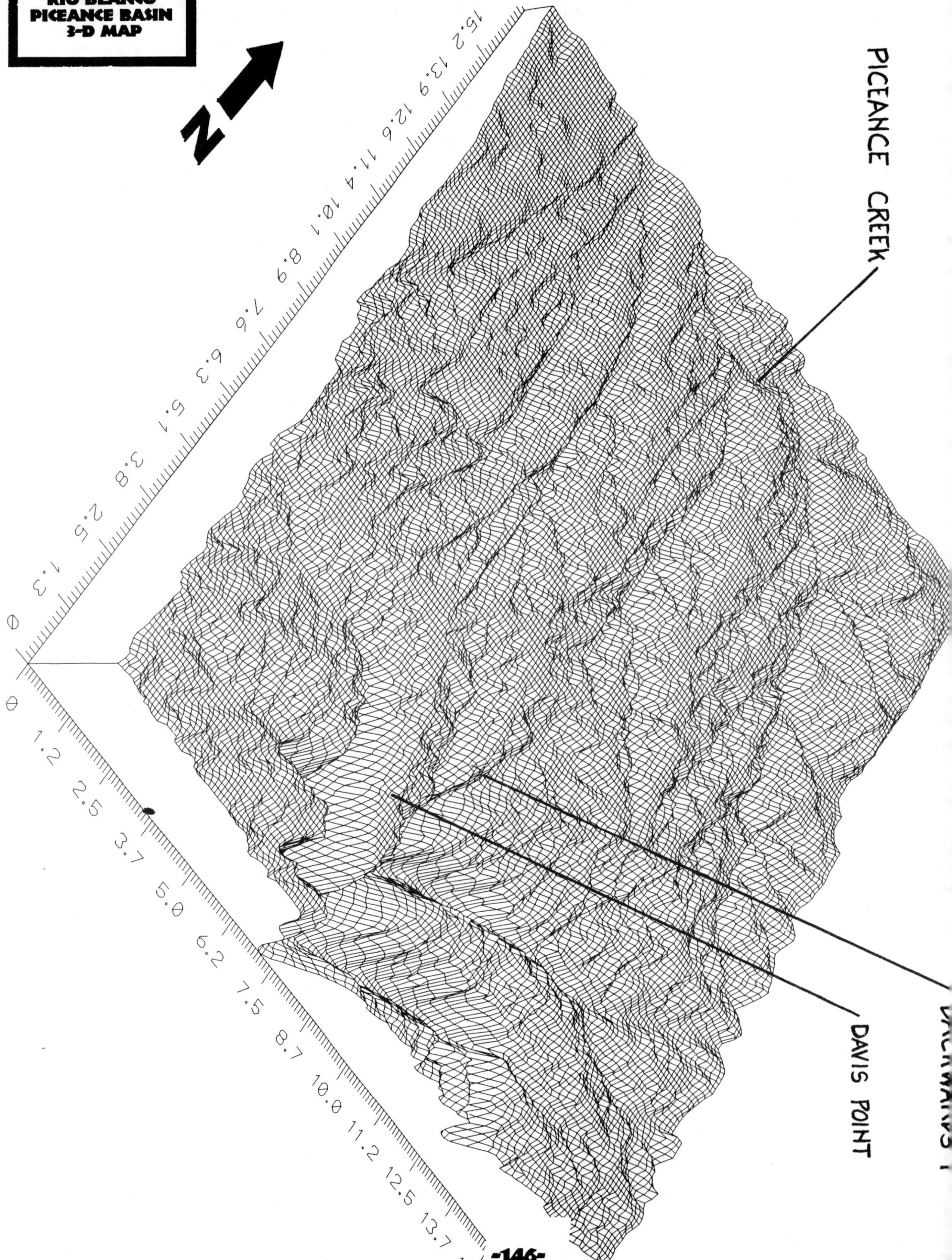

Rio Blanco

(Reprinted from USGS Douglass Pass map)

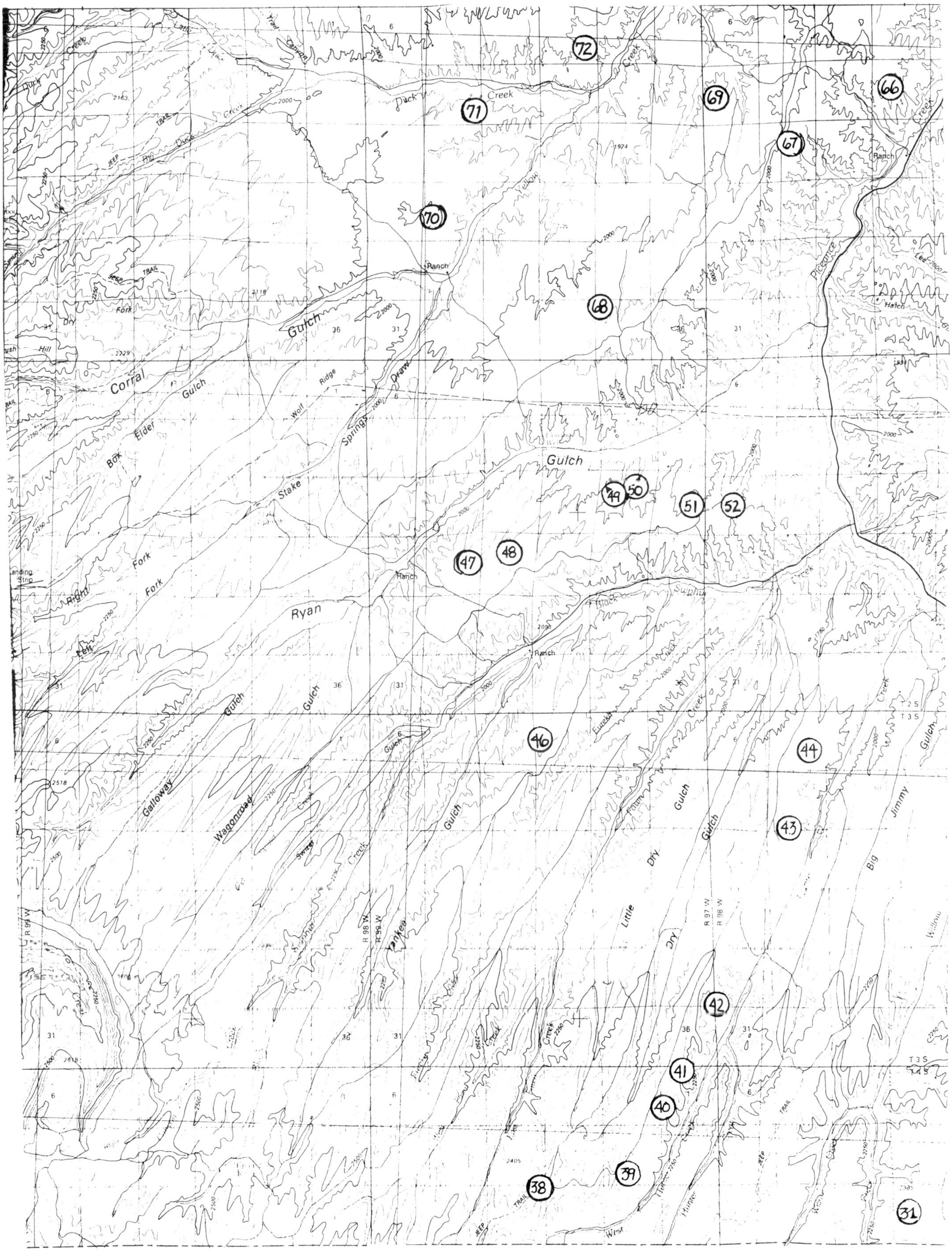

**RIO BLANCO
PICEANCE BASIN
3-D MAP**

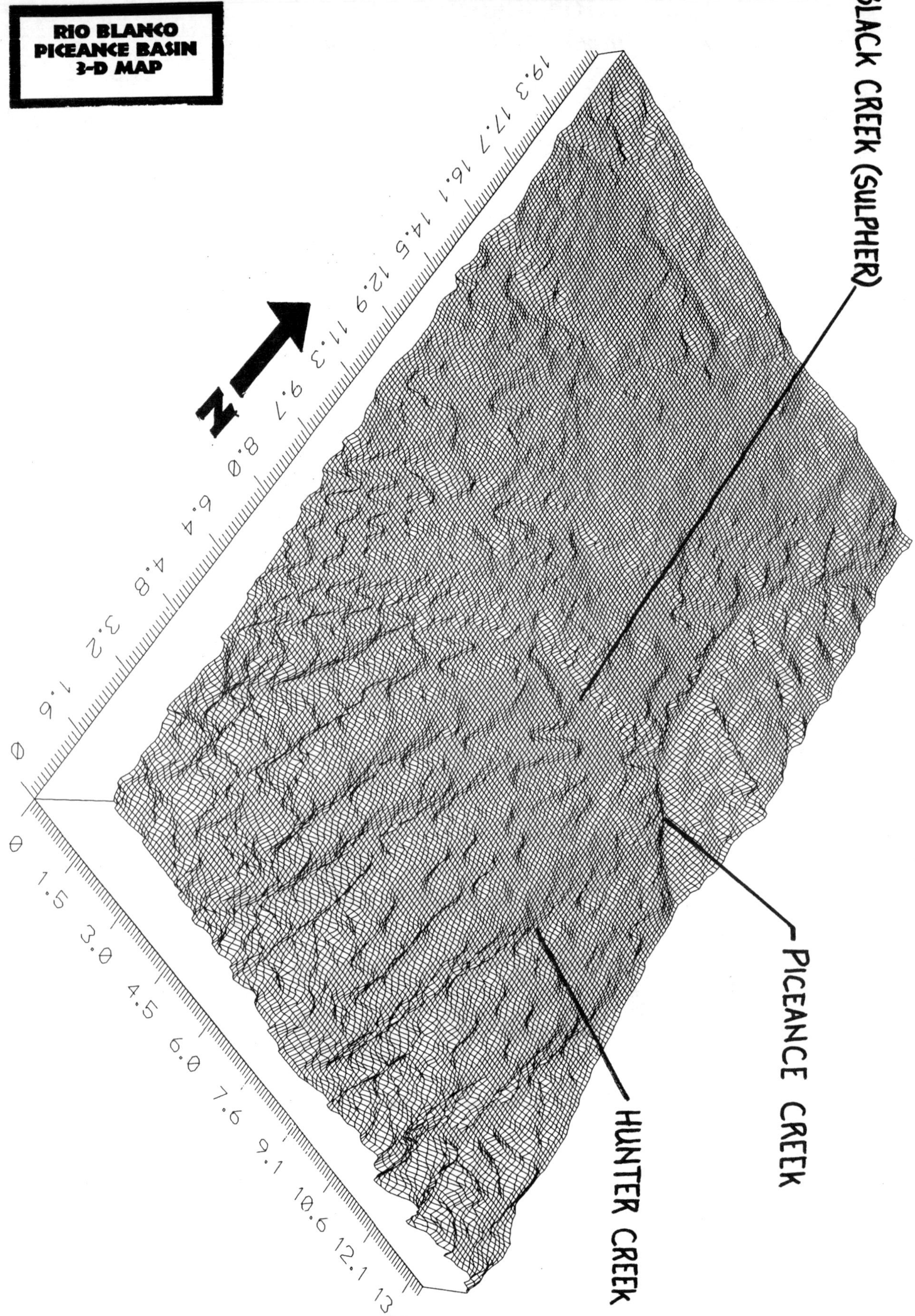

Rio Blanco

(Reprinted from USGS Douglass Pass map)

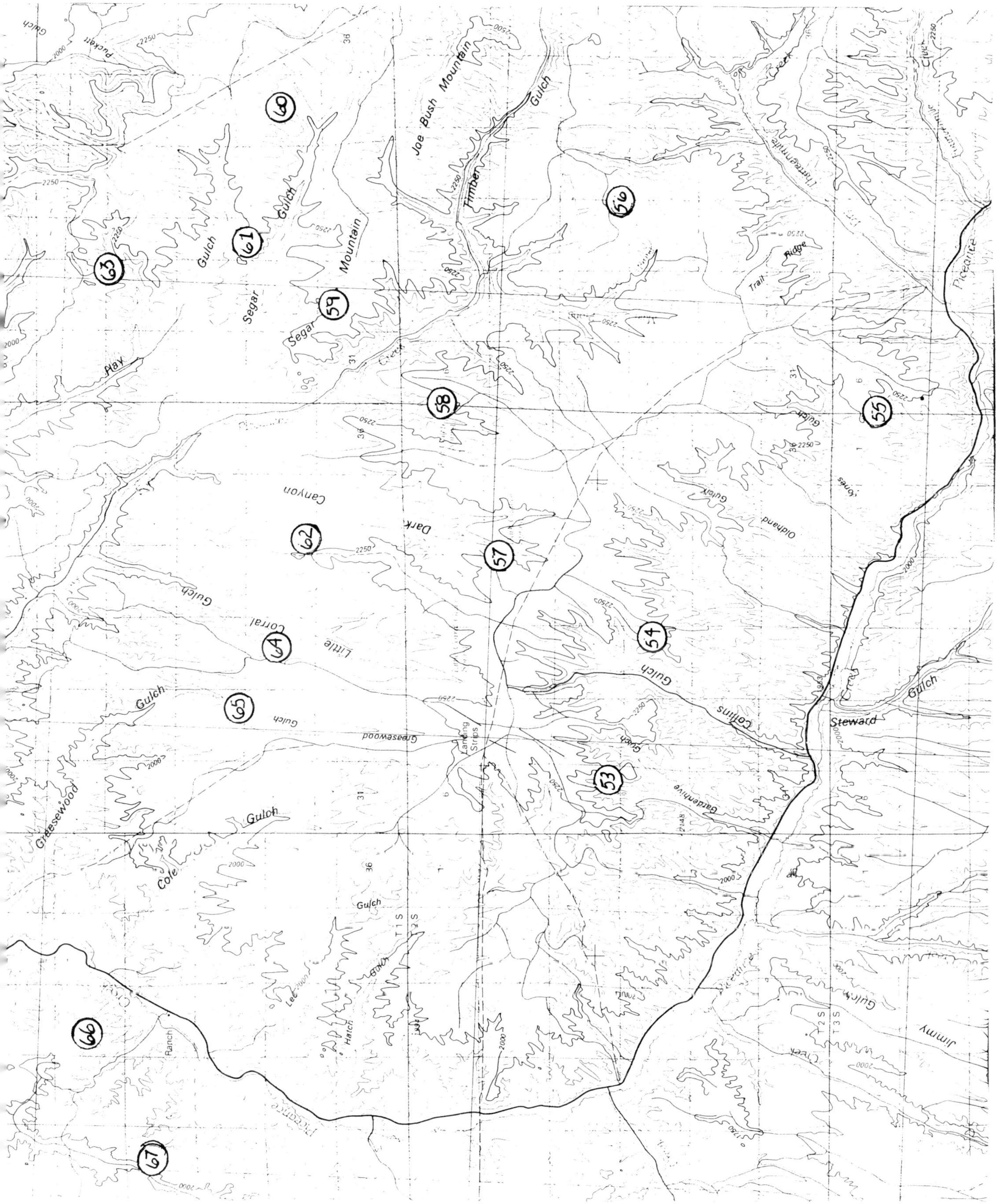

**RIO BLANCO
PICEANCE BASIN
3-D MAP**

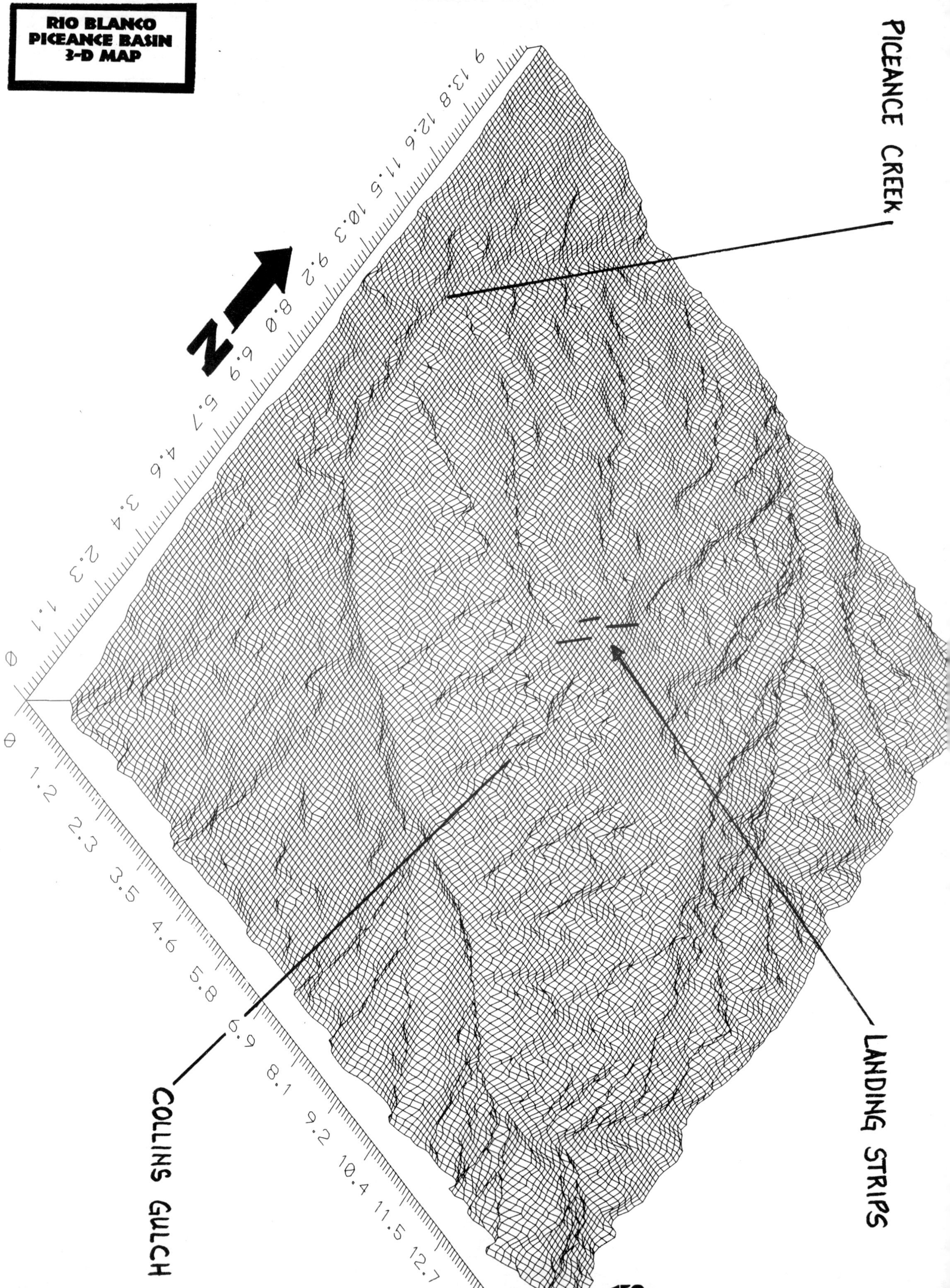

Rio Blanco

(Reprinted from USGS Douglass Pass map)

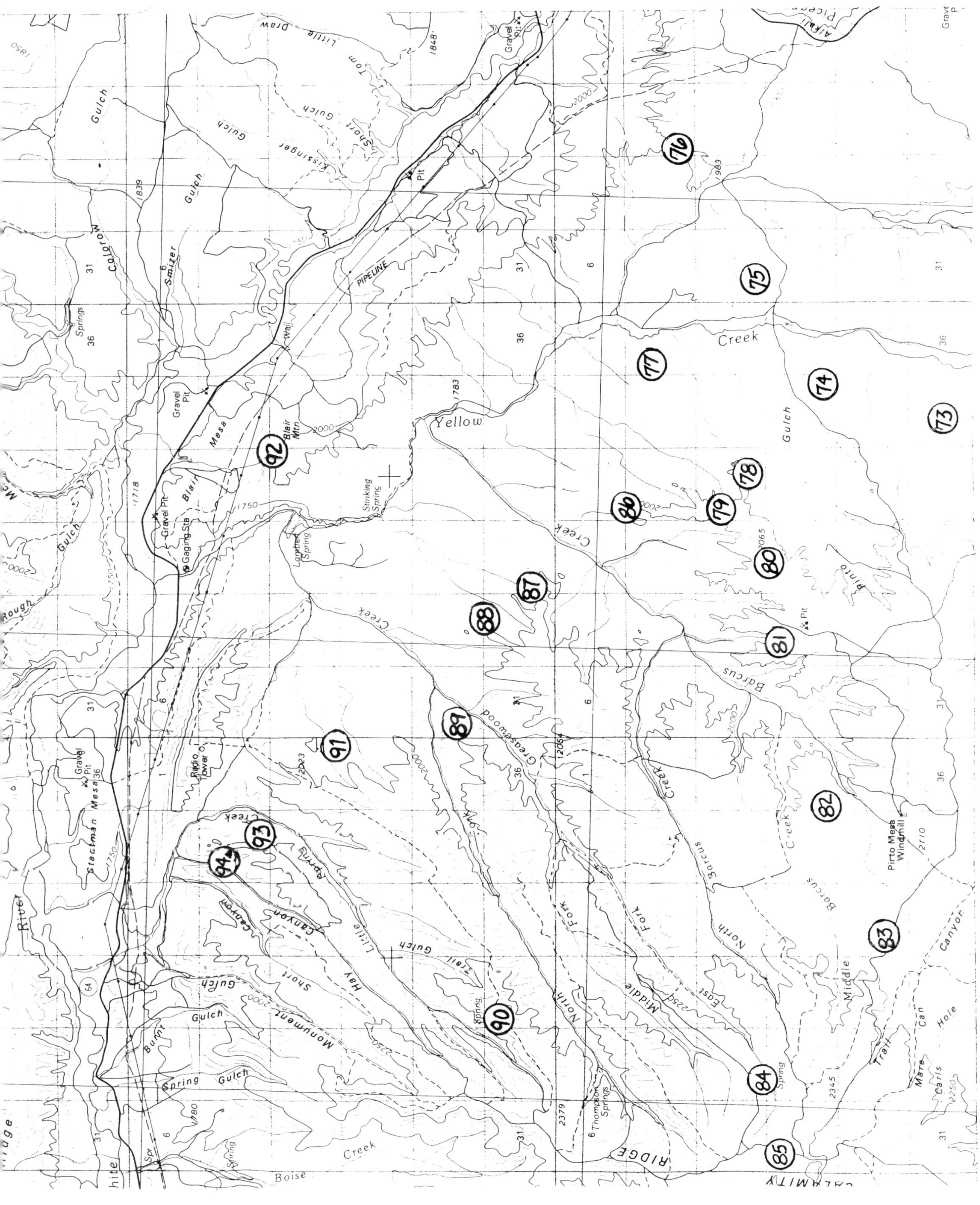

**RIO BLANCO
PICEANCE BASIN
3-D MAP**

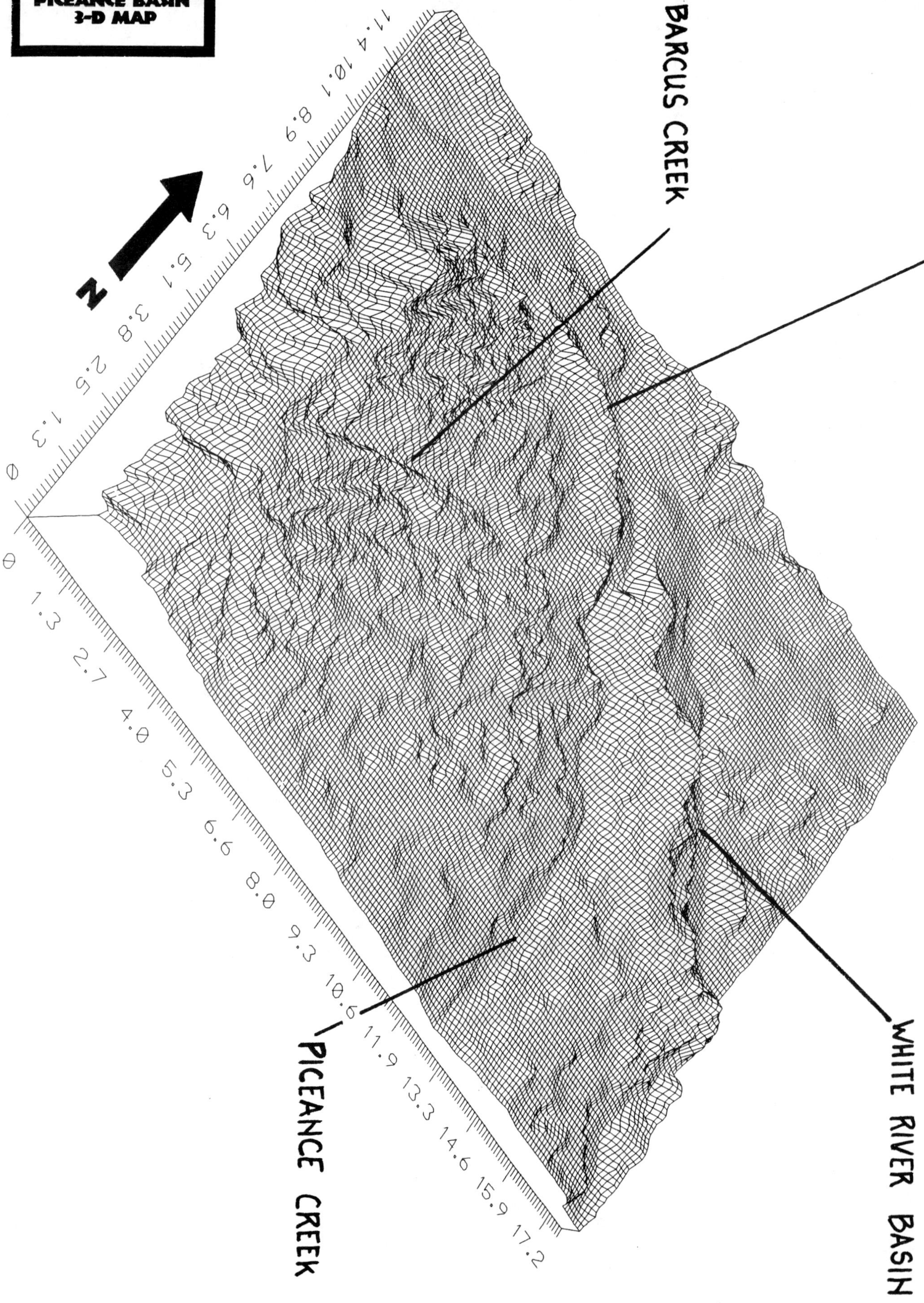

Ryder Peaks Area

Big Game Hunting Unit(s): 17

How To Get There:
Take I-70 west from Denver to the Highway 40 exit (40 miles). Drive north on 40 through the towns of Winter Park, Granby and Kremmling. From there drive to Muddy Pass where you will intersect Highway 14. Go northeast on 14 toward Walden. Approximately seven miles from the Highway 14/Highway 40 intersection you will see an access road for Indian Creek which you will take and head back south. Go approximately three miles on the dirt road until you reach the National Forest border.

Coming back after a morning hunt in the Ryder Peaks area.

How to Hunt this Area:
The terrain in this area consists of thick lodge pole pines intermittent with lush meadows created from the springs seeping out of the sides of the mountains. There are also some open parks up toward the top of the saddles by the higher peaks. The timber is primarily dark pine, but there are some aspen groves on the south facing slopes. There are a lot of old logging roads through the forests that provide optimal hunting access. By walking on those roads you can quickly get back into an area without making any noise.

The elevation in this area goes from roughly 9,000 feet all the way up to 9,900 feet at the peak tops. The area offers good hunting opportunities during all the seasons because it doesn't get as much snow as other areas, but is still high enough to remain cool most of the year.

All through this area ranchers have put out mineral licks for the cattle that graze the open range. We found large elk and deer trails going to the licks. They're great ambush spots.

Spot 01: **6 Point**. Approximately 3/4 of a mile after you enter the National Forest boundary, on the right hand side of the road will be a lush meadow. It's a good place to park your vehicle and begin walking uphill. Follow the gully up because it has water year round and pulls in the elk.

Guy:

> A few years back Fish and I went to this spot during the second rifle season. Although we had never been there, it was highly recommended by a friend at a local sporting goods store in Granby. We parked there at first light and walked up the gully. Within 25 minutes we ran into a herd of elk containing a six point bull and five cows. We both had permits yet we failed to take an elk. The reason was that we became a little nonchalant during the climb up and started talking with one another. Suddenly, out of the corner of my eye I saw the herd. The bull turned his harem around by hooking them with his rack and quickly disappeared over the ridge. At first we sat there dumbfounded. Then we began to laugh because we couldn't believe how foolish we had been. We walked over to where the elk had been and found six sets of tracks in the fresh snow.

Spot 02: **Mineral Lick Knob**. If you continue up the valley a little bit farther it will flatten out around a knoll. There is a mineral lick right in there. You'll easily find it because every trail in the entire area goes right to it. We found this spot late in the day and therefore were not able to pattern the game. They could be coming in morning or evening. If you have some time to spend, or a member of your hunting party can't walk far, this would be an ideal spot to sit in ambush.

Spot 03: **North Ryder Peak**. This spot is located on the northwest face of North Ryder Peak. This is where the elk we saw at Spot 01 ran to. Up there are some patches of dense timber and downed timber that are extremely hard to get through. But that's where you'll see the most animals. Fortunately, it's not very steep, so you can easily circle the peak staying level and cover a lot of ground. There are also some high points where you can sit and have an easy 100 to 200 yard shot at anything that passes by.

Spot 04: **Big Saddle**. There are some open saddles between North and South Ryder Peaks where you can get a shot two to three hundred yards down the south facing slope. If you sit there on opening morning before the elk have been spooked or become nocturnal you'll more than likely get something into your scope. It's also a good spot for ambushing with a muzzle loader or bow.

Guy:

A few years back my buddy Greg Sheets was sitting in this particular spot right between a patch of aspen and black timber. We had placed him there to watch the saddle while Spence and I worked farther down. It wasn't surprising that we spooked a herd of deer right past him. Greg said he heard a bunch of noise. He thought it was us running back to him. Then suddenly a nice three point came running through. Immediately thereafter a nice four point, and immediately behind him was a five point. He said all he could do was sit there and watch each of them bound through his scope as each one got bigger. He didn't even take a shot. Don't let this happen to you. Be prepared and take the first animal you are willing to settle for. I think he was a little greedy.

Spot 05: **Indian Ponds**. This spot is located on the east side of Indian Creek Road right next to a pond. This is ideal elk country and there are also some nice timber bucks to be had. In there we saw a lot of sign - chewed up bark, dozens of rubs and torn up ground from bulls sparring. We didn't actually see the animals, just the sign. But they're in there. It's a good sleeper spot which has limited access.

Spot 06: **Bear Pond**. This spot is located adjacent to a small pond back on the south side of Indian Creek Road. You will be hunting a little lower in elevation where there are more open meadows. It's much easier to walking down there. In addition to elk and deer sign, we came across bear tracks around the pond. A few years back, when baiting for bear was still legal, someone had put out bait right next to the pond. There was a tree stand over the bait, but it looked like the hunter hadn't used it in a while. Too bad for him because the bear had been in to feed, and he had missed his opportunity.

Spot 07: **Valley Of The Campers**. This is where we camped several years ago and hunted the area quite extensively. While the spot contained more deer sign than anything else, elk were also scattered around in small groups up toward Ryder Peak. There are also some ridges directly to the west and south that are good spots to hunt. The ridges are not named on the maps, but once you get there you won't have trouble finding them.

Spot 08: **Hidden Pond**. There is a pond in this area that does not show up on the quadrant map. It's located right between two peaks and is always wet. The sign around that pond is tremendous. It looks like a highway for deer, elk and moose.

Guy:

I sat around that pond for about two hours one evening without any animals coming in. But then as I started to walk back down the hill, I heard some noise coming from the trail I was walking on. So I stepped not more than three feet off the trail behind a large tree. A few seconds had passed when I saw them. Up the trail came a cow and a calf elk, the cow leading. They were coming at a mild trot. I did not move. They did not see me and couldn't smell me as I was downwind of them. The cow passed probably within six yards of me and kept walking. As the calf passed me I moved so it could see me in an attempt to get it to stop. Stop he did. He tried to figure out exactly what I was but couldn't. Next he continued on his way, never being spooked. I would have taken the cow elk had it not been for the calf. It was just fun to get that close with him not having any idea that I was there. I am confident they were going up to the pond I'd just left. In light of this, I think it would be a good place if you are willing to sit over it late and walk back in the dark.

Spot 09: **Spencer's Gully**. This spot is located just north of the Continental Divide and just south of Spot 06. The vegetation in the area is mostly dark timber.

Spence:

Four years ago I took a decent sized buck mule deer in this spot. I was amazed at how big and healthy the deer was. His fur was a glossy reddish color with gray and silver that I had never seen in a deer. They must find excellent forage in the area.

I hadn't hunted with or even shot a rifle in a long time and was pretty proud of my shot. Some other hunters kicked the buck out from below and he ran across the field in front of me. I hit him on the run at about 150 yards. I've always wondered if I could do that again.

Spot 10: **Ryder Lakes**. This spot is located south of Ryder Peak. In order to get there you will have to walk up a trail that has been closed to vehicular travel. You'll see it at the first hairpin turn you come to along Indian Creek Road. It's pretty easy walking. You'll only have to go about a mile. Once you get over the ridge you will drop down into some lush meadows. This is one of the first spots we checked out because it looked so good on a topographical map. Although we didn't get anything in there, we did run into one guy who shot a nice five point bull elk due east of the lakes.

Guy:

I've sat there many nights with no luck. But that doesn't mean that I haven't seen animals. I've seen several cows and some lesser bulls that I was not willing to settle for. They came and grazed the meadows around the lakes.

Spot 11: **Chimney Rock**. This spot is located just west of Chimney Rock. You'll be hunting in an expansive valley. From there you can see all the way to the Gore Mountains which are nearly forty miles away. A little creek that has willows growing along its edge runs along the bottom of the valley. It attracts numerous big bucks that eat the buds off of the willows. You'll be hunting way out in the open where you can take long shots.

Spot 12: **Several Ponds**. This spot is located between Ryder Lakes and Chimney Rock. It's the least accessible spot in the entire area and therefore gives you the best chance at taking a fine animal. However, you will have to pack it out quite a ways as there are no roads in. The vegetation consists of sparse trees and open meadows. The best way to hunt there is to keep your back up against a tree and glass as much terrain as you possibly can with your binoculars.

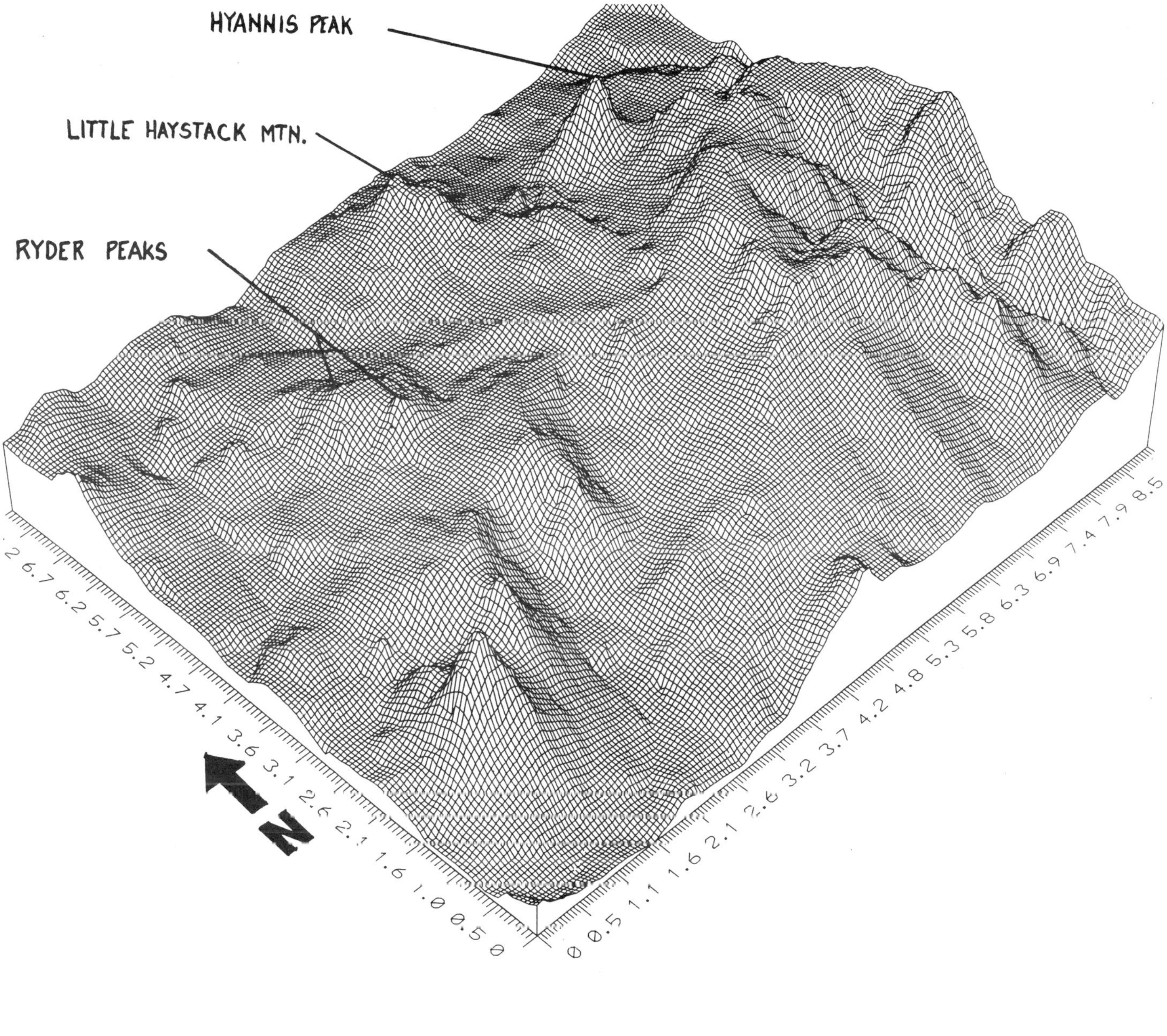

RYDER PEAKS 3-D MAP

Ryder Peaks Area

(Reprinted from Routt National Forest map)

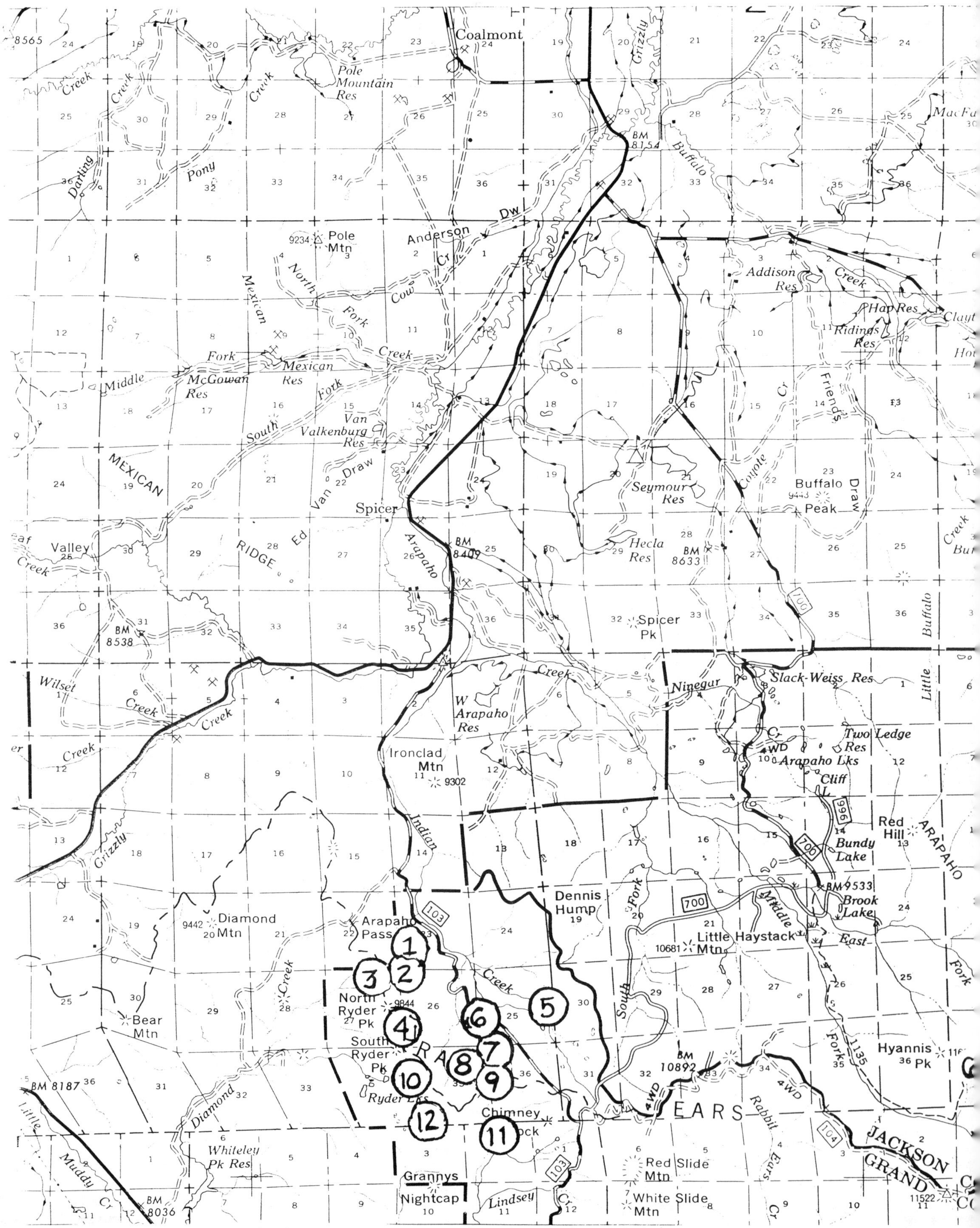

Salt Park/Sleepy Cat Area

Big Game Hunting Unit(s): 12 & 24

How To Get There:

These two areas are located north of the Flat Tops Wilderness. The Sleepy Cat Peak area is in White River National Forest while the Salt Park area is located in Routt National Forest. To get there take Highway 40 90 miles north from I-70 miles through Steamboat Springs, then on to the small town of Craig. Continue south on Highway 13 to Hamilton and then east to Pagoda on Road 317. From there you will go south on Road 67 to the spots we've marked on the map.

You will need a four by four to get back into many of the spots we've profiled. If you come in from the north into Salt Park, you will probably have to hike in three and half, maybe four miles which will take you about 2 hours. If however you decide to hunt the Sleepy Cat Peak area we recommend coming in from the Buford side. You can take the Lost Creek trail road all the way up about four miles and you will only have to walk two miles.

How To Hunt This Area:

Guy:

> The hunting in this area is going to offer archers and especially muzzle loader hunters an excellent opportunity to take both a trophy bull elk and big high country bucks. If I had to guess, from what I've seen of this area I would say your chances of muzzle loader success would be in the 95 percentile for deer, and 75% for elk. It's also very good for rifle hunting. But remember, there's a four point restriction in these units.

The elevation in this area is relatively high, from 9,000 to 11,000 feet. You will be hunting in the Beaver Flat Tops, which is directly north of the Flat Tops Wilderness. This section of country is good feeding ground for elk. It supports the largest elk herd in western Colorado as well as some of the finest trophy buck hunting anywhere, and we do mean anywhere.

Due to the uncharacteristically heavy precipitation this area gets, the forests are thick which makes for excellent close cover hunting, much like you would do back east. An effective tactic is to place tree stands over heavily used game trails. The heavy cover and downed timber acts as a barrier, concentrating game onto well beaten paths that provide easier travel. Trail hunting is best in late morning (8:00 to 10:00 AM) and early evening (3:00 to 6:00 PM) when the game is going to and from the open fields.

During mid-day, you will want to slowly work the thick cover, being sure to walk into the wind. You'll be looking for bedded animals. Quite often they will sit back in the woods in a position where they can watch an open field. Usually they will be on a bit higher ground or a bench where the wind will blow your scent up to them.

When the elk are in full rut there should be no reason why you can't call the bulls to within a few yards for an excellent shooting opportunity. You can expect to make shots anywhere from 20 yards all the way up to 150 yards (rifles only at that distance). Remember, because the woods are so thick, the animals will rely more on their sense of smell and hearing than their eyesight. You can eliminate their hearing advantage by moving slowly, or not moving at all if they are coming to you. Their keen sense of smell is harder to deal with because as they get closer your smell will get stronger and easier for them to detect. What you should do is always walk into the wind, and carry a bottle of cover scent that has a spray adaptor. When they are getting close, spray the scent into the air around you.

For those of you hunting during the rifle season you need to get there early and secure a good place to camp. There's enough game in there for everybody, but to improve your chances it's best to get in early and walk up higher than everybody else. That way the other hunters will push animals to you.

Spot 01: **Salt Park**. This spot is located at 9,200 feet on an east sloping hill around several beaver ponds. You get there via Trail 1114. This is a great place to check for the freshest elk sign available (elk moving to and from the area). It's all heavily wooded with no large open meadows or parks to speak of.

During the archery and muzzle loading seasons try bugling on the ridges to get a response down in the valley. During the rifle season hunt between the ridge and Corral Creek.

Spot 02: **Berry Creek Drainage**. Walk Trail 1113 all the way up to the base of Berry Creek where you'll find a big open meadow. Then turn and go back to the southwest up Berry Creek to the beaver ponds. Right where the beaver ponds end is the start of an open meadow in which elk feed. Sit down and watch the meadow with your binoculars. It's best in the early morning.

Spot 03: **Upper Lost Creek**. This spot is located in an area called Lost Park. The upper end of the creek breaks off into two different drainages. You can hunt either one, but stay on the high side and don't walk through the middle or the elk will spot you. Remember not to silhouette your human figure against the horizon, or the elk below you will pick you out.

If you happen to catch a bull elk out in the meadows below you, stay back in the timber and do some cow calls. It's a lot easier to pull a bull into cover rather than out of cover.

Guy:

I've seen 20 or 30 elk in the upper drainages of this park, mostly cows. There were only a couple of raghorn bulls in there, but I know there were big ones somewhere near. I think the big boys were up higher toward Sleepy Cat Peak.

Spot 04: **Sleepy Cat Peak**. Although you'll be hunting at 10,200 feet in elevation, this spot is still not above timberline. In the earlier part of the season the elk and deer are going to be up high on the peak. If it has been warm the elk will stay in the dark timber where it's cooler. Hunt the fringes of open fields and the areas where aspen pockets border dark timber. After the leaves fall, you'll find it much easier to hunt the aspen stands. In late October and November there will be quite a bit of snow at 10,200 feet. Once the snow becomes so deep that they find it hard to dig for their food, they will move down lower. The best place to hunt is just along the snow line. By the rifle season they will have moved down to lower Lost Park.

Spot 05: **Mt. Baldy**. This spot is located on the north side of Sleepy Cat Peak. Continue up Trail 1114 until you cut across a ridge the locals call Baldy Mountain. The terrain goes from dark timber to a few open meadows where you can take longer shots. There are dense stands of aspen where you will find lots of elk feeding on the grasses that grow between the trees.

Baldy Mountain has a few meadows up on top of it where in the past we've spotted herds of 15-20 elk. This area doesn't get as much pressure as the Flat Tops because you have to hike farther to get there, but it is equally as productive. Plus, the game will be undisturbed and easier to hunt. Just make sure you are in good shape, and you will have no problems.

Spot 06: **Ell's Mountain**. This spot is located even farther to the northwest of the previous one. You will be losing altitude as you walk the ridgeline down from Baldy Mountain. There are several trails crisscrossing the ridge. One of those goes down to the open parks below. Walking the ridgeline to the bottom also takes you to the parks. The lush grass down there draws a lot of elk. Also down lower are aspens that are heavily scarred by elk chewing their bark.

This area borders private property. Hunt the boundary between private and public land as the game will move between the two. Also, look for the numerous transition zones where one type of vegetation starts and another stops. The greater variety of food types along those zones pulls in more game than single vegetation areas.

Spot 07: **Upper North Fork Of The White River**. There are several ways to get to this spot. You can walk up Missouri Creek or take Road 250 all the way to the top of Sand Peak. Early in the season the open areas to the north and west of Sands Peak are great places to spot and stalk elk that are out feeding. Even later in the rifle season when the snow drives them out of the high country you will still find elk in there. The wind blows snow off the face permitting them to stay up high. There is also good hunting along Dead Horse Creek.

Spot 08. **Pagoda Peak**. Continue up the jeep trail from Sand Peak until you reach the thick woods around Pagoda Peak. Hunt the fringes where aspen and lodgepole pine stands meet. Walk the level ridgeline toward the northeast. It's easy walking on top of the ridge. You will not gain more than 200 feet in elevation. Elk will usually move up a gully, cross the ridge and then head back down into a gully on the other side. Look for spots where they have recently crossed, and follow. Also, look for places where they may be crossing back and forth daily, and set up an ambush.

Spot 09: **Vaughn Lake/Ripple Creek Pass**. This spot is located farther to the east of the previous one. To get there take the Ripple Creek Pass Road northeast over the top and down the back side about two miles to Vaughn Lake. There is a campground there, and several productive elk hunting spots right around the lake. Another good spot is in the lodge pole pines and aspens on both sides of the pass itself. Hunters pull big bulls out of there every year. However, if you're hunting during the rifle season, you'll be in there with a lot of other people. During archery and muzzle loader seasons you won't see many other people.

Spot 10: **Ripple Creek**. This area is known for its excellent big game hunting. An outfitter who has a lodge located at the bottom near the White River takes hunters back up on top of the Flat Tops. We've been contemplating this or another outfitter to get us farther back into the wilderness area.

Guy:

If you do decide to hunt the wilderness area a drop camp is a great way to go, especially with the success spots we are giving you. Drop camps offer a reasonable alternative to the expense of a fully guided hunt. It will cost anywhere from $650 all the way up to $1,000, depending upon what options you choose, and how long you stay.

Spot 11: **Upper Ripple Creek Valley**. Driving up the valley you'll notice an increasing amount of open sagebrush on the south facing slopes. Those are great places to catch the elk out feeding in the morning. They like the grass that grows between the sage. Plus, the open range allows them to see approaching hunters from a long way off.

The hills along the bottom of Ripple Creek are very steep and difficult to walk. The best thing to do is to glass the slopes above and only walk up when you see something worth walking for. Sooner or later you are going to spot elk.

Salt Park/Sleepy Cat Area

(Reprinted from White River National Forest map)

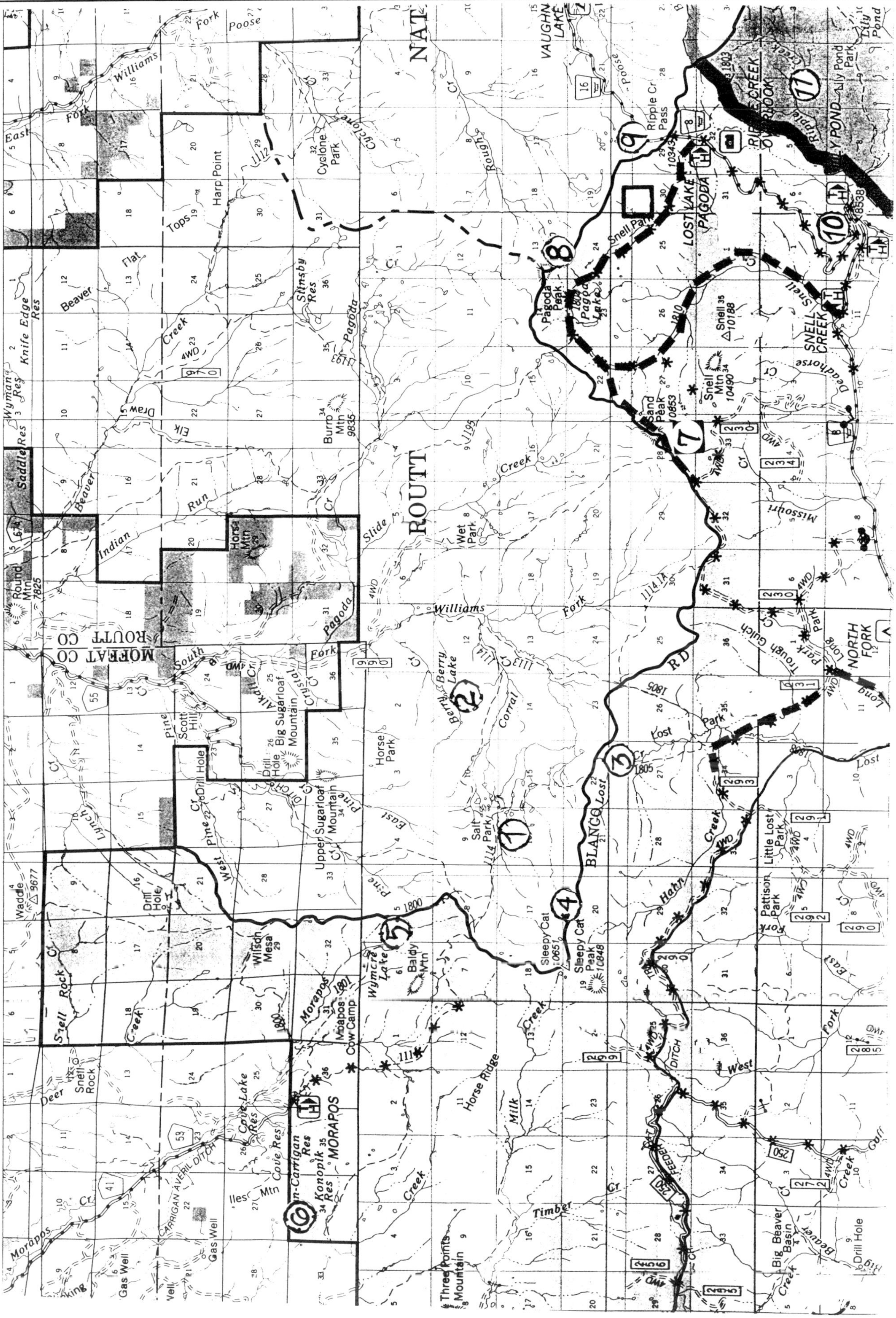

SALT PARK/ SLEEPY CAT PEAK 3-D MAP

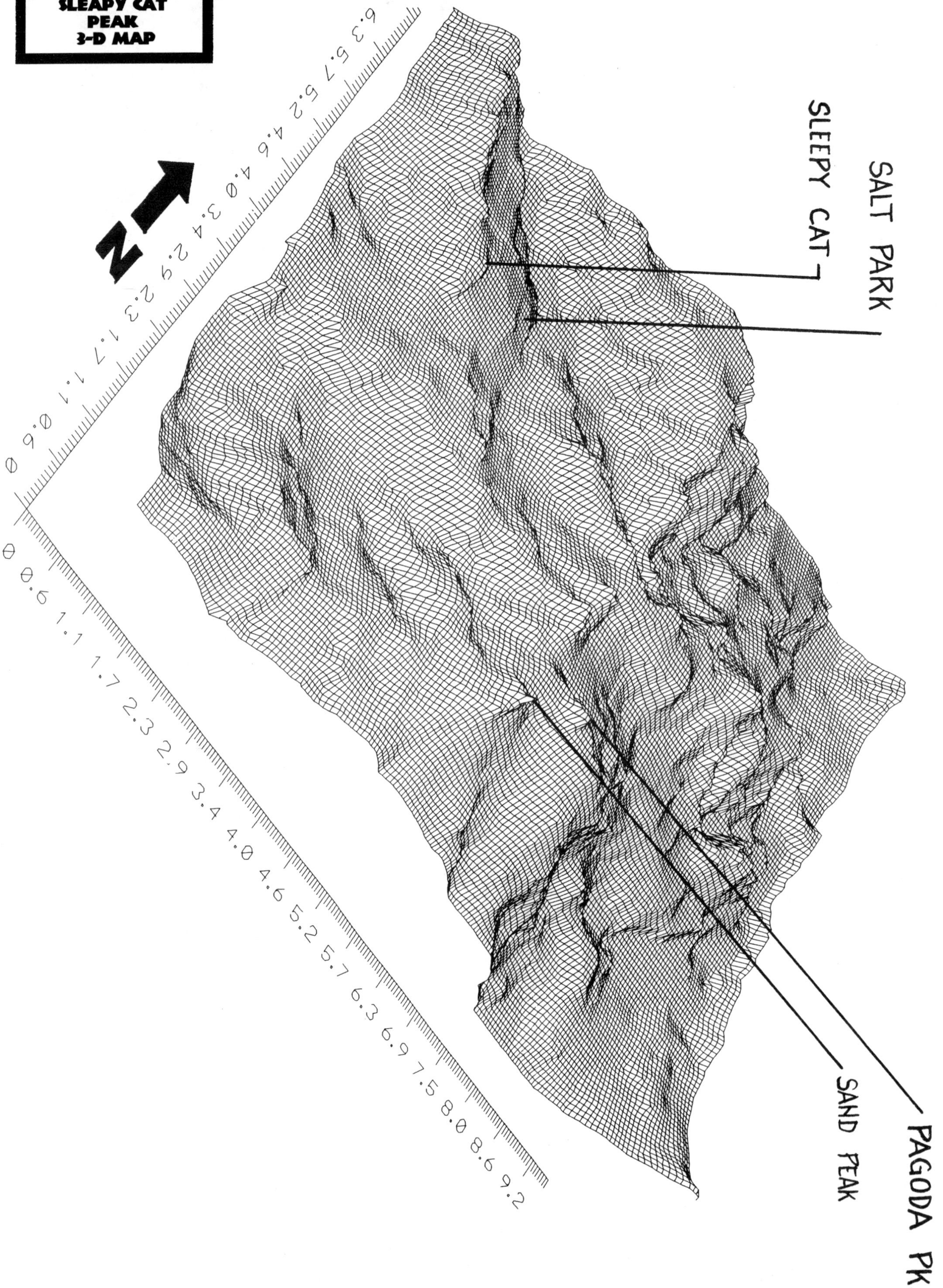

Silver Creek

Big Game Hunting Unit(s): 28

How To Get There:

From Denver take US 70 west past Idaho Springs, to the Highway 40 turnoff. Cross Berthoud pass and head north past the Silver Creek Ski Area. About a mile before you hit Granby take the road heading east. Access to this area is a little difficult because the local ski area has tried to make it hard for hunters to get in. But if you're willing to walk, you'll be glad you did.

How To Hunt This Area:

The vegetation in this area consists of dark timber mixed with sage. The timber is very closely packed and brushy. You'll notice a lot of little offshoot branches lower down on the trees than you would expect. Driving up from Winter Park you will be surprised at how thick the clumps of timber look. But you can still pass through them. Usually there are logging roads you can walk.

Stay a little back into the timber and watch the sage fields from as far in as will still permit binocular spotting. There are a lot of deer in the area as well as elk in the late season. They feed just along the perimeter of the sage. Because the trees are so thick, it's hard to spot an animal if it's standing anywhere but out in the fields. If the animals are in the timber, you just have to move slowly and utilize back lighting. Try to walk so you are always looking toward an open spot where you can pick out silhouettes and movement.

When they're not walking the pine/sage transition zone, the elk follow the timbered ridgelines. Rather than cross saddles from one valley to the next, they move down from one ridgeline, cross the saddles and head back up to the next ridge. This behavior may be the result of too much hunting pressure. We scouted this area during the third rifle season. However, if this behavior holds true, it's critical that you don't assault a ridge from the side. You will be backlighted by the sage behind you. Instead, follow a saddle up, then head up the ridgeline from the saddle with the wind in your face. You will either come up behind the animals, or will walk directly into one another.

If you are hunting for deer in this area, look for small clumps of trees out in the middle of the sage. Nine times out of ten you will kick deer out of those clumps because they provide the only spot where the deer can bed down under cover.

Spot 01: **West Silver Creek Valley.** This spot is located on one small patch of BLM land on the west side of the Silver Creek valley just north of the ski area. You can walk up the Silver Creek valley to it. The vegetation is mostly sage brush, except for two large patches of timber just below the rocky ridgeline. The deer hang out in those patches most of the daylight hours. It's a great flush and shoot spot.

Spot 02: **Elk Hill.** On the east side of Silver Creek, just north of the ski condo area is a knob hill that elk like. It gives them a good view of the valley below and they can quickly move into the rough terrain of DeBerard Draw if they need to. This spot attracts elk in the late season after snow has fallen.

Spence:

> My wife Becky and I were staying at the ski resort during the third rifle season. One morning we saw over 50 elk including three bulls standing on that knob in the middle of the afternoon. We walked toward them and as we got closer the whole side of the hill looked like it just turned into a river of elk. We counted over 200 running. They moved to the top of the hill and stared down at us. Becky had never really seen this many big animals thundering through the sage. She was very worried they would turn and trample us. I couldn't get her to go any closer. We moved off into the woods and then they just went on feeding. On the edge of the woods we spotted a beautiful 6 X 6 which we watched for some time. We went back the next day and ran into two hunters who told us that the day before, at 4:30 in the afternoon a hunter had taken that 6 X 6 we had spotted.

Spot 03: **Ridge - DeBerard Draw.** There's a ridge between DeBerard Draw and Silver Creek. The elk walk this because it gives them a good view of both valleys while they remain in thick cover. At night, they feed in the valleys below.

Spot 04: **Saddle - DeBerard Draw.** A gully runs up from DeBerard Draw to form a saddle between it and Silver Creek. Elk cross between the two quite frequently. Also a herd of about 12 deer hang out on the west side of the saddle right where the sagebrush starts.

Silver Creek

(Reprinted from Arapahoe National Forest map)

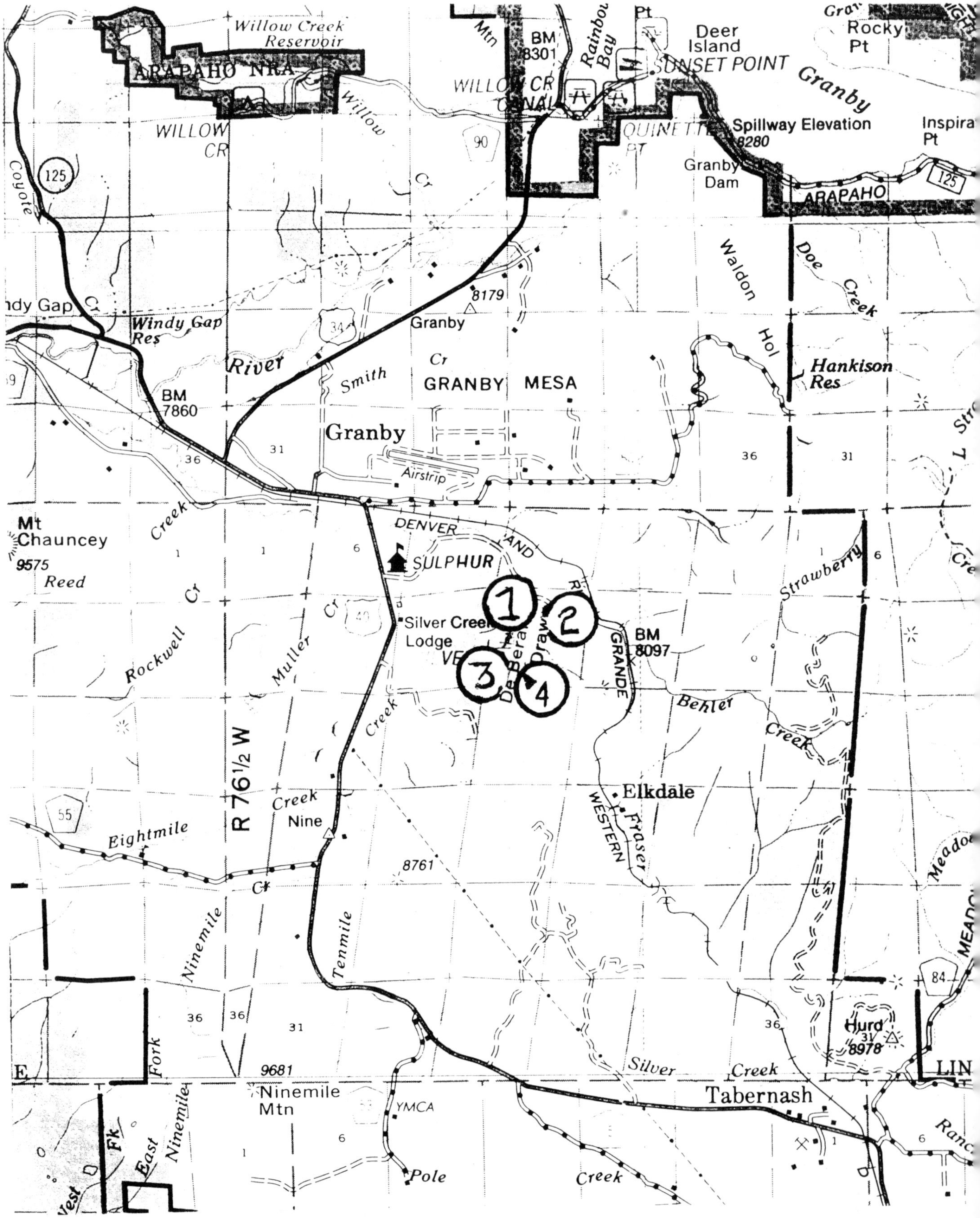

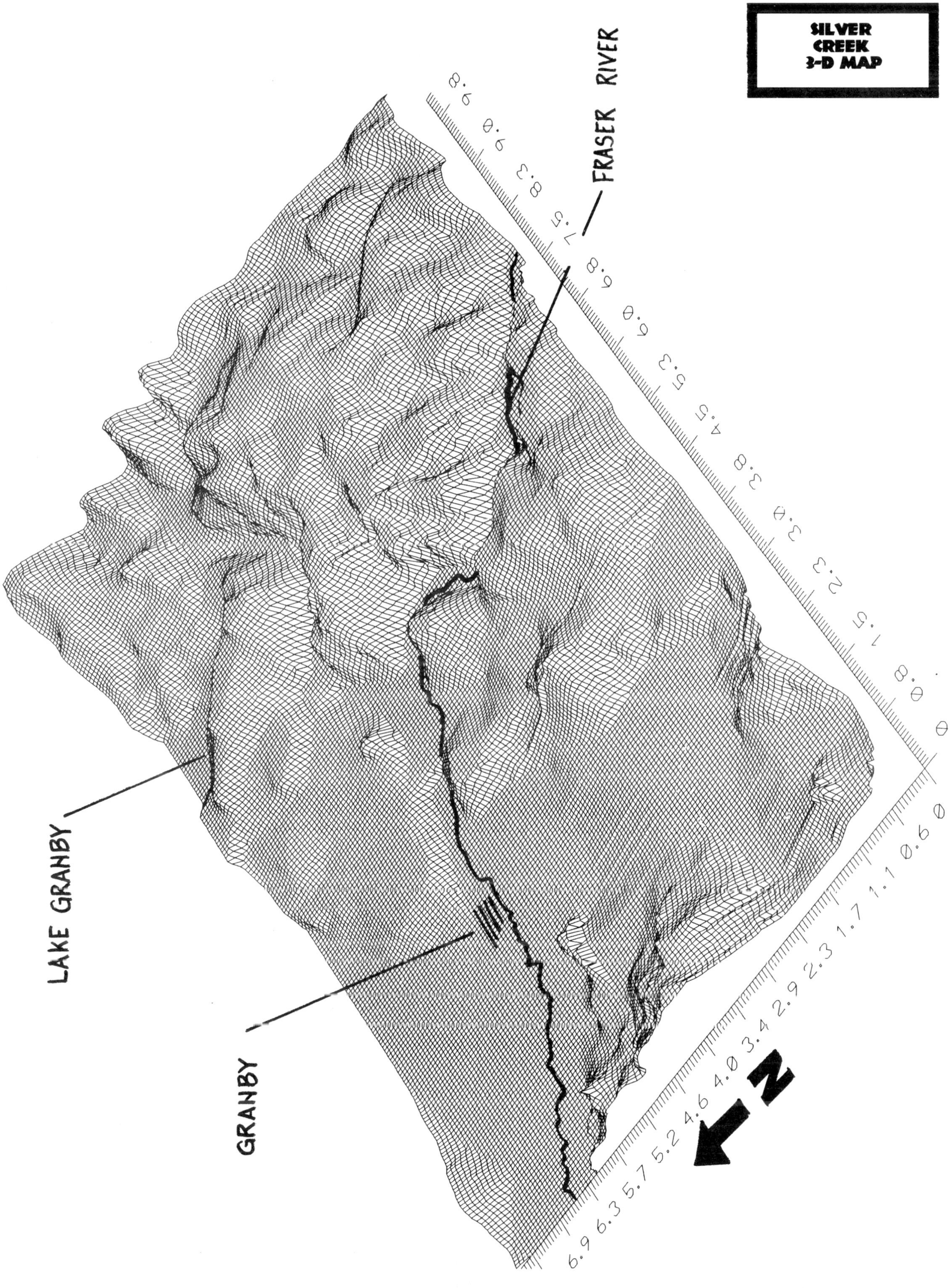
SILVER CREEK 3-D MAP
FRASER RIVER
LAKE GRANBY
GRANBY
N
0 0.8 1.5 2.3 3.0 3.8 4.5 5.3 6.0 6.8 7.5 8.3 9.0 9.8
0 0.6 1.1 1.7 2.3 2.9 3.4 4.0 4.6 5.2 5.7 6.3 6.9

South Park Area

Big Game Hunting Unit(s): 50

How To Get There:

To get there from Denver take Highway 285 southwest all the way over Kenosha Pass (65 miles) and down into South Park through the town of Jefferson. Just before the town of Como turn left on CR 15 and head south to the spots marked on the map.

How To Hunt This Area:

This is mostly an antelope and deer area, although you may see elk in there during the late rifle season. Deep snow will push elk out of the high country and onto the open plains, but don't count on it unless the mountains get some really heavy snow.

The way you hunt this area varies greatly from many of the other areas we've profiled because the terrain is very open and sparse. Often times, the animals will be out in an area that doesn't even have a bush. The only way you will be able to get close to them is to use low lying hills and humps as cover.

Down in the valleys which get a little more water there's quite a bit of sagebrush that provides a little better cover. There's also a few windmills with waterholes underneath which attract game. One good way to hunt the waterholes is to make a platform stand inside the framework of a windmill and wait for the antelope to come in for water. You can also try a shaded pit blind that gives you a good view of the water while remaining hidden. Another way to hunt them is to use an antelope decoy. Decoying is by far the hottest new way to attract antelope during the September-October pre-rut and rut.

Spot 01: **Como**. This spot is located on BLM land right where you turn off from Como on PCR 15. There is always a herd of antelope grazing right there off the side of the road. Sometimes they walk down toward the creek and back up again. Setting up an ambush along that route may work well. A lot of people overlook this spot because they don't realize it's on public land.

Spot 02: **Park Gulch**. This spot is located just to the south of Road 15 along the creek bed. A herd of antelope wanders from one side of the road to another. There are also a few big mule deer that hang around the creek bed. Just like the previous spot, hunters rarely stop there because they don't realize it's all BLM land.

Spot 03: **Windmill Flats**. Drive approximately three to four miles down PCR 15. On the west side of the road you will see some windmills that are located on BLM land. We've seen several dominant antelope bucks in that area herding up does and chasing off lesser bucks. If you're looking for trophy sized antelope, this is one place where you won't be disappointed.

Spot 04: **The Big Miss**. Follow PCR 15 back to the National Forest boundary. Once inside the boundary the road will "T" and you will turn left (you should be heading north after the turn). Approximately two miles up on the west side lies a grove of ponderosa and pinion pine trees. Antelope sit under those trees to escape the heat. Note: This type of terrain isn't what hunters typically look for when scouting antelope which is why the area gets so little hunting pressure.

Guy:

> By those trees I took a shot at a big buck antelope a couple of years ago. I stalked to within 35 yards before I raised to shoot. Unfortunately right as I released my arrow the antelope that had been stationary for some time made a sudden turn. I think he may have heard my aluminum shaft whistling as it came at him. My arrow flew true and whizzed within inches of that big buck. He was probably in the fourteen inch class so he wasn't huge, but he was definitely a nice trophy.

Spence:

> I talked to a guy who last year took three shots at antelope from his blind. Each time he shot the buck actually jumped his arrow. He's going to carbon shafts this year because he's heard they make less noise and the antelope can't jump them. It's amazing how agile they are.

Spot 05: **Ruby Gulch H2O Hole**. This spot is located just to the east of Eagle Rock in a creek bed that runs along the bottom of Ruby Gulch. The creek dries up before antelope season but due west of Eagle Rock, one waterhole remains. Around the waterhole is a good place to dig a ground blind. You will do a lot of sitting and waiting which can be quite boring - bring a book. The antelope will usually come in to water twice, and sometimes three times a day if it's really hot.

Spot 06: **East Berkeley Creek**. This spot is located in a group of deep arroyos northwest of Eagle Rock. The antelope stay on the flat tops above and between the arroyos which is a perfect setup for a hunter. You can stay down in the arroyos and easily stalk to within shooting range. Buck antelope hunters may have a more difficult time because as the season progresses, the bucks become more wary of the gullies.

Spot 07: **Observatory Rock**. This spot is located farther to the north of the previous one, well off the road. Due to the seclusion of this spot, the you'll find a lot of deer as well as a few elk. Many of the trees have been stripped by bull elk rubbing their antlers to remove their velvet. However, later in the rifle season, hunting pressure will push game out of this area. We recommend that you hunt there during the black powder season, bow season and opening day of rifle season.

South Park Area

(Reprinted from Pike National Forest map)

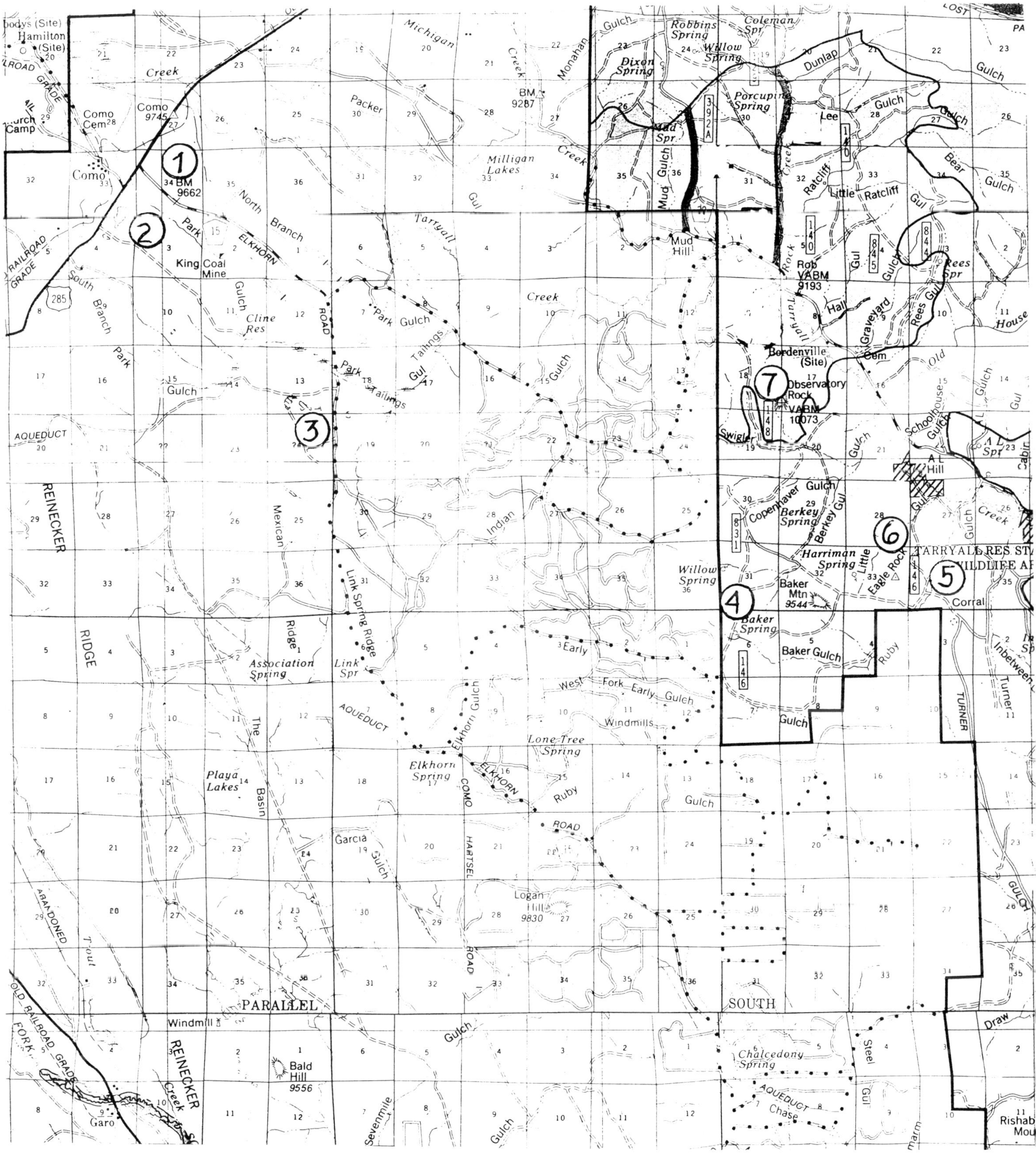

SOUTH PARK AREA 3-D MAP

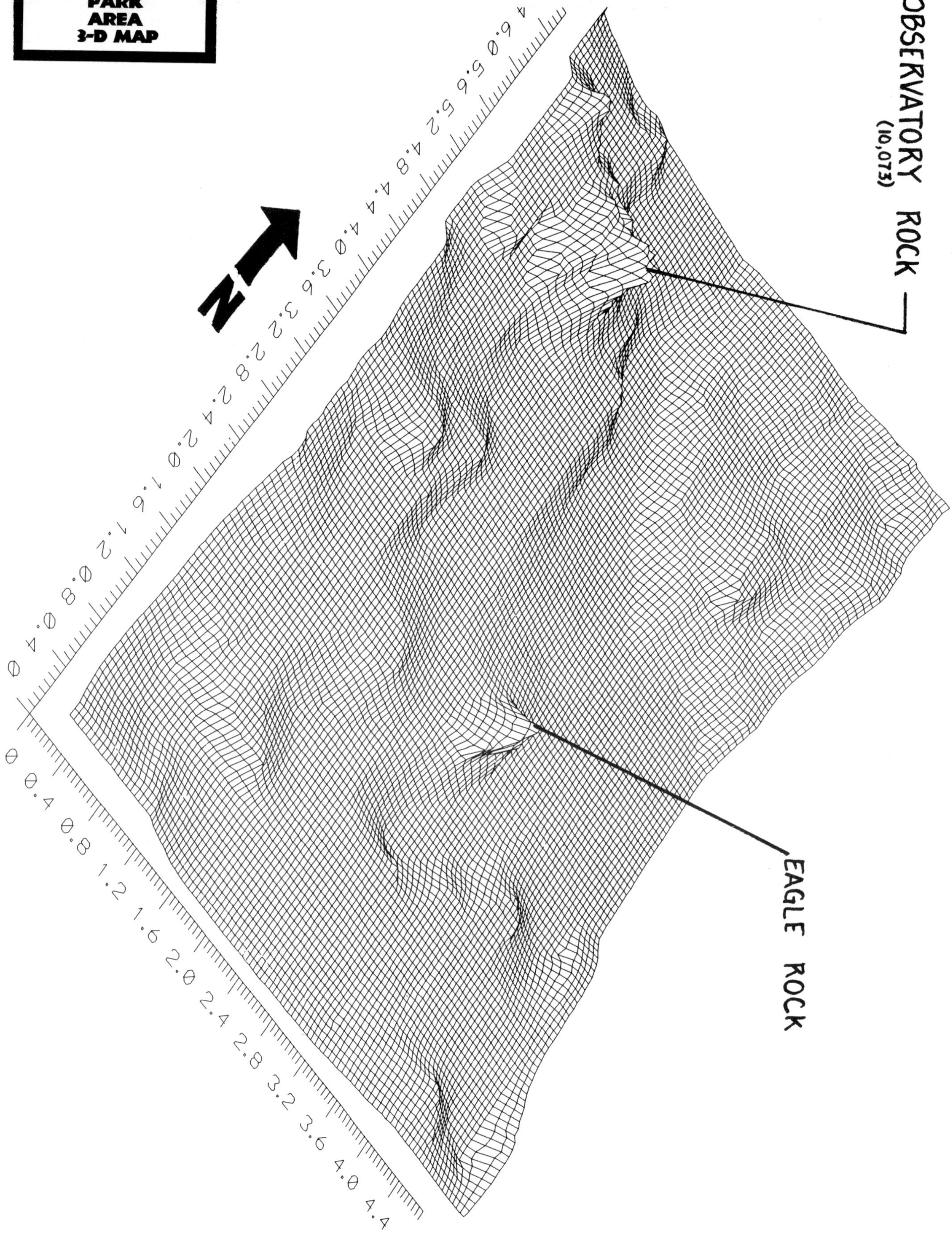

SOUTH PARK AREA 3-D MAP

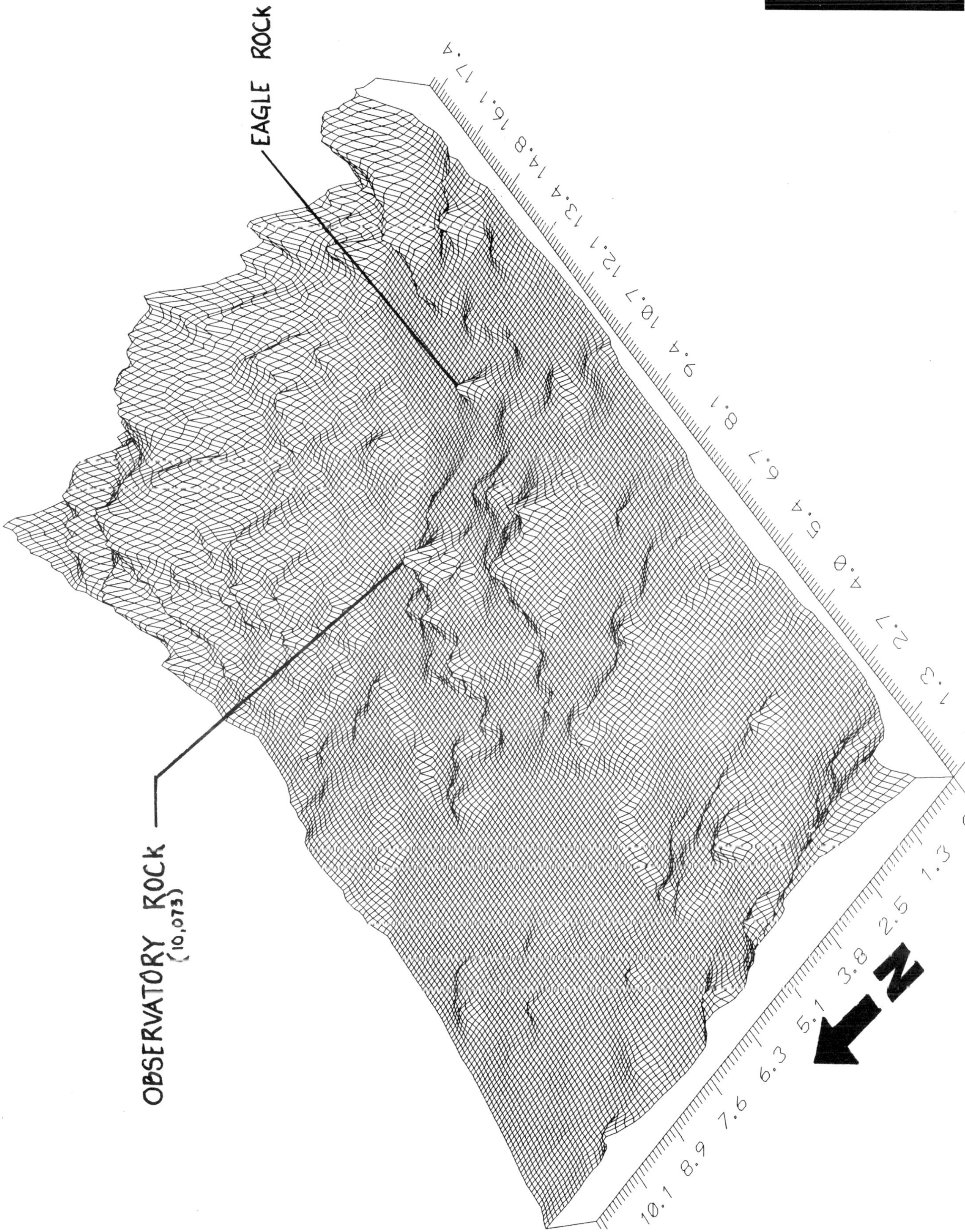

Big Game Hunting Unit(s): 17

How To Get There:
From Denver drive west on I-70 to Highway 40 then north to Granby. Just past Granby turn off on Highway 125 and drive over Willow Creek Pass. Turn left on Forest Service Road 106 and drive to Troublesome Pass. It becomes a four wheel drive road up toward the top.

It's not uncommon to see elk like these feeding in the open meadows around Troublesome Pass in the early morning.

How To Hunt This Area:
When you do see mule deer in this area, they will usually be trophy size. Elk herds usually number less than 20. There are also a large number of moose, so make sure the elk you have in your sights is really an elk. The Division of Wildlife is extremely harsh on people who shoot the wrong species.

Spence:

> A few years back I heard about a hunter shooting a moose he thought was an elk. The funny thing was, he was a wildlife officer from California.

The terrain in this area consists of thick lodge pole pines broken by a few clear cuts, but not very many. The elevation is high, around 12,000 feet. There are several high mountain bowls which hold a lot of elk in the early archery and muzzle loader seasons. They go there to escape the heat and bugs below. Plus, early on there's lots of lush grass up there. When the first freeze hits, and the upper slope grasses turn brown, the elk move down low, sticking to the still green vegetation of the lower altitudes. Eventually though, the freeze hits down low, and they head back up high where the grasses have cured and are no longer bitter.

The places where aspen and pine groves meet are always productive. During the early morning, sit along those transition zones, preferably in a spot overlooking a meadow that has a well used trail running into it. During the day when the elk are bedded, walk with the wind in your face, moving slowly through the dark timber. Look specifically for spots where they can stay in dark timber, but get a good view of a meadow or other open area from which danger might come.

Due to the remoteness of this area, and the exceptional hunting, there are quite a few outfitters who take hunting parties into the backcountry. They usually come from the Arapaho National Forest side of the pass and work the remote country down along the Troublesome Creek area. Some of the spots we profile will be south of where they hunt.

Spot 01: **Haystack Creek**. Follow Road 106 until it ends at a large brush pile. Then take the trail 3/4 of a mile over the top of the Continental Divide and down into Haystack Creek. At the point where Haystack Creek meets the other arm of the adjoining creek lies a big open meadow. The ground in the meadow is moist and consequently is a great place to look for fresh tracks. You're sure to find a lot.

Spot 02: **Headwaters of Haystack Creek**. There is no trail directly to this spot. To get there take Trail 55 down along Haystack Creek to the north arm of Haystack Creek which you will follow back up to the northeast. At the headwaters of the north arm is some thick timber you can hunt. It's very wet up there and you will be able to spot many tracks left by the animals that feed on the thick growth. Also look for wallows around the springs. Remember, elk use wallows even in the late rifle season when they have ice on them. Wallows will always be productive. However, this spot usually has too much snow for the late rifle season. It's really only good in the first and possibly the second seasons.

Spot 03: **Haystack Springs**. This spot is farther up the canyon from the previous one. The canyon branches out and forms numerous open meadows right along the Continental Divide. You'll be hunting in a saddle next to a small peak. You can get there one of two ways: (1) Go back down Haystack Creek and hunt up through the other arm until you reach the top, or (2) Drive Road 730 until you hit the Continental Divide and then walk a half mile south.

Elk feed in those meadows in the early morning and late evening. It's a great place for spotting with binoculars or a spotting scope. Mid-day, the elk bed down on the north slope.

Spot 04: **Long Draw**. To get to this spot continue down Trail 55 approximately three more miles from where you cut off to go to Spot 02. Off to the right will be a little creek called Long Draw. Head to the northwest of that about 400 yards up the drainage. You'll notice several springs that get a lot of elk activity. By the springs are a couple of nice wallows that the elk use quite frequently, especially right before and during the rut. They stir it up with their horns and hooves then urinate all over themselves and roll in the mud.

To the south of the draw is another spot where you'll find several more wallows. It would be a good idea to hang up a tree stand downwind of one. You may sit there for a couple of days without seeing a thing, but sooner or later a big bull will come.

Spot 05: **Upper Troublesome Creek**. This spot is located just a little bit farther to the west of the previous one up along the Continental Divide. The saddles in this area are heavily used by elk. But they don't just pass through. They are attracted to the abundance of food and the fact that this area gets very little hunting pressure (because it's located away from the trails). You'll find dung piles and rubs all around this spot.

Spot 06: **Hyannis Peak**. Take Trail 1135 to Hyannis Peak. The summit of this peak is at about 11,600 feet. You'll be hunting in the saddle that is located between the peak and the continental divide. Elk continuously cross through the saddle. There is a hiking trail through the saddle that you can use to get around faster. Hunting the saddle will work best if you have a rifle and can take long shots. Archers are going to have to work the timber down lower where they can get in for a closer shot.

Spot 07: **Middle Troublesome Creek**. Take Trail 57 up to the big basin located at the headwaters of Troublesome Creek. You'll probably have it all to yourself. There are a lot of big mule deer bucks up there. A few big bull elk are also taken out of the area each year. Specifically, you want to look for bucks bedded under the trees and shrubs around the big meadow where the three branches of the creek meet. Lower down the draw toward Matheson Reservoir you will see more moose sign, so be careful to positively identify your game before you shoot.

Spot 08: **Upper Matheson Reservoir**. Along Troublesome Creek just above Matheson Reservoir is a marshy area elk feed in and around. It's a great place to find fresh sign. You can also find elk feeding along the banks of the reservoir during the evening and at night.

Spot 09: **Lower Troublesome Creek**. This spot is located on BLM Land farther down the creek from Matheson Reservoir. The valley you'll be hunting in has a lot of dark timber and open meadows where the elk come out to feed in the evening and early morning. The area doesn't get much hunting pressure because the outfitters concentrate their hunts lower down in the valley. An aggressive hunter can really score in a sleeper area like this.

Spot 10: **Continental Divide**. This spot is located at the end of Pack Trail 1135 which goes up over the Continental Divide. You'll be hunting a transition zone where dark timber opens to big alpine meadows. Anywhere you find those zones the elk won't be too far away. The area is so large that to effectively hunt it, you may need to backpack in and stay a few days. We are hopefully alleviating some of the difficulties of hunting a vast area like this by giving you some specific places where you can go. Due to the high altitude and strenuous hiking, you need to be in good shape before you hunt this type of terrain. Being fit can save you a lot of agony later, especially if you have to pack out a mature bull elk or trophy mule deer buck.

Spot 11: **Arapaho Ridge**. Walking this long ridge northwest you will come to a group of saddles that elk use to get to the open meadows above. Take Pack Trail 1135 to get there. The elk will come out to graze in the meadows at dawn and dusk. But if you want to hunt them at other times of the day, check out the gullies and creeks on both sides of the ridge like the East Fork. We once watched 50-60 elk cross the ridge, including several nice bulls. They stayed up there and fed all night until early morning. Just after sunrise they began to work their way back down into the timber. If you plan it right you can sit downwind of their travel routes and get a shot off.

Troublesome Pass - Haystack Mountain Area

(Reprinted from Routt National Forest map)

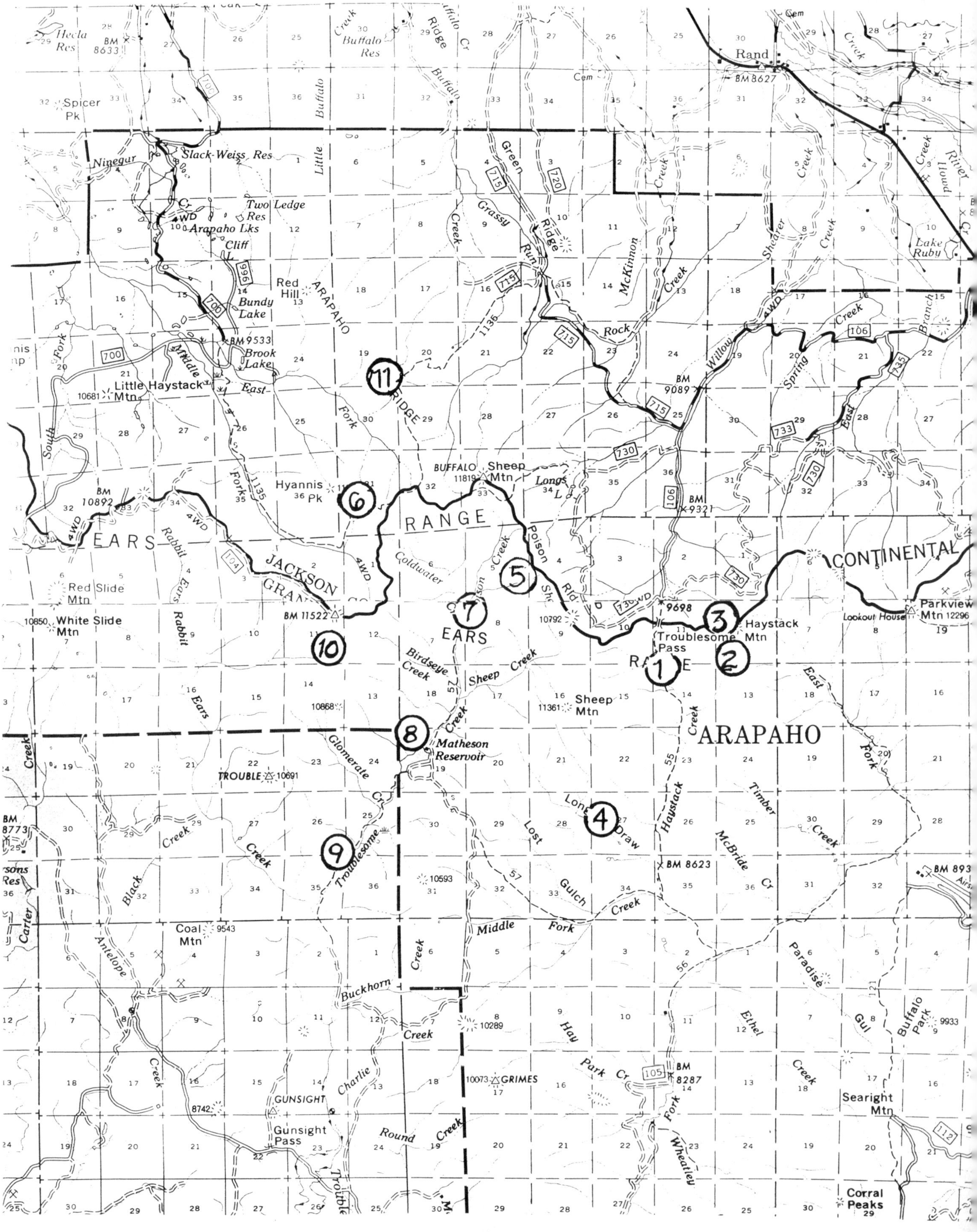

TROUBLESOME PASS/HAYSTACK MOUNTAIN 3-D MAP

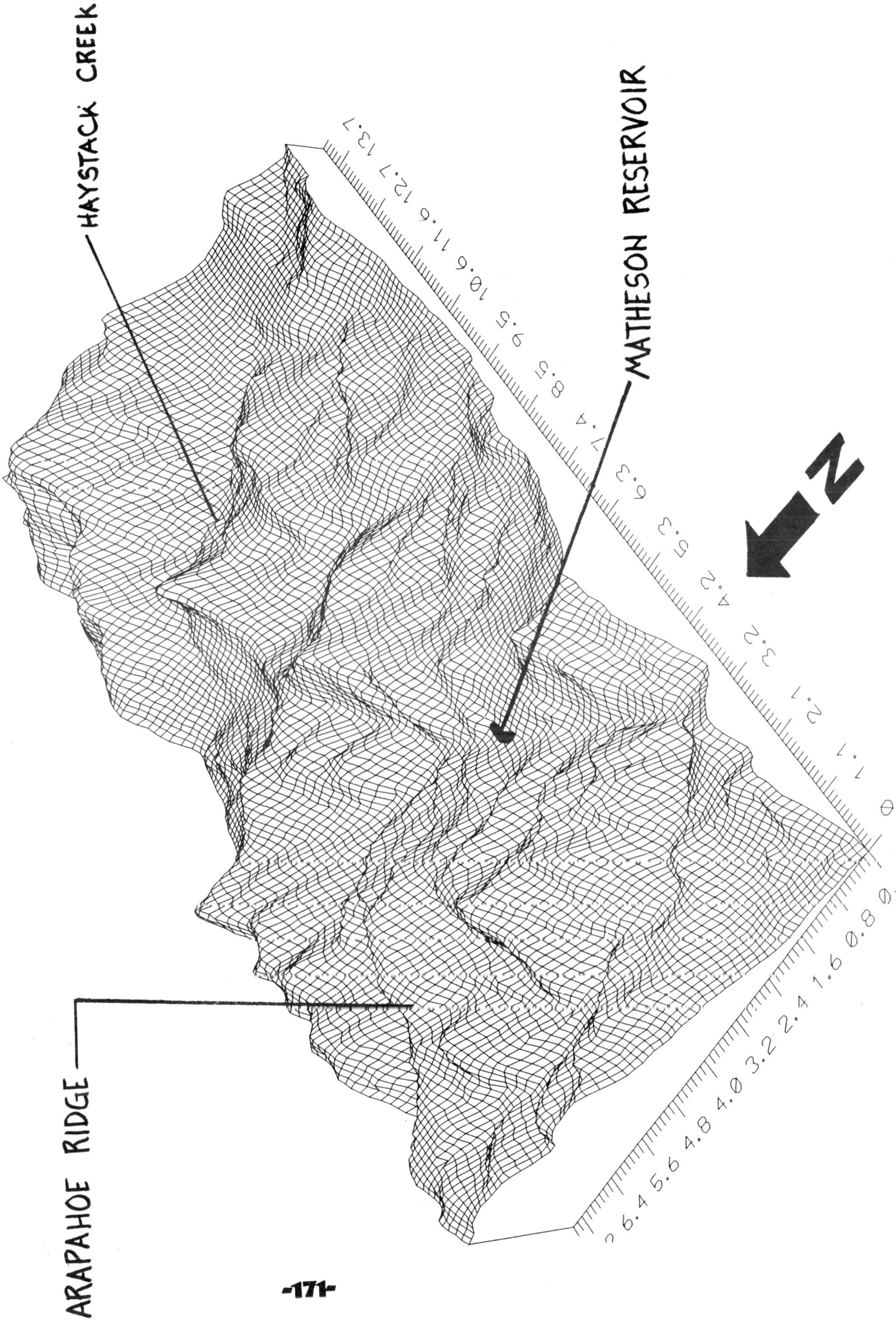

Williams Fork

Big Game Management Unit(s): 37, 28

How To Get There:

To get to the first couple of spots we've marked, take US 70 west from Denver to Highway 40. Where the road turns to head up Berthoud pass, continue going west up Jones Pass.

To get to the other spots, take US 70 west to the Dillon/Silverthorne exit. Then take Highway 9 north to the Ute Pass turnoff heading east over the Williams Fork Mountains.

How To Hunt This Area:

The vegetation in this area is mostly thick mature pines broken by clear cuts in various stages of regrowth. Clearings with a lot of small, densely packed new growth pines are productive, but more difficult to hunt because of lower visibility. You'll find elk and deer at the edges of those open areas in the early morning and at dusk. Stumps and brush piles provide excellent ambush spots. Be prepared to continuously scan edges with your binoculars. It only takes deer or elk seconds to get out in the open and leave again. We can't count the times we've glassed a spot, looked away, and less then a minute later looked at the same spot and seen an animal. They're quick. Also, don't forget to scan above timber line. Some elk stay up high as long as weather will permit, only coming down into the upper rocky treeline areas in the late morning to bed.

Although there are not a lot of deer in this area, the timber bucks you do see will be huge. Guy took this huge buck in the hills to the north of Williams Fork.

Loggers always seem to leave the low thick areas that have a lot of water uncut. They're good spots to find animals in the evening before they go to the cuts to feed. Also, they sometimes move through those areas for a last drink on their way out of the cuts in the morning. Waterholes way out in the open only get activity at night, so you're wasting your time to sit over them.

Some of the hillsides are extremely steep. Walk up or down one of the deeper gullies that has water. Because the ground is more moist in the bottom, tracks are easier to find. It may take a while, but eventually, you'll find fresh tracks you can follow. They'll probably horizontally traverse the steep hillside. Lots of times, if they're browsing slowly, you can catch up to them when they bed down. Use the same tactic by walking old logging roads where you can quickly cross a lot of terrain without making any noise.

Spence:

> Last year, I used this tactic to take a cow elk. I found a fresh set of tracks crossing an old logging road, and followed them to a herd that had bedded down for the afternoon. They stood below me, oblivious to my presence. When I shot, the forest erupted with elk running every which way. But the funny thing was, they kept coming back to the one I'd shot. I think I shot the lead cow because the others milled around confused. Even an hour later, I continued to jump elk that wouldn't leave an area that obviously had hunters in it. I could have easily shot several more elk that hung around.

Spot 01: **Bob Tail Creek**. Cross over Jones Pass then drive as far down as the road will permit. Park at the SW most gate and head up the trail. The valley opens up at the top where most of the game is found. During the archery season, we spotted over 100 elk in that valley, including over 30 bull elk. However, just a few days later, they had moved across the pass to the upper section of South Williams Fork. Without horses, it was impossible to follow.

Spot 02: **Steelman Creek.** From the gate mentioned in the previous spot, walk the logging road that runs northwest. Stay on the road that remains completely level, not the one that drops down to the creek. If you have a mountain bike, bring it. You can save yourself at least an hour of walking. Half way up the valley, on the left you'll notice an open treeless brushy area running straight up the mountain. This is an avalanche chute where heavy winter snow slides down the side of the mountain, uprooting any trees in its way. Deer frequent that spot when there isn't any snow. We spotted 3 large timber bucks there, and tracks for a lot more deer. Farther up the valley, you'll need to cut away from the road and continue to the open meadows at the top of the pass. We've seen very heavy elk sign there during the archery season.

Preparing to hunt down from one of the many logging roads found in the Williams Fork Area. Notice how thick the forests are.

Spot 03: **Upper South Fork/Williams Fork & Short Creek**. From the South Fork Campground, drive Road 142 as far back as it will permit. Then take the trail all the way up the valley (about 9 miles). This is where game goes that is pressured in Bobtail Creek and Steelman Creek. If you want to hunt unspooked game, go there. But be prepared for an expedition type hunt. You can't walk up there and back all in one day. You have to be prepared to back-pack in, or use a horse. Before you make the trip, you may want to try glassing the open hillsides in the evening from above the Eisenhower tunnel off of US 70.

Spot 04: **Upper South Fork/Williams Fork SW Hillsides**. This is the "one day hunt" alternative to the previous spot. Walk up the trail a few miles back, then head up the hillsides to the southwest. About halfway up the mountainside there are a few flat spots overlooking the creek gullies. For years those benches have been good spots for elk. The farther up the valley you go, the better it gets, because game is pushed there by hunters who aren't willing to walk as far. Be prepared for a lot of physical exertion.

Spot 05: **Old Baldy**: Where Road 142 ends, head northeast up the side of Old Baldy. Locals told us that you can spot elk feeding there up above timberline early in the morning. One hunter took a 5 point bull elk up at timberline during the third rifle season. He had climbed up in the dark and caught them out in the open just as it got light.

Spot 06: **Eisenhower Tunnel.** Hike the valley north from the west side of Eisenhower Tunnel. This can only be done in the archery/muzzle loader season, and maybe the early gun season if there isn't too much snow. Elk can be found in the high alpine meadows on either side of the divide. Walk the ridgetop above timberline and look for fresh tracks leading down into the woods.

Spence:

I hiked up this valley in August and ran into a couple of guys who had backpacked all the way over to the headwaters of Williams Fork. They said that once you got on the other side of the ridge, there was elk sign everywhere. Their exact words were that it "smelled like a zoo." But be prepared for a tough 3 1/2 hour hike in extremely thin air (12,000 feet in elevation) to get there.

Spot 07: **Lost Creek**. Just northwest of Horseshoe Campground, on the left side of the road you'll see a road going to a little Forest Service hut. This is the beginning of the trail to a really good spot. Once again, it's tough to get there, but worth the effort. You will walk for about 2 1/2 hours across some land owned by the mining company to get to the Forest Service land which you can hunt. We found extremely heavy elk sign from the beginning of the Forest Service land up the hill.

Spence:

Right where the Forest Service land starts, we bugled in 3 different bull elk from one spot. One came in silently circling down wind as he hit the creek bottom. He smelled us and bolted up the hill to the south, spooking the other two. Later, on the hill to the north, Guy passed up a 30 yard shot (muzzle loader) at a 5 pt mule deer because he couldn't see if it was 4 or 5 points until it ran. Everyone in camp hassled him about it.

But the next weekend, he took a 5 X 6 in the same area. It must have been fate.

Guy skinning out a big buck.

Spot 08: **Haystack Mountain**. Instead of driving over Ute Pass, continue northwest on highway 9 past Green Mountain Reservoir. Head west on Road 200 up Haystack Mountain. The bottom part of the road is very muddy if the weather has been wet. You really need a 4WD. If it's dry you can make it up, but you may have to cut your hunt short if the weather changes. Directly east of the windsock (used by hang-gliding enthusiasts), on the back side of the mountain, you'll find an area heavily browsed by elk.
The only reason we know about this spot is that guy in a hang glider flew over it and spotted the elk from the air. We initially tried to get to the spot from the Williams Fork Valley, but there was no access despite the appearance of access on the Forest Service map.

Spot 09: **Williams Peak Ridge**. From the previous spot, hunt southeast along the flat top of the ridge. The aspen along the top of the ridge are heavily scarred by elk. When there isn't any snow, elk feed up to the top then cut back down the east side of the ridge. When there is a lot of snow, they stick to the side of the ridge facing Green Mountain Reservoir where there's more sun. Road 200 is in good condition until you drive around Williams Peak. Then it gets extremely "hairy."

Spot 10: **Williams Peak Bald Spot**. Drive down Road 200 to Williams Peak. On the east side of the mountain is a bald spot. The woods at the bottom of the bald spot are full of Elk, but there's no easy way to get there. It's a tough one hour hike down, and two back up. It gets even better as hunting pressure increases. But it's a very difficult hike down. It's so steep, we'd even thought of winching meat from anything we shot up the hill. Eventually, despite the number of elk, we moved on to another area that was easier to get to.

Spot 11: **North Of Williams Fork Reservoir**. Just north of the Williams Fork Reservoir dam is prime deer habitat. Herds of deer move up from the Colorado River and down to the spillway. This is BLM land and may be inaccessible, depending on current cattle leases, etc. Check for posting before you hunt. If it is open, be prepared to see a lot of big brush bucks. It's very open. Use group hunting tactics for best results.

Spot 12: **Church Park**. Take Road 139 east from Horseshoe Campground then take Road 133 north until you hit the second dirt road going west. Stay on top. If you begin to lose a lot of altitude, you've missed the turn. The road goes a lot farther back than indicated on the map. Go all the way to the end. You'll pass some large mounds of bulldozed dirt to the right, which have caused a watering hole to form. We found a number of elk rubs around the watering hole. A small herd of 20 elk frequents the waterhole at night during late summer and early fall. We also found black bear tracks along the road. The bear had headed south into the wooded gully. The road ends at some more large bulldozed mounds. Walk from there northwest and look for tracks crossing to either side of the ridge. The terrain consists of open clear cuts that have regrown with tightly packed saplings. The ground is powdery and tracks are easy to read. Some people really like to hunt this kind of terrain due to the easy tracking.

Spot 13: **Beaver Creek/Strawberry Creek**. Take Road 133 southeast from Highway 40 about three miles past where you enter Forest Service land. Elk cross over between Beaver Creek and Strawberry Creek. Driving down Road 133 we spotted 7 elk (one 4 point bull and one fork horn) bedded in the willows by the creek. They jumped up and headed up the hill over to Strawberry Creek. Dry weather may push herds down from on top. That little group liked it so much they stayed for the afternoon.

Williams Fork

(Reprinted from Arapahoe National Forest map)

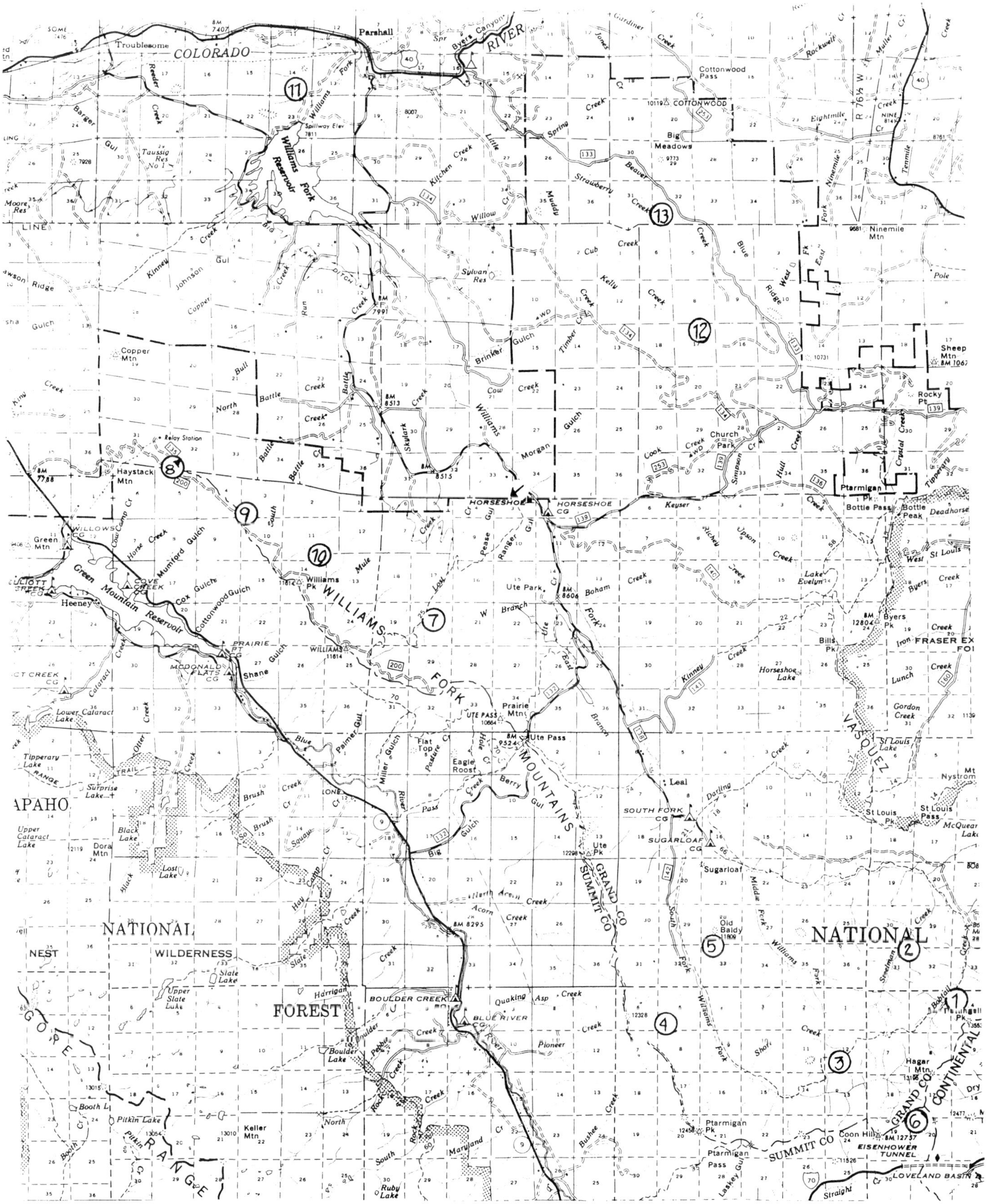

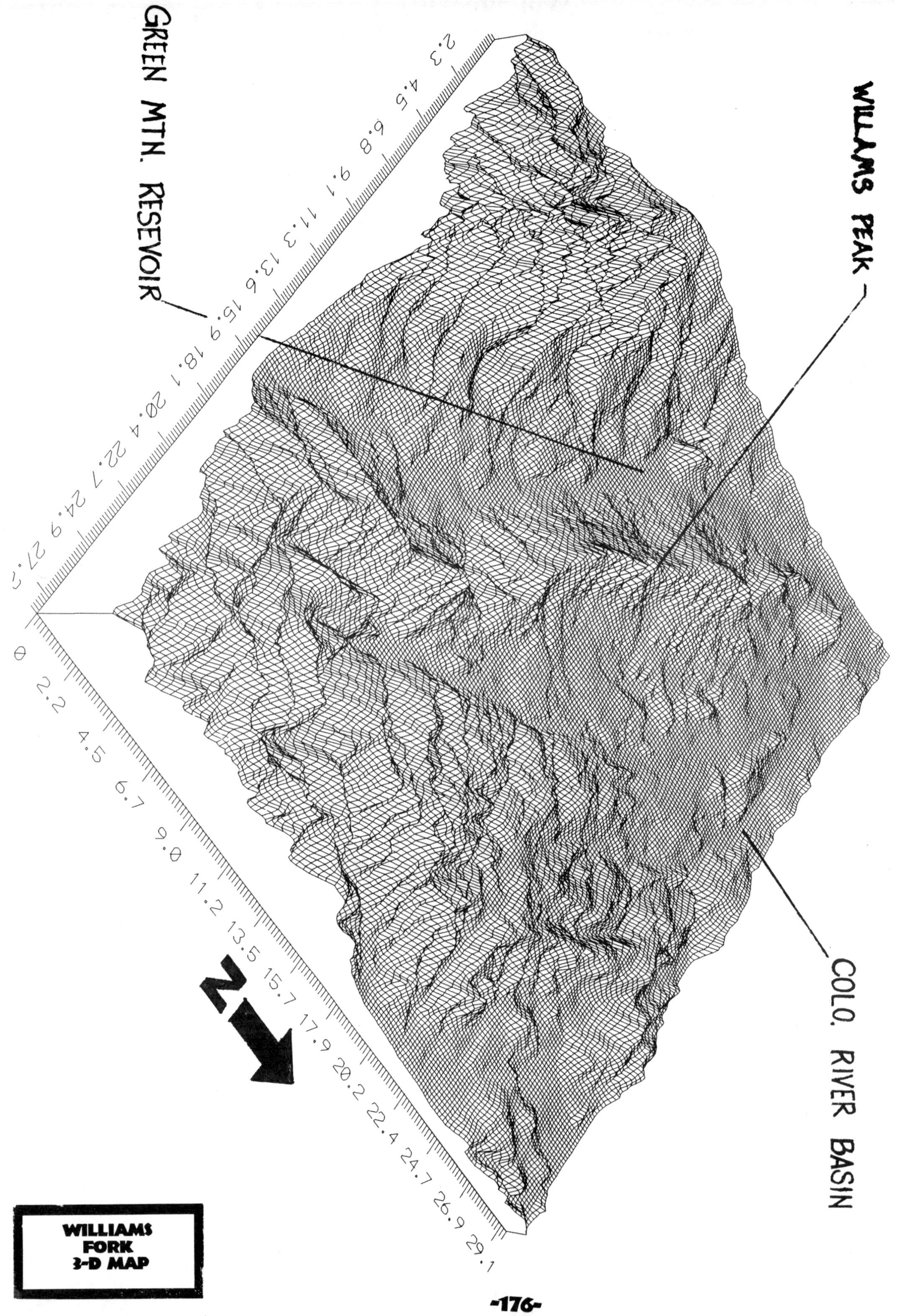

WILLIAMS FORK 3-D MAP

Parting Words

By Spencer Kluesner

Twilight in the Colorado forests.

Guy really hasn't left any specific instructions for what is to be done if he were to pass away, but I have. There's a hunting spot that's not on our maps because we were only permitted to hunt there once in the fall of 1986. In this spot I saw more elk and bugled in more bulls in one day than I probably will in all the combined hunts of the rest of my life.

Something tells me that if my ashes are spread over my favorite hunting spot of all time, I'll spend an eternity hunting big elk. And I kind of wonder. If I die before Guy and Fish, and they were to get back onto that land and hunt, maybe in the evening just at dusk, while the elk are bugling up a storm, they might get a glimpse of something, possibly the left-over spirit of me coming back from a fresh kill, and moving off into the hills, deep into twilight hills, to a place where they dare not follow.

Best of luck in your hunting endeavors from all of us.

Spencer Kluesner & Guy Collier
Colorado Gamefinders
1993

Appendix A

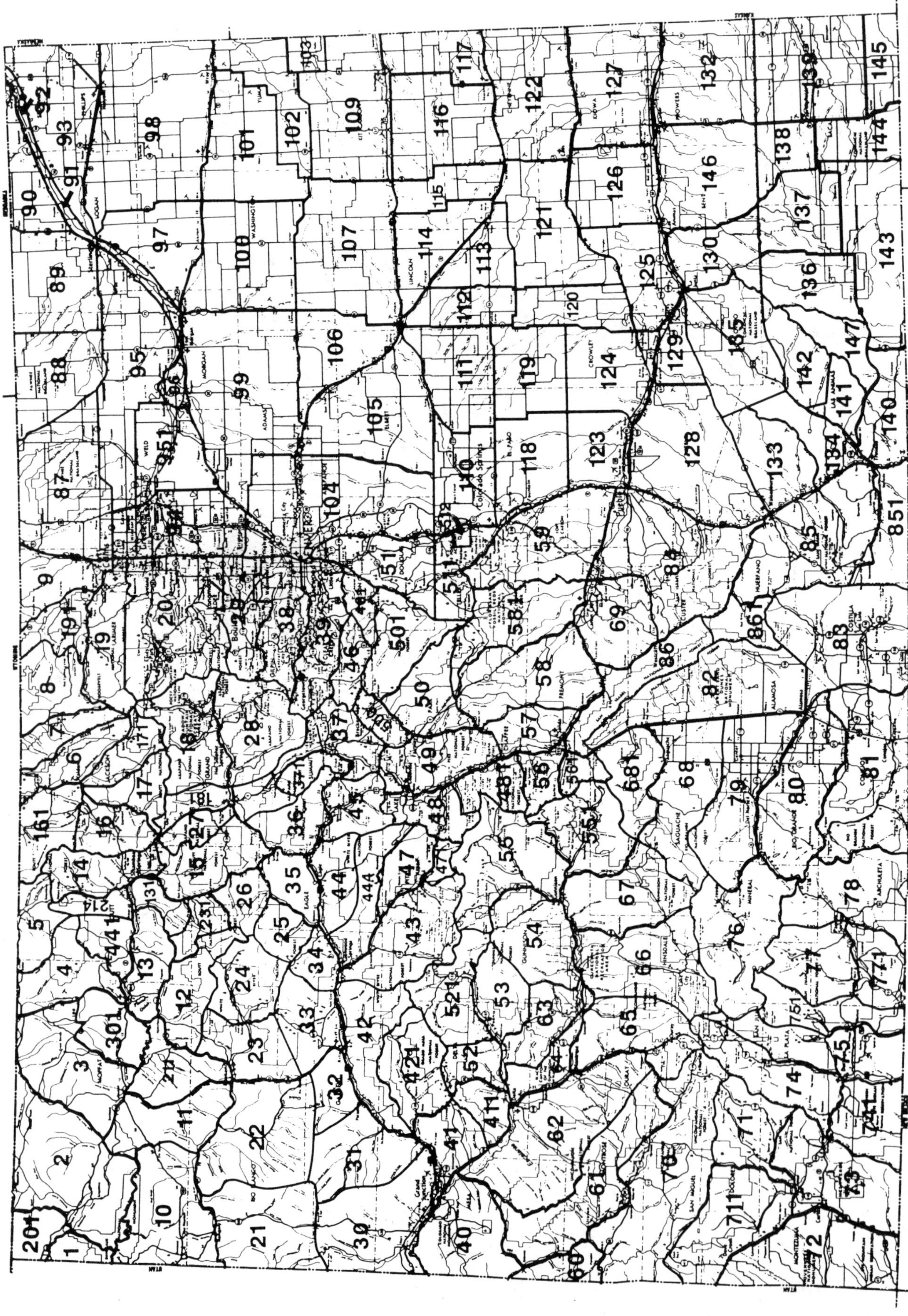

GAME MANAGEMENT UNITS

MAY 1993